HISTORY OF R

THE DAWN
AND TWILIGHT OF
ZOROASTRIANISM

R.C. Zaehner was born in 1913 and educated at Tonbridge School and Christ Church, Oxford where he gained first class honours in Persian and Avestan. In 1936–37 he studied Pahlavi with Sir Harold Bailey at Cambridge where he began work on his monumental *Zurvan, a Zoroastrian Dilemma*. During and immediately after the war he served at the British Embassy in Teheran. Appointed Lecturer in Persian at Oxford in 1950, he returned to Teheran in 1951 with the rank of Counsellor for a period of one year. On his return to Oxford he was elected Spalding Professor of Eastern Religions and Ethics. R.C. Zaehner died in 1974.

OTHER TITLES IN THE PHOENIX PRESS
HISTORY OF RELIGION SERIES

The Gods of Prehistoric Man by Johannes Maringer

THE DAWN
AND TWILIGHT OF
ZOROASTRIANISM

R.C. Zaehner

PHOENIX
PRESS

5 UPPER SAINT MARTIN'S LANE
LONDON
WC2H 9EA

A PHOENIX PRESS PAPERBACK

First published in Great Britain
by Weidenfeld & Nicolson in 1961
This paperback edition published in 2002
by Phoenix Press,
a division of The Orion Publishing Group Ltd,
Orion House, 5 Upper St Martin's Lane,
London WC2H 9EA

Phoenix Press
Sterling Publishing Co Inc
387 Park Avenue South
New York
NY 10016-8810
USA

A CIP catalogue record for this book
is available from the British Library.

Printed and bound in Great Britain by
Clays Ltd, St Ives plc

ISBN 1 84212 165 0

To
JOHN CAUTE

CONTENTS

PREFACE   15

INTRODUCTION   19

The Historical Setting—The Iranians—The Medes—The Persians and
the First Persian Empire—Macedonian and Parthian Interregnum—The
Sassanian or Second Persian Empire—The Parsees—Sources and
Tradition—The Avesta—The Inscriptions—The Pahlavi Books—
Difficulties of Interpretation

PART I—DAWN

1 THE PROPHET   33

His Place and Date—The Economic and Political Background—Truth and
the Lie—The Traditional Religion—Free Will—The Two Spirits—Zoroaster and his God—The Bounteous Immortals—God and the Two Spirits—
The Two Spirits in the Dead Sea Scrolls—The Holiness of God—God,
the Sole Creator—Post Mortem Judgement—Heaven and Hell—Influence on Judaism—The 'Second Existence'—Summary of Doctrine

2 THE SEVEN CHAPTERS   62

Divine Beings beside God—The Wives of Ahura Mazdāh—The Old
Religion—Ahura and Varuṇa—Mithra—The 'Preservers-Creators':
Ahura and Mithra—The Nature of Zoroaster's Reform—Prototype of
the Holy Spirit—Changed Tone of the Seven Chapters—Veneration of
Material Things—Minor Prophets—Haoma

3 THE CULTUS   79

The Yasna—The Yashts—The Vidēvdāt—The Three Forms of Zoroas-
trianism—The Fourfold Confession of Faith—Ahuras and Daēvas—
Zoroaster and Animal Sacrifice—Sacrificial Bull and Haoma Rite—
Haoma, the Drink of Immortality of the Indo-Iranians—Haoma, as
Sacrifice and Sacrament—The Liturgy—Origins of the Cult—Haoma,
Victim, Priest, and God—Sraosha—Sraosha the Mediator

4 MITHRA   97

The Yashts—Iranian Mithra and Roman Mithras—The Pre-
Zoroastrian Mithra—Mithra, Compact and Warlord—Mithra and
Indra—The Daēva-Worshippers and Mithra—The Separation of
Mithra from Ahura—Analysis of Mithra Yasht—Mithra as Contract
and King—Mithra as Terrible Warlord—Mithra as Light—Mithra,
Sraosha, and Rashnu—Mithra's Heavenly House—Mithra's Plaint to the
Wise Lord—Mithra's Descent to Earth—Haoma Consecrates himself
Mithra's Priest—Mithra Initiated into the 'Good Religion'—Ahura and
Mithra Reunited—Mithra and the Holy Spirit—The Revised Cult of
Ahura and Mithra

9

5 MITHRA—YIMA—MITHRAS   121

The Daēvas and their Worshippers—The Daēva-Worshippers and
Mithra—Roman Mithras and his Immolation of the Bull—Yima and the
Bull-Sacrifice—Ahriman's Slaughter of the Bull—Bull-Sacrifice at the
End of Time—Ahriman-Areimanios in the Mithraic mysteries—The
Bull-Sacrifice of Man's First Parents—Yima again—The Vedic Yama—
The Avestan Yima—Yima's Golden Reign—His Subterranean Paradise
—Yima and the Sun—Zoroaster and Yima—Yima's 'Lie'—Yima,
Mithra's Twin—Nōrūz and Mihragān—Yima the Prototype of Ahri-
man?—Yima and Mithra in the Avesta—Cautes and Cautopates in the
Mithraic Mysteries—Conclusion

6 FRAVASHI—VAYU—KHWARENAH   145

Ahura Mazdāh's Veneration of other Deities—The Fravashis—Vayu—
Vayu and Zurvān—The Khwarenah

7 ACHAEMENIDS AND MAGI   154

Primitive and 'Catholic' Zoroastrianism—The God of Darius the
Great—The 'Zoroastrianism' of Darius—The Daiva-Inscription of
Xerxes—Xerxes' 'Un-Zoroastrian' acts—Artaxerxes II and III—The
Magi—Zoroaster and the Magi—Magavan—Popular Religion in
Western Iran—Zoroastrianism and the Popular Cults—The Religion
Described by Strabo—Decline and Fall of 'Catholic' Zoroastrianism

PART II—TWILIGHT

8 IN SEARCH OF AN ORTHODOXY   175

Revival of Zoroastrianism by the Sassanians—In Search of an Ortho-
doxy—Three Sects—The 'Mazdean' Dualists—The 'Monotheists'—The
Zurvanites—Zurvanism Predominant in the Third Century AD—The
Eclecticism of Shāpūr I—The High Priest Kartēr and the 'Zandīks'—
Āturpāt and the 'Fatalists'—The Zurvanism of Yezdigird II and his
Grand Vizier—The Synthesis of Khusraw I—Study of Indian and
Greek Works—The Second Decline and Final Fall of Zoroastrianism

9 THE VARIETIES OF ZURVANISM   193

The Pahlavi Books—Priestly Brothers: Mānushchihr and Zātspram—
The Influx of Greek and Indian Ideas—The 'Zandīks' and 'Dahrīs'
—'Classical' and Materialist Zurvanism—The Zandīk Ontology and
Metaphysics—Mēnōk and Gētēh—Creative Evolution—The Dualist
Interpretation of Evolution—A Zurvanite View of Evolution—The
Three Types of Zurvanism—Zurvanite Fatalism—'Classical' Zurvanism
—The Zurvanite Myth—Zurvān and the Pact between Ohrmazd and
Ahriman

10 CLASSICAL ZURVANISM   211

Zurvān, the One and the Many—Zurvān's Doubt—Ohrmazd and
Ahriman in Mythological Zurvanism—Main Differences between
Zurvanism and Orthodoxy—Aberrant Versions of the Zurvanite

Myth—The Sect of Gayōmart—The Four Elements and their Proto-types—Infinite and Finite—Emergence of the Finite from the Infinite—The Emergence of Consciousness and the Genesis of Evil—The Changelessness of Created Being—Āz, the Weapon of Concupiscence—The 'Endless Form' or Macrocosm—The Zurvanite and the Manichaean Āz—Āz, a Borrowing from Buddhism?—Essential 'Zoroastrianism' of classical Zurvanism—The Gender and Sex of Āz—The Wickedness of the Female—The Defection of Woman to Ahriman—The Defilement of Man by Woman

11 ZURVĀN   236

The Sevenfold Zurvān—Macrocosm and Microcosm—Zurvān, the God of Fate—The God of Death—The God of the Resurrection—The Fatalism of Firdausī's Epic—The Orthodox Attitude to Fate—Man's Response to Fate—Orthodoxy's Reaction to the Three Types of Zurvanism

12 OHRMAZD AND AHRIMAN   248

The Orthodox Cosmogony—Finite and Infinite in the Orthodox Account—The Nature of God—The First Creation—Ahriman's Reaction—The Weapons of Ohrmazd and Ahriman—The Limiting of Time—The Perdurance of Ohrmazd's Creation—Ohrmazd's Instrument, the Endless Form—Ahriman's Instrument, Concupiscence—Zurvanite Origin of these 'Instruments'—Creation of Truth and Falsehood—Ohrmazd's Offer of Peace—Ahriman Laid Low—Creation of the Bounteous Immortals and their Demonic Counterparts—The Material Creation—The Heavenly Sphere or Macrocosm—A Variation Derived from India—Man the Microcosm—Man's Fravashis Consent to Descend to Earth—Ahriman's Revival and Assault against the Material World—The Fall of Man

13 MAN   265

Ahriman Imprisoned in the Material World—The Re-creation of Plant and Animal Life and of Man: Man's Second Fall—Soul and Body—Body, Vital Spirit, Soul, Image, and External Soul—The Fravashi or External Soul—Essential Goodness of Man—The Soul's Free Will—Soul and Reason—Relationship of Soul to Body—Concupiscence, the Enemy of Soul and Body Alike—The Interconnexion of Bodily Health and Virtue—Primacy of Spirit over Matter—Moderation in All Things—Self-love the Foundation of All Love—The Solidarity of Mankind—The Indwelling of the Good Mind—Contemplation and Action

14 THE RELIGION AND THE KING   284

The Interconnexion of the Zoroastrian Religion and the Sassanian Empire—The Doctrine of the Mean—The Mean as Cosmic Principle—The Mean as the Treaty between Ohrmazd and Ahriman—The Mean, the Essence of Reason—Virtue, the Mean between Contrary Vices—Wisdom or Reason in Man and God—Wisdom as Creative Principle—Ahriman's Lack of Wisdom and Reason—Concupiscence, the Misuse of Reason and Desire—Man's Khwarr (Khwarenah) and Concupiscence—The Good Religion in Essence and Manifestation—Religion and

Royalty—The Function of Royalty—Royalty the Material Complement of the Good Religion—The Virtues of Kings—Royalty the Bond between God and Man

15 THE END   302

The Soul's Fate at Death—The Nature of the Discarnate Soul—Heaven—Hell—The Frashkart or Final Rehabilitation—Ohrmazd's Master-plan for the Overthrow of Evil—The Three Phases of Ohrmazd's Plan—The Beginning of the End—The Destruction of Āz and Ahriman (Zurvanite Version)—The Meaning of Ahriman's Destruction—The Disintegration of Evil (Orthodox Version)—The Resurrection of the Body—The Role of Saoshyans and the Final Bull-Sacrifice—Purgation by Molten Metal—The 'Final Body' and Renewal of All Things—The Marriage of Matter and Spirit

ABBREVIATIONS USED IN THE NOTES   323

NOTES   325

BIBLIOGRAPHY   339

APPENDIX   349

INDEX   361

LIST OF ILLUSTRATIONS

1. Two pages from the *Avesta, Bodleian Library, Oxford* (Photo: Bodleian Library).
2. The symbol of Ahura Mazdāh, Persepolis (By courtesy of the Oriental Institute, University of Chicago).
3. The tomb of Cyrus the Great (*d.* 529 BC), Pasargadae (Photo: Paul Popper).
4. Relief of Darius the Great (*c.* 549–485 BC) carved in rock, Bīsitūn (By courtesy of George C. Cameron, The University of Michigan, and the American Schools of Oriental Research).
5. Darius' Inscription, Bīsitūn (Photo: British Museum).
6. Darius, from southern doorway of the Council Hall, Persepolis (Photo: Paul Popper).
7. Head of Darius, Bīsitūn (By courtesy of George C. Cameron, The University of Michigan, and the American Schools of Oriental Research).
8. Darius the Great and Xerxes, Persepolis (Photo: Paul Popper).
9. The tomb of Darius, Naqsh-i Rustam (Photo: Paul Popper).
10. Ruins of Persepolis (Photo: Paul Popper).
11. The palace of Darius I, Persepolis (Photo: Paul Popper).
12. Xerxes' Hall of a Hundred Columns, Persepolis (Photo: Paul Popper).
13. Medes and Persians, from the frieze at Persepolis (Photo: Paul Popper).
14. The *Daiva* inscription of Xerxes (By courtesy of the Oriental Institute of the University of Chicago).
15. Tomb of one of the Achaemenian Kings, Persepolis (Photo: Ella Maillart).
16. Achaemenian fire temple, Bishāpūr (By permission of Professor R. Ghirshman).
17. Achaemenian fire temple, Naqsh-i Rustam.
18. Artaxerxes I, Persepolis (Photo: Paul Popper).
19. Zāl and the Magi, manuscript page of a *Shāhnāma, c.* 1310, *Museum of Fine Arts, Boston* (By courtesy of the Museum of Fine Arts, Boston).
20. The Battle of the Issus, mosaic, *Museo Nazionale, Naples* (Photo: Alinari No. 12050).
21. An Islamic miniaturist's interpretation of the Battle of the Issus, *Bodleian Library, Oxford* (Photo: Bodleian Library).
22. Darius III, detail from the Battle of the Issus, mosaic, *Museo Nazionale, Naples* (Photo: Alinari No. 12050c).
23. Alexander the Great, detail from the Battle of the Issus, mosaic, *Museo Nazionale, Naples* (Photo: Alinari No. 12050a).
24. Antiochus I of Commagene and Mithra, Namrud Dagh (By courtesy of Theresa Goell, Director of the Namrud Dagh Excavations).
25. Deus Arimanius *c.* AD 190, *Vatican Museum* (Photo: Alinari No. 35666).
26. Deus Arimanius, second or third century AD, *Vatican Museum* (Photo: Alinari No. 35667).
27. Mithras slaying the bull, *Musée du Louvre, Paris* (Photo: Alinari No. 22665).
28. Mithras slaying the bull, *British Museum* (Photo: Mansell Collection).

29. The Goddess Anāhitā, *British Museum* (Photo: British Museum).
30. Investiture of Ardashīr I by the god Ohrmazd, AD 226, rock relief, at Naqsh-i Rustam (Photo: Paul Popper).
31. Shāpūr I and the Emperor Valerian, AD 260, rock relief, Naqsh-i Rustam (Photo: Paul Popper).
32. The god Ohrmazd, rock relief, Shāpūr, *c.* AD 273 (Photo: Paul Popper).
33. The High Priest, Kartēr.
34. Detail of the Inscription of Kartēr.
35. Yezdigird II (AD 438–457), *British Museum* (Photo: British Museum).
36. Sassanian fire temple, Shāpūr (Photo: Paul Popper).
37. Ruins of Ctesiphon (Photo: Paul Popper).
38. Mashyē and Mashyānē, Islamic miniature, *University Library, Edinburgh* (Photo: University Library, Edinburgh).
39. Jamshīd sawn in two, Islamic miniature, *Bodleian Library, Oxford* (Photo: Bodleian Library).
40. Gushtāsp entertains King Isfandiyār, Islamic miniature, *Bodleian Library, Oxford* (Photo: Bodleian Library).
41. The justice of Khusraw I, Islamic miniature, *Bodleian Library, Oxford* (Photo: Bodleian Library).
42. Parsee Priests officiating in a Bombay Temple.
43. A Parsee 'Tower of Silence'.
44. A modern Parsee marriage ceremony (By courtesy of Dasturji Khurshed S. Dabu and the New Book Company Private Limited, Bombay).
45. The Parsee *Naojote* ceremony (By courtesy of Dasturji Khurshed S. Dabu and the New Book Company Private Limited, Bombay).

PREFACE

OF ALL the great religions of the world Zoroastrianism presents the most intractable problems; for it was a religion founded by a prophet who claimed to have had a revelation from the one true God and who nonetheless lived in a traditionally polytheistic society not yet ripe to receive the totality of his message. In the event a modified version of the older religion was grafted on to the Prophet's original message, and the very cultus of Zoroastrianism, the religion of the Prophet Zoroaster, was borrowed from an ancient rite that dated back to a very remote antiquity. Later again, when the Zoroastrian religion, in its modified form, was adopted by the royal house of the first Persian Empire, it came to be controlled by a priestly caste, the Magi, with which it originally had nothing to do. So much is admitted by nearly all Zoroastrian scholars.

For the present writer, once a specialist in Zoroastrian studies and now a teacher of the comparative study of religions, Zoroastrianism has taken on a new interest; for its whole development, as interpreted by the great majority of specialists, is unparalleled elsewhere. While adhering in the main to the traditional interpretation as originally laid down by those giants of Zoroastrian scholarship, K. F. Geldner and Christian Bartholomae, I have been forced to diverge from them in some respects. Thus, while I can understand that the followers of Zoroaster could tolerate the reintroduction of the older gods into the Prophet's strictly monotheistic creed in the role of created spirits, I cannot understand how the central rite of Zoroastrianism, centring as it does round the Haoma plant (pp. 85–93), could possibly have arisen within the Zoroastrian community, apparently without any voice of protest ever being raised, if, as is generally maintained, this very rite had been denounced and outlawed by Zoroaster himself. For this reason I have devoted more space than some may think justified to the development of the liturgy.

In any book not primarily designed for a specialized audience there are bound to be omissions. In this book I have tried to concentrate on what seem to me to be the essential features of Zoroastrianism, both in the history of its early development and in the final forms it crystallized into during its silver age in the third to the seventh centuries AD; namely, the gradual adaptation of a prophetic religion to a still predominantly pagan society in the first instance, and the working out of theological positions the object of which was always to preserve intact the absolute goodness of God, in the second.

Most books on Zoroastrianism devote chapters to the study of the nature and functions of the various deities that had made their way into the later Avesta. This I have scarcely done at all since these deities are prominent in only one transient phase of Zoroastrianism and because they play no essential part in the liturgy. An exception, however, has been made for the great god Mithra, first because he was originally intimately associated with Ahura, the prototype of Zoroaster's own Ahura Mazdāh—the Wise Lord—who, for the Prophet, was the one true God, secondly because to this day the holy of holies of the Zoroastrian temple is called the 'place of Mithra', and thirdly because the cult of Mithras in the Roman Empire which derived from the Iranian Mithra was for long a rival to Christianity in its early centuries. I have devoted more space to the relationship between the Iranian Mithra and the Roman Mithras than is perhaps justifiable, and my very tentative conclusion on how the one could develop into the other will, no doubt, be hotly contested. In the main, however, I have not departed from the 'orthodox' interpretation of Zoroastrianism nor have I taken into consideration the highly individual views of either Herzfeld or Nyberg; and since I regard these as radical perversions both of Zoroaster's own teaching and of historical truth, I have printed Professor Henning's admirable critique of their methods (if such they can be called) in an appendix.

The present volume differs too from its predecessors in that it omits all account of the elaborate system of taboo worked out in the *Vidēvdāt* (p. 81) and maintained down to the present day by the orthodox. This I have done both because it is of no interest to the general reader and because it is the least attractive and the least worthwhile aspect of an otherwise attractive religion. It differs too from previous general surveys in that it devotes as much space to the theology of the Zoroastrian silver age as it does to the early historical development—and this proportion seems to be right, for, apart from the message of the Prophet himself, the interpretation of that message by the theologians of a much later date seems to be the only thing of real and vital interest to the comparative theologian as opposed to the student of comparative mythology. The problems that faced these Zoroastrian theologians are the problems that face all religions that are in any sense monotheist, and, this being so, what they have to say is bound to have a universal and abiding interest. Moreover, a full account of their beliefs—of their solutions of the problem of evil and their enthusiastic acceptance of this world as being good in itself—

may serve as some slight corrective to the modern tendency to turn to a bastard form of Buddhism or Vedāntism, imperfectly understood, in order to shirk the responsibilities that living in this world imposes on us. Thus, in my own estimation, the second part of this book no less than chapters I and VII which describe the monotheistic faith of Zoroaster and Darius respectively, has much more than a specialized interest, for it sets forth, to the best of its ability, the religious perspective of a world-accepting faith that once commanded the allegiance of a very great people.

It remains for me only to thank the Oxford University Press and Professor W. B. Henning for their kind permission to reproduce a long section of Professor Henning's *Zoroaster*, Enrad M. F. Kanga for his great kindness in supplying material for the illustrations and Mr P. S. Lewis for the time and trouble he gave in helping me to check the references.

All Souls College, Oxford   R. C. ZAEHNER

INTRODUCTION

The Historical Setting—The Iranians—The Medes—The Persians and the First Persian Empire—Macedonian and Parthian Interregnum—The Sassanian or Second Persian Empire—The Parsees—Sources and Tradition—The Avesta—The Inscriptions—The Pahlavi Books—Difficulties of Interpretation

'*Also sprach Zarathustra. . . .*' 'Thus spake Zarathushtra. . . .'

Who was Zarathushtra? and what words did he speak?

Even today the average educated man knows nothing of Zarathushtra except that he is the mouthpiece used by Nietzsche to pronounce his doctrine of the superman. Yet never has a great religious thinker been more grossly travestied—travestied by his own followers who straightway obscured the purity of his monotheistic vision, travestied by the Magi in the Levant who presented him to the Graeco-Roman world not only as the author of a rigid religious dualism which made good and evil two rival and co-eternal principles, but also as a magician, astrologer, and quack, travestied by Nietzsche himself who fathered on him doctrines he would have found little to his taste, travestied again in these latter days by men reputed as scholars whose fuddled imaginations have seen in him either a witch-doctor bemusing himself with the fumes of Indian hemp or a political intriguer plotting behind the scenes at the court of the Persian king of kings.

The Historical Setting

Zarathushtra or Zoroaster as he is commonly called in the West, was none of these things: he was the Prophet of ancient Iran who, according to tradition, flourished in the seventh and sixth centuries BC. In his day the Iranian peoples had fanned out throughout not only modern Persia and Afghanistan but also large parts of what is now the Soviet Union—Turkmenistan, Uzbekistan, and Tajikistan. They included not only the Medes and Persians so familiar to the West through both the Bible and the Greek historians, but also the Parthians and beyond them to the east the lesser-known tribes—Chorasmians, Soghdians, Bactrians, and many more. It was among these tribes which seem to have composed a loose federation under the hegemony of Chorasmia that Zoroaster proclaimed his religion which in the end came to be accepted by the ruling house of Vishtāspa soon to be extinguished by the military might of Cyrus the Persian.

The Iranians

The word 'Persia' we owe to the Greeks. Strictly speaking it refers only to the south-west province of modern Persia (more correctly called Iran) and corresponds to the modern province of Fārs or Pārs (the 'Persis' of Herodotus). To the north of it lay Media with its capital at Ecbatana (the modern Hamadān). The Medes were closely akin to the Persians, but differed from them slightly both in dialect and in manners. The Medes and Persians were, however, the two most westerly of the Iranian tribes and those, therefore, most familiar to the Greeks. The Iranian nation itself formed part of a wider grouping, the Indo-Iranians, themselves forming but one member of the huge Indo-European family of nations from which all the peoples of modern Europe with the exceptions of the Hungarians and Finns derive. Linguistically and culturally the Indians and Iranians were very closely linked, the Sanskrit in which India's most ancient and most sacred texts, the *Vedas*, are written being very close both to the language of the Avesta, the Zoroastrians' own sacred book, and to that of ancient Persis (the prototype of modern Persian) in which Darius the Great inscribed his exploits on the towering rock of Bīsitūn which today overhangs the highway from Baghdad to Teheran at a point just beyond Kermanshah.

The Medes

Both the Indian and the Iranian branches of the Indo-Iranian family called themselves *Āryas*—Aryans, a word later used to mean simply 'noble' or a 'gentleman'; and the word 'Irān', derived from an earlier form *Aryānām*, simply means '[the country] of the Aryans'. These Aryans or Iranians, though differing in dialect, formed a self-conscious national whole which must have felt itself racially one since they were careful to distinguish themselves from the *an-āryas*, peoples 'not Iranian'. Of these Iranians the first to make an impact on the West were the Medes. Established in the north-west of the Iranian plateau overlooking the basin of the Tigris and Euphrates, the Assyria and Babylonia of the ancients and what is now modern Iraq, they swooped down upon the Mesopotamian plain and extinguished for ever the Assyrian power that had, among other things, carried Israel off into captivity. And so, as a religious by-product of this first appearance of the Iranians in the Western world, Israel was once again free to return to the Holy Land. Meanwhile in her encounter with the Medes and Persians, Israel had found a kindred monotheistic creed in the religion of the Prophet Zoroaster, and one of her own prophets, Isaiah, did not hesitate to salute Cyrus, her liberator, as the Lord's anointed.

From this religion too she learnt teachings concerning the afterlife altogether more congenial to her soul than had been the gloomy prospect offered her by her own tradition (p. 57–8), teachings to which she had been a stranger before.

The Persians and the First Persian Empire

The spread of Iranian power westwards was, then, initiated by the Medes. With the conquest of Nineveh, the Assyrian capital, northern Mesopotamia passed under their control and further incursions were made into Asia Minor. The Median dynasty founded by Deïoces, however, came to an end in 550 BC when the last of the line, Astyages, was handed over by his own soldiery to the Persian rebel, Cyrus.

Cyrus the Great took over the Empire from the Medes and thereby founded the purely Persian dynasty of the Achaemenids, named after his ancestor Hakhāmanish or Achaemenes as he was known to the Greeks. Not only did he complete the conquest of Asia Minor, thereby extending his rule over non-Iranian peoples; he also subjugated the Iranian tribes to the east, thereby extinguishing the Chorasmian royal house of Vishtāspa, the patron of Zoroaster. The infant religion was, then, no longer under direct royal patronage, but had for a time to make its own way in its struggle with the old paganism that was the common heritage of the Indian and Iranian peoples.

The status of the Zoroastrian religion under the Achaemenids has been a matter of endless and tedious controversy and will have to be discussed in some detail later. Suffice it to say here that the Zoroastrian priesthood soon fell into the hands of a priestly caste of Median nationality called the Magi (pp. 161–5). The Magi, however, like the Brāhmans in India, were a hereditary sacerdotal caste whose presence was indispensable at any Iranian religious ceremony, whether Zoroastrian or not, and they it was who presented so curious and so distorted an image of the Prophet Zoroaster to the West. Though it is wellnigh certain that Darius adopted at least the basic doctrines of Zoroaster (pp. 156–8) and that Xerxes formally adhered to his religion, we cannot say with absolute certainty that Zoroastrianism became the religion of the Achaemenian kings until the reign of Artaxerxes I (465–425 BC), for it was he who introduced a Zoroastrian calendar. From the reign of Artaxerxes, then, until the death of Darius III and the overthrow of the Empire by Alexander the Great in 330 BC Zoroastrianism was the official religion of the royal house. The older cults continued to exist beside it and in course of time succeeded in corroding the hard monotheistic core of the Prophet's teaching. This was a long and complicated story and will of necessity occupy us in a later chapter.

21

Macedonian and Parthian Interregnum

The collapse of the first Persian Empire destroyed both the unity of the Iranian peoples and the privileged position of the Zoroastrian faith, and for a century and a half the greater part of the Iranian lands were ruled by Macedonians. These in turn gave way to a native Iranian dynasty, the Parthian Arsacids (250 BC–AD 226) who, though good Iranians by blood, seem to have been totally indifferent to the religion of the Iranian Prophet.

Of the fortunes of the Zoroastrians during the centuries of Seleucid and Parthian dominion we know practically nothing; and, indeed, as we shall see in the sequel, Zoroastrianism had so transformed itself during the later Achaemenian period that, unless we are careful to define our terms, we cannot speak of Zoroastrianism as a single religion at all, for every form of Iranian religion had now adopted the Prophet's name and used its authority to dignify and authenticate teachings that were very far from being his. It was not until AD 226 that the fortunes of the 'Good Religion', as the Zoroastrians now called their faith, revived, for it was in that year that Ardashīr of the House of Sāsān, who traced his lineage to the last of the Achaemenids, rose in rebellion against his Parthian overlord, overthrew him, and, according to the legendary account, restored the Zoroastrian faith as the official religion of the land.

The Sassanian or Second Persian Empire

Ardashīr was a Persian in the strict sense of that word. Like the Achaemenids before him he stemmed from the province of Pārs in the south-west, and the 'Sassanian' Empire he founded is thus rightly styled the second 'Persian' Empire, for the reigning house was not only Iranian, as the Parthians also were, but 'Persian', that is, native to the province of Pārs. The Sassanian Empire differed from its Achaemenian predecessor in that its western frontier never for long extended beyond Mesopotamia: it was then more homogeneously Iranian, less cosmopolitan, and therefore more consciously nationalist. So it was that Zoroastrianism, the religion founded by an Iranian Prophet, received official support as the national religion of all Iran: it became the state religion, and church and state thereby became inextricably interfused. For four long centuries Zoroastrianism was the religion of an empire which, in power and pomp, alone could rival Rome. It had, however, never fully recovered from the disaster it had suffered at the hands of Alexander, and it fell to the first Sassanian kings to re-establish it as a homogeneous religion complete with a system of dogmatics, fit in all respects to meet the challenge of a nascent

Christianity and later of the religion of the Manichees which too made a universal appeal. The Sassanian kings thus not only revived the ancient national faith but also sought to impose upon it its own orthodoxy. And so the Zoroastrian 'Church' not only became the religion of state, it became an intolerant and at times a persecuting faith. Its link with the crown, however, in the end proved its undoing, for when another prophet arose in the Arabian desert and when his successors, like Alexander before them, swept aside the whole vast apparatus of Persian imperial power, the fate of Zoroastrianism as a world religion was sealed.

But between the Muslim conqueror and Alexander there was an enormous difference. The conquest of the Iranian lands by Alexander had indeed introduced the Iranians to Greek ways and Greek manners, but it had no serious religious contribution to make. Indeed, the reverse was true, for the Iranians, whether truly Zoroastrian or not, did influence Greek thought though it is impossible to trace that influence with anything like certainty in any given case. The Muslims, however, came in the name of the One God who would brook neither rival nor equal: they came with a faith which was vital and simple and new. They came and they conquered; and the Zoroastrians, once again deprived at one blow of all official support and doctrinally disunited among themselves, were unable to meet the challenge. The collapse of the Empire brought with it the slow death agony of a once great religion which had claimed a universal validity.

The Muslim conquest of the Persian Empire in AD 652 really marks the end of Zoroastrianism as a living force. Iran, thenceforward, was to be a Muslim land, and the Zoroastrians, whose numbers declined from year to year, were to play no part in the national revival when it came. Tolerated at first, they were later to be the object of intermittent persecution; but the will to survive had gone, and the total number of Zoroastrians living in Iran today probably does not exceed 10,000 souls of whom the great majority live in the until recently inaccessible townships of Yazd and Kerman.

The Parsees

A small minority, however, preferred exile to Muslim rule. According to their tradition these set sail from the island of Hormuz in the eighth century AD and made for Gujerat in India. There they were granted asylum by the local ruler, and there, to this day, they remain, concentrated mainly in Bombay. Through the centuries they have practised the religion of the Iranian Prophet, adhering to it out of tradition rather than conviction. Only in the nineteenth century did they, at the behest of British orientalists and missionaries, begin to take a serious interest in their own religion, and it is thanks to Parsee benefactors that the Pahlavi books (pp. 27, 193–5) which form so important a part of their sacred literature, have been printed at all.

The Parsees (for so they are called after their native Pārs) have preserved their ancient rituals intact. In matters of doctrine they have tended to adapt themselves to the dominant religion—Christianity under the British dominion, Hinduism at the present time. This has not been difficult for them since the history of their own religion, even in its heyday, has been so chequered that a Parsee would have no difficulty in finding scriptural evidence to justify a total monotheism, an uncompromising dualism, or even a barely disguised polytheism. Being a small and highly Westernized community of less than 100,000 souls, they have not been exempt from the wave of secularism that once engulfed Europe and is now enveloping the whole world. Faithful still to the basic injunction of their creed—'good thoughts, good words, good deeds'—they have largely turned their backs on the observance of their rituals (irrational and repellent to the modern mind as many of them are) and have concentrated on the more serious business of public charity, education, and good works. In enriching themselves and in giving abundantly of what they have honestly earned, they remain true to a religion which has always regarded wealth as the material counterpart to moral excellence, and which rates honesty or righteousness and generosity as the cardinal virtues. Thus, though it is possible that Zoroastrianism will shortly become extinct as a cult owing to a dearth of candidates for a hereditary priesthood, its ethical values, which are largely those of commonsense and moderation, are likely to be retained.

Sources and Tradition

Yet, though Zoroastrianism is represented today mainly by a small Gujerati-speaking community in India which has long ceased to understand its ancestral tongue, it was in its great days, like Judaism, a national religion. But, unlike Judaism, Zoroastrianism was, in the long run, unable to stand up to the strict monotheism of Islam, and this for a variety of reasons.

Of these perhaps the most important is that Zoroastrianism does not show a coherent development of an original deposit of faith as do, for example, Judaism and Christianity. Like Judaism, which had its prophet in Moses, Zoroastrianism had its prophet in Zoroaster, but whereas the original deposit of revelation in Moses was further refined by later prophets and by rabbinic tradition, and the content of

Judaism thereby remained recognizably the same, Zoroastrianism possessed no such tradition, and indeed at a very early date lost the key to its own sacred language in which the Prophet had composed his hymns.

Thus before we can proceed to any analysis of Zoroastrian beliefs, we will have to consider the nature of the Zoroastrian sacred books as well as our other sources for this ancient Iranian religion. Strictly speaking there is only one sacred book, the Avesta, and of this only a fraction survives—that fraction only which is used in the liturgy. According to Zoroastrian tradition the original Avesta was written in gold ink on ox-hides and was deposited in the royal library at Istakhr[1]: this precious copy, which consisted of some 12,000 hides, was destroyed by Alexander the Great and only a third of it remained in the memories of men. The existence of such an original Avesta is almost certainly pure legend, but legend, as usual, probably enshrines some grain of truth. It is indeed extremely unlikely that the Avesta had ever been committed to writing before the downfall of the Achaemenid Empire, for the administrative and commercial *koiné* of the Empire was Aramaic whereas a simplified form of cuneiform had been devised for the royal rock inscriptions. The Avestan language, on the other hand, is an East Iranian dialect in which no inscriptions of any sort have been found or are likely to be found; and in all probability the words of the Prophet and his successors were transmitted by word of mouth from generation to generation precisely as were the *Vedas* in contemporary India. At the time of the invasion of Alexander, however, it seems unlikely that anything like a Zoroastrian orthodoxy had developed, and the confusion and acute hellenization that followed on the conquest must have caused the loss of much of this oral tradition.

The Avesta
At some time, however, a canon of the oral Avesta seems to have been drawn up. It is said to have consisted of twenty-one *Nasks* or books, a summary of which is found in the Pahlavi book of the *Dēnkart* which, in its present form, dates from the ninth century AD. Of these twenty-one *Nasks* only a fragment remains today. This fragment, however, is of considerable size, being about one and a half times as long as the Koran.

The oldest part, which is written in an earlier form of the language than the rest of the Avesta, is the *Gāthās*, 'hymns' or 'songs'; and these are generally considered to be the work of Zoroaster himself. These hymns form the kernel of the main liturgy or *Yasna* which constitutes one of the three principal divisions of the surviving Avesta. Analogous to the *Yasna* is a shorter liturgy called the *Visp-rat* or *Vispered* which, however, contains little that is not in the *Yasna*. In the *Yasna* itself, and sandwiched in among the *Gāthās*, is another ancient section called the *Haptaṅhāiti Gāthā* written in the same dialect as the genuine *Gāthās* of Zoroaster but very different in theological content.

Next in importance, and in date later than the *Gāthās*, though probably earlier than the main portion of the liturgy, are the *Yashts* and ancillary texts known as the *Khurda Avesta* or 'Little Avesta', which consists of a series of hymns addressed to a variety of deities. Last of all comes the *Vidēvdāt*, often wrongly called *Vendidad*, or 'Law against the Demons', which is largely concerned with ritual purity.

The language of the Avesta very soon seems to have become a purely liturgical language which was no longer spoken and only very imperfectly understood. Thus whereas in the *Gāthās* we feel that what we cannot explain is due to our own ignorance, we can feel tolerably certain that in the *Vidēvdāt* what appear to be gross grammatical blunders are genuinely so. Indeed, in the *Vidēvdāt* we have the impression that the authors are not only writing in a language that is not their own, but are doing so in one the rudiments of whose grammar they had quite failed to master. This in itself is surprising, for this phenomenon does not, so far as I know, occur, at least to this degree, in any other religious tradition. Neither the Latin of the Medieval Schoolmen nor the Arabic in which the earlier Persian-born theologians of Islam chose to write (often impeccably) offers any parallel to the grammatical anarchy exhibited by the latest portions of the Avesta.

The Inscriptions

The period covered by the Avesta dates probably from the late seventh century BC to perhaps the fourth or even the third. In addition to the Avesta, however, we have a series of inscriptions by the Achaemenid kings, some of which, notably those of Darius the Great and Xerxes, are of very considerable importance. Between the last of the inscriptions and the end of the Avesta on the one hand and the rise of the Sassanian dynasty in the third century AD on the other there is no evidence of how the Zoroastrian religion fared from any native source, and for our information during this period we have to rely on the Greeks.

The Sassanian period inaugurated a revival in the fortunes of Zoroastrianism, for during this period it was proclaimed the official religion of the Empire. Thus the focal point of the Zoroastrian religion now moves from the east to the south-west, the province of Pārs or Fārs, the equivalent of the ancient Persis; and for the earlier Sassanian period we have one extremely important inscription by the religious reformer Kartēr who flourished under Shāpūr I and his successors.

For the rest we have to rely on our second great corpus of native sources on Zoroastrianism—the Pahlavi books.

The Pahlavi Books

In their present form these were mostly written in the ninth century AD, but they almost certainly reflect the theological views of the last century of Sassanian rule, and have often preserved passages in translation from lost Avestan books. Among these Pahlavi books there are also translations of the surviving Avesta except—and this is note-worthy—the *Yashts*. These translations again illustrate the total lack of tradition among the Zoroastrians. The situation is quite unlike that which obtained in India where it is clear that the commentators on the *Rig-Veda*—though there were, of course, passages which were no longer clear to them—really understood the texts they sought to elucidate, whereas the Pahlavi commentators on the *Gāthās* understood nothing at all and did not hesitate to set down a meaningless concatenation of words which was supposed to render the thoughts of their Prophet. Only in the *Vidēvdāt* with its dreary prescriptions concerning ritual purity and its listing of impossible punishments for ludicrous crimes do the translators show a tolerable understanding of the text. It thus seems clear that even in the Sassanian period the clergy themselves no longer understood the liturgy they recited, for they freely admitted that the language in which it was written, and which their opponents described as 'unknown and cryptic', 'passed all comprehension of men'.[2]

Briefly then, the principal sources for the study of Zoroastrianism are the Avesta and the Pahlavi books on the literary side and the Achaemenid and Sassanian inscriptions on the epigraphical. In addition we have some fairly extensive accounts of the religion of the Western Iranians preserved in Greek sources, the principal of which are Herodotus, Strabo, Plutarch, and Agathias.

From this brief account of the sources it will be seen that the history of Zoroastrianism falls into two distinct periods: first from the appearance of the Prophet probably in the seventh century BC until the fall of the Achaemenid Empire in the fourth, and secondly the period covered by the second Empire under the Sassanians from the third to the seventh century AD. About the fortunes of the Zoroastrian religion in its homeland during the intervening odd five centuries we know practically nothing.

In the first part of this book we shall have to consider first of all the Prophet himself, the nature of his message, and the kind of religious milieu in which he can be presumed to have grown up, secondly the remaining writings of the Avesta, thirdly the inscriptions of the Achaemenid kings, and fourthly the main Greek accounts of the religions of the Iranians. In the second part we shall be turning to developments during the Sassanian period together with the conflict that seems to have arisen between the strict dualists and the so-called Zurvanites who raised the principle of Infinite Time above the two principles of Good and Evil, thereby imposing some kind of unity on to a fundamentally dualist system.

Difficulties of Interpretation

Anyone who attempts to give a coherent account of Zoroastrianism immediately stumbles on two difficulties. The first is linguistic, and since there is no adequate exegetical tradition to the Avesta, and the bulk of the Avesta itself is small, we are frequently forced to fall back on mere guesswork, supported by the use of comparative philology, which, however, is rarely of any real value in establishing the exact meaning of a word. This perpetual uncertainty about the meaning of the text is most serious of all in the *Gāthās* which, being the Prophet's own words, are obviously the most crucial part of the whole of the Zoroastrian sacred literature. In the Pahlavi books we are more fortunate from the linguistic point of view since Pahlavi (which should more correctly be called Zoroastrian Middle Persian) is so near to New Persian that the actual meaning of a word is rarely in doubt. The text of some of the books and particularly the *Dēnkart* which is, from the theological point of view, far the most important, is sometimes desperately corrupt and appears to make no sense whatever. The second difficulty is the extent of the difference in doctrine and emphasis we find between our principal sources, and this not only between the Avesta, the inscriptions, and the Greek sources, but also between the different strata of the Avesta itself. It is true that in other religions we find later accretions added to the original deposit of faith, but in no other does the original doctrine appear to have been so radically changed as in the earlier phases of Zoroastrianism. The only close parallel would seem to be the radical transformation of Islam by the Sūfīs from a strict and austere monotheism into a full-blooded dogma-less pantheism in which ecstasy was pursued as an end in itself through the artificial aids of song and dance. Sūfism, however, was merely an aberrant movement within the wider framework of Islamic orthodoxy: it never succeeded in changing the transcendent monotheism that was and is the essence of that faith.

In Zoroastrianism things were very different. It would seem clear that Zoroaster transformed the national Iranian religion in which he was brought up into an almost pure monotheism quite different from anything that either Iran or India had ever seen before. The reform, however, was too radical and too far-going for the majority of the people to accept and, with changed political conditions, much of the 'paganism' and its attendant polytheism which preceded the reform crept back into the religion that was now associated with his name. In the earlier period there is, then, no clear development in either doctrine or cult that can be traced with any certainty. The sources are so sparse and the contradictions that exist between them so many that no historical reconstruction can claim finality; and despite the great advances that have been made in the field of Iranian philology during the last few decades, there are still far too many passages which remain obstinately obscure and refuse to deliver up their secrets. This is particularly true of the Prophet's own *Gāthās* and of the *Dēnkart*.

All this accounts for the disarray into which Zoroastrian studies have fallen. Excited rather than dismayed by the uncertainties that meet them wherever they turn, scholars have built the most elaborate and improbable religious structures which they would have us believe are authentic representations of Zoroastrianism. Professor Henning has already demolished two such structures in his *Zoroaster, Politician or Witch-Doctor?* and my own effort to make sense of Sassanian theology has met with much well-deserved criticism. I hope that I have taken due account of this criticism in the present volume.

In this volume my aim has been to interpret Zoroastrianism from the texts themselves as I understand them. My approach to the Avesta has been on the whole liturgical, while my assessment of the Pahlavi books has been mainly theological; and since historically the heyday of Zoroastrianism coincided with the great days of the first and second Persian Empires, I have divided the book into two parts which I have called *Dawn* and *Twilight*, for what should have been the midday of this ill-fated religion was in fact an almost total eclipse.

I have rarely attempted to criticize or refute the views of other scholars as this would be unsuitable to the series of which this volume forms part, nor have I at all frequently offered philological justification for my own translations from the Pahlavi. Such justification will, it is hoped, appear in one of the learned journals. Above all I have tried to treat Zoroastrianism not so much as a problem to be solved as a faith by which a great nation once lived. This does not mean that I have been blind to the obvious defects which its lack of sound tradition itself reveals and which in the end resulted in its downfall, but it does mean that I have tried to gain an insight into what gave this religion the power for so long to attract the assent and loyalty of men.

Part I

DAWN

CHAPTER ONE

THE PROPHET

His Place and Date—The Economic and Political Background—Truth and the Lie—The Traditional Religion—Free Will—The Two Spirits—Zoroaster and his God—The Bounteous Immortals—God and the Two Spirits—The Two Spirits in the Dead Sea Scrolls—The Holiness of God—God, the Sole Creator—Post Mortem Judgement—Heaven and Hell—Influence on Judaism—The 'Second Existence'—Summary of Doctrine

His Place and Date

THE traditional date the Zoroastrians assign to their Prophet is '258 years before Alexander', and for the Persian or Iranian the name 'Alexander' can only have meant the sack of Persepolis, the extinction of the Achaemenian Empire, and the death of the last of the kings of kings, Darius III. This occurred in 330 BC, and Zoroaster's date would then be 588 BC, and this date we may take to refer to the initial success of his prophetic mission which consisted in the conversion of King Vishtāspa when Zoroaster was forty years old.[1] Since he is traditionally said to have lived seventy-seven years, we will not be far wrong in dating him at 628–551 BC. It seems also to be generally agreed that the Prophet's sphere of operation in which his message was proclaimed was ancient Chorasmia—an area comprising, perhaps, what is now Persian Khorasan, Western Afghanistan, and the Turkmen Republic of the U.S.S.R.[2] There is, however, evidence to show that Zoroaster was not a native of these lands, for he himself complains to his God that he is persecuted in his homeland and asks him to what land he shall flee.[3] Ultimately he found refuge with King Vishtāspa who was, according to Henning, the last paramount chief of a Chorasmian confederation finally overthrown by Cyrus. The only place in the Avesta which is brought into connexion with Zoroaster is Raghā (the classical Rhages and modern Ray, now a suburb of Tehran) which is described as 'Zarathushtrian'.[4] It is then rather more than possible that Zoroaster was a native of Rhages in Media and that he fled from there to Chorasmia where he finally found a patron in Vishtāspa. Yet even at the court of this prince, it would appear, he found no rest, for there are constant references to continuing hostile action on the part of his enemies even after he was assured of the royal protection.

The Economic and Political Background

The moral dualism between *Asha* and *Druj*, Truth and the Lie, Righteousness and Unrighteousness, which is so characteristic of the *Gāthās*, can be seen as a universalization of a concrete political and social situation in which a peaceful pastoral and cattle-breeding population was constantly threatened by the inroads of fierce nomadic tribes. To these latter Zoroaster habitually refers as the *dregvants* or *drvants*, the 'followers of the Lie', whereas his own supporters are the *ashavans*, the 'followers of Truth or Righteousness'. The 'Lie', however, which both in the *Gāthās*, in the later Avesta, and the much later Pahlavi books, is the term used to represent the very principle of evil— Angra Mainyu or Ahriman, the 'Evil' or 'Aggressive Spirit' being only its leading personification—is not only the opponent and denial of *Asha* or abstract truth: much more essentially, in the *Gāthās* at least, it is predatory aggression against, or subversion of, good government and a peaceful agricultural and pastoral order. 'This do I ask thee, Lord,' the Prophet asks his God, 'What retribution will there be for him who would secure the kingdom (political power) for the follower of the Lie, for the evil-doer who cannot earn a livelihood except by doing violence to the husbandman's herds and men, though they have not provoked him (*adrujyantō*, lit. "not lying to or harming him').'' [5] The nomad is the aggressor and the word used to represent and, to some extent, to personify his aggressive impulse, is *Aēshma*, 'violence' or 'fury', from a root *aēsh-* meaning 'to rush forward' or 'violent movement'.[6] This violence is directed against both men and cattle, the latter being sought after not only as booty but as sacrificial victims. The plight of the ox, indeed, which finds itself defenceless in a world of violence, forms the subject-matter of a whole *Gāthā*. Its soul appeals in anguish to Ahura Mazdāh, the 'Wise Lord', who is also for Zoroaster the one true God and to the 'Bounteous Immortals' (*amesha spentas*) who at once surround him and are yet inseparable from him in that they are his most characteristic attributes.

'For whom did ye create me?' the soul of the ox demands. 'Who was it that fashioned me? Violence, fury, cruelty, frightfulness, and might hem me in. No other husbandman have I but you; so assign me good grazing lands.[7]

To this Ahura Mazdāh replies:

'None has been found to be thy master and to judge concerning thee in accordance with Righteousness; for the Creator fashioned thee for the herdsman and the husbandman. In agreement with Righteousness did the Wise Lord create for the ox the sacred formula of the oblation of fat[8] and for parched(?) men [did he], bounteous in his ordinances, [create] milk.'[9]

This answer seems far from satisfactory to the soul of the ox who replies: 'Whom hast thou from among men, who, being well disposed to us[10] (the ox and the cow) would take care of us?' 'This man [alone] have I found here,' the Wise Lord replies, 'who has given ear to [my] ordinances, Zarathushtra of Spitama's lineage.'

Now what is the significance of this singular dialogue? The soul of the ox complains that it has become the object of violence and rapine, and this despite the fact that it has or believes it has divine protectors ('No other husbandman have I but you'). Yet, far from comforting it, the Wise Lord replies that no one exists who can be its master or pass judgement concerning it according to Righteousness, for the Wise Lord himself in agreement with Righteousness had created for it 'the sacred formula of the oblation of fat' whereas its milk was to assuage the thirst of men. This is as much as to say that in the original dispensation the bovine species was destined not only to nourish man with its milk but also to serve as a sacrificial victim. This Ahura Mazdāh had decreed 'in agreement with Asha', that is, Righteousness or Truth.

Now of all the 'Bounteous Immortals'[11] who surround and partake of the nature of Ahura Mazdāh, Asha alone is of demonstrably Indo-Iranian origin, that is to say, as a major religious concept it is common to both the earliest stratum of Indian religion found in the *Rig-Veda* and to the Avesta. *Vohu Manah*, the 'Good Mind', on the other hand, is a purely Iranian concept and is probably an invention of the Prophet Zoroaster himself. So it is that the soul of the ox asks whether no man exists who would take care of cattle *in accordance with the Good Mind.*[12] Such a man, Ahura Mazdāh replies, is to be found in Zoroaster.

This would seem to indicate that the Prophet did not regard himself as 'doing away with the law and the prophets' that preceded him *in toto*, rather he was adding a new dimension to the old religion in so far as it was represented by Ahura Mazdāh (if indeed he existed before his time) and Asha. Hence he continues to refer to his own followers as *asha-vans*, 'followers of Truth or Righteousness' and to his opponents as *dreg-vans*, 'followers of the Lie', that principle which violates the natural order.

Now it is obvious from the *Gāthās* that Zoroaster met with very stiff opposition from the civil and ecclesiastical authorities when once he had proclaimed his mission. The soul of the ox, when it learns that the powers above have entrusted it to him, cries out in genuine dismay and barely concealed derision: 'What, am I to be satisfied with a protector who has no power, with the word of a feeble man, I who crave [a protector] who exercises his sovereignty at will?[13] Will a man ever exist who will give him [effectual] aid with his hands?'[14] Zoroaster

35

too was conscious of his weakness and of how formidable the opposition to his teaching was: he complains of being persecuted by his own community because he is master of only a few cattle and men[15] whereas his enemy is stronger than he.[16]

Once, however, he becomes confident of the patronage of King Vishtāspa his tone changes and he sets himself up as the judge between the two parties:

'Remembering your laws we proclaim words to which those who cleave to the laws of the Lie and lay waste the worldly goods of the [followers of] Truth, will not listen, [words] most good, forsooth, to those who have given their hearts to Mazdāh. Though, maybe, the better path to choose may not be plain for all to see, yet will I face you all, for Ahura Mazdāh recognizes [me as] judge between the two parties, for it is we who live in accordance with Truth.'[17]

Truth and the Lie

The Prophet knew no spirit of compromise and, as prophets do, he saw things very much in black and white. On the one hand stood Asha—Truth and Righteousness—on the other the Druj—the Lie, Wickedness, and Disorder. This was not a matter on which compromise was possible: it was literally a matter of life and death, for he promised to bring as 'an offering the life of his own body, the first-fruits of his good mind and deeds to Mazdāh and to the Truth. Through these are his hearkening (s(e)raosha) [to the Word] and his Kingdom (khshathra).'[18] For him the issue is crystal clear and the battle is on.

There would seem to be little doubt that an actual state of war existed between the two parties, Zoroaster and his patron Vishtāspa standing on the one side and the so-called followers of the Lie, many of whom he mentions by name, on the other; for not only does the Prophet forbid his followers to have any contact with the 'followers of the Lie',[19] but he also asks his God directly to which of the two opposing *armies* he will give the victory.[20] Like Muhammad, Zoroaster relied on the sword to enforce the efficacy of his prophetic word.

'A true enemy of the follower of the Lie and a powerful support of the follower of Truth':[21] that is how Zoroaster describes himself. There can be no question of compromise with what the Prophet considers to be evil: the enemy must be either vanquished or converted. 'He who, by word or thought or with his hands, works evil to the follower of the Lie or converts his comrade to the good, such a man does the will of the Wise Lord and pleases him well.'[22]

Now who were these followers of the Lie whom Zoroaster so

vigorously attacks? Primarily they were worshippers of the *daēvas*, a word that, in Zoroastrianism, comes to mean simply 'demon'. Originally, however, the *daēvas* were not demons, they were a class of gods that were common to the Indians and Iranians alike. This is made certain by the fact that in the *Rig-Veda* in India two classes of deity are distinguished, the *asuras* and the *devas*, the former being more remote from man and the latter being closer to him. In the *Rig-Veda* the greatest of the *asuras* is Varuna, the protector of Truth, who is the guardian of the moral law, whereas the greatest of the *devas* is Indra, the war-god of the Aryans, who is the very personification of victorious might and who is not at all concerned with the moral order. The fate of the two classes of deity was very different in India and Iran; for whereas, in India, the *asuras* in the course of time sank to the rank of demon, in Iran it was the *daēvas* (= *devas*) who met with the same dismal fate, largely as a result of the direct onslaught that Zoroaster unleashed against them.

The leaders of Zoroaster's opponents, the followers of the Lie as he calls them, are usually called *kavis* and *karapans*. It has generally been assumed that the latter were a priestly caste, and the word itself has been shown to mean 'mumbler',[23] a reference, presumably, to the recitation of a traditional liturgy. The former term *kavi*, however, is not so clear, for it seems to have a quite different meaning in the Indian and the Iranian traditions. In India the word means a composer of hymns, but in the *Gāthās* Zoroaster uses the word not only to denote the leaders of his opponents but also as an epithet of his own patron Vishtāspa. Moreover, in the later Avesta the word is used to mean 'ruler' or 'king' and is regularly applied to the legendary kings of Iran, and the same development is maintained in the later languages. Despite the Indian evidence, then, it would appear that the *kavis* (of whom Zoroaster's patron was one) were local rulers who in the normal course of events would be supporters of the old religion which Zoroaster attacked. His enemies, then, were the established civil and religious authorities which supported the ancient national religion.

What this religion was is made fairly clear by Zoroaster's own attacks on it.

The Traditional Religion

That it is a traditional religion he is attacking is made quite clear by the fact that it is Yima, the first man according to the ancient Iranian tradition, whom he singles out for especial abuse. 'Among those sinners,' he says, 'was Yima, the son of Vivahvant, for so have we heard, who, to please our men, gave them portions of the flesh of the ox to eat. As to these, O Mazdāh, I leave the decision to thee(?).'[24] Zoroaster is here attacking a practice said to have been instituted by Yima who was both in the Indian and Iranian tradition[25] the first man, and which must therefore have been a national institution. Yima's crime would seem to have been not so much that he had introduced meat-eating among his people as that he had slaughtered cattle in sacrifice to the ancient gods. This sacrifice would appear to have been associated with the equally ancient rite of the consumption of the fermented juice of the Haoma plant which appears to have been associated with ritual intoxication.[26] 'When wilt thou strike down this filthy drunkenness,' the Prophet exclaims, 'with which the priests (karapans) evilly delude [the people] as do the wicked rulers of the provinces in [full] consciousness [of what they do].'[27] More strangely Yima and his co-religionists are accused not only of laying waste the pasture lands but of declaring that the sun and the ox were 'the worst things to see'.[28] This seems very odd indeed since Yima himself was almost certainly a solar figure, and there seems no ready explanation for so extraordinary an accusation except that the rite alleged to have been instituted by Yima consisted of the ritual slaughter of a bull or cow in a sunless place or at night. This is so strikingly similar to the Mithraic mysteries which were later to be practised in the Roman Empire and which were certainly of Iranian origin, that scholars have maintained that these rites were performed in honour of Mithra. We shall have to consider this view when we come to deal with the god Mithra as he appears in the Avesta.

From the passage we have been discussing, however, it would seem clear that Zoroaster is attacking a traditional cult in which a bull was slaughtered at night or in a sunless place in honour of the *daēvas*: this rite was accompanied by another in which the juice of the Haoma plant was extracted and ritually consumed. This juice must have been fermented and was certainly intoxicating. What is strange, however, is that already in the later Avesta the Haoma rite had become central to the Zoroastrian liturgy itself, and the whole of the later liturgy shows that in its original form animal sacrifice must have been prominent. So in *Yasna* 11, which forms part of the liturgy dedicated to Haoma, both the ox and Haoma are represented as complaining of being ill-used; but the ox does not, as one might expect, complain of being slaughtered but merely accuses the priest of not distributing its sacrificial flesh equitably, while Haoma complains that the priest withholds from him the jaw, tongue, and left eye of the sacrificial animal which had been allotted to him by his father, Ahura Mazdāh.

This, indeed, is one of the most puzzling aspects of early Zoroastrianism, for the whole liturgy of the *Yasna* (of which the *Gāthās* of the Prophet form part) centres round the Haoma rite, one form of which was certainly condemned by Zoroaster, and it is clear that although the rite as performed in later times did not involve animal sacrifice, it certainly did so in its earliest form, for among the offerings mentioned are both the 'beneficent ox' and the 'living ox'. In the historical development of the ritual the 'living ox' was represented by milk, but in its original form it seems clear that an ox must actually have been immolated in sacrifice. How such a radical distortion of the Prophet's express wishes can have come about we shall shortly have to discuss when we come to deal with the later Avesta. For the moment it is sufficient to note that the so-called 'followers of the Lie' must have been worshippers of the traditional gods whose liturgy included the slaughter of an ox and the consumption of the fermented juice of the Haoma plant. Zoroaster sees himself as a prophet sent by God not only to proclaim a new doctrine but also to reform ritual practices claiming immemorial antiquity.

What this traditional religion was is fairly clear in its broad outlines both from the later Avesta into which much of the earlier 'paganism' has been readmitted, and from the parallel religion of the *Rig-Veda* in India which was never subjected to any radical reform. In the *Rig-Veda*, as we have seen, two types of deity were recognized, the *asuras* and the *devas*—the former being more remote and more directly concerned with the right ordering of the cosmos, the latter being nearer to man, more active, and more nearly associated with the victorious advance of the Aryan tribes then swarming into India. So too in Iran these two types of deity must have existed side by side before the Zoroastrian reform, and it is amply clear from the *Gāthās* themselves that the *daēvas* (= the Indian *devas*) were considered by Zoroaster to be no gods at all but maleficent powers who refused to do the will of the Wise Lord. Further evidence of this is supplied by the later Avesta where we find some of these demons' names, and these names correspond exactly to the names of some of the most prominent gods of the *Rig-Veda*. Thus the most popular of all the Rig-Vedic gods, Indra, the patron war-god of the Aryans, turns up in the later Avesta as a demon. So too we meet with Saurva corresponding to the Indian Śarva or Rudra, the most sinister of the Vedic gods who was later to be known as Śiva, and Nāñhaithya corresponding to the two Nāsatyas or Aśvins of the Vedic texts. Never, however, does Zoroaster attack the other class of deity, the *ahuras* (= the Indian *asuras*), and yet he, pointedly perhaps, refrains from mentioning any of them by name. It would, however, not be true to say that he ignores their existence, for he twice speaks of

39

ahuras or 'lords' in the plural,[29] thereby indicating that he had not, at least at the time when the two hymns in question were composed, entirely rejected the *ahuras* existing alongside his own supreme God, Ahura Mazdāh, the Wise Lord. It is, however, fair to say that he found them inconsistent with his own religion and therefore studiously avoided mentioning them by name.

Zoroaster's world-view is rooted in the actual conditions of his time. From the old religion he takes over the antithesis—already attested in the *Rig-Veda*—of Truth (*asha*) and the Lie (*druj*), and in this respect his religion may be called an ethical dualism, but, unlike the *Rig-Veda*, he thrusts this fundamental antagonism right into the forefront of his religious teaching. He does not, however, start from any abstract principle, he starts from the concrete situation as it faced him in Eastern Iran. On the one side he found a settled pastoral and agricultural community devoted to the tilling of the soil and the raising of cattle, on the other he found a predatory, marauding tribal society which destroyed both cattle and men, and which was a menace to any settled way of life. Their gods were like unto them: never were they good rulers, delivering over, as they did, the ox to Fury (*aēshma*)[30] instead of providing it with good pasture.

In his war against the 'followers of the Lie' Zoroaster neither offers nor seeks a compromise: for him his opponents are evil incarnate, and they are to be treated as such. In an astonishing passage he says: 'Whether a man dispose of much or little wealth, he should show kindness(?) to the follower of Truth, but should be evil to the follower of the Lie,'[31] for the man 'who is most good to the follower of the Lie is himself a follower of the Lie'.[32] There can, then, be no question of loving your enemies because they embody the Lie, and so long as they do so, they are evil creatures to whom no mercy should be shown. So in his colloquy with the Good Mind[33] Zoroaster describes himself as a 'true enemy of the follower of the Lie' and a 'strong support of the follower of Truth'.[34] The Prophet, however, did not believe that the followers of the Lie were necessarily irretrievably damned, for every man is free to choose between the two parties for himself. So long as they persist in adhering to what he considers to be a false religion they must be attacked, but the possibility of conversion is always at the back of his mind. 'He who by word or thought or with his hands works evil to the follower of the Lie or converts his comrade to the good, such a man does the will of Ahura Mazdāh and pleases him well.'[35] His ultimate aim, indeed, is not merely to make war on the followers of the Lie, but rather to convert them and all men to the new religion he proclaimed.[36]

Free Will

Zoroastrianism is the religion of free will *par excellence*. Each man is faced sooner or later with making his choice between Truth and the Lie—the true religion which the Prophet claimed had been revealed to him and the false religion which his contemporaries had inherited from their forebears. Zoroaster, however, projected this basic opposition between Truth and the Lie which he saw working itself out here and now on earth on to the purely spiritual sphere: on all levels were the two principles opposed, and so he came to see that the whole cosmos, both material and spiritual, was shot through with this fundamental tension: over against a transcendental Good Mind stood the Evil Mind, over against the Bounteous Spirit the Evil or Destructive Spirit, over against Right-Mindedness Pride and so on; and on every level a choice had to be made, Ahura Mazdāh, the Wise Lord, himself not being exempt.

On the lowest level the ox has freedom to choose between the good husbandman and the man who is no husbandman, and 'of the two it chose the husbandman who would tend it, a master who follows Truth and cultivates(?) the Good Mind; no share in the good news shall the man who is no husbandman have, however much he strive.'[37] The free choice which is the privilege even of the animal kingdom was God's free gift to his creatures at the very beginning of existence, for 'in the beginning, O Mazdāh, by thy mind didst thou create for us material forms (*gaēthā*) and consciences and rational wills (*khratu*), for thou didst establish corporeal life—deeds and doctrines that men might thereby make their choices in freedom of will.'[38] The choice that must be made is ultimately always that between Truth and the Lie. 'For our choice,' the Prophet says, 'Truth has been presented for our own benefit, but to the [false] teacher the Lie for his own undoing.'[39] Thus though there is no doubt at all in Zoroaster's mind that Truth is exclusively on his side, he realizes that the freedom of the will entails freedom to make the wrong choice, freedom, that is, to err; and it is interesting that the word *varena* which in Avestan means 'free choice' comes, in its Pahlavi form *varan*, to mean 'heresy'—an exact parallel to the development of the Greek word *hairesis* in Christianity. 'Both he who speaks true and he who speaks falsely, both the wise and the fool, raise their voices in accordance with [what is in their] hearts and minds.'[40] Both parties are entitled to proclaim their doctrines and there would seem to be no obvious way of deciding which doctrine is true unless some universally accepted authority is recognized. This difficulty was fully apparent to Zoroaster for he asks of his God who is really a follower of the Truth and who a follower of the Lie,[41] thereby conceding that his enemies may have been sincere in holding their false views. To solve the difficulty and because he sincerely saw himself as a prophet of God, he claimed such authority for himself and set himself up as judge between the two parties. 'Though,' he says, 'maybe, the better path to choose may not be plain for all to see, yet will I face you all, for the Wise Lord recognizes [me as] judge between the two parties, for it is we who live in accordance with Truth.'[42]

It is in this capacity of judge, perhaps, that Zoroaster in *Yasna* 30 summons all men to make the great decision. 'Hear with your ears,' he prophesies, 'behold with mind all clear the two choices between which you must decide, each man [deciding] for his own self, [each man] knowing how it will appear (?) to us at the [time of] great crisis.'[43] With these words he introduces the myth of the primeval choice that the two Spirits whom he calls 'twins' had to make at the beginning of time:

'In the beginning those two Spirits who are the well-endowed (?) twins were known as the one good and the other evil, in thought, word, and deed. Between them the wise chose rightly, not so the fools. And when these Spirits met they established in the beginning life and death that in the end the followers of the Lie should meet with the worst existence, but the followers of Truth with the Best Mind. Of these two Spirits he who was of the Lie chose to do the worst things; but the Most Holy Spirit, clothed in rugged heaven, [chose] Truth as did [all] who sought with zeal to do the pleasure of the Wise Lord by [doing] good works. Between the two the *daēvas* did not choose rightly; for, as they deliberated, delusion overcame them so that they chose the most Evil Mind. Then did they, with one accord, rush headlong unto Fury that they might thereby extinguish (?) the existence of mortal men.'[44]

The Two Spirits

It is impossible to say whether this myth of the two twins was original to Zoroaster himself or whether he was reformulating a more ancient myth in accordance with his own ideology. In the myth, however, he projects the concrete situation he saw on earth—where the followers of the Lie represented destructive forces hostile to physical life, and the followers of Truth the life-conserving and life-enhancing forces—on to the spiritual world. Here the basic duality of Truth and Falsehood, Righteousness and Wickedness, Order and Disorder are personified in a pair of Primal Twins whom he calls the Bounteous or Holy Spirit—for the word *spenta* usually translated as 'holy' implies increase and abundance—and the Destructive or Evil Spirit (*Angra Mainyu*, the later Ahriman), the one the bringer of life and the other

42

the author of death. These two Spirits stand over against each other, irreconcilably opposed to each other in a total contradiction.

'I will speak out,' the Prophet proclaims, 'concerning the two Spirits of whom, at the beginning of existence, the Holier thus spoke to him who is Evil: "Neither our thoughts, nor our teachings, nor our wills, nor our choices, nor our words, nor our deeds, nor our consciences, nor yet our souls agree." ' [45]

In the *Gāthās* the Holy or Bounteous Spirit is not identical with Ahura Mazdāh, the Wise Lord, who is also the supreme God, but is only an aspect of him, one of his 'sons'. But even Ahura Mazdāh himself must make his choice between Truth and the Lie, between good and evil. In a strange passage in which both men and *daēvas* are represented as making supplication at the divine court Zoroaster says:

'Family, and village, and tribe, and you *daēvas* too, like me, sought to rejoice the Wise Lord [saying]: "Let us be thy messengers that we may keep at bay those who hate thee." To them did the Wise Lord, united with the Good Mind and in close companionship with bright Truth, make answer from his Kingdom: "Holy and good Right-Mindedness do we choose: let it be ours." ' [46]

So does God himself make the choice that all must make between good and evil. United with the Good Mind and in close companionship with Truth or Righteousness, God chooses the good and utterly condemns the old religion which he identifies with evil.

'But you, you *daēvas*,' he exclaims, 'and whosoever multiplies his sacrifice to you, are all the seed of the Evil Mind, the Lie, and Pride; doubtful(?) are your deeds for which ye are famed throughout the seventh part of the earth. For ye have so devised it that men who do what is worst should thrive [as if they were] favoured by the "gods" (*daēvas*)—men who depart from the Good Mind and break away from the will of the Wise Lord and from Truth. So would you defraud man of the good life and immortality even as the Evil Spirit [defrauded you], you *daēvas*, through his Evil Mind— a deed by which, with evil words, he promised dominion to the followers of the Lie.' [47]

So does the Wise Lord unequivocally condemn the old religion and take the part of Truth which he identifies with Zoroaster's reform.

Zoroaster and his God
Zoroaster, on his side, saw himself as a prophet and a visionary. He was also a priest[48] and therefore, presumably, must originally have been connected with the earlier cult which he was later to condemn. He saw himself as a prophet speaking to God and hearkening to his

43

word. He is 'the Prophet who raises his voice in veneration, the friend of Truth'[49] and God's friend.[50] His relationship to his God is not one of servility, rather he asks his help—the kind of help that a friend grants to a friend.[51] His mission was foreordained, for he was chosen by God 'in the beginning',[52] and he claims to have seen him in a vision which transported him back in time to the beginning of the world. 'Then, Mazdāh, did I realize that thou wast holy when I saw thee in the beginning, at the birth of existence, when thou didst ordain a [just] requital for deeds and words, an evil lot for evil [done] and a good one for a good [deed]: by thy virtue [shall all this come to pass] at the last turning-point of creation.'[53] Repeatedly he asks to see his God and the entities associated with him.[54] 'When will I see thee in Truth, and the Good Mind, and the path [that leads] to the Wise Lord, the most mighty, [the path that is] to hearken [to his word]?'[55] The word *sraosha* which we have translated as 'to hearken' and which is usually translated as 'obedience' or 'discipline' probably originally meant the Prophet's relationship to God, the one hearing and obeying the divine message, the other hearkening to the prayers of his prophet. Although Sraosha, the genius of hearing and obeying, was later to become more fully personalized and anthropomorphized than almost any other deity, surviving right down into Islamic times as Surūsh, the messenger of God sometimes identified with the angel Gabriel, yet the original meaning of his name was never wholly lost, for the Pahlavi translators often render it with the Pahlavi word *nighōshishn* meaning 'listening' or 'hearkening'; and this meaning of the Avestan word too can still be detected in *Yasna* 56.1 in the phrase 'May the listening to [the word of] the Wise Lord be present here'. Thus Zoroaster not only sees his God, he also hears the words he speaks. This 'hearing' of God's voice he expresses in the most concrete possible imagery: he asks God to speak to him 'with the tongue of his mouth'.[56] He hears God and he sees him, and seeing him knows him as he is in Truth: 'Now have I seen him with my eyes, knowing him in Truth to be the Wise Lord of the Good Mind and of [good] deeds and words.'[57] Zoroaster realizes the holiness of God not by thought or concentration but by a direct vision of his goodness, truth, and eternity. 'Then did I understand in my mind,' he confesses, 'that thou art the ancient, thou the [ever] young, the father of the Good Mind, when I comprehended thee with my eyes—[thee], the very creator of Truth, Lord of [all] creation in thy works.'[58] For the Prophet this vision is self-authenticating: he has *seen* God as the holy and good, as the eternal, the primeval being who is yet ever young, the first and the last, and the origin of all goodness: he sees him with his eyes and grasps him with his mind. It is, if you like, an intellectual vision of God's holiness. 'Then did I realize that thou wast holy, Wise Lord . . .' is the refrain that runs throughout *Yasna* 43: it is an intensely personal *experience* of the reality of God's goodness.

The Avestan word we have translated as 'holy' is *spenta*, but we might equally translate 'bounteous'. The Pahlavi translators render the word by the Pahlavi equivalent *abhzōnīk*, an adjective derived from *abhzōn* ('increase'). Holiness, for Zoroaster, also meant abundance, growth, and health. The divine nature is seen as an overwhelming giving of self, as superabundant life both in the spiritual and the material realm; for Zoroastrianism is in all its phases a religion that enthusiastically and thankfully accepts and blesses all the good things of *this* world as well as those of the next: indeed, in the *Gāthās*, the work of the Prophet himself, it is often exceedingly difficult to decide whether he is referring to a concrete situation here on earth or whether he is speaking of the last things.

The Bounteous Immortals

God is *spenta*: he is holy and he gives abundance. Ahura Mazdāh, however, the Wise Lord, is not identical with *Spenta Mainyu*, the Holy Spirit, who, as we have seen, is the eternal antagonist of the Evil or Destructive Spirit 'who chose to do the worst things'. The relationship between the Holy Spirit and those other entities that are close to the Wise Lord is not easy to define. Very soon after the Prophet's death these 'entities' were drawn into a closed system, forming a heptad of so-called *amesha spentas*, 'Holy' or 'Bounteous Immortals'. Ahura Mazdāh, the Wise Lord, came to be identified with the Holy Spirit, though nowhere in the *Gāthās* is such an identification made, and beside him were six abstractions, all of which figure prominently in the *Gāthās*—the Good Mind, Truth or Righteousness (*asha*), Right-Mindedness (*ārmaiti*), the Kingdom, Wholeness, and Immortality. In the *Gāthās* Ahura Mazdāh is spoken of as the father of the Holy Spirit,[59] as he is the father of Truth,[60] the Good Mind,[61] and Right-Mindedness;[62] but paternity in God is not to be understood in any crude sense, for he is also said simply to have *created* Truth or Righteousness by an act of will (*khratu*). Zoroaster's idea of paternity in God, then, is very like its Christian counterpart: Holy Spirit, Good Mind, Truth, and Right-Mindedness are thought into existence by the Wise Lord who is the supreme Being. Of these various entities the Holy Spirit, Truth, and the Good Mind stand nearest to God and are rightly regarded as his hypostases. Right-Mindedness, on the other hand, is rather the attitude of man towards God, it is an attitude of humility, the opposite of pride,[63] while the Kingdom, though it is an essential attribute of Ahura Mazdāh, being his by right, may on occasion be usurped by the followers of the Lie.[64] Wholeness and Immortality are indeed attributes of God, but in Zoroaster's thought they are also regarded as being primarily his gifts to man.[65] Indeed, of the 'Bounteous Immortals' only the Holy Spirit is exclusively appropriated to God: the others belong to God by nature but can be and are bestowed on man if he lives according to Truth. So intimately are the spiritual and material worlds connected that very soon after the Prophet's death each of the Bounteous Immortals came to be identified with physical 'elements'— the Good Mind with cattle, Truth with fire, the Kingdom with metals, Right-Mindedness with the earth, Wholeness with water, and Immortality with plants. This linking up of the spiritual with the material world in so concrete and apparently arbitrary a manner seems to date back to Zoroaster himself. Already in the *Gāthās*, Ārmaiti or Right-Mindedness seems to have been identified with the earth, for it is said to have been created as a pasturage for the ox[66] and plants are made to grow for it,[67] whereas in *Yasna* 51.7 Wholeness and Immortality seem to be equated with water and plants.[68] Moreover, already in the *Gāthās*, fire is a symbol of Truth and has its power,[69] while the Good Mind is closely connected with cattle.

Yet in Zoroaster's thought all this is subsidiary: the Bounteous Immortals are primarily aspects of God, but aspects in which man too can share. Wholeness and Immortality are pre-eminently the divine qualities which the Wise Lord bestows on the followers of Truth, and it is the Good Mind which unites man to God[70] and, so to speak, activates Righteousness in him; and it is through Righteousness or Truth that the just man treads the paths of the Good Mind.[71] Yet it is quite impossible to assign any definite role to these Bounteous Immortals in the *Gāthās*: they are little more than the agencies through which God acts. The Good Mind is simply God's mind, though this does not prevent man from participating in it. Truth is what it is because it is God's creation, and he himself is not only *spenta*, 'holy' or 'bounteous', he is also *asha-van* 'truth-ful'.[72] That the Bounteous Immortals were not conceived of by Zoroaster as having an existence separate from God seems to be shown by the fact that God usually appears as the agent and his various divine operations take place *through* one of the Bounteous Immortals, and it is for this reason that, grammatically, they so frequently appear in the instrumental case. Typical of the way in which Zoroaster sees God and his Bounteous Immortals in mutual interdependence is the following stanza: 'May the Wise Lord give us Wholeness and Immortality through the Holy Spirit and the Best Mind, through deeds and words [that are] in accordance with Truth, and through the Kingdom and Right-Mindedness.'[73]

Here all the Bounteous Immortals appear together—two being God's direct gift to man—Wholeness and Immortality, the other five being the instruments through which he operates. This 'instrumental' role of the Bounteous Immortals can perhaps be better understood if we compare it to the formulae of Christian prayer. Christianity too is a monotheistic religion, but its God is not an absolutely pure monad but a Trinity: so the ending of a well-known Catholic prayer is *per eumdem Dominum nostrum Jesum Christum Filium tuum, qui tecum vivit et regnat in unitate Spiritus Sancti Deus per omnia saecula saeculorum*—'through the same Jesus Christ, thy Son, our Lord, who liveth and reigneth with thee, in the unity of the Holy Spirit, God, world without end.' Man prays to God through Christ just as God creates through the same Christ, his Son and pre-existent Word. So, too, in Zoroastrianism, it is through the Good Mind that God communes with man, and through the Holy Spirit that he creates, both the Good Mind and the Holy Spirit being his 'sons'. He also reigns in virtue of the Kingdom which is his by right in union with the Holy Spirit, and his reign lasts for ever and ever because he is possessed of Wholeness and Immortality.

It is true that there are traces of a specific relationship between Right-Mindedness and the earth, and between Wholeness and Immortality and water and plants in the *Gāthās* themselves, but this is because Zoroaster saw the spiritual and material worlds as being the opposite poles of a unitary whole intimately linked together. The link is only weakened with the appearance of the Lie and its most illustrious representative, Angra Mainyu, the Destructive Spirit, who first introduces death into the world. In the later tradition man is the earthly counterpart of Ahura Mazdāh himself, the ox of the Good Mind, fire of Truth, the earth of Right-Mindedness, water and plants of Wholeness and Immortality. None of this does violence to the Prophet's own thought, for physical life in its perfection is the mirror of the divine life: earth and water which give rise to plants, plants which provide fodder for cattle, and cattle which furnish both milk and meat to man are all part of the universal life-process, of the universal natural harmony that is only marred by the violence and corruption introduced by the Lie. But since the Lie is with us and is likely to remain with us as long as the world lasts, man needs weapons with which to defend himself, he needs the metals which are the earthly counterpart of the Kingdom, but which, like the Kingdom itself, can be filched from him and used against him by his enemies. Finally there is the fire which Zoroaster made the centre of his cultus[74] because in its power to destroy darkness it is the symbol of Truth itself whose brilliance too destroys the darkness of error.

Very much has been written on the 'origin' of the Bounteous Immortals, and the mere fact that scholars are in such total disagreement on this subject only goes to show that we know nothing certainly. Asha who is Truth, Righteousness, and Order, we also know in the *Rig-Veda* as *Rta*; and we can therefore be certain that the concept is inherited from Indo-Iranian times, as is its opposition to the Lie. In the case of the Kingdom (*khshathra*), Wholeness, and Immortality, it would seem rather futile to look round for an origin at all since these are concepts that are common to almost all religions. As to the Good Mind and Right-Mindedness, these would seem to be further and more specific elaborations of the basic antithesis between Truth and the Lie that gives its especial flavour to Zoroastrianism. Over against the Good Mind is set the Evil Mind,[75] just as the Holy Spirit on a yet higher level is opposed to the Destructive Spirit. There is, however, this difference: the Holy Spirit is conceived of as being totally divine whereas the Good Mind, though divine and of divine provenance, can be shared by man, and it is this selfsame Good Mind which envelops the Prophet when he comes to the realization of the holiness of God;[76] and it is the Good Mind whom he consults[77] and with whom he seeks union.[78] Similarly Ārmaiti, Right-Mindedness, is opposed to Tarōmaiti or Pairimaiti, 'pride'. Right-Mindedness, then, is predominantly a human excellence, and because this is so, it is Right-Mindedness rather than Truth that the Wise Lord chooses when he himself is required to make his irrevocable choice between truth and falsehood; for Truth and the Good Mind are his from all eternity whereas Right-Mindedness is rather the right and fitting response of man to the Good Mind of God in accordance with Truth.

It would, then, seem quite likely that both the Good Mind and Right-Mindedness on the one hand and their opposites, the Evil Mind and 'perverted-mindedness' or 'pride', are concepts developed by Zoroaster to fill out the overall picture of the great antagonism between Truth and Lie he had inherited from his forebears. That Zoroaster felt himself to be especially close to the Good Mind seems clear from the following passages. In *Yasna* 29 where the soul of the ox complains of ill-treatment at the hands of the 'followers of the Lie', neither Truth nor the Wise Lord himself can or will grant the ox a protector. On the contrary: 'In agreement with Righteousness did the Wise Lord create for the ox the sacred formula of the oblation of fat and for parched(?) men [did he], bounteous in his ordinances, [create] milk.'[79] The soul of the ox, then, appeals directly to the Good Mind and in return the latter appoints Zoroaster as his protector. Thus the Good Mind is represented as modifying an eternal ordinance promulgated by the supreme Being and his Truth, but he does this not of himself but at the behest of Ahura Mazdāh himself, who chooses him as his vehicle of prophecy through which he inspires him not indeed to abrogate his ordinances but to reform what in them had been corrupted. Similarly in what is perhaps the most personal of all the revelations vouchsafed to Zoroaster it is the Good Mind who envelops him and asks him who he is and what his credentials are. 'Who art thou? Whose son art thou? By what token wilt thou appoint a day that I may question thee concerning thy worldly goods and thy self?'[80] To this the Prophet replies: 'First I am Zarathushtra, a true enemy of the follower of the Lie as far as lies within my power, then a powerful support for the follower of Truth.' Thus it is to the Good Mind that Zoroaster confesses himself to be a genuine follower of Truth, and again it is through him that he establishes the fire as the centre of his cult. There is then good reason to suppose that the Good Mind at least was a personal invention of Zoroaster's—the Good Mind which was the manifestation of the divine mind to him personally.

It should not, however, be supposed that the modification of an age-old ordinance of the Wise Lord and his Truth by the Good Mind indicates any tension within the personality of the divine heptad, for Truth and the Good Mind are always represented as being intimately united:[81] the Good Mind is merely the more active partner, the agency through which God prefers to reveal himself to Zoroaster. Both are intimately associated with the supreme Being, and Professor Duchesne-Guillemin is quite right to refer to the three combined as the divine 'Triad'. Truth and the Good Mind are inseparably united to Ahura Mazdāh in a way that the other Bounteous Immortals are not.

The very originality of Zoroaster's conception of these divine entities which surround his God has disconcerted scholars ever since the Avesta was discovered. The theories that have been elucidated to explain them in fact explain nothing at all and are scarcely worth even a cursory notice. They have been likened to the Ādityas of early Indian mythology despite the fact that not one single name is common to the two groups; or, because their number is seven, they have been likened to the Babylonian planetary system with which they have nothing whatever in common. More recently the distinguished French scholar, Georges Dumézil, has seen in them the representatives of the 'three functions' into which, he maintains, all Indo-European society was divided—Truth and the Good Mind representing what he calls the function of sovereignty, the Kingdom representing the warrior function, and Wholeness and Immortality representing the pastoral and agricultural activity of the peasant. This hypothesis, though not wholly implausible, really explains nothing, and it is further vitiated by the parallels that Dumézil and his disciples attempt to draw between Zoroaster's Bounteous Immortals and specific Vedic deities: the parallels are not parallel at all. The defenders of this latest fashion, quite undaunted by the fact that none of the Zoroastrian 'entities' correspond in name with the Vedic deities they are supposed to resemble or by the fact that their nature and function are quite different, seem indifferent to the acknowledged fact that the *Asha*—Truth and Righteousness and Cosmic Order—of the *Gāthās* corresponds most exactly, in etymology and in function, to the *Rta* of the *Rig-Veda*. This, at least, can safely be said to form part of a common Indo-Iranian heritage, and, for lack of any evidence to the contrary, we must suppose that the other 'entities' were developed from very rudimentary beginnings by Zoroaster since they are only faintly adumbrated in the *Veda*. The Prophet's originality may be disconcerting, but it is none the less real for that. That his thought was indeed profoundly original becomes glaringly obvious once we compare his *Gāthās* both with the hymns of the *Rig-Veda* and with the later Avesta. The parallels between these latter two are unmistakable: in the *Gāthās* we are in a totally different religious world. Both the *Rig-Veda* and the later Avesta are frankly polytheistic or—if one prefers the more ambiguous phrase—henotheistic, whereas in the *Gāthās* we meet with a pure monotheism that not only has the stamp of a profoundly experienced revelation but also gives the impression of having been deeply thought out.

God and the Two Spirits

Yet, just how far are we justified in describing the religion of the *Gāthās* as being an ethical monotheism? Earlier in this chapter we had occasion to quote two crucial passages depicting the eternal antagonism that exists between the twin Spirits, Spenta Mainyu and Angra Mainyu, the Holy Spirit and the Destructive Spirit. Whence did the Destructive Spirit arise? The answer would seem to be clear enough, for the two Spirits are explicitly said to be twins, and we learn from *Yasna* 47.2–3 that the Wise Lord is the father of the Holy Spirit. In that case he must be the father of the Destructive Spirit too—a conception that has recently been described as 'absolutely absurd in the mental framework of the *Gāthās*'.[82] In actual fact the logical conclusion we are bound to draw from our texts, namely, that Ahura Mazdāh is the father of the Destructive as well as of the Holy Spirit is only 'absurd' if we persist in judging Zoroaster's own teaching by the standards of a very much later dualist orthodoxy: and there are very good reasons for refusing to do this. First it is undeniable that in many respects as, for example, in the matter of animal sacrifice the later tradition grossly distorts the Prophet's teaching. Secondly, the later tradition identified Ahura Mazdāh, the Wise Lord, with the Holy Spirit, whereas the *Gāthās* ascribe paternity of the Holy Spirit to the Wise Lord. Thirdly, the later tradition assimilates the Wise Lord, now identical with the Holy Spirit, to light and the Destructive Spirit to darkness, whereas the *Gāthās* declare that the Wise Lord creates both light and darkness.[83] Lastly, the later tradition is divided on the interpretation of the stanzas in question; for the rigid dualism of late Sassanian orthodoxy did not hold the field alone. Orthodoxy, indeed, maintained a rigorously dualist position—there were two eternal distinct and separate principles of good and evil, the good principle being Ahura Mazdāh whom tradition had erroneously identified with the Holy Spirit. Zurvanite heterodoxy, however, drew the obvious conclusion from the Gāthic text that describes the two Spirits as twins and argued that, if they were twins, then they must have had a common father. Since Ahura Mazdāh was already identified with the Holy Spirit, he could no longer be considered to be the latter's father. So, for reasons that are obscure, they made the two Spirits the sons of *Zrvan Akarana* or Infinite Time. Yet another sect maintained that the Evil Spirit arose from a single evil thought of the supreme Being. Since, then, two sects among the later Zoroastrians themselves interpreted this stanza (*Yasna* 30.3) as meaning that the Evil Spirit derived from God himself, it seems a trifle wayward to condemn such a notion out of hand in the case of the Prophet himself.

All that we can say is that, by describing the two Spirits as 'twins', Zoroaster implied that the Evil Spirit too must derive from God, but he differs from the later Sassanian orthodoxy in that, for him, the Evil or Destructive Spirit is not an evil substance—he is evil by choice. Like Lucifer he '*chooses* to do the worst things'; he is not forced to do so either by God or by any inner compulsion of his own nature: the misery he brings upon himself and upon his followers is entirely his own fault and will inevitably lead to his destruction.

The Two Spirits in the Dead Sea Scrolls

An almost exact parallel to this solution of the problem of evil is to be found in the *Manual of Discipline*, perhaps the most interesting document of the Dead Sea sect of Qumrān. That Judaism was deeply influenced by Zoroastrianism during and after the Babylonian captivity can scarcely be questioned, and the extraordinary likeness between the

Dead Sea text and the Gāthic conception of the nature and origin of evil, as we understand it, would seem to point to direct borrowing on the Jewish side. According to the account given in the *Manual of Discipline* God:

'created man to have dominion over the world and made for him two spirits, that he might walk by them until the appointed time of his visitation; they are the spirits of truth and of error. In the abode of light are the origins of truth, and from the source of darkness are the origins of error. . . . And by the angel of darkness is the straying of all the sons of righteousness . . . and all the spirits of his lot try to make the sons of light stumble; but the God of Israel and his angel of truth have helped all the sons of light. For he created the spirits of light and of darkness, and upon them he founded every work and upon their ways every service. One of the spirits God loves for all ages of eternity, and with all its deeds he is pleased for ever; as for the other, he abhors its company, and all its ways he hates for ever.'[84]

Here, in a Jewish setting, we have an exact parallel to the attitude of Ahura Mazdāh to the Holy and Destructive Spirits. Like the Jewish God, Ahura Mazdāh abhors the company of the Destructive Spirit, and 'all its ways he hates for ever'; but his hatred is based on rather more rational grounds than is his Jewish counterpart's, for he did not create the Evil Spirit evil: he only becomes such by choice. Yet though there seems to be no valid reason for doubting the Wise Lord's paternity of the Destructive Spirit, repulsive though such an idea may have seemed to a later orthodoxy, it cannot be denied that there is a basic dualism underlying the Prophet's monotheism; but it is not the dualism between the Holy Spirit and the Destructive Spirit who are what they are by their free choice, but between Truth and the Lie, that is, the twin objects of all choice. Zoroaster does tell us indirectly how the Destructive Spirit came into existence and how and why he went wrong; he does not tell us how the Lie originated but leaves us rather to infer that it was there from the beginning. This dualism is basic to all his teaching, and it is this one idea, which he took over from his Indo-Iranian heritage, that he developed and expanded as the corner-stone of the new religion. His followers who elaborated the later orthodoxy merely systematized a doctrine that was already there.

Yet, though Zoroaster's whole vision of the cosmos is dominated by this mortal antagonism between Truth and the Lie, Ahura Mazdāh, the Wise Lord, stands above and beyond them, wholly committed though he is to the side of Truth. In the *Gāthās* the Destructive Spirit does not presume to set himself up as a principle independent of and antagonistic to the supreme God: he is content to measure his strength against the Holy Spirit which emanates from God yet is not God. The *daēvas* too, those ancient gods who had been dethroned, perhaps by Zoroaster himself, do not forget their divine origin, for, by asking the Wise Lord that they may still be allowed to be his messengers, they show that they too acknowledge him as supreme Lord.

'Family, and village, and tribe, and you *daēvas* too, like me, sought to rejoice the Wise Lord [saying]; "Let us be thy messengers that we may keep at bay those who hate thee." To them did the Wise Lord, united with the Good Mind and in close companionship with bright Truth, make answer from his kingdom: "Holy and good Right-Mindedness do we choose: let it be ours." '[85]

Here we are allowed a glimpse of the old order: the dethroned *daēvas* appeal to the God whom they too acknowledge as supreme, against the new authority claimed by the Prophet Zoroaster. Plainly the followers of the old religion did not lightly acquiesce in being dubbed 'followers of the Lie', for they too must have claimed to be *ashavans*, 'followers of the Truth'; and Zoroaster himself seems to be aware of this, for he exclaims:

'This I ask thee, Lord: answer me truly. Which of those whom I consult is the follower of Truth and which the follower of the Lie? On which side is the aggressor (*angra*)? [Is it I?] or is he the aggressor, the follower of the Lie, who seeks to thwart thy bounty (*savah*)? How do things stand? Surely it is he, not those near me, that must be held to be the aggressor.'[86]

So it would seem that Ahura Mazdāh, the Wise Lord, was recognized as the supreme Being by the worshippers of the *daēvas* themselves, and these are rebuked for not taking pains to associate with Truth and for not consulting with the Good Mind, the inference being perhaps that though they may have claimed to be 'followers of Truth', this was not apparent from their behaviour. In accusing them of not consulting with the Good Mind, however, Zoroaster contrasts them with himself, for his very claim to prophethood is based on the close communion with the Wise Lord he experiences through the Good Mind.

The essence of Zoroaster's reform would appear to be that he immensely raised the stature of Ahura Mazdāh, seeing in him not merely the 'greatest and best of the gods' but the sole creator and preserver of the universe, omnipotent and omniscient Lord. We have seen that he is called the 'father' of the Holy Spirit and the Good Mind, of Truth and Right-Mindedness, but these entities are not brought into being by any crassly physical act of generation, they are thought into existence as eternal attributes of God himself. Truth, for instance, is created by God's will or wisdom (*khratu*)[87] and it is by Truth that he maintains his own Good Mind. Again at the beginning of existence

God *thinks*, 'Let the wide spaces be filled with lights',[88] and it is so. Again it is by thought, that is, by the Good Mind operating within him, that Zoroaster comes to the realization that God is the eternal, the ancient and the ever new;[89] and it is by the Good Mind, the exteriorization of the divine thought, that the world is brought into existence, 'by [his] mind, in the beginning, [he] fashioned forth corporeal things, consciences, and wills, [he] created bodily life, and deeds and doctrines among which men could freely make their choices'.[90] Man's free will, then, so passionately insisted on in the *Gāthās*, is also a direct creation of God's, his deliberate plan for humanity.

The Holiness of God

In *Yasna* 43 Zoroaster adopts the refrain 'Then did I realize that thou wast holy when . . .', and it will repay us to see in what he considers this holiness and bounty to consist. First he realizes God's holiness when he receives the Good Mind from his hand which holds the destinies of both good and evil men; secondly when he 'sees' him 'at the birth of existence' deal out their lots of weal and woe to good and bad and when he sees him pass judgement at the end of time; thirdly, when at the urgent behest of the Good Mind, he makes his confession of faith and resolves to be a 'true enemy of the follower of the Lie and a powerful support to the follower of Truth'; fourthly when, once more impelled by the Good Mind, he vows to venerate the fire as the symbol of Truth; fifthly when he first hears God's words, puts aside all trust in men, and resolves to do whatever God tells him is best; sixthly when he glimpses eternal life in God's Kingdom which is his alone to grant or withhold; seventhly, when his 'silent thought' teaches him not to attempt to curry favour with the followers of the Lie who pretend that evil men are good.

Zoroaster, then, recognizes God's holiness first in the act of revelation itself which is transmitted to him through the illumination he receives from the Good Mind, secondly in the content of that revelation. And the content is this: that God is just and that he will judge men according to their good and evil deeds; that evil which is the Lie exists and must be fought; that Truth exists and is to be reverenced in the sacred fire; that God is to be obeyed and that no trust is to be put in men; that God will reward whom he will with eternal life; and lastly that it is wicked to dress up evil in the garb of good. In short, God is a just judge.

God, the Sole Creator

God is judge; and he is the creator of all things,[91] both spiritual and material, and since he thinks all things into existence, his creation is *ex nihilo*. He is omnipotent for he 'rules at will',[92] that is to say, though his Holy Spirit may be pitted against the Destructive Spirit, this happens by his will and consent. His being is in no way circumscribed by the forces of evil as it is in later Zoroastrianism : and it is he who will judge all men according to their deeds in the last days. God's creative activity is magnificently portrayed in a series of rhetorical questions that go to make up the bulk of *Yasna* 44 :

'This I ask thee, Lord : answer me truly. Who is the primeval, the father of Truth through [generation and] birth? Who appointed their paths to the sun and stars? Who but thou is it through whom the moon waxes and wanes? This would I know, O Wise One, and other things besides.

'This I ask thee, Lord : answer me truly. Who set the earth below and the sky [above] so that it does not fall? Who the waters and the plants? Who yoked swift steeds to wind and clouds? Who, O Wise One, is the creator of the Good Mind?

'This I ask thee, Lord : answer me truly. What goodly craftsman made light and darkness? What goodly craftsman sleep and wakefulness? Who made morning, noon, and night to make the wise man mindful of his task?

'This I ask thee, Lord : answer me truly. Is the message I proclaim really true? Will Right-Mindedness [among men] support Truth by its deeds? Hast thou illumined (lit. taught) thy Kingdom with the Good Mind? For whom didst thou fashion the pregnant cow that brings prosperity?

'This I ask thee, Lord : answer me truly. Who created Right-Mindedness venerable with the Kingdom? Who made the son dutiful(?) in his soul to his father? Recognizing thee by these [signs] as the creator of all things through thy Holy Spirit, I [go to] help thee.'[93]

God, then, is the creator of all things, both spiritual and material, and he is the creator of free will. Man, then, enjoys an awful responsibility for his own actions, and though he will be judged by God, it is really he who automatically condemns or saves himself by his evil or good deeds. This is made amply clear in the following passage : 'At the last, glory will be the portion(?) of the man who adheres to a follower of Truth. A long age of darkness, foul food, and cries of woe—to such an existence will your own consciences lead you because of your own deeds, ye followers of the Lie.'[94]

Yet though man earns his own heaven and his own hell by his own good and evil deeds, it is Ahura Mazdāh who passes judgement[95] or this judgement is delegated to Sraosha ;[96] for Sraosha is not only man's hearkening to the word of God, he is also God's all-hearing ear which nothing escapes; and so it is that in the later Avesta Sraosha becomes God's chosen instrument for the chastising of the *daēvas* and all evil men.

Post Mortem Judgement

In later Zoroastrianism there is both an individual judgement at death and a universal ordeal by fire and molten metal at the end of time. Both ideas are present in embryo in the *Gāthās*. The individual soul is required to cross the 'Bridge of the Requiter' where those who have performed good works will receive a just return for their righteousness (*asha*) and the kingdom by their good mind.[97] Here, as so often in the *Gāthās*, we cannot be certain whether 'righteousness' and 'good mind' refer to the divine entities which are hypostases of the Wise Lord or to the righteousness and good thoughts of individual men. The underlying idea, however, would appear to be that when the good man crosses the Bridge of the Requiter the righteousness and good thoughts that had accompanied him on earth are united with substantial Righteousness and Truth and with the Good Mind of God which are themselves the source of all earthly goodness and truth. This thought is elsewhere expressed as union with the Good Mind.[98]

The good man's guide across the bridge is Zoroaster himself. He leads the souls of his followers across the dreaded Bridge and conducts them into the House of the Good Mind[99] where they will come face to face with their creator who dwells together with Truth and that same Good Mind.[100] The wicked meet with a very different fate: 'their souls and consciences trouble them when they come to the Bridge of the Requiter, guests for all eternity in the House of the Lie'.[101]

The Bridge of the Requiter at which the soul is judged figures prominently in the later tradition.[102] On it the deeds of the soul are weighed in the balance of Rashnu, the just judge *par excellence* who is himself the Requiter,[103] and the gods Mithra and Sraosha assist him. This was probably the traditional picture as it existed before the Zoroastrian reform, and, if this is so, it shows how great the Prophet's zeal on behalf of Ahura Mazdāh, whom he regarded as the one true God who could brook no rival, was, for in the *Gāthās* it is not Rashnu nor even Sraosha who had been accepted into the Prophet's system, but Ahura Mazdāh himself who is the Requiter and judge of pure and impure alike.[104]

Heaven and Hell

Heaven and hell are variously described in the *Gāthās*; they are the best[105] and the worst[106] existences, and these quite unlocalized conceptions of the future life survive in the Persian language today: *behesht*, heaven, meaning originally simply 'the best', and *dūzakh* meaning 'a wretched existence'. That the 'best' existence is regarded as being on a mental and spiritual level is shown by the fact that the opposite of the worst existence is not simply the best existence but the best Mind.[107] Similarly heaven and hell are the House of the Good Mind[108] and the house of the Worst Mind,[109] or, more typically, the House of Song[110] and the House of the Lie.[111] Unlike Muhammad, Zoroaster does not describe the joys of heaven in physical terms; the blessed attain to 'long life', that is, presumably, eternal life and the Kingdom of the Good Mind;[112] they will be blessed with ease and benefit[113] and will be possessed of Wholeness and Immortality, God's supreme gifts to the faithful.

Oddly enough, the torments of hell are more fully described than the joys of heaven. The damned will be oppressed with discomfort and torments,[114] condemned to 'a long age of darkness, foul food, and cries of woe'.[115] Unlike later Zoroastrianism in which the souls of the damned are released in the last days, the Prophet seems to have regarded the torments of the damned as being eternal, for whereas the souls of the just will be granted immortality, the souls of the damned will be tormented in perpetuity (utayūtā).[116]

Influence on Judaism

Zoroaster's doctrine of rewards and punishments, of an eternity of bliss and an eternity of woe allotted to good and evil men in another life beyond the grave is so strikingly similar to Christian teaching that we cannot fail to ask whether here at least there is not a direct influence at work. The answer is surely 'Yes', for the similarities are so great and the historical context so neatly apposite that it would be carrying scepticism altogether too far to refuse to draw the obvious conclusion. The case for a Judaeo-Christian dependence on Zoroastrianism in its purely eschatological thinking is quite different and not at all convincing, for apart from a few hints in the Gāthās which we shall shortly be considering and a short passage in Yasht 19.89–90 in which a deathless existence in body and soul at the end of time is affirmed, we have no evidence as to what eschatological ideas the Zoroastrians had in the last four centuries before Christ. The eschatologies of the Pahlavi books, though agreeing in their broad outlines, differ very considerably in detail and emphasis; they do not correspond at all closely to the eschatological writings of the inter-testamentary period nor to those of St Paul and the Apocalypse of St John. They do, however, agree that there will be a general resurrection of body as well as soul, but this idea would be the natural corollary to the survival of the soul as a moral entity, once that had been accepted, since both Jew and Zoroastrian regarded soul and body as being two aspects, ultimately inseparable, of the one human personality. We cannot say with any certainty whether the Jews borrowed from the Zoroastrians or the Zoroastrians from the Jews or whether either in fact borrowed from the other.

The case of rewards and punishments, heaven and hell, however, is very different; for the theory of a direct Zoroastrian influence on post-exilic Judaism does explain the sudden abandonment on the part of the Jews of the old idea of *Sheol*, a shadowy and depersonalized existence which is the lot of all men irrespective of what they had done on earth, and the sudden adoption, at precisely the time when the exiled Jews made contact with the Medes and Persians, of the Iranian Prophet's teaching concerning the afterlife. Thus it is Daniel, allegedly the minister of 'Darius the Mede', who first speaks clearly of everlasting life and eternal punishment. 'Many of them that sleep in the dust of the earth,' he writes, 'shall awake, some to everlasting life, and some to shame and everlasting contempt.'[117]

Thus from the moment that the Jews first made contact with the Iranians they took over the typical Zoroastrian doctrine of an individual afterlife in which rewards are to be enjoyed and punishments endured. This Zoroastrian hope gained ever surer ground during the inter-testamentary period, and by the time of Christ it was upheld by the Pharisees, whose very name some scholars have interpreted as meaning 'Persian', that is, the sect most open to Persian influence. So, too, the idea of a bodily resurrection at the end of time was probably original to Zoroastrianism, however it arose among the Jews, for the seeds of the later eschatology are already present in the *Gāthās*.

The 'Second Existence'

In later Zoroastrianism there is a well-defined eschatology: at the end of time the Saoshyans or 'Saviour' will come to renew all existence. He will raise the bodies of the dead and unite them with their souls, there will be a mighty conflagration, and all men will have to wade through a stream of molten metal which will seem like warm milk to the just and be in very truth what it is to the wicked. The sins of the damned are, however, purged away in this terrible ordeal and all creation returns to its Maker in joy. The ideas from which this eschatology developed are present in the *Gāthās* but not systematically worked out; moreover there is no looking forward to a time when the damned will be released from hell.

It would seem that Zoroaster first looked forward to himself 'reforming' existence here on earth, and that only later was the coming of God's Kingdom indefinitely postponed. So in *Yasna* 34.6 he asks God for a sign which will be 'the total transformation of *this existence*'[118] here and now, and begs him to make existence 'most excellent' (*ferasha*)[119]—

again apparently here and now. Even clearer is his prayer that it may be 'we who make existence most excellent'.[120] Similarly the Saoshyans in the *Gāthās* is no eschatological figure but Zoroaster himself. This seems to be certainly so in *Yasna* 48.9 and 45.11 whereas in *Yasna* 53.2, the only *Gāthā* composed after Zoroaster's death, the 'religion of the Saoshyans' which Ahura inaugurated must be the religion of Zoroaster. Again, when the word is used in the plural[121] it probably refers to Zoroaster and his earthly allies, although this cannot be regarded as absolutely certain.

Yet alongside a belief that the world was to be made anew here and now by the Prophet, there was also a belief in 'last things'—a 'second existence'[122] at the end of time when all things will be re-created in perfection. Then 'at the last turning-point of existence'[123] the evil will be allotted their final doom and the just their eternal reward. The judgement will be in the form of an ordeal by fire and molten metal; and here again we almost certainly have another example of that inter-penetration of the two worlds—the material and the spiritual—which is so characteristic of Zoroaster's thought, for the trial by ordeal certainly refers to an ordeal to which the Prophet himself must have submitted in order to prove the truth of his message as well as to an eschatological ordeal which will decide the lot of the two parties for ever and ever.[124] This fire it is which allots portions of weal and woe to the two sides[125] both here on earth and at the final reckoning.

The Zoroastrians have always been known as fire-worshippers and have, not unnaturally, resented this appellation; but it is quite clear that the Prophet himself revered this element 'which possesses the power of Truth'.[126] Its association with the Wise Lord is, however, far less apparent in the *Gāthās* than it is in the later Avesta where it is habitually called his son, but 'his' fire is indeed bestowed on Zoroaster along with the Good Mind as his special protector, and it is through this fire that he will make Righteousness to thrive at the expense of the followers of the Lie.[127]

Zoroaster's own eschatology is not identical with the more familiar eschatology of the later Avesta and the Pahlavi books. The Saoshyans is not yet an eschatological figure and the *Frashkart* or Final Rehabilita-tion of existence is only very vaguely adumbrated in the *Gāthās*, for it is Zoroaster himself who will make existence *frasha*, that is, 'excellent'. In the *Gāthās* there appears an individual judgement at death when souls are judged at the Bridge of the Requiter and a final universal ordeal by fire when the two parties are allotted their eternal destinies of weal and woe. This is in marked contrast to the later doctrine in which there is one individual judgement only: the final eschatological ordeal is not in any sense a judgement but a purgation by molten metal in which the sins of the damned are burned away. By this final purification they are made fit for eternal life and eternal joy.

Summary of Doctrine

The main doctrines preached by the Prophet Zoroaster can, then, be summed up as follows:

(1) There is a supreme God who is creator of all things both spiritual and material. He thinks his creation into existence by his Holy Spirit: he is holy and righteous, and by holiness are also understood creativeness, productivity, bounty, and generosity. He is surrounded by six other entities of which he is said to be the father and creator. Three can be said to be inseparable from his own essence—the Holy Spirit through which he creates, the Good Mind, and Truth. He dwells in his Kingdom, which means, no doubt, that he is absolute Lord of all that he has created—a kingdom which is now marred by the onslaughts of evil but which will be restored to its purity in the last days. Wholeness and Immortality, too, are inseparable from his essence, but they are also the reward he promises to those who do his will in Right-Mindedness. This last 'entity' or virtue is common to God and man and represents a right relationship between the two. God, the Wise Lord, stands beyond the reach of the powers of evil.

(2) The world as we know it is divided between Truth and the Lie. Truth is created by the Wise Lord or is his 'son'. About the origin of the Lie the Prophet is mute. This dualism between these two opposite poles, these two alternatives offered to the free choices of men, is basic to Zoroaster's thought; and although there are dim parallels to it in the sister tradition of India, nowhere in that civilization are they so tremendously and so uniquely emphasized.

(3) The creatures of the Wise Lord are created free—free to choose between Truth and the Lie. This applies as much to spiritual beings as it does to man. So Angra Mainyu, the Destructive Spirit, described surprisingly as the twin brother of the Holy Spirit, 'chooses to do the worst things'. This he does of his own free will as do the daēvas, the ancient gods whom, on account of the violence associated with their worship, Zoroaster considered to be evil powers.

(4) Since the will of man is entirely free, he is himself responsible for his ultimate fate. By good deeds he earns an eternal reward: Wholeness and Immortality are his. The evil-doer too is condemned by his own conscience as well as by a just God to the eternal pains of hell, the 'worst existence'.

(5) The outward symbol of Truth is the fire; and it is the fire-altar that becomes the centre of the Zoroastrian cult. It is by an ordeal of fire and molten metal that the Prophet vindicates the truth of his message, and it is by fire and molten metal that all humanity will be judged in the last days.

These would appear to be the salient doctrines taught in the *Gāthās*. Characteristic for the whole teaching is the word *savah*, 'benefit' or 'increase'. The word is used both for prosperity on earth and for the joys of heaven. Zoroaster is the Prophet of life, and of life ever more abounding.

CHAPTER TWO

THE SEVEN CHAPTERS

Divine Beings beside God—The Wives of Ahura Mazdāh—The Old Religion—Ahura and Varuna—Mithra—The 'Preservers-Creators' : Ahura and Mithra—The Nature of Zoroaster's Reform—Prototype of the Holy Spirit—Changed Tone of the Seven Chapters—Veneration of Material Things—Minor Prophets—Haoma

IN THE extant Avesta the *Gāthās* form part of the liturgy called the *Yasna* and occupy chapters 28–34 and 43–53 of that text. The intervening sections (35–42) form the so-called *Gāthā Haptaṅhāiti* or *Gāthā* of the Seven Sections or Chapters. This the Zoroastrians themselves have always regarded as not being a *Gāthā* proper, but rather as a part of the liturgy. This *Gāthā* of the Seven Chapters is unique in that it is written in the same archaic dialect as the 'genuine' *Gāthās* themselves and not in the apparently later dialect of the rest of the Avesta. It would then seem fair to conclude that it was composed not long after the Prophet's death and therefore earlier than all the other Avestan material that has come down to us. Unlike the *Gāthās* composed by Zoroaster and the last *Gāthā* which was composed after his death to celebrate the marriage of his youngest daughter, Pouruchishtā to one of his patrons, Jāmāspa, the *Gāthā* of the Seven Chapters is written in prose. And not only does it differ from the five 'genuine' *Gāthās* in this respect; it differs very considerably in content.

We have already seen that although Zoroaster recognizes a difference between the spiritual and material worlds, he does not regard them as being in any way antagonistic: they tend to blend into one another. Throughout his work, however, the emphasis is, for the time and place in which he lived, quite astonishingly on the spiritual and intellectual. God, through his Holy Spirit, thinks the material world into existence, and the material world thus only has reality as seen against the background of the spiritual; yet it is this very interdependence of the two worlds that gives the battle between the followers of Truth and the followers of the Lie its eternal actuality here on earth. The earth, then, and all it brings forth, is holy, for it is the creation of the Wise Lord and has a mysterious *rapport* with Ārmaiti or Right-Mindedness, herself the 'daughter' of the Wise Lord.

In the *Gāthā* of the Seven Chapters two things seem to be happening. First there seems to be some attempt to systematize Zoroaster's ideas—

the 'Bounteous Immortals', for instance, are mentioned for the first time as a group, though they are not individually named—and secondly there is an obvious tendency to adapt the teachings of the Prophet to a form of religion far closer to nature than was his without actually reintroducing into the reformed religion anything that the Prophet had specifically condemned.

Divine Beings beside God

The *Gāthā* of the Seven Chapters, then, stands midway between the genuine *Gāthās* and the rest of the Avesta: it represents the transitional stage between the 'reformed' doctrine of Zoroaster and the eclecticism or 'catholicity' of the later Avesta. Like the greater part of the *Yasna* proper it is a purely liturgical text concerned with the worship of Ahura Mazdāh and his attendant deities. The nature of these attendant deities will now be our principal concern. The Seven Chapters open with these words:

We worship the Wise Lord who is associated with Truth (*ashavan*), the Judge of Truth; we worship the Bounteous Immortals whose Kingdom is good, the beneficent; we worship the whole realm (*stī*) of the righteous, both that which is spiritual and that which is material, with the rite of goodly Truth, with the rite of the Good Religion of the worshippers of Mazdāh.

Here are mentioned by name for the first time the *Amesha Spentas* or Bounteous Immortals as a group and the Good Religion of the worshippers of Mazdāh, the *daēnā māzdayasni*. The first term, as we have seen, came to be used as a generic term for the six beings most closely associated with the supreme God, Ahura Mazdāh, in the *Gāthās*— *Vohu Manah*, the Good Mind; *Asha*, Truth or Righteousness; *Khshathra Vairya*, the Desirable Kingdom; *Ārmaiti*, Right-Mindedness or Humility; *Haurvatāt*, Wholeness; and *Ameretāt*, Immortality. It is, however, not at all certain that the term was restricted to these entities alone in the *Gāthā* of the Seven Chapters: nowhere are these six entities listed by name, and two of them—Wholeness and Immortality—are not mentioned at all. Moreover, the whole *Gāthā* ends up with the words, 'We worship all Bounteous Immortals', which gives the impression that the term means all the divine beings which have been mentioned throughout the Seven Chapters. Further in *Yasna* 39.3 we read: 'We worship the goodly Bounteous Immortals, both male and female, who live for ever and prosper for ever and dwell with the Good Mind.'

This would seem to imply that the Good Mind was not included among the Bounteous Immortals at this time. It would not, perhaps, be surprising to find that nowhere in the *Gāthā* of the Seven Chapters are the six Bounteous Immortals of the later literature listed together were it not for the fact that such lists do occur and that they differ from the later standardized version. Thus in *Yasna* 37.5 we find the Good Mind, the Kingdom, Right-Mindedness associated not, as one would expect, with Truth, Wholeness, and Immortality, but with the Good Religion and the Good Reward (*fseratu*). It would, then, appear that for the *Gāthā* of the Seven Chapters the Bounteous Immortals meant all the abstract concepts referred to both in the Seven Chapters and in the 'genuine' *Gāthās* of Zoroaster, not only the seven entities which are specifically associated with Ahura Mazdāh. These would include such concepts as 'zeal' (*īzhā*), 'energy' (*yaokshti*), 'consultation', 'fortune' (*ashi*), 'good desire' (*īsha*), the 'oblation', 'fame', and 'prosperity',[1] all of which are objects of veneration. Among them would also be the *Daēnā Māzdayasni*, 'the Good Religion of the Worshippers of Mazdāh' which is venerated along with Truth.[2]

'The Good Religion of the Worshippers of Mazdāh' was later to become the official designation of the Zoroastrian religion, and it is perhaps significant that the Zoroastrians style themselves worshippers of Mazdāh rather than of Ahura. This would seem to indicate that the term *Mazdāh* ('wise') as applied to *Ahura* ('the Lord') was added to the divine name by the Prophet himself, and that his religion thereby came to be called 'worship of Mazdāh' rather than worship of Ahura, the latter word having been used for a whole class of deity before his time.[3]

In content the *Gāthā* of the Seven Chapters is quite different from the *Gāthās* of Zoroaster. It might almost be called the *Gāthā* of Truth, for it is Asha, Truth or Righteousness, that dominates the whole of its seven chapters. In this *Gāthā* the Good Mind to which Zoroaster owed his inspiration has completely retreated into the background, and we are constantly being brought back to the Wise Lord and his Truth. 'We give, proclaim, and dedicate songs of praise and veneration to the Wise Lord and the Best Truth',[4] the bard proclaims, and it is fellowship or union with the Wise Lord and the Truth 'for ever and ever'[5] rather than fellowship with the Good Mind that is now the object of the worshipper's quest. Moreover, in the *Gāthā* of the Seven Chapters it seems that Asha is not, as in Zoroaster's *Gāthās*, simply the Truth as opposed to the Lie, Righteousness as opposed to Unrighteousness, Order as opposed to Disorder. It is a far more generalized conception and is now much more clearly associated with light: it is 'most fair, bounteous, immortal, made of light' and it is 'all good things'.[6]

The Wives of Ahura Mazdāh

If, then, Truth is here associated with Light, this is even more marked in the case of the Wise Lord himself. No longer is he regarded as a pure spirit who thinks creation into existence out of nothing, the creator of light and darkness: he also has a bodily form which is the sun, 'the highest of the high', and 'these lights' which may refer to the other luminaries or simply to the daylight.[7] And not only has he this fairest material form, he has also taken to himself wives, for we read: 'We venerate this earth together with women, this earth that supports us, and we venerate the goodly wives that thou hast in accordance with Truth, O Ahura Mazdāh.'[8] These wives are called *Ahurānīs* ('female Ahuras'), and they are in fact the waters. 'We venerate the waters,' the same text goes on to say, 'when they surge forward, come together, and flow forth, the wives (*ahurānīs*) of Ahura—beneficent, easy to cross, good to swim and bathe in, a gift for both the worlds.'[9] We have travelled a long way from the Prophet's exalted conception of the Wise Lord, his one true God who completely transcended his creation.

The strangeness of this passage, however, consists not so much in the fact that it is in such sharp contrast to the Prophet's own conception of the deity, but that it is quietly ignored in the later Avesta[10] and in the Pahlavi books. There we do occasionally come across a spouse of Ahura Mazdāh, but this spouse is not the waters but Ārmaiti, the 'Right-Mindedness' of the *Gāthās*, later identified with the earth. It seems, then, clear that these *Ahurānīs*, the wives of Ahura, are relics of the old religion and are certainly quite foreign to the spirit of the Zoroastrian reform. It is also worth noting that they are described as the wives of Ahura, wives of the Lord, not as wives of Mazdāh; and this would tend to confirm the theory that Zoroaster took over the worship of the god Ahura, the Lord *par excellence* (even going so far as to admit the existence of a plurality of 'lords'[11]), but that, in adding the qualifying epithet 'Wise', he purified the whole concept and quite changed the nature of the old religion.

The Old Religion

This would seem to be a convenient point at which to consider just what the old religion can be presumed to have been. The oldest evidence we possess for the religion of the Indo-Iranians is an inscription found in the village of Boghaz Köy in Eastern Anatolia which celebrates the conclusion of a treaty in the fourteenth century BC between Matti-waza, an Aryan ruler of the kingdom of Mitanni, and the Hittite king Shuppiluliumash. Here we meet with five divinities, all of which were to play a leading part in the *Rig-Veda*, the earliest literary monument

E

we possess of the religion of the Indian branch of the Indo-Iranian family. These gods are Mitra, Varuna, Indra and the two Nāsatyas.[12] The names of the first two gods are preceded by the word *ilāni*, meaning 'two gods', and this indicates that they (Mitra and Varuna) must have been so closely connected as to be spoken of in their own Indo-Iranian language as a single compound deity in the dual number. This does indeed actually occur in the *Rig-Veda* where Varuna and Mitra form an almost inseparable pair and frequently appear in the dual as *Mitrā-varunā*, the '*Mitra-Varunas*'. The other gods mentioned in the inscription are also well-known, Indra being the warrior-god of the Indo-Iranians, and the Nāsatyas or Aśvins as they are more usually called in the *Rig-Veda* being, among other things, the divine physicians.

We have already seen that the Vedic pantheon was roughly divided into *asuras* and *devas*, though the distinction is never absolute. Of the five gods mentioned in the Mitanni inscription Mitra and Varuna are predominantly *asuras*, while Indra and, to a lesser degree, the Nāsatyas are essentially *devas*. In Iran the Prophet Zoroaster reduced the *daēvas* to the rank of demons while, on the whole, he preferred to ignore the *ahuras* with the single exception of Ahura Mazdāh, the Wise Lord—the epithet *Mazdāh* ('wise') probably being his own creation. In the later Avesta both Indra and Nāñhaithya (= Vedic Nāsatya) turn up, and, as we might expect, they are numbered among the *daēvas*, by this time unmistakably demons. Mithra (= Vedic Mitra), who, before Zoroaster's time, had been numbered among the *ahuras*, reappears in the later Avesta as perhaps the most important god next to Ahura Mazdāh himself.

What happened to Mithra's companion Varuna in Iran is not immediately clear. That such a god existed in ancient Iran seems almost certain both because he is the most exalted of all the *asuras* in the sister tradition of the Indians and because he appears on the Mitanni inscription which probably antedates the separation of the Indian and Iranian tribes. It has been frequently pointed out that Zoroaster's Ahura Mazdāh has much in common with the Vedic Varuna, and the very considerable differences between them, the principal of which is that Ahura Mazdāh is no longer *primus inter pares* but the one true God, the sole creator and Lord, are rightly attributed to the religious genius of the Iranian Prophet. The resemblances between the Indian Varuna and the Ahura or Ahura Mazdāh of the *Gāthā* of the Seven Chapters are, however, quite striking, and it is a fair assumption that the 'greatest and best of the gods' before the Zoroastrian reform was a god closely akin to Varuna, called either by the same name (*Vouruna in Iranian) or, more probably simply Ahura *tout court*, the 'Lord'.

Ahura and Varuna

We have seen that in the *Rig-Veda* Mitra and Varuna are so closely connected that they form together a dual compound *Mitrā-varunā*, the 'Mitra-Varunas'. Similarly in the *Yasht* dedicated to Mithra we find a similar compound *Mithra-ahura*,[13] the 'Mithra-Ahuras', or again in the reverse order *Ahura-mithra*.[14] This must correspond to the *Mitrā-varunā* of the Indian tradition, and it is therefore safe to say that a god called simply Ahura, the Lord, existed before Zoroaster's time and that this god bore a very close resemblance to the Varuna of the Indian tradition.

That Zoroaster took over this god Ahura, *the* Lord, and filled out his personality by adding the epithet *mazdāh* to his name seems clear enough from the fact that in his own *Gāthās* the double name is not yet fully fixed; the order of the two words is not always the same, and they are frequently separated from each other. In the later Avesta, on the other hand, the order is almost always *Ahura Mazdāh* not *Mazdāh Ahura*, whereas in the Achaemenian inscriptions the two names have coalesced into one word *A(h)uramazdā*, from which the later Middle Persian form *Ohrmazd* derives.

In the *Gāthās* proper the stamp of Zoroaster's genius makes itself felt everywhere. Ahura Mazdāh is the god of prophetic revelation, the one true God revealing himself to the Prophet through the Good Mind. Though he is in some ways comparable to the Vedic Varuna, he is not recognizably the same God, so transformed and spiritualized has he become in the Prophet's fiery spirit. The Ahura Mazdāh of the *Gāthā* of the Seven Chapters, however, is recognizably an Iranian counterpart of the Vedic Varuna. He is an amalgam of Zoroaster's God and the earlier Ahura whom Zoroaster's Ahura Mazdāh was designed to replace.

We have seen how the Ahura Mazdāh of the *Gāthā* of the Seven Chapters is connected almost exclusively with Asha, Truth, rather than with the Good Mind. This too is typical of the Vedic Varuna. He, like Ahura Mazdāh is *rtāvan* (= Avestan *ashavan*), 'possessed of truth' or 'maintaining order',[15] he is the guardian of Truth (*rtasya gopā*),[16] the 'lord of Truth and light who increases Truth by means of Truth itself'.[17] Again we have seen that in the *Gāthā* of the Seven Chapters Ahura Mazdāh is given one or more consorts called *ahurānīs* who are identical with the waters. So too in the *Rig-Veda* we meet with Varunānī, the consort of Varuna,[18] while in the *Yajur-veda*[19] of slightly later date the waters are explicitly referred to as Varuna's wives, and in the later literature he became the god of the sea. He and Mitra are constantly invoked to bestow rain, and they are said to possess milch-cows who give sweet milk,[20] this being the standard metaphor used in the *Rig-Veda* to denote the rain-bearing clouds. Similarly the Ahurānīs, the spouses of Ahura, in the *Gāthā* of the Seven Chapters are the 'pregnant waters, the mothers, the milch-cows who care for the poor'.[21]

Again the attribute of sovereignty (*kshatra*) is in a predominant manner appropriated to Varuna[22] and we have already seen that the Kingdom (*khshathra = kshatra*), later to become the fourth of the Bounteous Immortals, is the rightful possession of Ahura Mazdāh in Zoroaster's own scheme of things. In the Seven Chapters too the author prays that 'we may attain to thy good kingdom, O Ahura Mazdāh, for ever and ever. May a good ruler (*hukhshathra*), whether man or woman, rule over the two worlds, O most wise among existent beings.'[23]

Further, Varuna and Mitra are distinguished from the other gods by their possession of *māyā*, 'mysterious power', and Varuna thereby becomes *māyin* 'possessed of mysterious power' to a superlative degree.[24] This *māyā* in the *Rig-Veda* may be used for either good or evil ends, but in the case of Varuna it is always regarded as being beneficent. So too in the Seven Chapters we read of Ahura Mazdāh: 'We acknowledge thee as the god (*yazata*) of good *māyā* (*humāīm*) as the possessor of good fortune (*īzhīm*) who accompanies Truth; mayst thou be for us life and substance in the two worlds.'[25]

We have seen that in the Seven Chapters the sun and the light of day are described as the visible form of Ahura Mazdāh, and in the later *Yasna* the sun is said to be his eye.[26] So too does Varuna prepare a broad path for the sun,[27] and the sun is his eye.[28] From this brief comparison between the two gods it seems clear that the Varuna of the *Rig-Veda* and the Ahura Mazdāh of the *Gāthā* of the Seven Chapters are the Indian and the Iranian derivatives of one and the same god. Both are intimately associated with Truth (*asha/rta*), with the Kingdom or sovereignty (*khshathra/kshatra*), with the waters which in both traditions are likened to milch-cows or are his wives, with mysterious power (*māyā*), and finally with light and the sun. Both are so intimately connected with Mitra/Mithra that we find the two names coupled in a single compound in the dual number, *Mitrā-varunā* in India, *Mithra-ahura* or *Ahura-mithra* in Iran. If then the *Gāthā* of the Seven Chapters represents a partial return to an earlier 'paganism' in which Ahura, the Lord, corresponded roughly to the Vedic Varuna, we might expect to find some trace of Varuna's partner, Mitra/Mithra.

Mithra

Some modern scholars have allowed their fancy free play on the subject of Zoroaster's supposed antipathy to the god Mithra, whereas Dr Gershevitch, in his excellent edition of the Mithra *Yasht*, has tended to the opposite extreme, considering that 'Mithra had every claim to Zarathushtra's affection' and that 'even the prophet may have felt a pang of regret' at Mithra's 'unavoidable exclusion from Zarathushtrianism'.[29] For Professor Duchesne-Guillemin, on the other hand, Mithra remained for long the great rival of Mazdāh, and Zoroaster's silence concerning him is a 'deliberate, hostile, passionate silence'.[30] Strong words indeed, for which there is not one shred of positive evidence, any more than there is for the opposite view that the Prophet excluded Mithra from his system with a heavy heart, so great were that deity's claims on his affections. That two so mutually exclusive views can be advanced by scholars of repute on one and the same subject is, of course, due to the fact that there just is *no* evidence as to what the Prophet thought about the god Mithra. The word *mithra*, however, originally means 'contract' and the god Mithra of the later Avesta is still primarily the god of the contract. It would then seem rather strange that Zoroaster should in fact use this word in its original meaning of 'contract',[31] if his hostility to Mithra were quite as pathological as has been maintained.

The most reasonable explanation of Zoroaster's silence on the subject of Mithra would appear to be that, in his drastic reform of the old religion which entailed the setting up of Ahura Mazdāh as the supreme God, creator and preserver of all spiritual and material beings, there could be no room for a co-creator with God. If Ahura, the Lord, was to become Ahura Mazdāh, the 'Wise Lord' and as such the one true God, then, plainly, Mithra would have to go. It is, of course, possible that Zoroaster's Holy Spirit through whom the Wise Lord creates, and with whom he is so inseparably one that a later Zoroastrianism could roundly identify the two, was simply Mithra in disguise, but this theory cannot be pressed although there is supporting evidence which we shall have to examine later. This view has, moreover, been held by some of the very greatest Zoroastrian scholars.

The 'Preservers-Creators' : Ahura and Mithra

In the *Gāthā* of the Seven Chapters a curious dual compound reminiscent of the same type of compound as that which unites Ahura and Mithra in the phrase *Ahura-mithra* does occur in the form *pāyū-thwōreshtārā*,[32] meaning literally 'the preservers-creators' or 'the preserver and the creator'. The verse in which the expression occurs shows a degree of inconsequence so far as the objects of veneration are concerned that is rare even in the *Yasna*: 'We venerate the mountains down which the waters flow; we venerate the lakes, containers of water; we venerate barley which brings increase; we venerate the two preservers-creators; we venerate Mazdāh and Zoroaster.'

It is far from clear what the two preservers-creators have to do with the mountains, waters, and corn in particular, nor what special relationship they have with Mazdāh and Zoroaster. The context therefore helps us not at all unless we are prepared to identify the 'creator' (more literally the 'fashioner') with Mazdāh and the 'preserver' with Zoroaster.

The Pahlavi translator, however, for once adds a gloss that may well go back to an authentic tradition. Unaware that the phrase is in fact in the dual number he translates 'the creative (*brīnkar*) protector', and glosses this with the words 'the god Mithra', and this gloss reappears in the parallel passage *Yasna* 57.2 where we read:

> We worship Sraosha . . .
> Who worshipped Ahura Mazdāh,
> Who worshipped the Bounteous Immortals,
> Who worshipped the two preservers-creators
> Who fashioned (*thweresatō*, dual) all creatures.

If the Pahlavi translator is right in stating that one of the two preservers-creators is Mithra, it would seem to follow that the other was Ahura—the Ahura, that is to say, of the pre-Zoroastrian religion—Ahura thus being the creator and Mithra the preserver. As has been pointed out,[33] the word *thwōreshtar* corresponds etymologically to the Vedic *Tvashtr* who usually appears in the Veda as an independent creator-god; but in *Rig-Veda* 4.42.3 we read: 'I [Varuna], knowing the two wide, deep, firmly established areas of space in all their grandeur, [knowing too] all creatures as their fashioner (*tvashtr*), I have created (*airayam*) both worlds and maintain them.'

If then the Pahlavi translator is right in identifying Mithra with one of the preservers-creators, it seems that the other must be the pre-Zoroastrian Ahura who corresponds so closely in the *Gāthā* of the Seven Chapters to the Vedic Varuna. Thus the pair of creators-preservers would appear to represent the ancient divine pair, Ahura and Mithra—the *Mitrā-varunā* of Vedic tradition.

The Nature of Zoroaster's Reform
So, by examining the *Gāthā* of the Seven Chapters which has preserved so much of the older religion of Ahura, the 'Lord', we have been able

to gain some insight into the extent of the reform that Zoroaster introduced. Zoroaster, however, attacked only the worship of the *daēvas*: so far from attacking that of the Ahuras he twice speaks of the Ahuras in the plural, which shows that, in the early days of his ministry at least, he did not fear to associate other gods with God. Moreover, the names of his own 'Bounteous Immortals', as they were later to be called, were not strikingly new, and their equivalents can all be found in the *Veda*. Thus *asha* corresponds to the Vedic *rta*, as we have seen, *khshathra* to *kshatra*, the Kingdom with which Varuna is particularly closely associated, *ārmaiti*, Right-Mindedness, Humility, or Devotion to *aramati*, 'devotion', *ameretāt*, 'Immortality' to *amrta*, etc. with the same meaning, and *haurvatāt* to *sarvatāt(i)*, 'Wholeness', used in both traditions of both gods and men. The only significant innovation in nomenclature would appear to be that of *Vohu Manah*, 'the Good Mind', and *Spenta Mainyu*, 'the Holy Spirit'—apart, of course, from the addition of the epithet *Mazdāh*, 'Wise', to *Ahura*, 'the Lord'.

What Zoroaster would appear to have done was to take over these traditional abstract terms to the exclusion of all purely personal deities. His religion could scarcely be more different from the polytheism of the *Rig-Veda*, yet the abstract concepts he was to make so peculiarly his own lay already to hand as the Vedic evidence itself shows. Zoroaster was not substituting abstract entities for personal gods as so many scholars both past and present would have us believe. He did away with all personal gods except Ahura Mazdāh himself and the Holy Spirit—who in his encounter with the Destructive Spirit is fully personalized—and developed to an unprecedented degree the concepts of Truth, Right-Mindedness, the Kingdom, Wholeness, and Immortality which he conceived of not simply as abstract notions but as part of the divine personality itself, as mediating functions between God and man, and as qualities which sanctified man can himself acquire through the Good Mind with which God illuminates him.

Prototype of the Holy Spirit

Of all the entities that came to be known as the Bounteous Immortals perhaps only the Holy Spirit has its counterpart in the religion that was current before Zoroaster's time. We have seen how the Holy and Destructive Spirits confronted each other at the beginning of time, and how the one introduced life and the other death into this world. This creation of life and death, later crystallized in the figure of Gayō Maretan meaning literally 'mortal life', was transformed in the later tradition into the Zoroastrian version of the first man. In the later legend Ahura Mazdāh does not simply create life as such, he creates the first man, also called the Truthful, Righteous, or Blessed (Pahlavi *ahrov* = Avestan *ashavan*) Man whom he destined to be immortal. This first man is slain by the Destructive Spirit (Angra Mainyu or Ahriman), but human life nonetheless continues as we shall see in the sequel. Now in the classical form of this story Ahura Mazdāh and Angra Mainyu are the protagonists, but in one of the Pahlavi accounts of this initial tragedy which brought death into the world, it is not Angra Mainyu or Ahriman, the Destructive Spirit, who brings death to the first man, but *Mithrāndruj*, 'he who lies unto Mithra' or 'he who breaks the contract'. The crucial passage runs as follows: 'Then [came][34] that fighter who lies against Mithra, and he destroyed life and wrought the grievous work of death. This is called *Gayōmart* which, being interpreted, means "dying life".'[35]

The antagonists here, then, are not the Holy Spirit and the Destructive Spirit but Ohrmazd (Ahura Mazdāh) who creates Gayōmart, the first man who is 'dying life', and 'the fighter who lies against Mithra' who slays him. Ahura Mazdāh has here taken over the role that his Holy Spirit fulfils in the *Gāthās* because the two had long since been identified; but the mere fact that his antagonist is here called 'he who lies against Mithra'—Mithra's enemy *par excellence*—would seem to indicate the existence of a myth, not yet forgotten even in post-Sassanian times, in which it was not the Holy and the Destructive Spirits who brought life and death into the world, but Mithra and his antagonist who lies against him. It would then seem likely that Zoroaster substituted for the older conception of an almost inseparable pair Ahura-Mithra an equally inseparable pair, Ahura Mazdāh and his Holy Spirit. This seems the more likely when we consider that Ahura Mazdāh is the father of Mithra[36] in the later Avesta as he is the father of the Holy Spirit in the *Gāthās*. This does not, of course, mean that the Gāthic Holy Spirit is identical with Mithra, but that it, in some respects, fulfils the function that Mithra probably fulfilled in the older religion. Had the correspondence been wholly exact, there would have been no need to reintroduce the ancient pair Ahura-Mithra either openly or in the disguised form of the preservers-creators.

All this has taken us some way from the *Gāthā* of the Seven Chapters, but the digression will have served its purpose if it has shown how much of the ancient religion reappears in that *Gāthā* and if it has shown that Zoroaster was not working in a religious vacuum but was adapting, elevating, and transforming traditional material that was already to hand. This is not to belittle his achievement which was radical and quite revolutionary in that it established a pure monotheism against a dualist background where, before, it would seem, there had been only a jumble of unco-ordinated ideas and myths. With the *Gāthā* of the Seven Chapters we witness the first stage in the refashioning of his work on lines less uncompromising and therefore more palatable to the popular taste.

Changed Tone of the Seven Chapters

There is no means of telling whether the *Gāthā* of the Seven Chapters is by a single author or by several. The arrangement of the seven chapters, however, does not seem to be altogether haphazard, for the first three chapters can almost be regarded as a résumé of some of the essential doctrines to be found in the *Gāthās*. One thing, however, is very noticeable in this *Gāthā*, and that is that although great emphasis is laid throughout on the Truth and its relationship to the Wise Lord, no mention at all is made of the Lie and the forces of evil against which the entire preaching of the Prophet had been directed. This seems to represent not only a return to an earlier state of affairs in which—if the Indian parallel of Varuna and his Truth can at all be pressed—the Lie cannot have hovered half as menacingly over the religious stage as it did in the preaching of Zoroaster, but it would also seem to represent a change in the fortunes and in the policies of the Zoroastrian community itself. Zoroaster was a prophet convinced of the truth of his message and consequently most unwilling to come to any compromise with the worshippers of the *daēvas* whom he roundly denounced as the 'followers of the Lie'. After his conversion of King Vishtāspa his whole tone changes, and he now sounds a note of exultation and confidence in his own strength. No longer do the princes and priests of the old religion subject mankind to their misrule;[37] the time has come for God to assign the true kingdom which is that of Truth and Right-Mindedness to the Prophet in person.[38] It is clear from remarks like these that once Zoroaster had secured himself the powerful patronage of Vishtāspa and his house, he had high hopes of dealing his opponents their death-blow and thus of establishing the 'second existence' here and now on earth.

If, as Professor Henning and the whole Iranian tradition maintain,[39] Vishtāspa was the last of a line of kings and 'if we see Vishtāspa, as we should, as the ruler of the Khwārezmian state of Marv and Herat in the first half of the sixth century, we understand why his dynasty and his state disappeared all of a sudden: his state suffered the fate that Babylon and Lydia had suffered, it lost its separate existence in Cyrus' gigantic empire'.[40] With the establishment of the Achaemenian Empire, then, under Cyrus the original Zoroastrian community, with its fierce intolerance of some of the ancient cults, ceased to hold a privileged position: it became simply one sect among many, and the new Imperial power was unlikely to be favourably impressed by a religious intolerance of traditional forms of worship which can only have impeded the slow process of the pacification of the immense areas that Cyrus had conquered. This new political situation is reflected in the *Gāthā* of the Seven Chapters. The Zoroastrian community is no longer associated with the ruling house; it no longer possesses the *khshathra*, the 'kingdom', that is, in this context, political power. The best they can do is to pray that, in the new order, there may at least be good government. 'May the kingdom belong to the best ruler,' we read, 'so that we may dedicate, proclaim, and lend to it our assistance for the sake of the Wise Lord and Truth which is Best.'[41] Or again: 'May we be granted thy good government (*khshathra*) for ever and ever, O Wise Lord. May a good governor, whether it be a man or a woman, rule over us in the two worlds.'[42]

The changed political situation, then, would account for the change in the tone of the *Gāthā* of the Seven Chapters. The original Zoroastrian community, having lost its royal patronage, would be forced on to the defensive. That there may have been Zoroastrian zealots who opposed this new trend is quite possible, but neither the later Avesta nor the evidence of the inscriptions in Western Iran indicates that they had much success, at least until the time of Xerxes. The *Gāthā* of the Seven Chapters marks a turning-point: it can be regarded as a first effort of the young community to adapt itself to changed conditions. Zoroaster's conception of the 'good' which makes no sense except in the context of his struggle with 'evil', is rendered innocuous, and a general benevolence takes its place. The formula 'good thoughts, good words, good deeds'[43] appears for the first time, and the Prophet's injunction to render evil for evil is passed over in silence. The choice is no longer the terrible one between two irreconcilable parties, but simply to think, say, and do what is in accordance with 'fair Truth'.[44] Even more eirenic is the recommendation that the community should urge all to tend their kine and give them pasture—all, whether they be 'hearers' (*surunvata*) of the doctrine or not, powerful or not.[45] By doing good zealously and tending his cattle the Zoroastrian is now promised his reward in union with Truth in both worlds. Whether Zoroaster's successors were conscious of having changed his message or not, they nonetheless looked to Ahura Mazdāh as their teacher.[46]

We have seen that Zoroaster established the fire as the symbol of Truth and made it the focal point of his cult. So, too, the second of the Seven Chapters is dedicated to the fire, and it is through the fire that God is approached by his worshippers. The fire is not only Ahura Mazdāh's very own (in the later *Yasna* it is addressed as the son of

Ahura Mazdāh), it is identical with his Holy Spirit: 'As fire thou art a joy to the Wise Lord,' we read, 'as the Most Holy Spirit art thou a joy to him—for this is thy most efficacious name.'[47] The fire, then, is now identified with the Holy Spirit and can be regarded as its visible form just as the sun and the light of day are the visible forms of Ahura Mazdāh. Spiritual and material are here brought into a far closer union than was ever contemplated by the Prophet, and one is again tempted to see in this a return to an earlier state of affairs. In the Prophet's own compositions Ahura Mazdāh is not associated with any natural phenomenon: he is indeed associated with light, but he also creates darkness. He is not especially connected with any particular aspect of the material world, all of which is his creation. In the Seven Chapters, on the other hand, he is especially associated both with the sun and the fire as well as with daylight in general, and again he appears in the west, surmounting the great inscription at Bīsitūn, as a human head rising out of the sun-disc with the sun's rays stretching forth on either side. Further his name survives in Khotanese as *urmayzde* and in Sanglechi as *ormōzd*, and in both languages the word means the sun.[48] It seems then probable that the original Ahura Mazdāh must have had solar connexions, but so complex is the nature of primitive deities that we are practically always wrong in assigning to them only one natural association, for the pre-Zoroastrian Ahura was more evidently still connected with the concept of Truth or cosmic order as well as with the waters than he was with light or the sun.

So far the Seven Chapters have not departed in any essential respect from the Prophet's own teaching: they have merely mitigated its vehemence the better to adapt his views to the changed political circumstances. So too the third chapter reaffirms Zoroaster's characteristic teaching of Ahura Mazdāh as the creator of all good things. He is praised specifically as creator of the ox, of Truth, of the waters and plants, of the goodly lights, the earth, and all good things. This list, oddly enough, does not correspond in detail to the order of creation given in the later books, and this would seem to show that no attempt at systematization had been made at the time of the composition of the Seven Chapters.

Apart from being worshipped as the creator Ahura Mazdāh is also worshipped by his name of Ahura, as the most Bounteous, and as *mazdā-vara*. This last epithet calls for comment. In his great dictionary Bartholomae translates it as 'pleasing to Mazdāh', but the root *var-* is, in the *Gāthās*, the root used for the choice that all must make between Truth and the Lie, and it would therefore seem natural that this normal meaning of the word is present here also. *Mazdā-vara* would most naturally mean 'whose choice is *mazdā*', i.e. 'whose choice is wisdom'. If this interpretation is correct, it would seem that the early generations of Zoroastrians understood their God's name to mean 'the Lord whose choice is wisdom'. This fits in nicely with the later tradition in which God is characterized by 'omniscient wisdom' as his opponent is by 'slowness in knowledge' or 'evil knowledge'.

The remainder of this short chapter is devoted to the glorification of Truth and other entities including the Good Mind, the Good Kingdom, and the Good Religion. It also mentions for the first time the 'Fravashis of men and women who follow Truth'. These Fravashis figure largely in the later Avesta and the Pahlavi books, and some account of them will have to be given later. For the moment it will suffice to say that they are the pre-existent external souls of all good men and women. They are nowhere mentioned in the genuine *Gāthās* and are, therefore, almost certainly a revival of an earlier popular cult.

Veneration of Material Things

We have seen that in the genuine *Gāthās* themselves there is no rift between the spiritual and material worlds: in the later sections of the *Gāthā* of the Seven Chapters the distinction almost entirely disappears. The earth, the waters, and the animal world rub shoulders not only with the followers of Truth but also with the 'good Bounteous Immortals, both male and female, who live for ever, prosper for ever, and dwell with the Good Mind'.[49] With the soul of the ox and its plaint to the Wise Lord we are already familiar. In the Seven Chapters, however, not only are this bovine soul and its creator venerated but also the souls of all useful animals; and as if there were no essential break between the brute creation and human kind, the author immediately goes on to venerate 'the souls of all men and women who follow Truth wherever they may have been born, [the souls of all men and women] whose good consciences (*daēnā*) are, were, or will be victorious':[50] and from these he passes on to the Bounteous Immortals who form the summit of the good creation.

It is clear that the ancient Iranian religion was firmly rooted in the soil: it was the religion of an agricultural people wholly dependent on its cattle. Thus the Prophet himself cannot distinguish entirely between the cosmic battle conducted by Truth and the Lie and the mundane battle between herdsmen and marauding nomads. Like man, the ox has a soul which cries aloud to God for justice: man and beast are inseparably linked, and the sufferings of the one are the sufferings of the other. In the *Gāthā* of the Seven Chapters this tendency is carried much further. Veneration is due not only to the immortals who preside over earthly things: it is due also to the earthly things themselves, for, in some way, they partake of the divine. Fire is holy because it is the visible form, indeed the Holy Spirit, of God, as is the sun and the daylight that proceeds from it. The waters are holy because they are the wives of the Wise Lord. For the Zoroastrians, however, in all the stages of their development, holiness does not mean so much purity as it so often does for us: it is rather *savah*, prosperity, usefulness, and plenty. Though they never express themselves in this way, it would appear that they regard man as being the meeting-place between the spiritual and material worlds, the mental and the physically alive. The whole of the physical world nourishes man in ascending scale: the waters nourish the plants, the plants the animals, and the animals man; and man, in his turn, needs 'wholeness' to partake of 'immortality' in order that he may be united with the Good Mind and Truth. Thus the whole material world is holy—mountains, lakes, the crops, earth, sky, and wind, waterways and roads[51]—for they all contribute to the well-being of man and in their way serve God's purpose in creation, and that is the union of both the spiritual and the material worlds in the society of God and his Truth.[52]

Minor Prophets

The author or authors of the *Gāthā* of the Seven Chapters plainly considered that they were transmitters of the word of Truth[53] and they do not hesitate to describe themselves as 'prophets' (*mānthran*)—a word used by Zoroaster only of himself. Moreover, they claim that their *Gāthā*, the 'strong *Gāthā* of the Seven Chapters, the truthful, an authority of Truth',[54] is an object of veneration: it is as fully canonical as the words of the Prophet himself. For them it is the conscious expression of the Good Religion of the worshippers of Mazdāh,[55] the communal expression of the faith of all who call themselves by that name: for the Avestan word *daēnā* which survives to this day in its Persian form *dīn* had hitherto meant the individual conscience or organ of faith of the individual worshipper, and even in the Seven Chapters it is still used in this sense,[56] but in the formula 'the Good *Daēnā* of the worshippers of Mazdāh' it stands for the faith of the whole community: it is the 'Good Religion' as established by the Prophet and as interpreted by the minor prophets of the Seven Chapters.

Haoma

We have already seen that this religion differs in many respects from the Prophet's own urgent message. It thinks nothing of assigning the waters as consorts to the Supreme Deity or of reintroducing the idea of the Fravashis, the pre-existent souls of all living things, into the reformed religion. Yet neither of these ideas runs directly counter to the Prophet's teaching. Rather different is the revival of the Haoma cult which practically all modern writers on Zoroastrianism believe the Prophet to have suppressed: for revival there is, and in the most explicit terms:

> We venerate the exalted golden Haoma,
> We venerate the glowing Haoma which makes physical life to prosper:
> We revere Haoma from whom death flees.[57]

We shall have occasion to discuss the Haoma cult in our next chapter when we come to deal with the liturgy, and we will merely note at this juncture that it was certainly practised at the time of the composition of the *Gāthā* of the Seven Chapters, that is, in all probability only a generation or two after the Prophet's death. Zoroastrianism, from this time on, became as intimately associated with this cult as had been the religion which it superseded: it now formed as much part of the liturgy as did the veneration of the sacred fire. This, then, would be the form of Zoroastrianism that was being propagated during the reign of Cyrus and his successors. The Prophet Zoroaster's message had triumphed thanks to the patronage of King Vishtāspa and his house. Under the Achaemenian Empire Zoroaster's successors seem to have made concessions to the older religion—to the worshippers of the great Ahura and his associated 'lords', but not to the worshippers of the *daēvas*—but this by no means deterred them from seeking proselytes. On the contrary the last words we read in the *Gāthā* of the Seven Chapters are these: 'We venerate the return of the fire-priests who go out afar desirous [of bringing] the Truth to [all] provinces. We venerate all Bounteous Immortals.'

The religion of the Prophet Zoroaster, as modified by the minor prophets that succeeded him, thus sets out to conquer the minds of the greatest Empire the Middle Eastern world had ever seen. Its centre of gravity now passed west from the Central Asiatic steppes to the new centres of power in the west—Media and Persia.

CHAPTER THREE

THE CULTUS

The Yasna—The Yashts—The Vidēvdāt—The Three Forms of Zoroastrianism—The Fourfold Confession of Faith—Ahuras and Daēvas—Zoroaster and Animal Sacrifice—Sacrificial Bull and Haoma Rite—Haoma, the Drink of Immortality of the Indo-Iranians—Haoma, as Sacrifice and Sacrament—The Liturgy—Origins of the Cult—Haoma, Victim, Priest, and God—Sraosha—Sraosha the Mediator

THE genuine *Gāthās* of Zoroaster and the *Gāthā* of the Seven Chapters which is sandwiched between them form part of the sacramental liturgy known as the *Yasna*. In the liturgy itself great veneration is paid to them. They are said to protect and defend the worshipper, they are his spiritual food, his sustenance and raiment. Great is the reward they will bring him at the separation of 'his bones from his consciousness'; and the reward they bring is one of Truth or Righteousness. They bring strength and victory, health and healing prosperity, increase, comfort, assistance and a state of blessedness (*ashavasta*).[1] Yet venerable though the words of the Prophet may be and rich though is the reward which they bring, they not only do not form the core of the liturgy, they are in a sense subsidiary to it: for the central act of the liturgy is not the recitation of the *Gāthās* but the symbolic immolation of the Haoma plant—the plant 'from which death flees' and which confers immortality on the worshipper.

The Yasna

We have seen that in the *Gāthā* of the Seven Chapters naturalistic features from the old religion were beginning to creep back into the reformed faith. Later, when we turn to the religion of the Achaemenian kings and of the Magi, we shall have to discuss whether either or both of them were Zoroastrians. The controversy that raged around this issue has been largely futile since authors have all too rarely defined what it is that they mean by the word 'Zoroastrian'. They have not always said whether they mean the strict message of the Prophet himself which survives in his own *Gāthās* and nowhere else or the religion of the later Avesta: nor have they always been careful to distinguish between the religion of the three main portions of the latter —the *Yasna*, the *Yashts*, and the *Vidēvdāt*.

The religion of the *Yasna*—of which, ironically enough, the *Gāthās*

79

now form part—is completely different from that of the *Gāthās*. It has recently been described as pantheism, but this conveys the wrong impression, for pantheism normally means the kind of nature mysticism we find in the *Upanishads* in India in which the All, in all its variety, is seen to be in some sense one with the One which is the source of all being. The religion of the *Yasna*, on the other hand, is rather 'animatism', for it sees the divine in all living things—whether really animate like the plants and animals, or inanimate like the fire, the waters, wind and mountain; whether material or, like the 'spiritual' gods, invisible to the eye of man. Ahura Mazdāh, the Wise Lord, it is true, is still the creator and preserver of all things, but he is no longer—in association with the Bounteous Immortals who formerly constituted his personality—the sole object of worship. A host of gods, fetched up from an older tradition and slightly refurbished to bring them more into accord with the new order of things, now share in his glory: and besides these, time and space and the divisions into which they are divided—the five periods into which the day is split up, the seasons and the years, as well as the territorial units into which the Empire was divided—become objects of worship, as do the luminaries—the sun, moon, and stars. Everything in the *Yasna* partakes of the divine except only Angra Mainyu, the Destructive Spirit, his attendant spirits like the Evil Mind and Pride, the *daēvas*, and their worshippers. These are renounced in the course of the liturgy, but we are not made to feel the omnipresence of the Lie as we are in the *Gāthās*.

The Bounteous Immortals themselves, though we are told for the first time exactly who they are,[2] play little part in the liturgy, and none at all at its most crucial points. In the *Gāthās*, though their number and function are not neatly defined as they are in the later texts, they are of vital importance to the Prophet's whole conception of God. Both in the later Avesta and the Pahlavi books, however, little more than lip-service is paid to them: they had ceased to play any vital part in the transformation of the Prophet's doctrine that unfolds itself in the *Yasna*.

The Yashts

The *Yashts* differ from the *Yasna* in this respect, that whereas the bulk of the *Yasna* consists of a monotonous invocation of every conceivable divine being, the *Yashts* are hymns—some of them of considerable length—addressed to various deities singly: they are hymns of praise devoted to the reinstated gods. Most of these gods—with the probable exceptions of Vayu and Verethraghna—belonged to the *ahura* class of deity before the Zoroastrian reform: few of them had ever been *daēvas*. Like Mithra they were those deities which Zoroaster ignored, without attacking them. Their reinstatement, then, did not necessarily do extreme violence to the Prophet's views; and Zoroastrians need not have been any more shocked at this return to a former 'paganism' than was the average Muslim at the introduction of the custom of venerating the tombs of Muslim 'saints'. What, however, is quite contrary to the whole spirit of Zoroaster's teaching is the humiliation Ahura Mazdāh inflicts on himself in not only venerating subordinate beings but in actually asking their help. Thus he asks the goddess Anāhitā to bring Zoroaster to think, speak, and act according to the Good Religion,[3] and—this is much more striking—he asks Vayu, the god of the wind, who was probably, in origin, not even an *ahura* but a *daēva*, that he may be able to vanquish the creation of the Destructive Spirit, as if he were unable to accomplish this himself.[4] Even more surprising is the Wise Lord's confession that but for the help he received from the Fravashis who are the pre-existent souls of men, both animals and men would have died out and the whole material world would have been given over to the Lie.[5]

The Vidēvdāt

Thus, if the *Yasna* represents a return to a form of 'animatism', the *Yashts*, although Ahura Mazdāh's supreme position as sole creator is still theoretically maintained, represent an overt return to the kind of polytheism that must have existed before Zoroaster appeared on the scene. The last of the books that compose the Avesta as we know it today is the *Vidēvdāt*, and this book, which is concerned largely with ritual purification, is fully dualist, the Lie being in all cases the ultimate source of impurity. This tendency is carried to its logical conclusion in the Pahlavi books where Ohrmazd and Ahriman (the earlier Ahura Mazdāh and Angra Mainyu), God and the Devil, are represented as co-eternal and mutually antagonistic principles.

The Three Forms of Zoroastrianism

Thus we must distinguish three separate forms of Zoroastrianism: first the primitive message of the Prophet which can conveniently be called 'primitive Zoroastrianism'; secondly the re-paganization of the Prophet's message in which some of the old gods are readmitted alongside the Wise Lord and in which all nature is regarded as being interpenetrated by the divine: this we will call 'catholic Zoroastrianism'. Thirdly we have the new dualist orthodoxy which only developed self-consciously and fully in Sassanian times, and this we will call 'reformed Zoroastrianism', for in this phase the Wise Lord once again asserts his absolute ascendancy over all the good creation, though he is

F

now again limited, as he was not in the primitive message, by an independent power, Ahriman, the Destructive Spirit, who, as a separate and co-eternal substance, can challenge him on his own terms. In the sequel, then, 'primitive Zoroastrianism' will be used to mean the original teaching of Zoroaster himself, 'catholic Zoroastrianism' to mean the syncretism of his doctrine with a revived nature-worship and polytheism which was the common heritage of the Iranian and Indian races, and 'reformed Zoroastrianism' to denote the stringent dualism that begins to appear in the *Vidēvdāt* and is systematically developed during the Sassanian period, finding its most complete expression in the Pahlavi books.

The Fourfold Confession of Faith

The Zoroastrians themselves seem to have been aware that their religion was not all of one piece. The *Yasna* begins with their confession of faith: 'I confess myself a worshipper of Mazdāh, a Zoroastrian, a renouncer of the *daēvas*, an upholder of the Ahuras (or Ahura).'

The second half of this formula which contrasts the *daēvas* (who are abjured) with the Ahuras (who are accepted) brings us right back to Indo-Iranian times, to the distinction between *daēvas* and *ahuras* in Iran on the one hand and between *devas* and *asuras* in India on the other. It seems certain that before the time of Zoroaster both classes of deity were worshipped; for, as we have seen, in *Yasna* 32 the *daēvas* claim to be on the side of the Wise Lord in that they offer to be his messengers. There is evidence, however, that even before Zoroaster's time there was a party which had rejected the worship of the *daēvas* and which confined its worship to the *ahuras*, principal among whom were Ahura, the 'Lord' *par excellence*, and Mithra, the preservers-creators of the *Gāthā* of the Seven Chapters. It is possible that Zoroaster himself was born into such a milieu, for he is said to have been *born* a 'renouncer of the *daēvas* and an upholder of the doctrine of the *ahuras*'.[6] This much he may be said to have inherited: what is new in the confession of his followers is that they proclaim themselves his disciples, 'Zoroastrians' (*Zarathushtrish*) and worshippers of *Mazdāh*, not only of Ahura or the *ahuras*.

Ahuras and Daēvas

We must now consider whether the ancient Ahura-worshippers were worshippers of one great Lord only or of one supreme Lord who, among many lesser lords, was *primus inter pares*. All the evidence goes to show that they were the latter. First the *Gāthās* themselves speak of a plurality of *ahuras*;[7] secondly the Seven Chapters speak of both one and many *ahurānīs* or female *ahuras*, and thirdly the title *ahura* ('lord') is still retained by the gods Mithra and Apām Napāt, 'the Child of the Waters', both of whom are of common Indo-Iranian origin. Further, in the later Avesta Verethraghna, the genius of victory, and the earth are Ahura-created,[8] whereas almost everything else is created by Mazdāh.

This fourfold synthesis which the Zoroastrian confession of faith attests is more clearly evident in *Yasna* 2.13[9] where we meet with one religion, two laws, and one tradition. First the 'holy word' in general is venerated, then specifically the 'law against the demons' (*vīdaēva*), the law of Zoroaster, the 'long tradition', and finally the 'Good Religion of the worshippers of Mazdāh'. It would seem reasonable to suppose that the 'long tradition' corresponds to the 'doctrine of the *ahuras*' of the confessional formula since the other three members correspond exactly in the two versions. Zoroaster's inherited religion, then, was an ancient tradition of worship of the *ahuras* and a repudiation of the *daēvas*. That he inherited both seems clear enough from the fact that his followers admitted two 'laws' as being valid, the one being Zoroaster's own law and the other being the law 'against the *daēvas*' into which Zoroaster is said to have been born. What Zoroaster inherited then was an ancient tradition of Ahura-worship which excluded the worship of the *daēvas*: what he himself introduced was his own 'law' and the worship of Mazdāh, that is, Ahura Mazdāh, the Wise Lord, the Creator of Truth and all good things.

This fourfold formula cannot have been adopted by the early Zoroastrians without their being fully aware of what they were doing. Zoroaster's own teaching, at least as handed down in the *Gāthās*, can scarcely have hoped to survive as a proselytizing religion under changed political circumstances unless it was prepared to compromise to some extent with other and older Iranian cults that had also abjured the worship of the *daēvas*. Hence, we may assume, other *ahuras* were readmitted alongside the Wise Lord on the one hand and a general veneration of natural phenomena was reintroduced into the new religion on the other. The veneration of water which could be identified with *haurvatāt*, the Bounteous Immortal who is Wholeness, was introduced beside the cult of fire (identified with Truth), and due honour was paid to the earth (identified with Ārmaiti or Right-Mindedness), winds, and mountains. All this was part and parcel of the ancient *ahura-tkaēsha*, the 'doctrine of the *ahuras*'—the 'long tradition'. All these divinities were subjected to Zoroaster's Wise Lord who was acknowledged as the creator of all things. At the same time the new 'catholic' Zoroastrianism still insisted that no worship of any kind was to be offered to the *daēvas* who were to be regarded simply as demons and of the House of the Lie. The Lie continued to represent the sum-total of evil, and the Destructive Spirit was the lord of this baleful kingdom.

Of the actual cult of primitive Zoroastrianism we know nothing except that it centred round the fire-altar. We do, however, know much more about the cult-practices denounced by the Prophet, and since the *Yasna* as we know it, the very liturgy of 'catholic' Zoroastrianism, seems to be an almost exact reproduction of what Zoroaster had condemned, we must once again study those passages in which the Prophet attacks the rulers and priests who conduct the cult of the 'followers of the Lie'.

Zoroaster and Animal Sacrifice

It has generally been assumed that when Zoroaster denounces *cruelty* to the ox, he means the cruelty inseparable from sacrifice. The priesthood of the old cult (*karapans* and *usigs*[10]) is accused by the Prophet of handing the ox over to 'fury' or 'violence' (*aēshma*) and the princes are alleged to make it cry out in pain.[11] The soul of the ox itself cries out, saying: 'Violence, fury, cruelty, frightfulness, and might hem me in'[12] and this is due to the plans of both *daēvas*[13] and men. Further, the 'followers of the Lie' are accused of not allowing the ox or cow to prosper;[14] they are, then, the enemies of the settled herdsman. Apart from these rather general attacks on the 'followers of the Lie' for gross ill-treatment of their cattle, there is Zoroaster's specific attack on Yima who, like his Vedic counterpart Yama, is the first man. Yima, whom Zoroaster describes as a sinner, is indicted for having 'given our men portions of the ox to eat';[15] he it is who speaks of the ox and the sun as 'the worst thing the eye can behold',[16] and who 'destroys the life of the ox with shouts of joy'.[17] The princes hostile to Zoroaster who continue to follow the old institutions handed down to them by Yima, the founder of their race, do everything in their power to suppress the Prophet's teaching in that they 'give aid to the followers of the Lie, saying: "Let the ox which sets ablaze [the deity] from whom death flees . . . be slain".'[18] The last phrase is as important as it is obscure. One thing, however, is certain, and that is that the deity 'from whom death flees' is Haoma, the sacred plant which was later to be the sacramental victim symbolically immolated in the Zoroastrian liturgy.

It has hitherto been assumed that Zoroaster, in these passages, is attacking both the sacrifice of bulls, oxen, or cows on the one hand and the Haoma cult that went with it on the other. This cult is assumed to be orgiastic since the slaying of the bull is accompanied by 'shouts of joy' and because Zoroaster elsewhere condemns the 'filth (literally, urine) of this drunkenness with which the priests of the old cult (*karapans*) evilly deceive(?) [the people] as do the evil rulers of the provinces in full knowledge [of what they do].'[19] The texts, indeed, taken together seem fully to confirm this view; and no scholar, so far as I know, has disputed it in recent times, so vehement does the Prophet's denunciation of the practice of slaughtering bulls 'with shouts of joy' to the accompaniment of drunken orgies stimulated by the fermented juice of the Haoma appear to be. And yet it seems contrary to the evidence of the history of religions that a cult which had been fervently denounced by the founder of a religion should have been adopted without protest or opposition by that founder's earliest disciples.

Sacrificial Bull and Haoma Rite

Two questions, however, are involved here. First there is the question of animal sacrifice, and secondly the cult of the Haoma plant. It seems that the combined cult which, as practised by the worshippers of the *daēvas*, must have been an unseemly and orgiastic affair, was explicitly condemned by the Prophet when he quotes his adversaries as saying: 'Let the ox which sets ablaze [the deity] from whom death flees . . . be slain'; he also condemned ritual drunkenness in the strongest possible terms. Yet there is nothing in the texts that forces us to conclude that Zoroaster condemned animal sacrifice and the Haoma cult as such. He does not censure Yima for the sacrificial slaughter of kine, but for giving the *people* portions of the sacrificial meat to eat. This need mean no more than that the Prophet objected to the consumption of the sacrificial food by the laity; and some substance is lent to this view by the fact that, in the Haoma ceremony as practised by the modern Parsees, the Haoma juice is consumed by the priests only at the first pressing.[20] Similarly it seems unlikely that Zoroaster should have condemned the Haoma cult as such, for it is almost unthinkable that the rite should, from time immemorial, have become the central sacrament of the religion he founded, if he had issued such a condemnation. The Haoma plant was regarded by the Indo-Iranians (in India the same rite centred round the Soma[21] plant) as the elixir of immortality and as such has the stock epithet *dūraosha*, 'from whom death flees'. If, then, Zoroaster wished to denounce the rite, he would scarcely have referred to it by the very epithet that attributes to it the power to conquer death. To explain the Prophet's use of the word as sarcasm, as has recently been done, seems a trifle frivolous.

What Zoroaster actually condemns is not the Haoma ritual as such but some peculiar combination of it with a bull sacrifice in which the plant appears to have been burnt. Such an interpretation would fit in very nicely with the *āzūtōish mānthrem* mentioned in *Yasna* 29.7. These words can scarcely mean anything other than the 'sacred formula of the oblation of fat', that is, the rite connected with the offering of the fat of the immolated animal. This rite was ordained by the Wise Lord himself 'in full agreement with Truth'. In mitigation of this eternal decree he, in association with the Good Mind, gives Zoroaster to the soul of the ox as its protector. Plainly if the rite of the 'oblation of fat' was originated by God himself, his Prophet could scarcely abrogate it. Had he done so the soul of the ox would hardly have complained that it had to make do with an 'impotent protector' and the 'word of a man without strength'. All that Zoroaster seems to have condemned, then, is a form of animal sacrifice in which the sacrificial flesh was given to the laity to consume and in which, perhaps—to judge from the reference to the *burning* of the Haoma[22]—the sacrificial meat was sprinkled with the sacred fluid and then roasted.

One last argument can be brought forward for our theory that Zoroaster never abolished the Haoma rite as such, and that is that in the *Yasna*[23] the Haoma is prepared for the satisfaction of the 'righteous Fravashi of Zoroaster'. It is, of course, quite true that the Zoroastrians of what we have called the 'catholic' period brought back a vast amount of 'pagan' material from the older national religion, but it is really incredible that *anyone* claiming to be a true follower of the Prophet should go so far out of his way to insult him as to offer to his soul a sacrificial and sacramental element that Zoroaster had himself outlawed.

So far as we can tell, the Haoma rite has been the central liturgical act of Zoroastrianism ever since that religion developed liturgical worship; and the central position it enjoys has never at any time been disputed. This is, however, not true of animal sacrifice: in later times this was practised by some but opposed by others. The *Yasna* ceremony, as it survives in the Avestan text, was, however, quite clearly originally an animal sacrifice as well as a sacrament involving the immolation of the Haoma plant. This emerges clearly enough from the offering of *gāush hudāo*, 'the beneficent ox (bull or cow)', and the *gām jīvyām*, 'the living cow' (still translated as 'meat' in the Pahlavi translation). Traces of it still survive in the *Yasna* as practised by the Parsees today, for the Haoma juice together with consecrated water is strained 'with the help of a ring entwined with the hair of a sacred bull'.[24] Originally this bull must itself have been immolated, and both the sacrificial flesh and the Haoma juice must have been consumed by the sacrificial priests. The flesh and the Haoma appear to have been mixed[25] and the actual slaughter of the animal is still mentioned in the Pahlavi translation of the *Yasna*.[26] Yet, though at the time that the Pahlavi books were written animal sacrifice was already on the way out, it survives in legend, for Saoshyans, the eschatological figure who brings about the resurrection of the dead, sacrifices a bull at the end of time and thereby inaugurates the 'second existence' which Zoroaster had prophesied and in which death will be no more.

'While the resurrection of the dead proceeds, Saoshyans and his helpers will perform the sacrifice of the raising of the dead, and in that sacrifice the bull Hadhayans will be slain, and from the fat of the bull the white Haoma will be prepared, [the drink of] immortality, and it will be given to all men. And all men will become immortal for ever and ever.'[27]

Zoroaster's fulminations against the ill-treatment of cattle are, however, so vigorous that it would seem unlikely that he actually performed any kind of sacrifice involving the immolation of an animal himself. Possibly he assisted at such sacrifices just as the Magi of a slightly later date stood by while the sacrificial animal was being slaughtered and contented themselves with singing what Herodotus calls a 'theogony'.[28] Again it is possible that Zoroaster did no more than humanize the method of sacrificial slaughter, for it is the *cruelty* of his opponents that he is for ever attacking, not the mere fact that they sacrifice. The method adopted by the later Zoroastrians was to stun the animal first with a log[29] and then to kill it. This process and the reasons why it was adopted are described in one of the Pahlavi books, and the words might apply to Zoroaster himself.

'The reason for striking the [sacrificial] kine with a log before [applying] the knife . . . apart from the ritual efficacy of cleansing the body from a number of demons . . . and [apart from] the prevention of the unjust and ill-considered slaughter of kine, is first pity for the beast and on this account the lessening of its fear and pain when the knife is applied to it, and the prevention of the slaughter of kine in an ill-considered manner, impulsively, or at any time when one feels a sharp urge [to do so].'[30]

What Zoroaster objected to in the worshippers of the *daēvas* would seem to be precisely this: they slaughtered cattle in vast quantities 'in an ill-considered manner, impulsively, and at any time they felt a sharp urge to do so'. Similarly he did not object to the Haoma rite as such, but to the *daēva*-worshippers' method of performing it. Their drunkenness probably disgusted him because it would have seemed to him sacrilege against the plant-god which was the sacramental centre of the cult.

From all the evidence it seems clear that the Haoma cult was practised before Zoroaster's day both by those who still worshipped the *daēvas* and those who did not, and we must now consider the cult itself as we find it in the *Yasna*.

Haoma, the Drink of Immortality of the Indo-Iranians

The *Yasna* ceremony is both a sacrifice and a sacrament: it is performed in honour of Ahura Mazdāh, the Bounteous Immortals, and all the other deities, both spiritual and material, which had crept back into the Prophet's religion since his death. In its original form there must have been a ritual immolation of a sacred bull or cow as well as the ritual pounding of the Haoma plant (from its description as yellow and glowing probably something very like our rhubarb, which is found in the Iranian mountains to this day) which, when bruised, became the elixir of immortality.

The Haoma cult goes back to Indo-Iranian times. In India it appears as *Soma*: it is the food of immortality, the food which the gods consume not only to ensure their own immortality but also to increase their strength in their struggle against their enemies and those of the Aryan people. In the *Veda* the Soma cult is associated primarily with the cult of the *devas*, only secondarily with that of the *asuras*; and, despite what we have said about Zoroaster accepting the cult in a modified form, it would seem that this must have been the case in Iran too. This is apparent when we consider the list of the *daēvas* that appear in the later Avesta:[31] these are Indra, Saurva, Nāñhaithya, Tauru, and Zairi. The first three of these are readily identified—they are the exact equivalents of the Vedic gods (*devas*) Indra, Śarva, and the Nāsatyas. Śarva is one of the names of the most sinister of all the Vedic gods, Rudra, the divine archer who deals out death and disease, whereas the Nāsatyas or Aśvins are gods of healing. Indra is the most prominent of all the Vedic gods and is above all others associated with the Soma cult. He it is who drinks enormous draughts of the intoxicating liquid to give him extra strength to deal with the various dragon-figures that stand in the way of the advancing Aryans, and it is made quite clear that on occasion he becomes disgracefully drunk in the process.[32] Moreover, only he and Vāyu, the wind-god, drink their Soma neat: for the Aśvins it is mixed with honey, while for Varuna and Mitra it is mixed with milk.[33] The Zoroastrians too mix the Haoma with milk, but we cannot be certain that this was original for the word for 'milk' (*gaoman*) may originally have meant 'ox-flesh', which is how the Pahlavi translators understood it.

The fourth of the demons named in the later Avesta, Tauru, is not easy to identify. The last, however, Zairi, can scarcely be other than

Haoma himself. The word means 'yellow' and corresponds to the Sanskrit *hari*, and this is perhaps the commonest of all the epithets of Soma in the *Veda* and frequently stands in place of his own proper name.[34] The personality of Haoma has thus been split into two; the substantive remains as a god, but the adjective becomes a demon! Under its own name Haoma is the plant that produces immortality, but under the name of Zairi, 'the yellow one', it is a demon. This may appear very strange to us, but the same has happened in the case of two other gods. Indra, as we have seen, had been reduced to the rank of a demon, but his stock epithet *verethraghna* (= Indian *vrtrahan*) remains a god.[35] A yet clearer case is that of the atmospheric god of the wind, Vayu, whom we meet with in the *Veda* as Vāyu. In the later Avesta and in the Pahlavi books this god has been neatly bisected: there is a good Vayu who protects the creatures of Ahura Mazdāh, and there is an evil Vayu who is little better than a demon of death.

The Vedic evidence that Haoma was more closely connected with the worship of the *devas* than with that of the *asuras* is confirmed by the evidence of the *Yasna* itself, for the first persons who are said to have performed the Haoma ceremony were Vivahvant, the father of Yima, the primal ancestor whom Zoroaster had seen fit to attack, Āthwya and Thrita. Now Trita Āptya (= Avestan *Thrita Āthwya*) is a well-known Vedic god intimately associated not only with Indra and Soma but also with Yama (= Avestan *Yima*). In the Avesta the two parts of his name have taken on distinct personalities of their own, and we are left not with one god but with two mythical heroes. We cannot, then, avoid the conclusion that originally the Haoma rite must have been more typical of the worshippers of the *daēvas* than it was of that of the *ahuras*. In all probability no clear distinction was made between the two until shortly before the birth of the Prophet; for the fourth person to have performed the Haoma ceremony was no less a person than Pourushaspa, the father of the Prophet himself. And 'this was the boon that he received,' we read, 'that thou, the righteous one, wast born to him, O Zarathushtra, in the house of Pourushaspa, a renouncer of the *daēvas* and a follower of the doctrine of the *ahuras*.'[36]

If, then, we are to absolve the early followers of Zoroaster from foisting a daēvic ritual into the very centre of his religion in defiance of his express command, we can only say that the Haoma cult was practised both by the followers of the *daēvas* and by those of the *ahuras* at the time when the Prophet saw the light of day. The daēvic cult was no doubt orgiastic, violent, and cruel, and it is this perversion of the cult, attributed in the *Gāthās* to Yima, that the Prophet attacks. Yima's sin would be all the greater in Zoroaster's eyes in that it was his own father who had instituted the cult in all its purity, and this primordial cult Yima had desecrated.

Whatever Zoroaster himself may have thought, the later tradition did not interpret his words as meaning either that he condemned anything but drunkenness in connexion with the Haoma rite or that he condemned animal sacrifice as such, but only the cruelty that could be associated with it and lack of moderation in the use that was made of it. With regard to the Haoma rite as practised by the Zoroastrians themselves we read: 'All other intoxicants are accompanied by Fury (aēshma) of the bloody spear, but the intoxication produced by Haoma is accompanied by Truth and joy: the intoxication of Haoma makes one nimble.'[37] From this passage it is clear that even in the Zoroastrian rite some degree of exhilaration resulted from the drinking of the juice of the sacred plant, but this would have been very different from the mūthrem madahyā, the 'excrement of drunkenness', that the Prophet so vehemently denounced.

Haoma, as Sacrifice and Sacrament

According to the Dātastān i Dēnīk,[38] a Pahlavi book written by Mānushchihr, High Priest of Pārs and Kirmān, in the ninth century AD the whole Yasna ceremony lasted from dawn until nightfall. During this time the officiating priests could neither eat nor drink, sleep or relieve themselves, nor were they allowed to utter any profane word. The core of the liturgy is the sacrificial immolation of the Haoma plant and its sacramental consumption first by the priests and then by the congregation.[39] The Haoma is the plant of immortality: 'it makes both soul and body immortal in righteousness';[40] and in this it differs from the animal sacrifice instituted by Yima, for 'they who devoured Yima's meat became immortal in body [only]'.[41] From this passage it would seem that the combined rite of the bull and Haoma sacrifices was considered to procure immortality both of body and of soul, bodily immortality deriving from the bull[42] and that of the soul from the Haoma. The sacrament on earth, however, is only in anticipation of the final sacrifice of the bull Hadhayans performed by the Saoshyans, the eschatological saviour who, in the last days, will rise up from the seed of Zoroaster to restore the whole of the good creation. From the fat of this ultimate sacrificial victim the white Haoma will be prepared, the drink of immortality, by which all men are made anew, perfect and whole in body and in soul.[43] The earthly Haoma was, at least for the Zoroastrians of the ninth century AD, only a symbol of, and a pointer to the eschatological reality. 'The fine-grown Haoma in its pure metal container [which is] the glorious earthly Haoma blessed by Zoroaster, is the symbol of that white Haoma [called] Gōkaren from which [springs] the immortality [that sets in] at the final Rehabilitation [of all things].'[44]

Yet in earlier times it would seem that there was more sense of a 'real presence' in the sacrament of the plant-god. Haoma, like the fire, is the son of Ahura Mazdāh,[45] ordained by his father to be an eternal priest who, as son of God, offers himself up in the form of a plant to his father on high.[46] The earthly sacrifice as performed by human priests is merely the re-presentation of the eternal sacrifice which the god Haoma offers 'on the highest peak of high Harā' where heaven and earth meet. The Haoma sacrifice and sacrament, then, is in every sense one of communion. The plant is identical with the son of God: he is bruised and mangled in the mortar so that the life-giving fluid that proceeds from his body may give new life in body and soul to the worshipper.

The Liturgy

Only the earlier part of the complete *Yasna*, however, is taken up with the sacrament of the Haoma; but because the *Yasna* is the central liturgical text of the Zoroastrians, a very brief description of it must be given here.[47] The Haoma sacrifice is performed twice, and on the first preparation called the *Paragnā* it is accompanied by the offering of sacred bread called *Draona* which is consecrated to the god Sraosha,[48] and, after consecration, ritually consumed. Then follows the recitation of the Haoma *Yasht*, three chapters in verse which we shall have to consider a little more carefully later. At the conclusion of these hymns in praise of the divine plant the priests consume the sacred liquid but do not distribute it to the laity. There follows the profession of the Zoroastrian faith in which Ahura Mazdāh is acknowledged as the good Lord 'whose is the ox, whose is Truth, whose is light . . . who created the ox and righteous man'. The *daēvas* are solemnly abjured as Zoroaster had abjured them when he held colloquy with the Wise Lord.

After the profession of faith there follows the recitation of the three most sacred prayers which are supposed to date back to Zoroaster himself. Then comes the second preparation of the Haoma, its consecration and consumption: in the second performance of this rite the laity are invited to participate. This concludes the strictly sacrificial and sacramental portion of the liturgy.

After the conclusion of the two Haoma sacrifices the priest goes on to recite the *Gāthās* of Zoroaster together with the *Gāthā* of the Seven Chapters from beginning to end, and then intones a prayer in honour of the *Gāthās* themselves. Sections 56–7 of the *Yasna* form the Sraosha

Yasht, a hymn in honour of the god Sraosha, who, from the liturgical point of view is far more important than any other deity, including the Bounteous Immortals. There are further songs of praise and invocation, and a final section in honour of the waters and the goddess who is their patron, Ardvī Sūrā Anāhitā, the Humid, Strong, Immaculate.

The whole ceremony from beginning to end centres round the sacred fire which is repeatedly addressed as the 'son of Ahura Mazdāh'. Apart from the return of many of the ancient gods, however, and the veneration of the waters which was to become as marked a characteristic of Zoroastrianism as was the veneration of fire and sun, the most striking feature of the *Yasna*, apart from its sacrificial and sacramental content, is the repeated veneration of units of time and space; and it is worth mentioning here that the entire ceremony ends with an invocation not of Ahura Mazdāh and the Bounteous Immortals, as we might expect, but with an invocation of 'Space which follows its own law, of Infinite Time, and of Time which follows its own law for a long time'. We shall be hearing a lot more about Infinite Time in some most surprising contexts.

Origins of the Cult

The bulk of the *Yasna* is written in prose. Apart from the *Gāthās* themselves the only other verse passages are the *Yashts* or Songs of Praise in honour of Haoma and Sraosha. These two deities alone receive especial honour in the *Yasna* because, with the sacred fire, they are regarded as being intermediaries between God and man. In the Haoma *Yasht*, Haoma is represented as a fully authenticated Zoroastrian deity. Zoroaster had claimed to speak to God face to face. Similarly once the sacrament of the god-plant Haoma had established itself as the central act of worship in the Zoroastrian community, Ahura Mazdāh's divine son, Haoma, is represented as drawing near to the Prophet as he is occupied in tending the sacred fire and chanting the *Gāthās* over it. 'What man art thou,' the Prophet asks, 'the fairest I have ever seen in the whole material world?'[49] Haoma tells him who he is and bids him collect him in his plant form, pound him in a mortar, squeeze out the juice and consume it. This the Prophet does and thereby gives his blessing to the cult. But it is made clear that this is no new cult that is being introduced, but rather a cult that goes back to the beginning of time. The author of the cult was Vivahvant, originally a sun-god, and in return for his institution of the cult he was granted a splendid son:

'Kingly Yima of goodly pastures, the most glorious of [all men] born [on earth], like the sun to behold among men, for during his reign he made beasts and men imperishable, he brought it about that the waters and plants never dried up, and that there should be an inexhaustible [stock of] food to eat. In the reign of Yima the valiant there was neither heat nor cold, neither old age nor death, nor disease created by the *daēvas*. Father and son walked together, each looking but fifteen years of age, or so did they appear, so long as Yima of goodly pastures, Vivahvant's son, held sway.'[50]

According to the pre-Zoroastrian legend Yima's golden reign, in which all men were immortal and enjoyed perpetual youth, lasted a full thousand years[51] until Yima sinned and men lost their immortality. We have seen that at the end of time there will be a last sacrifice of the bull Hadhayans and that from his fat the white Haoma will be prepared by which all the human race will be restored in body and in soul, immortal and unageing for ever and ever. So too, according to the ancient Iranian religion, did the world begin, and it was through the sacramental rite of the god-plant Haoma that the sun-god Vivahvant had instituted, and the sacrificial immolation of a sacred bull that his son, Yima, had added, that death, old age, and disease were banished from this material world.

Of Āthwya and Thrita who were the next to perform the sacred rite we need say no more than that Thrita too is said to have been involved in the slaying of a bull,[52] thereby carrying on a tradition that had originated with Yima. The last person to perform the rite before the advent of the Prophet was his own father, and it was thanks to his father's acceptance of the rite that so great a son as Zoroaster was born to him. Zoroaster, far from repudiating the rite he had inherited from his father, enthusiastically adopts it; and the Wise Lord himself puts the seal of his blessing on the marriage of his divine son with the Good Religion by girding him with the sacred 'girdle, studded with stars and fashioned in the spiritual world, [which is] the Good Religion of the worshippers of Mazdāh';[53] and just as the initiated Zoroastrian is inseparable from the sacred girdle he first puts on on attaining to man's estate, so is the Good Religion inseparable from Haoma, and 'until a man has drunk of the Haoma, he has made no [real] profession of the Religion'.[54]

Haoma, Victim, Priest, and God
Haoma is both sacrificial victim, priest, and god. As priest he appears to function both in the immolation of himself and in the immolation of the bull which is the emblem he bears on his standard.[55] As men are strengthened and made immortal by drinking the juice that flows from his ritually mangled body, so, we may suppose, is his own strength revived by the flesh of the sacrificial bull of which the Wise Lord, his

father, has allotted him the jaws, the tongue, and the left eye.[56] He is the priestly intermediary between God and man, for Zoroaster prays to him and he, in turn, prays to yet higher intermediaries that stand between him and his father. The boons that Zoroaster craves of him are, as might be expected, not only immortality, the 'best existence of the followers of Truth', that is, eternal life in heaven, a 'light containing every bliss', but also health of body, long life, earthly power and prosperity, victory in battle over the Lie, and the power to forestall thieves, robbers, and wolves.[57] Haoma, however, is no more than an intermediary consecrated as priest by the Wise Lord, and his priestly function he exercises principally in the worship of Mithra[58] and Sraosha,[59] who are themselves no more than intermediaries between man and God. This curious anomaly would seem to indicate that the Haoma cult was originally connected with the worship of Mithra rather than with that of Ahura [Mazdāh].[60]

The Haoma cult as found in the *Yasna* is not just tolerated: it is brought into the closest connexion with the Prophet himself, but it is never represented as having been introduced by him as something new; it is part of the old religion which he inherits and adopts into his reformed system. Once adopted it becomes the central sacramental act of the new religion. Moreover, not only is the rite of the dying plant-god adapted to the new theology, the concomitant sacrifice of a sacred bull or cow, which the Prophet had censured in the worshippers of the *daēvas*, is also made welcome in the new system. In the course of time the latter was abandoned, but only after a long struggle, for even in the Sassanian period we hear that Yezdigird II 'multiplied the sacrifice of white bulls and shaggy he-goats to the fire',[61] and Christians are specifically warned not to soil themselves 'with the scum of sacrifice and filthy pus'[62]—whereas Bahrām Chūbīn, who rebelled against Khusraw II in the last years of the sixth century AD, sacrificed no less than 7,000 bulls.[63] In Achaemenian times we hear of similar sacrifices performed by Xerxes[64] and the Magi in general.[65] It would seem that only after the Muhammadan conquest of Iran did the custom die out though there always was a party in Iran which opposed these 'immoderate' holocausts as the Prophet had done before them. Against the Haoma rite itself, however, no voice of protest was ever raised.

Sraosha

Apart from Haoma, whom we have had to consider at some length, there is only one god who is sufficiently prominent in the ritual to deserve special notice—Sraosha. We have already seen that his name means literally 'hearing' or 'listening', and as a passage from the *Gāthā* of the Seven Chapters makes clear[66] 'those who hear' are those who listen to God's word as opposed to those who pass it by. For the Iranians as for the ancient Hebrews, hearing also means obeying; and Sraosha, the faculty by which man listens to God's word,[67] thereby comes to mean 'obedience' to God's will and the 'discipline' that is necessary to ensure such obedience. But Sraosha is also God's all-hearing ear which listens for the cries of men wronged on earth by the *daēvas* and those who think like them; but he does not only listen, he comes down to earth to combat and chastise them. Thus Sraosha, once personified as an independent deity, is both the mediator of the divine Word and the chastiser of the wicked who refuse to hear and to obey.

In the *Gāthās* the word can always be translated as 'hearkening' or 'obedience'—much the same as the 'hearing and obeying' of Hebrew prophecy; and Zoroaster himself 'brings the life of his body as an offering, the first-fruits of his good thoughts and deeds, to Mazdāh and to Truth. Through these are his hearkening to the Word and his Kingdom.'[68] Sraosha is the bond of obedience that unites man to God: he is the intermediary between them and can thus be spoken of as the 'path' to God or his 'throne' (*gātu*).[69] No sacrifice to the Wise Lord is valid unless he is present at it,[70] for it is he who carries up to heaven the sacrifice of himself that Haoma makes to his father. He is the 'peace and the covenant' between God and man, 'the Most Holy One's watcher over the Lie',[71] and he is the Incarnate Word.[72] As such he receives the Good Religion from the Wise Lord[73] and teaches it to men:[74] as such, too, he was the first to recite the *Gāthās* before the Bounteous Immortals and to spread the *barsom*—the sacred twigs used in the *Yasna* ceremony—before them.[75]

As the Discipline by which God rules unruly men he does battle with evil-doers on this earth, chastises them, and then returns to the assembly of the Bounteous Immortals[76] who, at his behest, themselves deign to come down to the material world.[77] The weapon with which he assails the demons and evil men is the weapon of prayer—the *Ahuna Vairya*, which is the most sacred of all the Zoroastrian prayers, and the *Gāthā* of the Seven Chapters.[78]

Sraosha the Mediator

As the mediator between God and man he is especially concerned with what happens in this world, and in the later tradition he is the lord of this material world as the Wise Lord is lord over the spiritual world above;[79] and just as the Wise Lord protects the soul, so does Sraosha protect the body.[80] And because the *daēvas* and all wicked things are most active at night, he descends to the earth after the sun has set and lays about Aēshma, the demon of Fury, Violence or Wrath[81] who is the mortal enemy of the Zoroastrian community and therefore of himself.

Like Mithra, with whom he has much in common, he cannot be deceived nor has he ever slept since the Twin Spirits created the world.[82] He is the particular friend of the righteous man and dwells in his house,[83] and he it is who conducts the soul of such a man to the Bridge of the Requiter where, along with Mithra and Rashnu, he judges the soul and, the judgement once passed, conducts him on his way to heaven.[84]

Sraosha is the true mediator between God and man, and as such he stands in front of the Wise Lord in the heavenly court whereas the Bounteous Immortals proper are ranged to the Wise Lord's right and left.[85] Being the ruler of this earth as the Wise Lord is the ruler of the spiritual world above, he it is who has the task of chastising the *daēvas* and their like who prowl around the world seeking to encompass the ruin of the souls of the creatures of Ahura Mazdāh. This sets him apart from the Bounteous Immortals who flank the Wise Lord on either side, and he is therefore worshipped separately[86] and enjoys an especially honoured place in the liturgy. Indeed, as 'Incarnate Word' he is the liturgy personified, the meeting-place of this contaminated world of time and space and the pure, uncontaminated world of eternal Truth and goodness—the world of the Good Mind, the Kingdom, Right-Mindedness, Wholeness, and Immortality.

It is not for nothing that the Manichees who, when writing for an Iranian audience, dressed up their very different dualism in Zoroastrian clothing, identified their own Column of Glory, which unites the world of pure light with this fallen world, with the Zoroastrian genius Sraosha. Theologically, the Bounteous Immortals are doubtless more important than is Sraosha: but though it is true that in Zoroaster's own preaching the Bounteous Immortals were living and real to the Prophet at least, once they had been duly pigeon-holed and classified and formed into a compact group, they lost all religious vitality and could easily have been expunged from the liturgy of the *Yasna* without any appreciable loss to the worshipper. In their place we find Haoma and Sraosha, the god incarnate in a plant and the god who 'hears and obeys' and who is the Incarnate Word.

CHAPTER FOUR

MITHRA

The Yashts—Iranian Mithra and Roman Mithras—The Pre-Zoroastrian Mithra—Mithra, Compact and Warlord—Mithra and Indra—The Daēva-Worshippers and Mithra—The Separation of Mithra from Ahura—Analysis of Mithra Yasht—Mithra as Contract and King—Mithra as Terrible Warlord—Mithra as Light—Mithra, Sraosha, and Rashnu—Mithra's Heavenly House—Mithra's Plaint to the Wise Lord—Mithra's Descent to Earth—Haoma Consecrates himself Mithra's Priest—Mithra initiated into the 'Good Religion'—Ahura and Mithra Reunited—Mithra and the Holy Spirit—The Revised Cult of Ahura and Mithra

---

THE *Yasna* constitutes the liturgy of the Zoroastrians and, as such, it stands at the heart of their religion; for the Zoroastrian it is what the Mass is for the Catholic. And just as the Mass celebrates not only the major saints but also some very obscure ones like Marcellinus, Felicity, and Perpetua, so does the *Yasna* commemorate not only the major deities like Sraosha and Mithra but also a host of quite minor divinities too numerous to receive individual mention. Only the two divine priests, Haoma and Sraosha, are honoured with special *Yashts* or hymns of praise; no other deity receives this honour in the 'canon' of the sacred text.

The Yashts

There is, however, a collection of such *Yashts* which forms an important and, from the purely literary point of view, the only notable part of the Avesta. These *Yashts* are twenty-one in number, unequal in length, unequal in interest, and unequal in importance from the point of view of the history of religions. The collection is obviously derived from sources other than primitive Zoroastrianism, for the *Yasht* devoted to the supreme Deity, Ahura Mazdāh, is little more than a dreary recitation of the divine names, later in date than the 'great' *Yashts* and devoid of any intrinsic merit whatever. Of the seven Bounteous Immortals—or rather six, since the Holy Spirit has already been assimilated to the Wise Lord—Asha (Truth) and Haurvatāt (Wholeness) are individually celebrated, while the remainder have to make do with a collective '*Yasht* of the seven Bounteous Immortals', in which they are celebrated along with a host of other deities from whom they are distinguished only by the now permanent title of 'Bounteous Immortal' in which the deities reabsorbed from the older religion may not share.

Of the remaining *Yashts* only eight are of any great importance, and of these, the tenth, dedicated to Mithra, is certainly the most interesting and rewarding. Next in importance and interest are the *Yashts* dedicated to the Fravashis (Yt. 13), the Khwarenah (Fortune or Glory—Yt. 19), Ardvī Sūrā Anāhitā, the goddess of the waters (Yt. 5), and Ashi, the goddess of plenty (Yt. 17). From the point of view of religious history the *Yashts* addressed to Verethraghna (Victory—Yt. 14) and to the wind-god Vayu (Yt. 15) are not lacking in interest, while the hymn addressed to the star Sirius (Tishtrya—Yt. 8) is the most rewarding of all from the literary point of view. From the point of view of the development of Zoroastrianism from its primitive to its 'catholic' phase, however, it is peripheral.

Mithra, the Fravashis, the Khwarenah, Ardvī Sūra Anāhitā, Vayu, and Verethraghna all had their contributions to make to the transformation of Zoroastrianism from the theological monotheism of the Prophet with its dualist ethical overtones into the capacious catholicity of the later Avesta, and all of them managed to survive, diminished but alive, the determined reaffirmation of the unicity of the Wise Lord that marked the beginnings of the Sassanian period. Mithra, indeed, yielded pride of place to Sraosha in the liturgy, but to this day the *Yasna* sacrifice is performed in the *Dar-i Mihr*[1] the 'portico of Mithra', where the sacred fire of the Prophet unfailingly burns. Both the Fravashis and the Khwarenah, that strange concept hitherto translated as 'Glory, *Glückglanz*', etc., but more recently equated simply with *Fortuna*,[2] have been and are inseparable from the Zoroastrian religion from the time of the composition of the *Yashts* (and in the case of the Fravashis from the time of the *Gāthā* of the Seven Chapters) to this day. Ardvī Sūrā Anāhitā, one cannot help feeling, never quite fitted into the framework of even 'catholic' Zoroastrianism. Though the *Yasht* dedicated to her makes it quite certain that this goddess of the waters was fully at home in Eastern Iran—where she is perhaps no more than the goddess of the Oxus or Jaxartes—her most sensational career was in the West. She was worshipped by Artaxerxes II,[3] she was known to Herodotus who unaccountably confused her with Mithra,[4] and her cult spread throughout Asia Minor in the wake of immigrant and perhaps dissident Magi. Vayu, originally a god of the atmosphere and wind and almost certainly a *daēva* by origin, not an *ahura*, had the strangest fate of all. Impossible to fit into even a catholic Zoroastrianism in his original form, he was split into two—a good Vayu and an evil Vayu: the one working for the Holy Spirit, the other for the Evil One. After the Sassanian reform he is transformed into the Void which, in eternity before time began, separated the kingdom of the Endless Light over which the Wise Lord held sway from the kingdom of the Endless Darkness where the Destructive Spirit dwelt in a beginningless malevolence. Verethraghna, too, the genius of victory, an essentially martial god, survived the theological reform of earlier Sassanian times, and though he may play little part in the predominantly theological thinking that looms so large in the Pahlavi books he nonetheless must have been a favourite with the Sassanian kings, many of whom seem to have regarded war as the natural order of things, for no less than five of their number adopted his name.

Iranian Mithra and Roman Mithras

For the moment, however, it is with the re-emergence of Mithra into the pantheon of catholic Zoroastrianism that we are principally concerned. Mithra alone, among the Iranian deities, made a direct impact on the West, for it is this god who, in his migration outside the strictly Iranian lands, became the centre of a mystery cult widely practised by the Roman soldiery throughout the Roman Empire, and whose religion seemed for a time to offer attractions no less powerful than those of a nascent Christianity. Yet the Roman Mithras is strangely different from the Mithra we meet with in the Avesta, for the Roman Mithras is the slayer of the sacrificial bull *par excellence*, and by this act he brings new life to the world and offers immortality to the soul; whereas in the Avesta, Mithra plays no such part—rather, he is concerned with the preservation of the life of the kine of whose 'wide pastures' he is the lord. Again the Roman Mithras is a saviour god who releases the human soul from the trammels of a purely mundane existence which is under the severe and hostile control of the Zodiac and the planets, the agents of an unseeing Fate, whereas the Mithra both of the Avesta and the Pahlavi books personifies the sanctity of contracts and thereby becomes the just judge who, with his associates, Rashnu and Sraosha, judges the souls of men according to their deeds. The gap between Mithras, the Saviour, who so nearly won the allegiance of the Western world, and Mithra, the Judge, who ranked second only to the Wise Lord in Iran, is very wide, but this does not mean that the attempt to bridge it is not worth undertaking.

The Pre-Zoroastrian Mithra

In recent years it has become fashionable to allege that at the time of the Prophet Zoroaster a specific Mithra religion was already in existence, and that this religion practised a bull sacrifice and the Haoma cult. This, we are told, was the religion of the worshippers of the *daēvas* that Zoroaster attacked. We have already tried to point out that even before the time of Zoroaster two forms of 'paganism' existed side by side, the *ahura-tkaēsha* or 'doctrine of the *ahuras*' and the *daēvō-dāta*, 'the law according to the *daēvas*', and we showed that while the worshippers of the *ahuras* had already rejected the *daēvas* as being unworthy of veneration, the *daēva*-worshippers not only honoured the *ahuras* as well as the *daēvas* but acknowledged the supremacy of one supreme *Ahura* whose messengers they claimed to be: and this seems to emerge from the later Avesta too.

Thus in the Mithra *Yasht* the armies of the *mithrō-druj*, those who are false to their contracts and thereby lie to the god Mithra (for the word *mithra* means literally 'contract') are attacked by Mithra and his two faithful allies, Sraosha and Rashnu, but undeterred by this unmistakable sign of the god's displeasure, they nevertheless complain that 'their swift horses are being led *away from* Mithra',[5] the implication being that since they too, in their way, were worshippers of Mithra, they might have expected to be brought into the presence of their god rather than to be driven away from him, harried and put to the sword by himself and his most loyal allies. Similarly, Mithra himself wishes to know who his true worshippers are: 'Who is it that considers me a god by worshipping me well, and who by worshipping me badly?'[6] This can only mean: 'Who, among those who acknowledge me as a god, worships me correctly, and who in a manner that is displeasing to me?' Similarly, the Prophet Zoroaster is represented as asking the goddess Ardvī Sūrā Anāhitā what happens to the libations which the worshippers of the *daēvas* offer her after sunset; and the goddess replies that so far from being honoured by her, they only serve to honour the *daēvas*,[7] and with these she has no truck. From these two instances—and there are more—it is clear that the so-called *daēva*-worshippers worshipped the *ahuras* as well, for it is to this class of divine being that both Mithra and Anāhitā surely belonged.

Mithra, Compact and Warlord
On reading the Mithra *Yasht* we have to ask ourselves whether the god as he appears in the *Yasht* that bears his name is in all respects identical with the god Mithra as he was known to Zoroaster. Mithra, of course, was no *daēva*; on the contrary, before the Zoroastrian reform he shared the throne of the all-highest Ahura (the Iranian equivalent of the Indian Varuna) as the dual compound *Ahura-mithra*, the divine pair so frequently invoked in the *Yasna*, conclusively proves. Yet in the Mithra *Yasht*, Mithra is not only the personification of the sanctity of contracts, the implacable enemy of those who violate their contracts: he is also a god of war whose treatment of his enemies, in its savagery,

recalls the wanton cruelty attributed by Zoroaster to the followers of the Lie. The principal agent of his vengeance is Verethraghna who furiously pursues his perfidious enemies in the form of a raging boar:

'We worship Mithra of wide pastures in front of whom speeds Verethraghna, Ahura-created—in the form of a boar, aggressive, sharp in tooth, a male—a boar, sharp in tusk, unapproachable, a killer at one blow—furious, slobbering at the snout, and mighty: iron its fore-feet, iron its hind-feet, iron its tendons, iron its tail, and iron its jaws. Filled with rage and a hero's valour he catches up with his enemies and violently(?) smites them down, nor does he deem that he has dealt them a blow or inflicted a wound until he has smashed the vertebrae, the pillars of life—the vertebrae, the springs of vitality. At one fell blow he hacks to pieces everything: bones and hair, brains and blood of men who break their contracts he mashes up together on the ground.'[8]

This savage massacre of the enemies of Mithra (who are given no chance to repent) is indeed the work of Verethraghna, whose *daēvic* origin we have already had occasion to note, but it is done not in his own name but in the name of Mithra, the embodiment of the sanctity of the contract. We have seen that what Zoroaster complained of in the *daēvas* and those who worshipped them was their violence (*aēshma*): they did not subscribe to *asha* which, besides being Truth, is also the natural, fitting order of things: this they violate (*druj-* = 'lying, violation') even as the enemies of Mithra, the Contract, violate the contract. What the worshippers of Mithra and of Verethraghna in his boar incarnation are doing here, however, is to condone in their deities the methods of *aēshma*, of violence, in putting down what they consider to be wrong; and this is just what the worshippers of the *daēvas* must have done since they too, impudently dismissed by Zoroaster as mere 'followers of the Lie', must have regarded themselves as 'followers of Truth'. Again, in the *Yasht* dedicated to him Verethraghna appears as the executive arm of Mithra and Rashnu: 'he ranges among the drawn-up ranks, with Mithra and with Rashnu he asks to right and left: "Who is it that lies unto Mithra? Who is it that rejects Rashnu? To whom shall I bring disease and death—I who have the power [to do so]?"'[9]

This attitude of exultant violence is surely typical of the religion of the *daēvas* which Zoroaster had hoped to suppress: it is in flat contradiction to the Prophet's own intuition that death is the work of the Destructive Spirit, not of the Wise Lord or of his Holy Spirit or of the Bounteous Immortals.[10] It is the supreme evil. The Creator of life may, in the cause of justice and Truth, be forced to condemn his creatures to an eternity of woe, but he does not destroy either the bodies or the souls of what he has created. Verethraghna, on Mithra's behalf, does just this—and not only Verethraghna but Mithra too, for he himself says: 'To whom shall I bring disease and death? To whom miserable(?) poverty—I who have power [to do so]? Whose noble offspring shall I slay at one fell blow?'[11]

Mithra may be just in his way, but his methods of chastising the wicked are violent, cruel, and arbitrary. They do not harmonize with his own nature which is not only the 'contract' but also 'friendship', for this meaning of the word *mitra/mithra* is attested in both the Indian and Iranian traditions. In Sanskrit, *mitra* (masc.) means 'friend', whereas in Middle and New Persian *mihr* (derived from *mithra*) means 'love' or 'friendship', while the derivative *mihr-bān* ('one who observes Mithra') is still the ordinary Persian word for 'kind'. In large sections of the Mithra *Yasht*, Mithra, though possessed of many excellences, is scarcely kind. And not only is he not kind: in a much quoted passage he is described as being positively evil: 'Thou, Mithra, art evil yet most good to the countries. Thou, Mithra, art evil yet most good to men. Thou hast power over peace and war among the countries.'[12]

Yet it would be a mistake to suppose that Mithra is arbitrarily good and evil in turn: he is only 'most evil' to those who deserve to be disciplined (*sraoshya*),[13] those who are false to their contracts. It is not the fact that Mithra is described as 'evil' that runs counter to Zoroaster's teaching, for he is evil only to those who break their contracts, that is, are false to Mithra himself, the personification of contract, while he is 'very good' to truthful men who are true to their word. Indeed, had not Zoroaster himself bid his partisans 'be friendly to the follower of Truth but *evil* to the follower of the Lie'?[14] What does run counter to Zoroaster's teaching is the violence Mithra displays in the subjugation of his enemies: he makes no attempt first to convert them by peaceful means. Zoroaster, on the other hand, regarded the ultimate aim of his mission to be the conversion of the world. The followers of the Lie must be given a chance to come over to the Good Religion,[15] not simply be mown down in battle: Mithra offers those who offend him no such alternative.

And yet this violent side to Mithra's character is so out of keeping with his original function of preserver of the sanctity of contracts and with the function of judge and mediator he was later to assume that we are forced to conclude that these *daēvic* characteristics have crept in from an outside source.

Mithra and Indra

It has long been maintained, and with justice, that many of Mithra's more sinister attributes, so seemingly at variance with his true nature, are attested of the Vedic Indra, not of the Vedic Mitra. Mithra's characteristic weapon is the *vazra*, his 'club' or 'mace', which is considered to be so holy as to deserve veneration in its own right:[16] so too is Indra's characteristic weapon, which was later identified with the thunderbolt, the *vajra* (showing the usual alternation of *z* and *j* as between Iranian and Indic). Both are 'charioteers' (*rathaēshtār/ ratheshthā*, 'mighty' (*aojah/ojasvant*), 'strong-armed' (*ughra-bāzu/ugra-bāhu*), and both have 'good horses' (*hvaspa/svaśva*). Both appear as gods of battle who lead their peoples to victory.

The case of Verethraghna is even more clear, for his name (apart from the suffix) is identical with the stock epithet of Indra in the *Rig-Veda—vrtra-han*, 'he who overcomes the defence'[17] or 'he who overcomes [his enemy's] valour'.[18] It is true that in the Vedic account Indra is constantly associated with the feat of slaying a dragon variously called Vrtra, Ahi (the Serpent), or Vala, and that in the Avesta these feats fall to the lot of a variety of mythical heroes, not of Verethraghna or of Mithra; but the Armenian historian, Moses of Chorene, tells us that Vahagn (= Verethraghna) 'fought with and vanquished dragons, his exploits surpassing even those of Heracles',[19] and in an inscription accompanying a statue of Verethraghna set up by Antiochus I of Commagene he is identified both with Heracles and with Ares: he is both a hero and a god of war. This is equally true of the Vedic god Indra.

In Vedic mythology Indra's dragon-slaying exploit is normally followed by the liberation of kine which the dragon had held in captivity, and these kine are sometimes referred to as 'waters' or 'rivers'. In the Veda, Indra plays a dual role: first, he is the hero who leads the Aryans to victory against the dark-skinned Dasyus or Dāsas, and, secondly, he is the god who releases the waters or the imprisoned kine. In this second role he is usually considered to be the god of the thunderstorm, but if this aspect of him were at all primary, it is most surprising that we practically never hear of rain in connexion with him.[20] It is much more natural to take his liberation of the kine literally; they are liberated in the same sense that peoples are 'liberated' today—they are conquered and taken over by an enemy. So too in the Avesta does the cow cry out to Mithra for liberation; 'driven into captivity she cries out for help time and time again, her arms outstretched [in prayer], longing for the herd: "When will male Mithra of wide pastures, driving from behind, bring us to the herd? When will he turn us to the path of Truth, driven as we are to the dwelling of the Lie?"'[21]

Between them, then, Mithra and Verethraghna perform functions that are characteristic of the war-god Indra in the *Rig-Veda*. Indra, however, was a *deva* and appears as a *daēva* in the later Avesta too: and for a Zoroastrian to be a *daēva* means neither more nor less than to be a demon. The case of Verethraghna, however, is no stranger than the case of Vayu who, though originally a *daēva* rather than an *ahura*, was chopped in two by the catholic Zoroastrians, one half of him succouring the Holy Spirit, the other half ministering to the murderous designs of the Evil One. Similarly in the case of Indra-Verethraghna, Indra in his own proper *daēvic* name became a demon, whereas Verethraghna, his stock epithet, became the genius of victory of the Zoroastrians themselves. The case of Verethraghna is neither more nor less strange than that of Haoma and Zairi.[22]

The Daēva-Worshippers and Mithra
The distinguished editor of the Mithra *Yasht*, then, shows little awareness of the facts and probabilities of religious history when he writes:

'To infer, as is often done, that the Avestan Mithra, in addition to representing the Vedic Mitra, is also heir of the Vedic war-god Indra, means to open the door wide to a reckless identification of gods that never had anything to do with each other, thus spelling the confusion, instead of the clarification, of Indo-Iranian religious history. If Mithra is called Mithra, and not Indra, whose name, moreover, duly occurs in Avestan as Indra, then the only possible excuse for grafting the Rigvedic Indra on the Avestan Mithra would be an association in Rigvedic hymns of Mitra with Indra as close as that with Varuna.'[23]

This kind of criticism, which is itself evoked by the very recklessness of much modern Zoroastrian scholarship, is in its turn marvellously unhelpful. The *fact*, not for once the theory, that certain characteristics of the Vedic Indra reappear not only in the Avestan Verethraghna but also in Mithra himself, does not mean that anyone is trying to graft anything on to anything else, let alone to open the door to reckless identifications. It is a phenomenon that calls for an explanation. If it is true—and of course it may well not be—that before the coming of Zoroaster there existed two parties, one of which worshipped the *ahuras* exclusively and the other of which worshipped both the *ahuras* and the *daēvas*, then we must ask ourselves what was likely to happen after the Zoroastrian reform which admitted only one Ahura as truly God and ignored the existence of the others almost entirely. Because the Prophet was convinced by his own intense inner experience that there was only one God, though operating through a variety of agencies which were no more than aspects of his personality, and because he recognized this God as 'Lord' (*Ahura*), he was bound to turn a blind eye on Mithra, hitherto so closely associated with the Ahura who, we have assumed, existed as the 'greatest and best of the gods'[24] before Zoroaster's time. Once Zoroaster obtained royal patronage we may assume that persecution of the *daēva*-worshippers set in, and it would therefore have been in their interest to come to terms with their former rivals who worshipped only the *ahuras*, and for whom Mithra ranked second only to the 'greatest and best of the gods', the Ahura *par excellence*. With Zoroaster's appropriation of the supreme Ahura and his transformation of him into Ahura Mazdāh, the Wise Lord and one true God, however, it would be natural for the older Ahura to lose ground to his close associate Mithra and for a religion centring primarily round this god to develop. To my mind the Mithra *Yasht* represents the fusing of certain *daēvic* ideas with the worship of Mithra, hitherto the god of the sacrosanct contract and of light. Thus not only is Mithra's entourage increased by the inclusion of Verethraghna—a not very heavily disguised version of Indra—but his own character is also filled out with martial characteristics borrowed from the same *daēva* which had till then been lacking. Indeed, if there is any one main theme in the Mithra *Yasht* it is this.

The Separation of Mithra from Ahura

Thanks to the Zoroastrian reform which had dissociated Mithra from his senior partner Ahura, Mithra developed along lines of his own; but after the Prophet's death neither side seems to have been happy about this dissociation, for Zoroaster's epigones were never, throughout their whole history, able to live up to their Prophet's monotheistic insights. So, as early as the *Gāthā* of the Seven Chapters, the two 'preserver-creators', almost certainly the old pair Mithra-Ahura, reappear, whereas in the Mithra *Yasht* it is Ahura [Mazdāh] who himself reintroduces the worship of Mithra at the latter's urgent request. And not only does he do this: he establishes Haoma as his high priest and thereby makes Mithra, like Sraosha, the mediator between the earthly sacrifice and his heavenly throne. At the end of the *Yasht* the two gods again come together and are once again conjointly worshipped as they had been in former times. The breach between the Wise Lord, the 'greatest and best of the gods', and Mithra, the guardian of the sanctity of compact and treaty, is now healed.

It now remains for us to analyse the *Yasht* in a little more detail. 'When I created Mithra of wide pastures,' the Wise Lord says, 'I made him as worthy of veneration and of reverence as I am myself.'

So does the Mithra *Yasht* begin, and it is thereby made clear that Mithra is what he is, not in his own right but by the creative power and grace of the Wise Lord. It has often been maintained that this opening section was added to the original *Yasht* by the catholic Zoroastrians when they readopted Mithra as their own, and that in the 'original' Mithra religion, of which we in fact know nothing, Mithra himself was the creator.[25] Some plausibility attaches to this otherwise implausible view because the Roman Mithras is said by Porphyry[26] to have created the world, and because, in the Middle Persian Manichaean texts in which every effort is made to 'translate' the Manichaean cosmology into Zoroastrian terms, the Living Spirit who, in the Manichaean system, is the demiurge-creator, appears as 'god Mithra' (*Mihr yazd*).[27] But against this must be set the term *pāyū-thwōreshtārā*, 'the two preserver-creators', which must almost certainly be Ahura and Mithra, of whom the first is, according to all the Avestan and Pahlavi evidence, the creator, the second the preserver. If, however, as we have argued, Ahura [Mazdāh] and Mithra became momentarily estranged after the Zoroastrian reform and if Ahura sank into a position of relative unimportance until the two deities were again united in the catholic Zoroastrian synthesis, then it is quite likely that Mithra will have taken on the creative function of his partner. Indeed, there seems no reason to suppose that Mithra's function in the old religion in which the two great *ahuras*—the 'greatest and best' Ahura and Mithra—formed an indissoluble pair, differed sensibly from that of the Holy Spirit in primitive Zoroastrianism, and that just as the Wise Lord creates through the Holy Spirit, so does the 'greatest and best Lord' create and preserve through Mithra. All this is not unlike the Christian idea of God the Father creating through his Son or Word—creation proper being appropriated to the Father, and redemption to the Son. So too we may, if we will, surmise that creation was 'appropriated' to the 'greatest and best Lord' and preservation to Mithra, though each must have shared in the activity of the other.

Be that as it may, on reading the Mithra *Yasht* one is forcibly struck by the complete hiatus that separates the opening stanza from what follows: for what follows is a strict injunction to the worshipper never to break a contract (the term *mithra* being used not in the sense of a god to be venerated as the Wise Lord himself is venerated, but simply in the sense of a solemn compact entered into between man and man). The first stanza, then, sets out at the very outset to tell us what catholic Zoroastrianism considers to be the relationship of the Wise Lord to Mithra. The Wise Lord is the sole creator, but he creates Mithra equal to himself. Elsewhere Mithra is his son,[28] just as Truth in the *Gāthās* is sometimes spoken of as the Wise Lord's son, or again he is his creature.[29]

Analysis of Mithra Yasht

The Mithra *Yasht* is divided into the following fairly distinct sections:

(1) 2–3: the sanctity of contracts.

(2) 4–6: the worshipper promises to worship Mithra.

(3) 7–11: the god is worshipped by armed charioteers as a god of war.

(4) 12–16: Mithra's triumphant progress from east to west in which he precedes the sun.

(5) 17–27: the god's prowess in war and his relentless chastisement of those who lie to him by violating their contracts.

(6) 28–34: Mithra as the dispenser of victory and prosperity to the followers of Truth.

(7) 35–43: Mithra, the lord God of hosts and 'levier of armies', the gruesome chastiser of those who dare to break their contracts, the god who manifests himself in murderous wrath.

(8) 44–46: Mithra the 'undeceivable master of ten thousand spies', whose abode is the whole earth and who cannot be deceived.

(9) 47–48: the terrible avenger once again.

(10) 49–52: the Wise Lord and the Bounteous Immortals build him a house whence he can survey the whole wide world.

(11) 53–60: Mithra's first complaint to the Wise Lord that he is not worshipped as other gods are worshipped.

(12) 61–66: Mithra as universal provider through whom the waters flow and the plants grow, the giver of flocks and herds, power and sons and life itself—he 'in whose soul is a great and powerful pledge to the Religion'.

(13) 67–72: the chariot of Mithra, the 'wrathful lord', drawn by white horses: its way is paved by the Religion of the worshippers of Mazdāh. Verethraghna precedes him in the form of a boar, grinding down all opposition.

(14) 73–87: Mithra's second appeal to the Wise Lord, not a complaint this time, but a joyful request which he knows will not be denied. The followers of Truth acclaim Mithra as the destroyer of their enemies, the protector of the poor and of the cow: they appease him with sacrifice and libation.

(15) 88–94: Haoma worships Mithra, having been installed in this function by the Wise Lord. This [new form of the] Religion receives the seal of approval from the Wise Lord and the Bounteous Immortals.

(16) 95–101: Mithra, with Sraosha and Rashnu, scours the earth at night, putting the Destructive Spirit, Aēshma (violence or wrath) and all *daēvas* and 'lies' to flight. The worshipper prays that he may not get in the way of the wrathful Mithra.

(17) 102–103: the Wise Lord appoints Mithra protector and overseer of the whole material world.

(18) 104–111: infallibly Mithra detects and chastises those who violate their contracts [because he hates the Lie]; hence he is supremely good. He is determined to enrich those who are true, but to deliver to death and destruction their enemies who offer him improper sacrifices.

(19) 112–114: the destruction of those who offer 'heavy sacrifices'.

(20) 115–118: various kinds of contract: Mithra's promise to thwart the Destructive Spirit.

(21) 119–122: the Wise Lord lays down the rite according to which Mithra is to be worshipped.

(22) 123–124: the Wise Lord worships Mithra in heaven, the House of Song.

(23) 124–135: Mithra rides forth from the House of Song in his fair chariot drawn by four white steeds. He is accompanied by the most righteous Chishtā, the Likeness of the Religion of the worshippers of Mazdāh and by the 'blazing Fire that is the strong Fortune of kings (*kavaēm khwarenō*)'. Description of his weapons and the discomfiture of the Destructive Spirit and his henchmen. Another prayer that Mithra will not strike the worshipper in his wrath.

(24) 136: his one-wheeled golden chariot.

(25) 137–139: Mithra's favour to the man who is an 'incarnate word' and who performs the rite correctly: his displeasure at the man who is no incarnate word and no follower of Truth and who, though he performs the rite correctly, does not win the approval of the Wise Lord, the Bounteous Immortals, or of Mithra.

(26) 140–141: Mithra worshipped as good, as a 'strong charioteer', the 'merciful', and the 'undeceivable'.

(27) 142–144: Mithra worshipped as the light that illumines the whole world.

(28) 145: 'by the *barsom* plant we worship Mithra and Ahura, the exalted [lords] of Truth, forever free from corruption: [we worship] the stars, moon, and sun. We worship Mithra, the lord of all lands.'

Mithra as Contract and King

Iranian society, like the society of its sister civilization in India, was broadly divided into three main classes—the priests, the warriors (*rathaēshtār*, 'riders on chariots'), and the mass of the country people or peasants. For the strict followers of the Prophet, Zoroaster himself was the titular head of all three groups;[30] but in the Mithra *Yasht* it is clear that Mithra, besides being pre-eminently the great war-lord, also preserves a priestly or at least a judicial function in that he not only ensures that contracts between man and man are kept sacrosanct, but also represents in his own person the inviolability of all contractual relationships. His care for the peasantry and the well-being of the whole community is shown by his seeing to it that there is rain by which the plants may grow (§61), and by his bestowal of flocks and herds, life and livelihood (§65). He is, then, the god of the whole Iranian nation—of its priests, its warriors, and the peasants who till its soil, 'the province-lord of all the provinces' (*vīspanām dahyunām daiñhupaiti*, §145): he is the divine image of the Achaemenian king of kings, and as such, his sphere of operation is, like Sraosha's, this earth. 'His abode is set in the material world [extending] throughout the whole breadth of earth, vast, unhampered, gleaming, widely stretched abroad' (§44): so he is both lord and judge, that is, both the secular and spiritual sovereign in the material world (§92). Like his human counterpart on earth he has a thousand ears and ten thousand eyes (§141 etc.) through which he knows all things and thanks to which he cannot be deceived. His eyes are not, as has sometimes been supposed, the stars in the sky: they are the 'eyes and ears of the King', identical with his 'spies', and corresponding to the network of informers that kept the king of kings informed of the mischief being perpetrated by his subjects.[31] Mithra, as king, protects his subjects and brings them justice, but just as in India it was the function of the king, who must be of the warrior caste, not only to protect his own subjects but also to wage aggressive war against his neighbours, so does Mithra wage war on the *mithrō-druj*, the violator of the treaty, who does not acknowledge the god's supremacy. For Zoroaster *druj*, the 'Lie', meant false teaching and wrong worship and enmity to Truth which is also the harmonious order of the cosmos. To the worshippers of Mithra it meant more specifically the violation of a contract and the denial of the god who incarnates the contract. What Truth is in primitive Zoroastrianism Mithra is in the Mithra *Yasht*: to outrage him is to outrage Truth itself.

Mithra as Terrible Warlord

Contract and King: both these is Mithra 'of wide pastures'. But he is also—and very markedly—a terrible warlord. He is quick to anger and easily outraged, and even his own worshippers have to pray that he will not visit them in his wrath (§98). This aggressiveness which impels the great god to deal out death and disease to all who oppose him is obviously not a natural development of the god's character as contract and king. The sacred mace with which he beats down all opposition and the sense of insecurity which his anger inspires even in his own worshippers must be characteristics borrowed from a daēvic source. In the Indian tradition they are associated with Indra and Rudra-Śarva. Both these had been relegated to the status of demon by Zoroaster, but they take their revenge by insinuating their more unlovable characteristics into the personality of Mithra, while Indra transforms himself into Verethraghna, the genius of Victory and irresistible might, shorn indeed of his original name, but still fully recognizable in his standing epithet—'he who breaks down valour'.

Mithra as Light

Mithra, however, is not only contract, king, and warrior. He is also light. He is the light that precedes the sun when it rises 'surveying the habitations of the Iranians' (§13) : he is 'that greatest god who in the morning illumines many a form, [who illumines] the creatures of the Holy Spirit, as he lights up [his own] body, [he who is] self-luminous like the moon' (§142). His one-wheeled golden chariot is drawn by four white horses (§§125, 136) as he courses through the sky. From these descriptions it is clear that Mithra is also a sun-god—not identical with the sun, but the god of light in general of which the sun is the source and origin. To deny that Mithra is, among other things, a sun-god, as has recently been done,[32] is as silly as to identify him with the night sky,[33] for just as Ahura Mazdāh's 'body' or 'material form' is said to be 'these lights' and the sun in the Gāthā of the Seven Chapters,[34] so is Mithra's body the sun in the Yasht dedicated to him. Both hark back to the concept of the 'preservers-creators', Ahura and Mithra, as they must have existed before the Prophet Zoroaster caused a spiritual revolution within the religion of Iran. The two gods, bound together in closest union, both stood as guardians of Truth and Order, both were united against the Lie—falsehood, disorder, the violation of the natural law and of the contract that embodies it ; both were gods of light, because it is light that reveals things as they are and thus, of all sensible things, most nearly approximates to truth ; and because they are gods of light, so is their material and visible form the sun. But, for all this, neither god is himself *identical* with the sun ; for throughout the Yasna and in the concluding stanza of the Mithra Yasht itself, the two gods are first worshipped together, and only then is homage paid to the sun, the moon, and the stars—the physical lights that most nearly represent them in the material universe. Things had not changed when Porphyry wrote of the god of the Magians that 'he resembled light in his body and truth in his soul'.[35] Neither Mithra nor Ahura *is* sun or dawn or night sky, but each and both are the source of light in all of them.

And what of Mithra and the night sky? All that is said of him in this connexion is that he traverses the whole breadth of the earth after the sun's glow has faded from the sky, 'sweeping across both boundaries of this wide, round earth whose ends are far apart : everything does he survey between heaven and earth, holding his mace in his hand'.[36] Scouring the earth for *daēvas* and evil men, he puts the Destructive Spirit and the demon of Violence and Wrath to flight. From this passage alone it has been concluded that Mithra was the god of the night sky. In Zoroastrian studies all things are possible.

Mithra, Sraosha, and Rashnu

Before we analyse the significance of the Mithra *Yasht* from the point of view of religious history, a word or two must be said about Mithra's relations with Sraosha and with Rashnu. As has often been remarked, Mithra and Sraosha overlap in many respects. Both pursue the *daēvas* after dark;[37] both are worshipped by Haoma;[38] both are drawn by four white horses whose hooves are shod with gold;[39] and both have palaces on the highest of mountains.[40]

It is probable that the purely mythological traits were transferred to Sraosha from Mithra (i.e. the horses and the palace) as also the worship of him by Haoma. In the case of their activity after nightfall, however, it is significant that Sraosha's particular enemy is Aēshma, the demon of Violence and Wrath, which plays so conspicuous a part in the *Gāthās*, whereas Mithra is matched with the Destructive Spirit himself as well as with Aēshma. This tends to confirm our earlier contention that the Holy Spirit of the *Gāthās* fulfils a function that had previously been fulfilled by Mithra.

From the time of the Mithra *Yasht*, Mithra, Sraosha, and Rashnu form an almost inseparable triad. Together they set about the chastisement of the wicked;[41] together are they honoured time and again in the *Yasna*; three brothers are they, sons of the Wise Lord, and Ashi is their sister;[42] together they mediate for the soul of the dead, and after Rashnu has weighed their good and evil deeds, Sraosha leads the blessed on to heaven;[43] and together they are invoked for the forgiveness of sins.[44]

How this close association came about it is not easy to see, for Sraosha, as we have seen, appears in the *Gāthās* and is therefore accepted by the Prophet into the reformed religion, whereas *Rashnu* seems simply to be an epithet of Ahura Mazdāh in *Yasht* 12.3–5, and, equally, he seems to be an epithet of Mithra in *Yasht* 10.79. *Rashnu* probably means 'judge', and his main function in the later literature is to judge the souls of the dead on the Bridge of the Requiter (the Requiter being Rashnu himself),[45] but in the *Gāthās* it is Ahura Mazdāh who is the judge on the Bridge. It seems then possible that Rashnu was originally no more than an epithet of both Ahura and Mithra in the old Ahura Religion, whereas Sraosha, the genius of hearing and obeying belongs both to the ancient tradition and to the reformed religion. As belonging to the first, Sraosha may be compared to the Indian *Śruti* (from the same root meaning 'hearing') which is the technical term used to denote the primal revelation enshrined in the Vedas: and the word 'to hear' is used in precisely this sense when the Prophet says that it has been *heard* that Yima was among those sinners who gave the people portions of beef to eat:[46] this was the oral tradition. But the word is also used in the sense of receiving and actually hearing a *new* revelation as when the Prophet *hears* the two primal Spirits holding colloquy together.[47]

Both Sraosha and the goddess Ashi were adopted into his system by the Prophet, but they both underwent a change of character, the one becoming not only hearing but also obeying, not only obedience but also discipline, and not only discipline but also the chastisement of evil thoughts, words, and deeds; while Ashi, who appears in the *Yashts* as a goddess of plenty, becomes in the *Gāthās* the lot of weal and woe that follows on good and evil. Both deities (or concepts, if you will) played an active part in both primitive Zoroastrianism and the 'Mithraism' that developed independently of it. Rashnu too, the judge, who seems originally to have been no more than an epithet of both Ahura and Mithra in that capacity, survived as an independent deity. Thus Rashnu, Sraosha, and Ashi kept a passageway open between the old religion over which Ahura and Mithra, the 'preservers-creators', presided and primitive Zoroastrianism in which Ahura Mazdāh ruled alone and supreme—creator, preserver and judge. The Mithra *Yasht* tells the story of how the two cults encountered each other again, but this time in a spirit of reconciliation which was to reunite the two great gods much as they had been united before.

The first part of the Mithra *Yasht* (§§2–48) is very largely devoted to a description of Mithra as a war-god. In this section the daēvic properties which, in the process of religious evolution, had passed into him from the deposed *daēvas*, Indra and Saurva, are given their full scope. Sraosha and Rashnu already accompany him in the carnage he makes of his enemies, but nowhere is he brought into relationship with the primitive Zoroastrian scheme of things except in the initial stanza where it is categorically stated that Mithra was created by the Wise Lord.

Mithra's Heavenly House
In §§50-1, however, the scene changes:

'The Wise Lord fashioned for him a dwelling above Harā, the lofty, gleaming [mountain] round which circles many [a star], where there is neither night nor darkness, neither cold wind nor hot, neither disease in death abounding, nor yet defilement wrought by the *daēvas*. No mists arise from high Haraiti. This [dwelling] did all the Bounteous Immortals build, with minds fore-knowing and trusting hearts, in close concord with the sun. From high Haraiti does [Mithra] survey the [whole] material world.'

Mithra, as we have already seen, is the god in charge of this world, and, unlike Rashnu, his principal concern is with the body rather than with the soul;[48] he is concerned with the 'giving of life to men and he keeps their bodies alive'.[49] In Middle Persian his name also means 'love' and in living things he is that self-love which keeps them alive. 'Mithra,' we read in a Middle Persian text, 'is one [only] . . . in all living creatures, greater in some and less in others.'[50] Of the triad, then, Sraosha both chastises and saves, Rashnu judges, and Mithra preserves human life and individuality. Of course, Mithra also partakes of the functions of his companions, and just as the Bounteous Immortals can be regarded as functions of the Wise Lord, so can Sraosha and Rashnu be regarded as functions or aspects of the central figure, Mithra, even though they operate independently.[51]

By building Mithra a dwelling above high Harā the Wise Lord and the Bounteous Immortals raise him up from the world below the sun and constellations to their own natural habitat, the spiritual world, which is located beyond the vault of the sky. This is the first time, in this *Yasht*, that the Wise Lord and Mithra are brought together: historically it may well mean that the Zoroastrians, after admitting the Fravashis, the Haoma cult, and Ahura-Mithra too under the cover of the 'preserver-creators', now went a step further; and it may be supposed that just as Ahura Mazdāh builds a dwelling for Mithra in heaven, so do his worshippers on earth build a shrine for Mithra on earth. If this is so, this shrine exists even today in the form of the *dar-i Mihr*, the 'portico of Mithra', the holy of holies of every Parsee fire-temple.

However that may be, the building of Mithra's heavenly house by the Wise Lord himself and by the Bounteous Immortals, re-establishes contact between the two great gods, and Mithra is not slow to complain of the neglect he has hitherto suffered. With arms outstretched in supplication he approaches the Wise Lord and reproaches him with the injustice of which he feels himself to be the victim. Though he is the beneficent protector of all creatures, yet do they not reverence him with prayers in which his name is mentioned as they do in the case of other gods.[52]

Mithra's Plaint to the Wise Lord

This plaint of the neglected god is no mere face-saving formula enabling the Zoroastrians to receive back the ancient *ahuras* (or even *daēvas* in disguised forms) into their reconstituted pantheon, for only Tishtrya, that is, the star Sirius, makes a similar complaint. In the case of Anāhitā, Ahura Mazdāh simply orders Zoroaster to worship her, whereas Vayu and Verethraghna, both of them of daēvic origin, dispense with even so much formal introduction. We have the impression, then, that the reunion of the post-Zoroastrian Mithra, enriched as he now is with daēvic properties, with his old associate Ahura, now transformed by the Prophet Zoroaster into Ahura Mazdāh, the Wise Lord, creator, sustainer, and judge of all things, was regarded by both sides as an advance of major importance in their religious evolution: for whereas Anāhitā, Vayu, and the rest of them could lead a more or less peripheral existence in the general scheme of catholic Zoroastrianism without impinging overmuch on the central liturgy, the admission of Mithra, who must have retained strong ties with the old Ahura, into the system over which Ahura's successor, Ahura Mazdāh, presided, meant a radical change in the Zoroastrians' attitude to Ahura Mazdāh himself. His supremacy as creator was indeed faithfully preserved, but he now creates Mithra as in every respect equal in dignity to himself.

Mithra's Descent to Earth
Neither on this occasion nor on the second occasion when Mithra appeals to Ahura Mazdāh, does the latter answer him directly: in each case it is the worshipper of the Wise Lord, the *ashavan* or follower of Truth who does so. Henceforth his name will be mentioned regularly in the liturgy and due libations will be poured out to him. And so it is that when Mithra, pacified and well pleased, drives in his 'high-wheeled chariot, fashioned in the spiritual world'—driving across the empyrean from east to west—it is not only Ashi, his own sister, who guides his chariot, but also the Religion of the worshippers of Mazdāh, now his adopted sister[53] who makes smooth his path before him.[54] Yet this new alliance has in no way diminished the furious onslaught of the 'wrathful lord',[55] for it is now that he is preceded by Verethraghna, the genius of victory in the form of a boar, who pulverizes and grinds to pieces all that dare withstand him.

We must assume that the Religion of the Worshippers of Mazdāh, who herself had cleared the way for Mithra and his avenging angel, Verethraghna, has surveyed the carnage wrought among those who violate their contracts, liars unto Mithra, and therefore *eo ipso* followers of the Lie and not of Truth, and has approved it all. For, once the victory is won, Mithra no longer *complains* that he is neglected by the 'followers of Truth', he joyfully raises his voice, confident now that his dignity as a very great god is already acknowledged; and, sure enough, the followers of Truth recognize him immediately as the destroyer of their enemies 'who slay the followers of Truth'; they recognize that, by protecting the countries in which his own cult is religiously carried out and by smashing those who deny him, he is fighting against the same Lie against which they themselves are pitted. Or is he? For in the preceding stanza the Mazdāh-worshippers pray that they may be in a position to protect their homesteads, and not be compelled to leave them, or to leave their country altogether and yield to their enemies. This Mithra alone can guarantee. This may perhaps mean that because Mithra was also worshipped by the 'followers of the Lie' or *daēva*-worshippers, as he doubtless was, he alone could save them from their depredations. The Zoroastrians would appear to be appealing to Mithra as a pan-Iranian deity who can and will help both sides in accordance with whether or not he is propitiated in the same way that he is propitiated, though unsuccessfully, by the 'followers of the Lie':[56] they acknowledge his efficacy as the lord god of battles. From this moment he is the protector of *their* poor and *their* cattle[57] as much as are the Wise Lord and the Bounteous Immortals themselves.

Haoma Consecrates himself Mithra's Priest

Yet to be invoked in his own name is not enough in itself: the great god must be invited to participate in the central rite of the worshippers of Mazdāh: so we are told that 'glowing Haoma, the healing, fair, and lordly [god] with golden eyes, venerated him on the highest height of high Haraiti called Hukairya by name—[he] the immaculate [venerating Mithra] the immaculate with immaculate *barsom*,[58] immaculate libation, immaculate words'.[59] Yet Haoma did not do this of his own accord: 'The Wise Lord who holds to Truth (*ashavan*) established him as priest, prompt to sacrifice and loud in song, as the Wise Lord's priest, as the priest of the Bounteous Immortals, he, the priest, prompt to sacrifice and loud in song, sacrificed with a mighty voice, [and] his voice reached up to the [heavenly] lights, encompassed this [whole] earth, and penetrated all the seven climes.'[60]

Prima facie it would appear that this was Mithra's first initiation into the Haoma cult, but this seems unlikely since later in the *Yasht* we will hear of ritual variations which are condemned out of hand. One thing is certain, and that is that the Haoma rite is here regarded as being *the* ritual act *par excellence* of the worshippers of Mazdāh, and it is in this central rite that Mithra is now asked to participate. Yet it is extremely unlikely that similar sacrifices, using the same ingredients, had not been offered to Mithra before his reception into the pantheon of the catholic Zoroastrians, but there must have been ritual differences to which, as is always the case, both sides attached inordinate importance. In all probability the rite offered to Mithra was that mentioned in *Yasna* 32.14 in which the Haoma stalks were immolated in fire.[61] However that may be, the significance of our present passage is that Mithra is now admitted on an equal footing with the Wise Lord and the Bounteous Immortals to partake of the sacrifice and sacrament of the Haoma who is both high priest and victim in this 'Mazdean' and Zoroastrian cult.

Mithra initiated into the 'Good Religion'
The Religion of the worshippers of Mazdāh is also the '*Good* Religion', and Mithra, admitted now to the mysteries of this Good Religion of the Wise Lord, no longer sends Verethraghna before him to hack and mangle the bodies of his enemies, but contents himself with prostrating them with his mace, bringing them thus to a frightened realization that after all he perceives *all* the wrongs that are perpetrated throughout the world; and with this realization the sinner is given the chance to repent—a chance that had not been vouchsafed him before. So the worshippers of the Wise Lord and followers of Truth can now say with no misgiving:

'There is no material man in existence who thinks evil thoughts to so great an extent as Mithra, the spiritual, thinks good thoughts; there is no material man in existence who speaks evil words to so great an extent as Mithra, the spiritual, speaks good words; there is no material man in existence who does evil deeds to so great an extent as Mithra, the spiritual, does good deeds.'[62]

The great god Mithra, so long excluded from the Zoroastrian fold, is thus welcomed back wholeheartedly into the religion that worships not only with sacrifice and fire, but also with the formula—which first appears in the *Gāthā* of the Seven Chapters—'good thoughts, good words, good deeds'. In accordance with this formula Mithra now asks: 'Who, considering me to be a god, worships me with a good sacrifice, who with a bad sacrifice?' Who, in other words, worships him correctly according to current Zoroastrian usage, and who according to rites that may be akin to those of the *daēva*-worshippers. To the first he promises riches, good fortune, bodily health, and a noble offspring, to their rulers a powerful kingdom and a numerous army; to the second he promises still illness, death, poverty, misery, and the destruction of their children; and their rulers will be deprived of their sovereignty because they have angered him by not honouring their treaties. Thus Mithra's 'goodness' which consists in upholding those who are faithful to their contracts and in punishing those who break them, is seen to coincide with Zoroaster's 'goodness' which consists in doing good to the good and evil to the evil. The morality of both is still 'an eye for an eye and a tooth for a tooth'. Mithra and Ahura Mazdāh thus shake hands in recognition of the fact that basically they have one common enemy— the Lie—falsehood and disorder—the Lie which manifests itself through the Destructive Spirit, violence, and the *daēvas* who incorporate these qualities. So, when Mithra's onslaught on the 'sons of those who offer heavy sacrifices'—a reference, certainly, to some kind of daēvic cult practice—is extolled, both he and Ahura (not Ahura Mazdāh) are invoked in their old dual form *Mithra-Ahura* to come to the assistance of their joint worshippers.

But this is not the end of the story of the reconciliation of the two great gods: the details of the cult have still to be worked out. The worshippers of Ahura Mazdāh are bidden to worship Mithra with 'small and large cattle and winged birds',[63] and with the libations of which Haoma is the pourer. Moreover, Mithra's worshippers according to the new rite are required to perform ablutions for three days and three nights before the sacrifice, and they must submit to thirty lashes of the whip. This emphasis on purity and self-mortification, characteristic of the Iranian Mithra, was later to be no less characteristic of his Roman offshoot, Mithras.

Ahura and Mithra Reunited
Having prescribed the type of worship and sacrifice that was to be paid to Mithra whom he had raised up to a dignity equal to his own, the Wise Lord, to demonstrate the extreme importance he attaches to the combined cult, himself worships Mithra 'with arms upraised to deathlessness, in the House of Song'.[64] Mithra, then, whose dwelling had been on earth, but for whom the Wise Lord and the Bounteous Immortals fashioned another abode above Mount Harā, is now himself venerated by the All-Highest in Paradise, and from thence he is once again dispatched in his splendid chariot drawn by four white, immortal steeds, reared in Heaven, their fore-hooves shod with gold, their rear-hooves with silver. Rashnu still stands beside him, but Sraosha is no longer there; instead Chishtā, the 'likeness of the Religion of the worshippers of Mazdāh' now stands at his left side, and behind him flies the mysterious 'Likeness of the Creator', the double of Verethraghna, for he too has assumed the form of a boar. Before him now flies the blazing Fire which is the strong Glory of Kings.[65] Down he comes back

again to the earth of which he is the king of kings, falling upon *daēvas* and men who are false to their contracts. The Destructive Spirit and Aēshma fall back before his irresistible onslaught, routed by his might. Now that the link between the 'greatest and best of the gods', now transformed into Ahura Mazdāh, the all-seeing, all-powerful, all-Wise Lord, with Mithra 'of wide pastures' has been re-established, the fate of the Destructive Spirit and the *daēvas* is sealed. Ahura Mazdāh remains in the House of Song unsullied by the fray, while Mithra lays about the powers of evil, a warrior still, in this world over which they still have power.

Throughout the Mithra *Yasht* there is an element of unpredictability about the god which ill fits in with his primary role of 'contract' and guardian of the contract. True, he is represented as wreaking his vengeance primarily on contract-breakers, *daēva*-worshippers, and followers of the Lie, but his own worshippers feel anything but secure when he is 'angered and outraged': as in the case of the Vedic Rudra it is felt that the divine wrath might, on occasion, override the divine justice. Once he is admitted into the circle over which Ahura Mazdāh presides, however, this element of unpredictability becomes less pronounced. Mithra aids those who perform the liturgy correctly and with reverence, but assails even those who perform it correctly but negligently and without the right dispositions.

'Hail to the man in authority,' said the Wise Lord, '. . . for whom, a priest, a follower of Truth, an incarnate word, who has experience of the world, offers sacrifice on the outspread *barsom*, uttering Mithra's name the while. Straightway does Mithra draw nigh to the dwelling of that man in authority if, thanks to the favour [Mithra shows] him, he performs the liturgy correctly both in utterance and thought.

'Woe to the man in authority,' said the Wise Lord, '. . . for whom a priest who is no follower of Truth, has no experience, and is no incarnate word, stands behind the *barsom*, spreads it out fully, and performs a long sacrifice: [such a one] does not please the Wise Lord, nor the other Bounteous Immortals, nor yet Mithra of wide pastures, for he thinks slightingly of the Wise One, slightingly of the Bounteous Immortals, slightingly of Mithra, slightingly of the Law, of Rashnu, and of Justice that promotes prosperity and increase in the material world.'[66]

Mithra and the Holy Spirit

In this passage two points deserve notice: first, Mithra for the first time joins the company of the Wise Lord and the *other* Bounteous Immortals. The use of the word 'other' shows that Ahura Mazdāh himself is now numbered among the Bounteous Immortals, for he is now reckoned to be fully identical with the Holy Spirit. Mithra, then, takes over the position held in primitive Zoroastrianism by the Holy Spirit—a position which, very possibly, he held before the Zoroastrian reform. Secondly, the priest who offers sacrifice according to the correct formula and with a devout heart, is himself described as an 'incarnate word': he is, then, the earthly representative of Sraosha, who thus appears as the divine minister of the *Word*. We can, then, say with some confidence that just as Haoma is the priest and victim of sacrifice and sacrament, so is Sraosha the divine mediator of God's Word to man and of man's response, in the correctly uttered liturgy, to God's Word. God's Word and man's response are in fact the same—both are the Avesta, 'which, being interpreted, means pure praise of God (or 'the gods'—*yazdān*)',[67] and Sraosha is thus both man's hearkening to the Avesta and God's listening to and accepting man's response.

In the Mithra *Yasht* it is Mithra himself who fulfils the role of Sraosha in the liturgy, for it is to him that Haoma sacrifices, and it is he who now stands next to the Bounteous Immortals as Sraosha does in the *Gāthās*: he fulfils the functions of both the Holy Spirit and the Sraosha of the *Gāthās*. Moreover, with his reception into the pantheon of catholic Zoroastrianism, his character is purged of some of the daēvic elements which had insinuated themselves into it: not only is he the 'mighty, strong charioteer' and the 'undeceivable', he is also the 'good' and the 'merciful'.[68]

The Revised Cult of Ahura and Mithra

Once again Mithra takes his rightful place at the side of Ahura, 'the greatest and best of the gods', but this greatest of the heavenly 'lords' is now the Wise Lord, the Ahura Mazdāh as seen by Zoroaster. The Prophet's reform, then, is now wedded to the cult of Mithra in which not only was the ancient worship of the *ahuras* represented, but into which some of the violence associated with the worship of the *daēvas* had also found its way; and the final invocation not only brings Ahura and Mithra together again in the old dual compound which the ancient Iranians had used to emphasize their intimate union, it also emphasizes the fact that both gods partake not only of the nature of Truth, but also of light, for they are now jointly associated with the sun, moon, and stars. 'By the *barsom* plant we worship Mithra and Ahura, the exalted [lords] of Truth exempt from corruption: [we worship] the stars, moon, and sun: ... we worship Mithra, the lord of all the lands.'[69]

The Mithra *Yasht*, then, can be viewed as a piece of religious history in the making: it shows how, once the old cult of Ahura and Mithra had been swept aside by the prophetic revelation granted to Zoroaster, and the latter, under the protection of King Vishtāspa, had declared open war on the *daēvas* and their worshippers, some of the latter, in self-defence, sought a *rapprochement* with the *ahura*-worshippers, and, by dropping the individual names of their own daēvic gods, like Indra and Saurva, ensured that the functions they represented persisted both in a fuller figure of Mithra whom they enriched with a warlike function and in subsidiary deities like Verethraghna whose name is nothing less than the stock epithet of their own Indra, now reduced by primitive Zoroastrianism to the status of a demon. With the overthrow of Vishtāspa's Chorasmian kingdom by Cyrus, it would seem that religious passions must have cooled. Primitive Zoroastrianism, coming under the influence of the Magi, sought to broaden its base: the old association between Mithra and Ahura may have served as a pretext, and so Mithra became once again the honoured partner of Ahura, now not just the 'greatest and best' of the gods of the Iranians, but the Wise Lord who alone eternally is, the one self-existent being from whom all others derive, the God who had revealed himself to the Prophet Zoroaster.

CHAPTER FIVE

MITHRA—YIMA—MITHRAS

The Daēvas and their Worshippers—The Daēva-Worshippers and Mithra—Roman Mithras and his Immolation of the Bull—Yima and the Bull-Sacrifice—Ahriman's Slaughter of the Bull—Bull-Sacrifice at the End of Time—Ahriman-Areimanios in the Mithraic Mysteries—The Bull-Sacrifice of Man's First Parents—Yima again—The Vedic Yama—The Avestan Yima—Yima's Golden Reign—His Subterranean Paradise—Yima and the Sun—Zoroaster and Yima—Yima's 'Lie'—Yima, Mithra's Twin—Nōrūz and Mihragān—Yima the Prototype of Ahriman?—Yima and Mithra in the Avesta—Cautes and Cautopates in the Mithraic Mysteries—Conclusion

THE re-establishment of the cult of Mithra alongside that of the God of the Prophet Zoroaster merely reinforces a trend within Zoroastrianism which had already begun in the *Gāthā* of the Seven Chapters. The puritanism and intolerance of primitive Zoroastrianism gives way to the eclecticism and 'indifferentism' of the catholic Zoroastrianism of the *Yasna* and the *Yashts*. Such a development was, indeed, in harmony with the spirit of religious tolerance that typified the earlier Achaemenian kings, and it is not until the reign of Xerxes that a royal reaction against the prevailing indifferentism would seem to have set in. Up to his reign it is reasonable to suppose that all forms of Iranian religion were tolerated in the genuinely Iranian portions of the Empire's vast population. The worship of the *daēvas* whose cult Xerxes seems to have suppressed,[1] was probably tolerated alongside a Zoroastrianism which, in reabsorbing into its system those ancient *ahuras* whom Zoroaster had indeed mentioned in the same breath as the Wise Lord but had deprived of any individuality, was rapidly forming itself into a religion with a pan-Iranian appeal. This new 'catholic' Zoroastrianism whose worship centred round the immolation of the divine plant Haoma, the giver of immortality, was open to every kind of influence from popular religion with but one notable exception: it would not receive the *daēvas* back into its fold, so long as they retained their old names.

The Daēvas and their Worshippers

Mithra, it will be recalled, prayed to the Wise Lord that he might be invoked with a 'sacrifice in which his name is mentioned'; and it must be assumed that the *daēvas* demanded a similar courtesy of their devotees. This indeed would seem to constitute one of the principal differences between the catholic Zoroastrians and the worshippers of the *daēvas*. Another is that they differed in the manner in which they performed the ritual, for both the Mithra *Yasht* and other passages we have quoted above show that Mithra's enemies sacrificed to him with 'bad' or incorrect sacrifice, or with a 'heavy' one, or that they brought the wrong sort of fuel to the sacred fire, or performed the wrong kind of ritual prostrations,[2] and so on. Moreover, their priests are 'no followers of Truth, have no experience, are not "incarnate words" '—in other words, they are not properly consecrated according to the Zoroastrian rite. So we read in a Pahlavi gloss on *Yasna* 32.11 that the *daēvas* and their worshippers claim that as householders they are also priests (*maghō(k)mart* = Magus). Such a claim was rejected by the orthodox.

From the glosses on this thirty-second chapter of the *Yasna* we learn quite a lot about the worshippers of the *daēvas*, or rather about them as they were seen through Zoroastrian spectacles. They teach that sovereignty comes not from the Wise Lord but from the Destructive Spirit (Angra Mainyu or Ahriman as he was later to be called) (§5), that they alone hold the secret of (eternal?) life (§11), that they slaughter cattle indiscriminately saying that life and joy are to be obtained thereby (§12). They value wealth more than virtue, seek advancement by bribery and preserve their position by pitting one man against another even to the death (§13). What is worse, they claim to be the true religious leaders and the true dispensers of the Word of the Wise Lord (ibid.). They consider themselves, then, to be the authentic teachers of the traditional religion as it had been practised before Zoroaster upset the whole religious equilibrium by proclaiming a message he claimed to have received direct from the Wise Lord who, he affirmed, alone was God. Nor did they easily give way before the advancing tide of the broadened and more widely based Zoroastrianism of early Achaemenian times, nor yet before the edict that Xerxes issued against them. On the contrary, they seem still to have thrived in Sassanian times, no longer, perhaps, daring to describe themselves as the true exponents of a religion now so ancient that none had any knowledge of what it actually had been, but claiming a rival revelation, a rival Word which they opposed to the 'pure Word of the Wise Lord'.[3] Even at that late date the Zoroastrians, now once again reformed, cannot refrain from presenting what can be no more than a spiteful caricature of their activities:

'The perverted, devilish, unrighteous rite of the "mystery of the sorcerers" consists in praising Ahriman, the Destroyer, in prowling around in great secrecy, in keeping home, body, and clothes in a state of filthiness and stench, in smearing the body with dead matter and excrement, in causing discomfort to the gods and joy to the demons, in chanting services to the demons and *calling on them by name* as befits their activity, in the worship of the demons (= *daēvas*) and in false religion, in thinking in accordance with the Evil Mind, in false speech and unrighteous action . . . and in all else that befits the devilish and is far from the godly.'[4]

From all this invective we can deduce little more than that the worshippers of the *daēvas* worshipped Ahriman and chanted services to the *daēvas* calling upon them by name, a privilege that Mithra had once craved of the Wise Lord and which was plainly as highly prized by the *daēvas* as it was by the *ahuras*. Ahriman, however, is no less a person than the Angra Mainyu or Destructive Spirit of the *Gāthās*, the eternal adversary of God's Holy Spirit. It is, however, clear that the worshippers of the *daēvas* did not worship only the evil powers, for they too claimed to be the true interpreters of the Word of the Wise Lord. They would, then, worship the 'demons' in order to turn aside their malice as all primitive peoples do, and as the Vedic Indians did in the case of Rudra, but they would also worship the 'gods' or good powers to ensure their protection against their adversaries. This kind of double insurance is an entirely normal religious instinct, and it needs so unusual a phenomenon as a prophet to challenge its validity. And for the Zoroastrians of all ages it must be said that, dilute and distort the Prophet's message as they did, they never compromised on this central issue.

The Daēva-Worshippers and Mithra

Mithra, however, was more pliable. Not only was he received gratefully into the Zoroastrian pantheon, but, it would appear, he was to be granted pride of place in the 'mystery of the sorcerers' which seems to be the root from which sprang the Mithraic mysteries that were to sweep through the Roman Empire; for great as is the difference between those mysteries and any form of Iranian religion we know from the original Iranian sources themselves, we can be certain of one fact at least, and that is that the mysteries are an offshoot not of Zoroastrianism either primitive or catholic, but of the worship of the *daēvas* which had wholly by-passed the Zoroastrian reform. Fortunately, Plutarch has preserved for us an account of a form of Iranian religion which, though it placed itself under the aegis of the Prophet, is plainly at variance with his teaching, for rather than face up to the Evil One in open warfare as Zoroaster had commanded, the sect described by Plutarch seeks to circumvent his malice by offering him propitiary sacrifice.

'Some [says Plutarch] recognize two gods—as it were rival artificers—the one the creator of good things, the other of bad: but others call the better [power] God, and the other a "daemon", as does Zoroaster the Magus. . . . He called the one Horomazes (Ahura Mazdāh, Ohrmazd) and the other Areimanios (Angra Mainyu, Ahriman); and he showed too that of all sensible things the former resembled chiefly light, but the latter, on the other hand, resembled darkness and ignorance. Between the two is Mithras, wherefore the Persians also call Mithras the Mediator. And he taught them to sacrifice to the one votive offerings and thank-offerings, but to the other offerings for averting evil, things of gloom. For pounding in a mortar a herb called Omomi (= Haoma, Pahlavi Hōm⁵) they invoke Hades and darkness: then, mixing it with the blood of a slaughtered wolf, they bring it out into a sunless place and throw it away. So too they think that certain plants belong to the good God and others to the evil daemon. So too with animals: dogs, birds, and hedgehogs belong to the good [power], while water-rats belong to the evil. Hence they count the man fortunate who has killed the greatest number of them.

'Moreover, they have plenty of mythical stories to tell about the gods, of which these are a sample. Horomazes proceeds from the purest light, Areimanios from the darkness, and they are at war with each other. And [Horomazes] created six gods, the first of Good Mind, the second of Truth, the third of Good Government, and of the rest the one was [the genius] of Wisdom, another of Wealth, and the last was the creator of pleasure in beautiful things(?). [Areimanios created], as it were, rival artificers to these, equal in number to them.'⁶

This account of Iranian religion preserved by Plutarch represents a half-way house between catholic Zoroastrianism and the Mithraism we meet with in the Roman Empire. The rigid dualism which is already present in the later Avesta, and which was to become so much more marked during the Sassanian period, is plainly there; and the protagonists, Horomazes and Areimanios, are plainly the Ohrmazd and Ahriman of the Pahlavi texts, the later version of the Ahura Mazdāh and Angra Mainyu of the *Gāthās*. Mithra too, whom we have already encountered as essentially the god of this world rather than of the supernal realm over which Ahura Mazdāh reigns, is said to be intermediate between Horomazes and his kingdom of light on the one hand and Areimanios and his kingdom of darkness on the other, just as he is the righteous judge and mediator among both spiritual and material beings.⁷ Similarly the six gods are obviously equivalent to the Zoroastrian 'Bounteous Immortals', the first three corresponding exactly to the Good Mind, Truth, and the 'Desirable Kingdom' of the *Gāthās*. Wisdom, too, is a hellenization of Right-Mindedness, and 'Wealth' a not inept rendering of 'Wholeness'. Only the 'creator of pleasure in beautiful things' fails in any way to render the Avestan original—in this case *ameretāt*, 'Immortality'. The wonder is that the correspondences are as exact as they are, not that there are some minor discrepancies. The counter-creations of Areimanios, again, are found both in the later Avesta and the Pahlavi books as is the division of the plant and animal kingdoms into creatures of Ahura Mazdāh and Angra Mainyu. So much, then, is common to the account of Plutarch and the Zoroastrianism we know from the Iranian sources.

What, however, divides the two is the worship accorded to the Lord of the realm of darkness, the pounding of the Haoma in his honour, and the mingling of it with the blood of wolves. In the Pahlavi books the animal creation of Angra Mainyu or Ahriman is divided into two categories—creeping things (*khrafstars*)[8] and the 'wolf species'[9]; and the rite in question is therefore indisputably a rite practised by the *daēva*-worshippers for whom, as for the 'Zoroastrians' of Plutarch's account, the *daēvas* were not just demons but elemental powers which could be more or less successfully manipulated by appropriate rites and magic formulas. Similarly, in Mithraism we find inscriptions *deo Arimanio*, 'to the god Areimanios', which would be unthinkable to even the most 'catholic' of Iranian Zoroastrians. Mithra's intermediary status between God on high and the Demon below is also reminiscent of the essentially earthly role of the hero-god Mithras as he appears in the Roman mysteries.

Roman Mithras and his Immolation of the Bull

However, sharply as Plutarch's account is to be distinguished from all forms of Zoroastrianism known to us from the Iranian sources, and near though it may be to Mithraism in that both recognize that Ahriman-Areimanios is a power to be propitiated rather than resisted, the differences that separate Plutarch from Mithraism are no less than those that separate him from Iranian Zoroastrianism, for the central rite of Mithraism is not any propitiation of the god Areimanios, but the re-enactment of a great bull-sacrifice which Mithras incarnate performed *in illo tempore*, that is, in a mythological setting, in order to bring life more abundantly to this earth. Of this rite Plutarch tells us nothing.

The Avesta, however, does tell us a little about bull-sacrifices, while the Pahlavi books appear to supply us with the key to the whole significance of the Mithraic rite: but, in the Pahlavi books, the bull is slain not by the god Mithra, but by Ahriman, the Destructive Spirit. His slaying of the bull again is on a cosmic scale, but the rite is repeated, on the authority of Zoroaster himself, by Yima, the author of the human race, and, according to the later tradition, by Mashyē and

Mashyānē, the first human couple of the Pahlavi books. In no passage either in the Avesta or in the Pahlavi books, however, is there any hint that Mithra was ever implicated in the sacrifice of bulls; on the contrary he appears rather as the protector of the bovine species.

So glaring is the discrepancy here that scholars have been at their wits' end to explain it. It has been pointed out that in the Indian tradition—in the *Yajur-Veda* and the *Satapatha-brāhmana*[10]—Mitra is persuaded against his will to join in the slaughter of Soma, the Indian equivalent of Haoma, and that Soma, who is also the moon, is represented by a bull. In these passages the result of Mitra's yielding to the pressure of the gods is his estrangement from cattle. The parallel with the Roman monuments on which the god Mithras plunges a dagger into the bull's side, averting his gaze towards the sun, is not very exact; moreover, it is questionable whether Indian sources other than the *Rig-Veda* can be legitimately used to explain the phenomena of Iranian religion since the later Vedas and the still later *Brāhmanas* tend to add purely local detail to an original deposit of Indo-Iranian mythology, and rarely restate Indo-Iranian myths unknown to the *Rig-Veda*. A more fruitful line of approach would seem to be to study the Iranian evidence in its entirety to see whether we cannot deduce from it how the Mithras of the Roman mysteries came to be the slayer of the bull. For this purpose we must return first of all to the *Gāthās*.

Yima and the Bull-Sacrifice

'Among those sinners was Yima, the son of Vivahvant, for so have we heard, who, to please our men, gave them portions [of the flesh] of the ox to eat.'[11]

According to the Pahlavi gloss on *Yasna* 9.1 those who consumed the flesh given them by Yima became immortal in body. Yima, then, was regarded by the Iranians in general, in sharp distinction to the primitive Zoroastrians, as having been the institutor of the bull-sacrifice which was believed to bring about bodily immortality. That this sacrifice took place after dark or in a sunless place (like the sacrifices to Areimanios in Plutarch's account) seems to be implied by Zoroaster's condemnation in the same *Gāthā* of those who say that the sun and the bull are the worst things the eye can see. Further the slaughter of the bull is said to have taken place amid shouts of joy and to have been accompanied by the setting alight of the Haoma twigs.

The resemblance between the rite attributed to Yima and the Mithraic bull-sacrifice is striking; the principal purpose of the sacrifice was to secure immortality, and this was almost certainly true of the Mithraic sacrifice too. Again the Mithraic sacrifice takes place in a cave, and this was probably true of Yima's sacrifice since his adherents speak of the sun as the worst thing for the eye to see. This must be a gross distortion of the views of the Prophet's opponents, for Yima is the son of Vivahvant, a solar deity, and is himself *hware-daresa*, 'like the sun' or 'having the glance of the sun'.

In the Pahlavi books Yima appears as Yam, and in new Persian he is Jam-shīd.[12] In both he is the centre of an incredible variety of popular legends and in Muhammadan times he assimilated much of the lore associated with the Solomon of the Koran. He and his magic cup in which he can see all that goes on in this world has always been a favourite topic of Persian poetry; and it is strangely ironical that whereas the Iranian Prophet remains without honour in his own country, royal Yima who once became the target of the Prophet's malediction, lives on, a romantic and well-loved figure in Iranian folklore. So, too, Persepolis whose ruins are to this day an impressive reminder of the pomp that was Achaemenian Persia, is popularly called the throne of Jamshīd, while the very names of Darius and Xerxes were long ago expunged from the national memory. To 'royal Yima', his bull-sacrifice, the many legends associated with his name, and to his Indian counterpart Yama, we shall shortly have to return, for in him, perhaps, lies the key to the mystery of the Roman cult in which Mithra, the judge and mediator, becomes so incongruously involved in the sacrificial immolation of a bull.

Before we return to him, however, we must consider three cases of the bull-sacrifice as they appear in the Pahlavi books. The first is the cosmic sacrifice which produces fertility throughout the earth, the second is the eschatological sacrifice which ushers in the 'second existence' prophesied by Zoroaster, whereas the third seems to be a description of a genuine daēvic sacrifice originally performed by man's first parents.

Ahriman's Slaughter of the Bull

The Zoroastrian cosmogony as it appears in the Pahlavi books will be fully treated in the second part of this book. The setting of the drama is as fully dualist as it is in Plutarch: there are two totally distinct principles, Ohrmazd (= Ahura Mazdāh) the good principle, who dwells in the light, and Ahriman (= Angra Mainyu), the Destructive Spirit who inhabits eternal darkness. Both proceed to fashion their own creations independently and the decisive moment comes when Ahriman invades the material universe created by Ohrmazd. One by one he overruns the material creations which Ohrmazd had fashioned after the likeness of the Bounteous Immortals—the sky, the waters, the earth, the plants, the 'lone-created Bull', and lastly Gayōmart, Primal Man, who is also called the Righteous or Blessed Man. This is the moment of Ahriman's triumph, and it would have been his final victory, for it seemed that not only had human life been extinguished, but also plant and animal life together with the fertility of the soil, the productiveness of which was essential if ever Ohrmazd, himself the genius of productivity, were finally to gain the upper hand.

The death of the cosmic bull, however, did not result in the destruction of life on earth as Ahriman had calculated. For when the bull expired, its brain and other organs were scattered over the ground and fertilized it, and from its severed members every kind of grain and healing plant sprang up while from its blood the vine arose 'from which wine is made'. Its seed was carried up to the moon where it was purified, and from this purified seed cattle and all the different species of animal were created—apart from the 'wolf species', which also includes the entire cat tribe, for these were created by Ahriman.[13]

The death of the cosmic bull, then, so far from being a tragedy for the creation of Ohrmazd, was, in the result, a blessing, for it gave rise to all animal and vegetable life on which the life of man depends. Ahriman's triumph had proved illusory, and the battle, so far from being won, had only just begun. Now the result of the slaying of the cosmic bull by the Destructive Spirit is precisely the same as that of the slaying of the bull by Mithras in the Roman mysteries; it ensures the fertility of the earth and the reproduction of animal life. So, too, on the Mithraic monuments depicting Mithras' sacrifice of the bull, the point of the sacrifice is made abundantly clear by the appearance of ears of corn on the tip of the slaughtered animal's tail. We may be reasonably sure that from the blood of the slaughtered beast the vine arose, for after Mithras has performed the life-giving sacrifice, he is represented as feasting sacramentally with the sun[14] after he had been translated to heaven. This feast is in all probability the Western counterpart of the sacrament of meat and Haoma which, as we have seen, constituted the climax of the *Yasna* in its original form.

Bull-Sacrifice at the End of Time

The eschatological sacrifice of the bull Hadhayans which Saoshyans, the 'saviour', performs at the end of time in order to bring immortality in body and soul to all men, has already been discussed. So, too, we may assume that Mithras' sacrifice of the bull not only guaranteed the continued prosperity and productiveness of the material world, but also the continued life of the soul after death.[15] Yet, arresting though these parallels are, it should not be forgotten that the mere existence of votive tablets dedicated 'to the god Areimanios' proves beyond doubt that the Roman Mithraists originated not from any sect of Zoroastrians acknowledged as such in Iran, but among the daēva-worshippers whom the Zoroastrians utterly condemned and whom they identified with sorcerers.

Ahriman-Areimanios in the Mithraic Mysteries

Unfortunately, what we can glean about the daēva-worshippers from the Iranian texts themselves is not very much; but one thing would seem to be certain, and that is that, for the daēva-worshippers, the daēvas were not, as they were for the Zoroastrians, just demons: by making use of the appropriate magic they could be harnessed to man's service. Moreover, they, on their side, seem to have been influenced by Zoroastrianism in that they took over the Destructive Spirit (Angra Mainyu, Ahriman) into their pandemonium, nor did they attempt to give him a less ill-omened name. Despite his name, however, they represented him, rather than his rival, as the source of power and earthly prosperity. This view may well have passed over into the Mithraism of the Roman Empire, for there can be little doubt that the lion-headed figure who, next to Mithras, is more often reproduced than any other deity and whom Cumont identified with Zurvān, the genius of Infinite Time, is none other than the Evil One himself. But he is not the Ahriman of orthodox Zoroastrianism nor yet of its principal heresy, Zurvanism, which elevated Infinite Time to a supreme position over and above the twin Spirits of good and evil: he is the Ahriman of the daēva-worshippers, the source of power and riches, the Prince of this World, who would prevent the soul from rising up again to its true home, which is the Endless Light of heaven.

Iconographically Ahriman-Areimanios is represented in human form, but he has the head of a gaping lion, and around his body is coiled a serpent which rests its head upon his head. He has two pairs of wings and in his hands he bears two keys. Sometimes his body is studded with the Signs of the Zodiac, and this led the great Belgian scholar, Franz Cumont, to believe that this was the Iranian god of Time and Fate, Zurvān. The objection to this view is that nowhere is Zurvān mentioned in the Mithraic inscriptions, that apart from Mithra no other god except Ahriman is venerated under his own Iranian name, and that whereas the other gods are disguised as Olympians, the lion-headed god is not: utterly un-Hellenistic in appearance, he can, by the grimness of his appearance, only be equated with the well-attested Areimanios-Ahriman of the inscriptions. Moreover, the lion and the snake alone give away his true identity, for of all the 'wolf species' created by Ahriman, the lion is the most to be feared, and of all the creeping things that infest the earth the serpent is the most deadly; and it is in the form of a serpent that Ahriman launched his attack upon the sky.[16] Moreover, among the *Ahl-i Haqq*, a semi-pagan sect that still survives in Luristan, both the lion and the dragon still guard the first and fifth heavens through which the soul has to pass if it is to reach its heavenly home above. The *Ahl-i Haqq* ('People of Truth'), then, would seem to have preserved to this day beliefs which once must have been held by the *daēva*-worshippers of old, for they too celebrate a bull-sacrifice in imitation of a similar sacrifice mythically enacted by an incarnation of the sun. The evidence they supply, moreover, enables us to see how Ahriman, in his lion and serpent forms, could also hold the keys of heaven; for it is clear that he would not open the doors of heaven to the aspiring soul unless the soul, in its ascent, were provided with the correct passwords and effective talismans. Ahriman, the Prince of this World of time and space, had to be circumvented by those valiant souls who dared to make the dangerous journey into eternity which was the realm of Ohrmazd, or, as he appears in Mithraism, of Coelus, the god of heaven or the sky.[17]

The Ahriman of the Mithraic mysteries, then, would appear to be a very different person from the Ahriman we meet with in the Zoroastrian texts, and it is at least comprehensible that he should not be the protagonist in the slaying of the bull as he is in the Pahlavi books, for he is intent on keeping the soul bound to this world of which he is master and on preventing it from reaching its immortal home. Moreover, from the Mithraic monuments themselves it is clear that he would prevent the elixir of immortality, which the blood of the bull contains, from falling into the hands of mortal man, for his serpent is seen to dispute the life-giving blood with the dog, the faithful attendant of Sraosha in the Zoroastrian tradition; and the scorpion, another of his creatures, creeps up to the dying beast's scrotum in the hope of cutting all further life off at its source. In Mithraism the evil powers seek to prevent the sacrifice which enables man to escape from the bondage of temporality, whereas in Zoroastrianism they seek to destroy all living things in this world, because this world is itself the creation of the powers of good and its defence against evil.

The Bull-Sacrifice of Man's First Parents

In the *Bundahishn*, a Pahlavi text largely concerned with the creation of the world, we again meet with a bull-sacrifice which, since it increases the power of the *daēvas*, should throw some light on the Mithraic cult. It concerns Mashyē and Mashyānē, the father and mother of the human race who themselves sprang from the seed of the dying Gayōmart. Like Adam and Eve they were not slow to sin, for no sooner had they hailed Ohrmazd as the creator than they changed their minds and declared that 'the Destructive Spirit created water, the earth, plants, and other things'; and for this they were damned to punishment in hell until the last days. Hitherto they had lived without eating, but soon they started to drink milk. This did not satisfy them and:

'They came upon a head of cattle, tawny, with white jaws, and they slew it; and on a sign from the spiritual gods they built a fire from the wood of the lote and box, for these two trees are the most productive of fire. And they made the fire to blaze with [the breath of] their mouths, and the first fuel they burnt upon it was straw and olive and stems of mastic and branches of the date-palm. And they roast the beast on a spit and left a quantity of meat [equal to] three handfuls in the fire saying: "[This is] the portion of the fire." And they threw another portion towards the sky saying: "This is the portion of the gods." And a vulture passed above them and carried it off from them: for (sic) the first flesh [to be consumed] was consumed by a dog.'[18]

The vulture and the dog immediately call to mind the Mithraic monuments on which a raven, presumably replacing the vulture, is sent down by the sun to observe the sacrifice executed by Mithras on earth, whereas the dog leaps forward to lap up the blood of the dying bull. We have seen that the daēva-worshippers probably worshipped both ahuras and daēvas, and there is nothing surprising, then, in the fact that Mashyē and Mashyānē act 'on a sign from the spiritual gods'. Yet despite the fact that both the sacred fire and the gods above receive their portion, the latter do not seem to approve, for Mashyē and Mashyānē are accused of ingratitude,[19] and it is only then that they complete their sacrifice to the daēvas.

The presence of a dog and a carnivorous bird at the bull-sacrifice and the participation of the daēvas indicate that this sacrifice is indeed the original of the bull-sacrifice celebrated in the mysteries of Mithras; and not only that, it would also seem to be identical with the sacrifice of Yima in which he 'gave our people portions [of the flesh] of the ox to eat', for Mashyē and Mashyānē too seem to have consumed the bulk of the sacrificial meat themselves: and this perforce brings us back again to Yima.

Yima again

There is scarcely a figure in Zoroastrian literature that presents us with more problems than does Yima, the son of Vivahvant. The difficulty in his case is not lack of evidence but the conflicting nature of a whole mass of evidence. His Indo-Iranian antiquity is beyond dispute, for he appears as Yama, the son of Vivasvant, in the *Rig-Veda* where he is as much a god as a man. In the later Indian literature his importance increases, for he becomes the lord of the land of the dead and hence Death itself.

The Vedic Yama

In the *Rig-Veda* Yama is the first man only in the sense that he is the first of the immortals to choose a mortal destiny: 'To please the gods he chose death, to please his offspring he did not choose immortality.'[20] It is he, King Yama, the son of Vivasvant, who first 'reconnoitred a path for many, collecting [all] men together [upon it]'.[21] 'He first discovered the way, and this pasture land none can avoid; the ancestors trod it before us, and all men who are born [on earth] must traverse it in turn',[22] for Yama's path is death [23] as he himself is death.[24] But in the *Rig-Veda* Yama chooses death of his own free will: he lays aside his immortality so that, himself passing through the valley of death, he may once again join the immortals and feast and carouse with them for ever 'under a fair-leafed tree'.[25] 'This is the abode of Yama called the palace of the *devas*: [here] is his flute blown, and [here] is he surrounded with song (*gīrbhih*).'[26]

In these passages from the *Rig-Veda* there are some curious parallels to the Avesta. Yama's path is also called a *gavyūti* or 'pasture-land', and the Avestan equivalent of this word, *gaoyaoiti*, is used of the 'wide pastures' of Mithra. The word used for Yama's carouses when he has reconquered immortality (*mad-*) is identical with the word used by Zoroaster for the 'drunkenness' (*mada*)[27] of the followers of the Lie among whom he counted Yima. His palace is the 'abode' (*māna*) of the *devas* (= Avestan *daēvas*) and in it he is surrounded with song (*gīr-*). So too is Zoroaster's own heaven known as the House of Song (*garō (de)māna*). The use of the word *deva* in connexion with Yama should not, however, be over-emphasized, for the distinction between *deva* and *asura* is not nearly so marked in the *Rig-Veda* as is that between *daēva* and *ahura* in the Avesta. Indeed in the tenth book from which our extracts are drawn the term *deva* is fast becoming the ordinary word for 'a god', while the word *asura* is already beginning to take on those sinister connotations which were to reduce this whole class of deity to the status of something very like demons. Moreover, Yama's connexion with the *asuras* is fully established, as we shall see.

As the House of Song is the highest heaven in the Zoroastrian literature, so is the abode of Yama in which the dead are assembled higher than the two heavens of the sun-god Savitr[28]: both are the abode of the blessed dead.

We have seen that the Avestan Yima's sacrifice of a bull bears a distinct family likeness to the bull-sacrifice which Mithras performs, apparently rather against his will, in the Mithraic mysteries practised in the Roman Empire; and we have also seen that the gods Mitra and Varuna, who correspond to the Mithra and Ahura of the Avestan tradition, form an inseparable pair in the *Rig-Veda*. Varuna, however, is also associated with Yama, and the soul of the dead is exhorted to advance boldly 'along the ancient paths which our ancestors trod of yore', the paths of Yama, that is, 'and you will see both kings, Yama and the god Varuna, carousing on immortal food(?).'[29] Nor is this the only occasion on which Yama is mentioned together with Varuna, for elsewhere[30] sinners ask to be delivered from the fetters of Varuna and Yama, and once a mysterious bird is described as Varuna's messenger in the abode of Yama.[31] In the first two of these passages at least it would appear that Yama replaces Mitra, the king who normally shares Varuna's throne.

In Iran Mithra was associated with the sun from the earliest times. In the *Rig-Veda* Yama is the son of Vivasvant, himself the sun, and in his abode the dead will see the sun again;[32] he is an earthly fire just as the sun is the heavenly fire: 'As Yama is [Agni (the fire)] born, and as Yama [does he beget] future generations.'[33]

The Vedic Yama, then, appears as a solar deity who willingly gives up immortality in order to conquer death and to lead mortal men on after him on the 'path of Yama' which leads through death to immortality. He partakes of the Soma and carouses with both gods and departed souls in his own palace where the dead will once again look upon the sun. In his immortal realm he shares the royal throne of Varuna, and thus occupies the place normally reserved for Mitra. With Varuna again he ensnares the feet of sinners, and in this joint action he again usurps the function of Mitra. His name, moreover, means 'twin', and one is tempted to see in him the 'twin' or double of Mitra; but whereas Mitra ever remains an immortal, Yama chooses to become mortal in order that he may conquer death and thereby enable future generations of men to partake of immortality. He is the son of Vivasvant, the Shining One, one of the many Vedic representations of the sun. In the later literature he is not only the god who brings death but also the ruler of the land of the blessed dead. They dwell with him in his assembly hall 'which has the brilliance of the sun, gleaming, assuming everywhere what form it will: it is neither too hot nor too cold, and it rejoices the heart. Neither grief nor old age is there, neither hunger nor thirst, neither affliction nor toil nor aught that irks.'[34] The correspondence between Yama's assembly-hall as described in the Indian epic and Yima's kingdom as described in the Avesta is remarkably exact.

The Avestan Yima

In the Iranian tradition Yima is a split personality. Originally he was the first man and the progenitor of the human race as he is in the *Veda*. For Zoroaster, however, he was a 'sinner' who forfeited his own immortality and with it the immortality of all his seed. The mass of legend that has woven itself around this at once romantic and tragic figure illustrates the tension between two diametrically opposed traditions. What is most strange, perhaps, is that the 'sin' for which Zoroaster denounced him and which consisted in distributing slices of sacrificial meat to the people, seems to have been almost entirely forgotten, and in the Pahlavi books, with the exception of the Pahlavi *Yasna*, we find no reference either to his institution of animal sacrifice or the introduction of irregularities into it, we hear nothing of the slaughter of bulls accompanied by shouts of joy, nor is the burning of the Haoma ever referred to again. His sin, when it is recorded in the later sources, is very much more grave: he set himself up as creator,[35] or, less heinously, he despised the Creator.[36] Other accounts, and among these what is probably the earliest of all,[37] make no reference to any sin at all, and this must represent the genuine popular view, the authentic Indo-Iranian tradition as it developed independently of the Zoroastrian reform.

Yima's Golden Reign

Yima was the first man and the first king. According to the earliest tradition he ruled for a thousand years[38] in which he 'deprived the *daēvas* of wealth and prosperity, of flocks and herds, of comfort and good name. In his reign did men eat food[39] and drink unfailing, cattle and men did not grow old, water and plants did not dry up. In his reign there was neither cold nor heat, old age nor death, nor yet disease created by the *daēvas*.'[40] Thus Yima's kingdom was a replica of Mithra's dwelling which the Wise Lord had fashioned for him above high Haraiti 'where there is neither night nor darkness, neither cold wind nor hot, nor disease in death abounding, nor yet defilement wrought by the *daēvas*'.[41] Mithra's dwelling is a heavenly paradise, Yima's an earthly one: 'he made the earth in fairness like unto the House of Song.'[42]

His Subterranean Paradise

During his golden reign Yima extended the earth three times to make room for all the 'cattle, great and small, men and dogs, birds, and red, burning fires'[43] that his reign of peace and plenty had done so much to multiply. The golden age, however, could not last for ever, and the Wise Lord, foreseeing this, 'brought together an assembly along with the spiritual gods—he who is renowned in Airyana Vaējah[44] and the good [river] Daityā; and royal Yima of goodly flocks [too] brought together an assembly along with the best of men—he who is renowned in Airyana Vaējah and the good [river] Daityā.'[45] The Wise Lord warns Yima that in future 'wicked' humanity will be afflicted by winter, and that he must carve out for himself a great hole under the earth into which he shall bring the tallest, best, and most beautiful men, women, and cattle, the largest and the most sweet-scented plants, and the most tasty and sweet-smelling foods. All this did Yima do and when winter came he and all that was best and fairest in the world retired underground 'where men live the fairest life [imaginable]'.[46]

Like the body of Mithra[47] which is the sun and like the palace of Sraosha, Mithra's companion,[48] Yima's dwelling glows with its own light.[49] There he will remain together with his elect until the signs foreshadowing the last days appear. Of these the worst will be a winter more terrible than any the world had ever seen before when it will rain and snow and hail for three long years.[50] Then will 'royal Yima' and the noble race he has reared emerge from under the ground to re-people the stricken and devastated earth.[51] The whole of this story of Yima's golden age, his excavation of the *vara*[52] or underground retreat, and his re-emergence to re-people the earth (the last episode occurs only in the Pahlavi books) must belong to a very old stratum of Iranian folklore wholly untouched by the teachings of Zoroaster.

In this tradition the figure of Yima is semi-divine: he rules in peace and plenty for a thousand years, disappears into his underground paradise, and re-emerges in the last days to re-people the earth. He does not die; and because he is deathless, he was worshipped as a god by such Iranians who had not accepted the Zoroastrian reform right down into Muhammadan times.[53] For the ancient Iranians Yima was, like the Yama of the Indian tradition, a god among men, for on earth he is seen to correspond to the Wise Lord in heaven[54] in much the same way as Mithra does.

Yima and the Sun

In the Avesta Yima's connexion with the sun is very much more apparent than is Yama's in the *Veda*. Both he and the sun are *khshaēta*, 'royal' or 'kingly', and Yima himself is *hware-daresa*, 'sunlike' or 'having the glance of the sun'. He is the son of Vivahvant who, like the Vedic Vivasvant, is a god of the sun. He is also first man and first king, and the human race is thus thought of as deriving from the sun. Traces of this theory are to be found in the later literature too, and to these we shall have to return.

Zoroaster and Yima

Zoroaster's condemnation of Yima, however, was to change considerably the ancient myth of Yima's golden reign, his hidden life in the bowels of the earth, and his re-emergence at the end of time; yet even the Prophet's wrath was not sufficient to destroy Yima's ancient glory. The primitive Zoroastrians, however, do seem to have made serious efforts to get rid of this contentious figure. Thus rather than accept him as the first man they invented a first man of their own, Gayō Maretan (Gayōmart in Pahlavi), whose name means literally 'mortal life'; and Gayōmart in his turn inherited certain of Yima's characteristics including his solar lineage. Thus when he dies two-thirds of his seed is taken from him and purified in the light of the sun,[55] and he himself is described as 'shining like the sun'.

In the Avesta, however, we hear little of Gayōmart. Yima, however, figures prominently in the *Yashts*, but only once is he still regarded as being the first man and the first king.[56] Zoroaster's condemnation of him is met half way; his golden age is not denied, but it is cut short: it lasts only so long as he had not 'lied', 'until he admitted a lying, untrue word into his mind'.[57] Till then he had been possessed of the 'Kingly Glory' (*kavaēm khwarenō*), the nimbus of high royal fortune which is the prerogative of legitimate kingship. Once the lie had entered into his soul, however, this glory departed from him and was received by Mithra for safe-keeping.[58]

Yima's 'Lie'

There are two questions which arise here: first, what was the nature of Yima's 'lie'? and secondly, why is it Mithra who takes charge of his departed glory? In the Pahlavi books, as we have seen, it is said that his sin was to despise the creator or that he himself claimed to be the creator. What, one wonders, is meant by despising the creator? Fortunately the Mithra *Yasht* enlightens us on this point: the man who despises the creator is the priest who is not a follower of Truth, who performs the sacrificial rites correctly, but thinks slightingly of the Wise Lord, the Bounteous Immortals, Mithra, the law, and Rashnu in his heart.[59] He is, in fact, a crypto-*daēva*-worshipper who performs correctly a Zoroastrian sacrifice but secretly offers it to the *daēvas*.

Such a sacrifice would seem to be identical with the sacrifice of Mashyē and Mashyānē we have already had occasion to describe. Like Gayōmart, Mashyē and Mashyānē are substitute figures for Yima,[60] and the sacrifice they offered must, then, be identical with Yima's sacrifice to which Zoroaster took exception. Yima's sin was that he sacrificed to the *daēvas* as well as to the *ahuras*. There is, however, one notable difference between Yima and Mashyē; for whereas Mashyē did no more than despise the creator, Yima claimed that he was himself the creator. Mashyē's sin was to associate the Destructive Spirit with the Wise Lord as a co-creator, Yima's so to associate himself. We are, therefore, forced to ask ourselves whether Zoroaster, whose onslaught on Yima is so disconcertingly violent, had not more or less equated him with the Destructive Spirit, or rather had radically reformulated a more ancient myth in which Yima performed the life-giving sacrifice of the primal bull and transformed it into a myth in which Angra Mainyu, the Destructive Spirit, takes the place of Yima, and the sacrifice, offered as it was at least partly to the *daēvas*, brings no longer life but death.

Yima, Mithra's Twin

The word *yima* means 'twin', as does the Vedic *yama*; and both in the Indian and the Iranian traditions Yama-Yima is supplied with a sister-wife, but in neither case does the female twin appear to be original, nor does such a consort-sister appear anywhere in the Avesta. In fact the only twins known to the Avesta are the primordial Twin Spirits, the Holy Spirit and the Destructive Spirit. We have seen that there is some reason to suppose that the Holy Spirit of the *Gāthās* corresponds to the Mithra of the old Ahura-worshippers. Was, then, Yima originally Mithra's twin? and if so, is he the prototype of Angra Mainyu, the Destructive Spirit? On the face of it this sounds preposterous, but there is a very curious legend which survives in a late New Persian poem in which Yima or Jamshīd, as he is now called, does appear precisely as the earthly counterpart of Mithra, now identified with the sun.[61]

In this legend Yima is visited by Sraosha, at this period simply God's messenger, and is asked to receive the Good Religion and to spread it abroad on earth. He is then carried up to heaven by the Good Mind and taken before the throne of God. God repeats his request that he should accept the Good Religion, but Yima again declines.

'He complained and said: "O Creator, I would that thou make me king."
He asked too for Mithra (the sun) and a throne and a diadem, and God
made him a king on earth. He did not accept [God's] Religion for the sake
of kingship: to him [God] gave kingship and the crown of greatness. When
he returned from heaven he came to the great mountain of Alburz
(= Avestan Harā). On that day when the people looked up to the heavens,
they beheld marvellous things; [for] they saw two suns in the heavens, each
rearing its head, as they hastened on. One reared its head in heaven, and
the other came down to earth. When Jamshīd alighted on the earth, the
people marvelled at him. They began to praise God [saying]: "We rejoice
at thy creation, O thou who showest the way. Thou hast made this thy
servant so fair of face that in brilliance he is like unto Mithra." '

It is true that the word *mihr* (the Middle and New Persian form of
mithra) is generally used to mean simply the sun, but when Yima asks for
Mithra and a throne and a diadem, he is not asking for the physical
sun but rather for the god who incarnates light and the compact, the
patmān or genius of moderation as it appears in the Pahlavi books, the
god who will enable him to establish the golden age on earth. Yima
rejects the new religion and opts for the older paganism under the aegis
of Mithra, for he is the human sun on earth just as Mithra is the
heavenly sun above. In this account the sun-god and the sun-man
appear to be twins; they are 'two suns' each ruling in his respective
sphere. This solar nature of Yima is brought out by Al-Bīrūnī in
another legend where Yima is translated not this time to the throne
of God but to the Devil's domain in the north.[62] Here the Evil One
held in captivity the Good Fortune (*baraka*) with which the earth was
normally blessed, thus depriving men of food and drink. Yima retrieved
this Good Fortune, brought it back, and the world returned to its
normal state. On his return 'he rose like the sun and light shone forth
in him, for he was luminous like light itself: and the people marvelled
at the rising of two suns, and all the wood that had been dry became
green'.[63] So was the Iranian festival of Nōrūz, the 'New Day' and feast
of the vernal equinox[64] instituted by royal Yima who became thereby
the sun on earth.

Nōrūz and Mihragān
The feast of Nōrūz survives as the greatest by far of all the national
holidays in Iran even now because it is genuinely national, a survival
from a long-forgotten pagan past, as little influenced by Zoroastrianism
as it is by Islam. Its founder was the mythical ancestor of the Iranian
race, 'royal Yima whose glance is of the sun.' The companion feast
which in old days ranked but a little below Nōrūz in importance was
Mihragān, the feast of the god Mithra which took place in the month

dedicated to him at the time of the autumnal equinox. Both feasts stand midway between the burning heat of summer and the bitter cold of winter; both are therefore feasts celebrated at a time when the earth again most nearly resembles the golden reign of Yima during which there was neither excessive heat nor cold, or Mithra's palace in the sky which is also free from these extremes. They are feasts during which Nature is in equilibrium, and both Mithra, who is *harvisp-patmān*[65] or 'he who observes moderation in all things' and Yima, who restores natural equilibrium to the world after the *daēvas* have disturbed it, are guardians of right order and the just mean in all things.

Mihragān, the old Persian *Mithrakāna*,[66] was the festival held in honour of Mithra and, according to a Greek account,[67] the Persian king would get drunk in the god's honour, and in Sassanian times the king would put on a crown in the shape of the sun, thereby showing that he too was a Mithra upon earth. Just as Nōrūz celebrated the return of Yima from the land of the *daēvas*, so did Mihragān celebrate the incarceration of Yima's murderer, the dragon-king Azhi Dahāka, who usurped Yima's royal authority and sawed him in two.[68]

From the above it would seem clear that in pre-Zoroastrian paganism and presumably among the *daēva*-worshippers even after Zoroaster's time, Mithra and Yima were intimately connected: possibly they were twins, the one the king whose body is the sun on high, the other the king on earth who, each year as the new year comes round, reveals himself as the sun among men. From the *Gāthās* we know that Yima was attacked by the Prophet for introducing a form of bull-sacrifice that was, from his point of view, ritually incorrect. If the sacrifice attributed to Mashyē was in fact the original form of sacrifice initiated by Yima, then Zoroaster's objection would appear to be that the proportion of the sacrificial meat offered to the gods was niggardly and that the sacrifice was in any case shared with the *daēvas*. Further, it involved unnecessary cruelty and the burning of the Haoma plant. This, however, does not seem enough to account for the very vehement tones in which he attacks the progenitor of his race. If, on the other hand, he saw in Yima not the twin of Mithra (the precursor of his own Holy Spirit?) but one who falsely claimed this impossible distinction, his fury would be understandable.

Yima the Prototype of Ahriman?
It is true that the sources in which Mithra, the sun-god and Yima, the sun-man, appear to be twins are all late, but they probably reflect an ancient tradition which derives from the worshippers of the *daēvas* and has nothing to do with any form of Zoroastrianism as we know it.

In the Pahlavi books it is Ahriman, the Destructive Spirit, who slays the primal bull from whose body all plant and animal life emerges, yet this would seem to be a 'Zoroastrianization' of an older pagan sacrifice in which Yima, the first man, performed the fructifying sacrifice that must have inaugurated the golden age, for the consumption of the sacrificial flesh that Yima supplied did, according to the Pahlavi *Yasna*,[69] result in bodily immortality. Thus, in the purely 'pagan' version of the story of Yima, Yima himself never dies but disappears underground with all that is best of the human race and all that is best among the animals and plants; and his disappearance from the world deprives man of his immortality. Those who remain on earth, who have learnt to do evil, are now subject to death and disease, old age and bitter winters, but Yima lives on in his subterranean kingdom, illuminating it with his own light, and he will return once again in the last days to re-people and revivify a dying world. By withdrawing his presence from the world Yima hands it over to death. If, however, even in Zoroaster's time, Mithra, the god of the contract and of light, and Yima, the first man whose father was the sun, were in fact regarded as twins, then Yima could be regarded as the wilful author of death in this world as Mithra was of life. From this interpretation of the myth the Prophet may have moulded anew the myth of the two twins (*yimas*) and transformed Mithra into the Holy Spirit and Yima, in so far as he was a deathless spirit and not merely a man, into the Destructive Spirit who brought death into the world. Such a development is, after all, not so very strange, for in India we find Yima's counterpart, Yama, developing from the first immortal who voluntarily chose death into the god of death and the ruler of the dead. If there is anything in our argument, then it is at least intelligible how Mithra should take over the life-giving sacrifice from Yima when the ancient cult finally made its way into the Roman Empire, for of all the Iranian gods Mithra was by far the most familiar to the Graeco-Roman world, and it would also explain how the same role falls to Ahriman in the later literature.

Yima and Mithra in the Avesta

So much can be tentatively deduced from the evidence. By the sacrifice of a bull Yima had brought bodily immortality to men in addition to the immortality of the soul conferred by his father, Vivahvant. But his golden reign was not to last for ever: either he was to retire to an immortal realm in the bowels of the earth whither he would take all that was most good and fair from the world above and illuminate it with his own immortal light, or he would blaspheme against the Creator and thus himself sin and die. In either case his work would have

been undone and the effects of his sacrifice made void; for bodily
death would once again return to the world, and man would need
another saviour who would restore to him year by year bright Yima's
vanished paradise, and give him the assurance that in the end all things
would be made anew, and that Yima would return again to give back
to all men shining bodies that could never die.

Who would this saviour be? We can do no more than guess: but this
at least we know, that in the legend in which Yima 'admits a lying,
untrue word into his mind', his *khwarenah* or 'royal fortune'[70] departed
from him in the form of a raven and was gathered up by Mithra[71]
'whose ear is quick to hear and who has a thousand senses'. But what
exactly was this 'royal fortune', and what did Mithra do with it?
Primarily Yima's 'royal fortune', his *khwarenah*, is that which gave him
power to bring wholeness and immortality, increase and abiding welfare
to his enchanted kingdom; or, in the words of the Pahlavi translation,
it is the 'work he had to do'—and the work of this ideal king was to
bring increase and bodily immortality to all his subjects. Mithra, then,
must carry on the work of his twin brother and renew the sanctifying
and fructifying sacrifice of the bull that Yima had inaugurated.

Cautes and Cautopates in the Mithraic Mysteries
And here we pass from the Iranian evidence to the Roman: and
the only link between them is the raven—the raven which, in the
Avestan legend, embodies Yima's royal fortune and kingly glory and
takes refuge with Mithra, and which, on the Roman monuments,
stands between the sun and Mithras as he slays the bull, his eyes fixed
upon the bird; and the bird itself stands mid-way between the sun
and one of the twin figures that so often accompany Mithras in his
exploits—Cautes and Cautopates, the twin torch-bearers; and the
torch of the one points upwards, the other down, doubtless representing both the rising and the setting sun, and the two equinoxes
—the genius of the vernal equinox with torch pointing upward to
symbolize the sun's increasing power, and the genius of the autumnal
equinox, with torch down-turned to figure forth the dark, cold months
to come. And this again brings us back to Iran: for there, as we have
already seen, the high feasts of the year are the two equinoxes—Nōrūz,
the feast of renewal, instituted by royal Yima, and Mihragān, the feast
of Iran's lovely autumn, over which Mithra of wide pastures presides.
But why is Yima, the sun-man, now two, not one? It may be that the
twins represent simply Yima and Mithra in their aspects of vernal and
autumnal equinox, or it may be that another Iranian legend is here
conserved and further developed; for in one of the Zoroastrian versions

of the Yima legend Yima met his end by being sawn in two.[72] It is possible that just as Yima's sacrifice of the bull resulted in increased plenitude on earth, so did the sacrifice of Yima himself bring back some of the glory of his golden reign, and that out of his body grew two Yimas, each the double of Mithra, and each, therefore, portrayed on the Mithraic monuments as of much less than Mithras' stature, the one named Cautes, the guardian of dawn, and the other Cautopates, the lord of dusk and autumn.

Perhaps this latter solution is the better, for the monuments tell us that Mithras is 'born of a rock' which is his mother (*genetrix*), and as he emerges from the rock full-grown he is flanked by the two torch-bearers who seem to encourage him on his mission. This could well mean that Mithras descended into Yima's underground abode and re-emerged therefrom encouraged by a Yima now divided into two, a deity of dawn and a deity of dusk, to carry on his work on earth. If this is so, then the Mithraic mysteries follow a version of the Yima legend that is nowhere found in our Iranian sources.

But who are Cautes and Cautopates, so mysteriously named? No one has solved this enigma,[73] yet the answer is, perhaps, not so far to seek, for the letters *au* probably conceal an Iranian *avu* or *avau* rather than simply *au* which usually appears in Graeco-Latin as *ō* or even *o* (as *Ōramasdes* for *Auramazdā*, *Dareios* for *Dārayavaush*). *Cautes* would then represent Iranian **kavauta* or **kavuta*. *Kav* is easily understood as Avestan *Kavi*,[74] a term generically used of the ancient Iranian kings, whereas **auta* (or **uta*) reappears as Pahlavi *ōtak* or *utak* (from Old Iranian **auta-ka* or **uta-ka*) which seems to be an epithet of Yima himself. The context in which the word occurs is that of the legend according to which poor Yima was sawn in two. The villain of the piece, Azhi Dahāka, the dragon-king, has now usurped the throne, and his subjects complain bitterly of the changed times.

'Yima [they say] warded off from the world need and misery, hunger and thirst, old age and death, mourning and lamentation, excessive heat and cold, and the intermingling of *daēvas* and men. This too: he was a "bringer of ease", for what he did brought ease to men; he was a "granter of desires", for he gave away good things; he was a "bringer of knowledge", for he brought knowledge of righteousness to men: he was *ōtak/utak*, for[75] royal Yima of goodly flocks whom you struck down unjustly and by guile, let his lambs wander free upon the earth, and stopped the veneration of the demons of Need and Misery, Straitness and Craving, Hunger and Thirst, Wrath (*ēshm* = Avestan *aēshma*) of the bloody spear, Want that has no pasture-land, Fear and Bane that moves in secret, Old Age whose breath is foul, and the demon of Concupiscence[76] too.'[77]

We cannot be sure what the word *ōtak/utak* means, but it is glossed as 'he let his lambs wander free upon the earth'. There is, however, a word *anōtak* (which can be analysed as 'not-*ōtak*') meaning 'strange, alien, foreign, or excluded', the opposite of *khwēsh*, 'kin'; *ōtak* would, then, mean 'kinsman', and *kavauta would thus be [Yima] the 'royal kinsman'.

And what of Cautopates? He will be either *kavauta-pati, the 'lord of the royal kinsman', or *kavauta pati, the 'royal kinsman, the Lord', or *kavauta-pāta, 'protected by the royal kinsman'. Philologically the last is the most likely since Persian *a* tends to be represented by *ē* in Greek, *ā* by *ā*; and it is perhaps more natural to put the dying day and the dying year under the protection of the new life that another day and another spring will bring than vice versa.

Thus, that there is a connexion between Mithra and Yima is clear, but we cannot say with any certainty what exact form of the Yima legend gave birth to Mithraism. This much, however, seems assured: the original sacrifice of the bull which made Yima's golden reign possible was performed by Yima himself; but after a thousand years his reign, in which men and kine knew neither death nor disease, came to an end, and Yima took all that was best of them to a dwelling underground. Mithra, meanwhile, took charge of his *khwarenah*, his 'kingly glory' and 'royal fortune', which was also the work he was sent to do on earth. So Mithra, in his turn, must descend on to the earth, both because he is Yima's twin and because his connexion with the earth is already close. There, watched by Yima's royal fortune in raven shape which hovers between Cautes-Yima, the 'royal kinsman', and the sun on the vertical plane, and between the sun and Mithras himself on a diagonal one, he plunges the dagger into the bull that Yima's reign may once again come true: man, though mortal still, is assured of final immortality, and once again will 'men eat food and drink unfailing, cattle and men will not grow old, waters and plants will no more dry up. Neither will there be heat or cold, old age or death, nor yet disease created by the *daēvas*'.

Conclusion

The Mithraism of the Roman Empire would, then, appear to be a development of a form of Iranian paganism, condemned by Zoroastrians of all shades of opinion as being a cult devoted partially to the *daēvas*: but it was none the less a daēvic cult that had been influenced by Zoroastrianism. Yima whose appeal to the Iranian nation was far too strong for him ever to be forgotten in his homeland becomes the subject of every kind of legend in his native country, and even the

Iranian Prophet's condemnation of him could not wrest from him the golden age associated with his name. In the Western migrations of the worshippers of the *daēvas*, however, his name is forgotten, unless he is indeed Cautes, the 'royal kinsman', and the sacrifice he inaugurated is taken over by his twin, Mithra, who brought the Iranian message of immortality and the earnest we have of immortality in the constant renewal of life on earth from the Iranian uplands to the furthest corners of the Roman Empire.

The old Iranian religion, however, passed through many metamorphoses before it reached the shores of the Mediterranean: from Zoroastrianism it borrowed Ahriman, perhaps a devilish caricature of bright Yima himself; and Ahriman too, in passing through Babylonia, became a Gnostic rather than an Iranian devil. He came to hold the keys of heaven, and needed to be propitiated if the soul, imprisoned in this world, was ever to be allowed to return to Mithras, its father in heaven. Identified with an inexorable fate, his body embossed with the Signs of the Zodiac, he held the world captive and thereby became the Prince of this World.

CHAPTER SIX

FRAVASHI—VAYU—KHWARENAH

Ahura Mazdāh's Veneration of other Deities—The Fravashis—Vayu—Vayu and Zurvān—The Khwarenah

THE policy of 'catholic' Zoroastrianism, whether consciously pursued or not, was not only to welcome back the *ahuras* who had been displaced by Ahura Mazdāh, but to allow elements of daēvic origin to be grafted on to them. This did not prevent the Zoroastrians, however, from maintaining an attitude of implacable hostility to those who still worshipped the *daēvas* openly under their own name. In actual fact, in the Zoroastrian system the old *daēvas* like Indra, Nāñhaithya, and Saurva survive only in name, and are succeeded by Zoroaster's own ethical constructions which alone retain any importance. The old gods, now reduced to the stature of demons, are scarcely heard of again though their less disagreeable characteristics reappear under different names either as individual deities like Verethraghna or as specific characteristics of universal deities like Mithra. The powers of evil are no longer permitted to conceal their true nature under the names of what had once been national gods: they are brought out into the open and called by their real names—the Destructive Spirit, the Evil Mind, Wrath, Pride, and so on.

Ahura Mazdāh's Veneration of other Deities
In the Mithra *Yasht* we saw how, by a slow process of assimilation, Mithra once again took his place beside the Wise Lord, and we saw too how the latter was not too proud to venerate him. This was, perhaps, the first great betrayal of the Iranian Prophet by his epigones. The process, however, has gone much further in some of the other *Yashts*. To add insult to injury, these *Yashts* often take the form of a colloquy between the Wise Lord and his Prophet, and the latter who, during his lifetime, had recognized no god but Ahura Mazdāh as creator and sustainer of the universe, as omnipotent and omniscient lord, is now peremptorily ordered to worship a variety of gods and goddesses whose very existence he had preferred to ignore. So he is commanded to worship Ardvī Sūrā Anāhitā, the 'Humid, Strong, Immaculate' Lady of the Waters whose estimable qualities the Wise Lord himself retails; and, as if this were not enough, he must be told

K

how the Wise Lord himself worshipped her and craved her aid, saying:
'Grant me this boon, O good, most powerful Ardvī Sūrā Anāhitā, that
I may incline the son of Pourushaspa, Zarathushtra, the follower of
Truth, to think in accordance with the Religion, to speak in accordance
with the Religion, to act in accordance with the Religion.'[1] The
goddess, in granting this boon to him, 'a suppliant', was gracious
enough to enable the creator of heaven and earth to persuade the
Prophet of his own choice to think, speak, and act in accordance with
his divine will; and it is, perhaps, worth noting in passing that the
goddess demanded from her worshippers the sacrifice of a hundred
stallions, a thousand bulls, and ten thousand heads of sheep—a scale
of sacrifice that even the most 'catholic' of Zoroastrians could scarcely
have deemed 'moderate'. So too in the *Yasht* dedicated to Vayu, the
god of the winds, we find the Wise Lord once again asking a boon of
this ambiguous deity, only one half of whom is favourable to the good
creation; and the boon he craves is not just that he may be able to
bring the Prophet to think in accordance with the Religion, but that
he may be able to vanquish the creatures of the Destructive Spirit, as
if he were not capable of doing so unaided. This is not untypical of the
whole tone of the *Yashts*; Ahura Mazdāh, the Wise Lord, no longer
stands above and beyond the conflict between his own Holy Spirit
and the Destructive Spirit. He is now identical with the first and fights
with the second on equal terms; he can no longer be sure of the
outcome, and although no other god is unequivocally called a creator,
and although creation still remains his sole privilege, yet he depends
on his own creation to strengthen his hand against his enemy; he needs
his creation as much as his creation needs him. And if this is true of the
gods, it is no less true of man.

The Fravashis

For man is not only composed of body and soul; from the beginning
of the world the whole human race is present before the Creator in the
form of the Fravashis, pre-existent external souls on whom the very
maintenance of the cosmos depends. It is through their might and glory
that the Wise Lord is able to sustain heaven and earth, through them
that he spread out the earth, through them that he causes the waters
to flow, the plants to grow, and the wind to blow, through them that
the foetus can grow unharmed in its mother's womb, and through them
that sun, moon, and stars follow their proper courses.[2] No longer is
Ahura Mazdāh the creator of all things in his own right: his creation
can only come to fruition through the spiritual power of the entire
human race, for:

'Had the strong Fravashis of the followers of Truth not granted me their aid, then would I here possess neither cattle nor men which are the best of [all animal] species, but the power would belong to the Lie, the kingdom to the Lie, yea, the [whole] material world would belong to the Lie. Between heaven and earth would he who is the Liar of the two Spirits have installed himself; between the heaven and the earth would he who is the Liar of the two Spirits have been victorious; nor would the victor, the Destructive Spirit, ever again have yielded to the vanquished, the Holy Spirit.'[3]

God, then, in order to vanquish the power of his eternal enemy, must rely on the help of that dynamo of unseen power which is the totality of the external human souls, both of the living and the dead and of those yet to be born. This much, indeed, is consonant with the Prophet's teaching, namely, that man has a vital part to play in the annihilation of the Lie; but never did it seriously occur to the Prophet Zoroaster that, but for man's contribution, the whole of the material universe between heaven and earth might collapse in ruin before the onrush of the powers of evil.

And yet, one cannot help feeling that the poet's object in painting this desperate picture of what might happen to the good creation if things went only a little wrong, is not so much that he would sow doubts in the minds of his audience that the ultimate issue of the battle can ever be seriously in doubt, as that he would exalt the power and glory of the immediate object of his praise—in this case the Fravashis. This does not mean, as has sometimes been supposed, that there was a proliferation of 'high gods' throughout the Iranian lands, each of whom was supreme to his own particular group of worshippers; it means simply that the poets who composed these hymns were returning to a technique similar to that employed by the poets of the *Rig-Veda*—a technique which is concerned with the exaltation of one particular god in any hymn addressed to him in such a manner that it would appear that he is surely the greatest of all the gods. The collection of these hymns into the one cycle of the *Yashts* creates a false impression of a greater degree of polytheism than probably existed in fact; for unlike the *Yasna*, which is a liturgical text, the *Yashts* are individual hymns in honour of individual gods and are parasitic to the main act of the liturgy which centres round the twin figures of Haoma and Sraosha, the sacrificial and the oratory mediators between God and man. The cult of the gods and goddesses whom the *Yashts* celebrate corresponds fairly closely to the cult of the saints in the Catholic Church; they are not essential to the basic structure of the religion, but were probably accorded particular veneration by individual families and clans. Veneration of the physical elements, and more especially fire and water, seems always to have been more fundamental in Zoroastrianism in all its forms than any cult of an individual god. Mithra, indeed, certainly maintained an immense popularity for a long time as the long list of names of which his own forms a part conclusively shows, but Ardvī Sūrā Anāhitā, though her cult enjoyed astonishing success in Asia Minor and Armenia, does not seem to have struck deep roots in Iran itself; and of the gods and goddesses venerated in the *Yashts* only Vayu played any significant part in the dualistic system which came to the fore in the Sassanian period. Even the Fravashis were relegated to the background, but the *khwarenah*, the 'glory' or 'good fortune', celebrated in *Yasht* 19, not only survived, but took on a cosmic significance that it lacked in the Avesta.

Vayu

It has been maintained[4] that Vayu was a 'high god' in his own right, but this is probably an over-simplification. One thing, however, is quite certain, and that is that he has not the faintest concern for the antithesis of good and evil that is so characteristic of Zoroastrianism. The natural element from which he derives his name is the wind, and this natural basis to his character remains with him. In the *Yasht* dedicated to him his epithets are all of impetuosity and violence; he is a mighty, rushing wind, pursuing, overtaking, and conquering the creations both of the Holy Spirit and of the Destructive Spirit,[5] but at the same time he is fully personified; clad in golden helmet, crown, and tunic, he rides on a golden chariot,[6] and in this anthropomorphized form he becomes the patron of the warrior caste.[7] Vayu, however, who in India was the close associate of Indra, was not the kind of god who could easily be fitted into Zoroastrian dualism; so already in the Avesta his personality has been split into two, a good Vayu and an evil one. So it is that we read: 'We venerate that Vayu who follows Truth, we venerate that Vayu who works on high, we venerate that Vayu of thine which is of the Holy Spirit.'[8] It follows, then, that there is also a Vayu which is of the Destructive Spirit, and so we meet with both a good and an evil Vayu in the Pahlavi books where the dichotomy of this once unitary deity is complete. In the Vayu *Yasht*, despite the somewhat pedantic veneration of that Vayu only 'which is of the Holy Spirit', the separation of the good from the evil aspect of the wind-god is only partial, and his elemental unconcern with the moral order is inexpertly concealed. Since he is described as overtaking and conquering both creations, he wins the epithet of 'all-conqueror'.[9] This apparent omnipotence attributed to the god Vayu, however, does not mean that, even in the *Yasht* dedicated to him, he is the supreme god. True, he is at liberty to play havoc with both creations, but there is no suggestion that he has power over either the Holy Spirit or the Destructive Spirit themselves. His field of operation is the material creation as it exists now, the so-called 'mixed state' in which good and evil struggle for the mastery. In the latter part of the Vayu *Yasht*, Vayu appears as the *tertius gaudens*, harassing both creations.

In the strictly dualistic system that Zoroastrianism was fast becoming, so arbitrary a god as Vayu was could have no fixed place. Originally he was almost certainly a *daēva*, for in the *Rig-Veda* he pairs off with Indra, forming with him a dual compound *Indrā-vāyū* in exactly the same way as Mitra pairs off with Varuna to form a morphologically identical compound *Mitrā-varunā*. The Zoroastrians of the syncretistic catholic period, however, had no hard and fast rule for dealing with the *daēvas*. Usually their names survive as minor henchmen of the Destructive Spirit, but their attributes are either constellated to form a new deity like Verethraghna, or used to enlarge the stature of a great god like Mithra. In the case of Vayu a different technique was adopted: the old god was neatly bisected, one half of him being assigned to the Holy Spirit, the other to the Destructive one. Like his Vedic counterpart, however, Vayu was originally a god of the atmosphere—the wind that is the breath of the macrocosm and therefore also the breath of life that keeps man, the microcosm, alive. Being the force that controls the movement of the air he also has the power to take away the breath of man, and he thereby becomes the god of death—a god still, and not just a demon.

'The path can be avoided which a running river guards: only the path of the pitiless Vayu can never be avoided.
'The path can be avoided which is guarded by a dragon of the size of a bull, that devours horses and men, that slays men and is pitiless: only the path of the pitiless Vayu can never be avoided.
'The path can be avoided which a dusky bear guards: only the path of the pitiless Vayu can never be avoided.
'The path can be avoided which is guarded by a robber who slays at one blow and is pitiless: only the path of the pitiless Vayu can never be avoided.
'The path can be avoided which [is commanded] by an army equipped with chariots and [lurking] in ambush: only the path of the pitiless Vayu can never be avoided.'[10]

Vayu and Zurvān

Here the 'path of Vayu' is, of course, the path of death—a path elsewhere said to have been created by Time.[11] The connexion between Vayu and Zurvān, the god of Time, who was later to become so prominent in the Zoroastrian cosmogony, is not immediately apparent, but it seems to be this. Vayu, when considered not as a personal god but as a natural phenomenon, is not only the wind or air, but the whole atmosphere between heaven and earth in which alone the wind can blow. This atmosphere is an enclosed space between a solid heaven built of shining metal and a solid earth in the centre of it: it is finite space, and the 'Time' that controls the path of death is likewise finite time. Finite time plus finite space equals the whole cosmos contained within the sky. The cosmos or macrocosm, like man, the microcosm, comes to be from the infinite and again passes away into the infinite: it is born and it dies: it is life and it is death. Hence Finite Time (Zurvān) and Finite Space (Vayu) control man's destiny from the cradle to the grave. At the same time, as we have seen, the whole of the macrocosm is kept in being by the Fravashis, the spiritual powers that are indissolubly linked with each and every human being and with humanity as a whole. Finite time-space, then, is not a *kenoma*, an empty nothingness, but a *pleroma*, a 'full' and vital organism which is the prototype of man, and just as this *pleroma* dissolves into the infinite at the end of time, so does man, at death, revert to the light from which he originally proceeded.

In the Avesta, Vayu is still an independent power that pursues at will both the good and evil creations, but in the Pahlavi books he has become not only two rather insignificant personal daemons—a god who assists the virtuous soul after death and a demon who drags the sinner down to hell—he has become the atmosphere between heaven and earth, the battlefield in which the struggle between good and evil must work itself out. He is the vital breath of the universe and he is the vital breath in man.[12] This highly ambivalent nature of the god Vayu causes great confusion in the cosmology of the Pahlavi books, but before we come to discuss this, it is as well to bear in mind that in the later literature three Vayus must be distinguished. First there is the evil Vayu who is simply a demon of death; secondly there is the good Vayu who both assists the righteous and is also the patron of the warrior caste. Thirdly there is the impersonal Vayu which is finite space and thereby identified with both *spihr*, the heavenly sphere, and *āsmān*, the sky, both of which are considered to be not only the heavenly vault but also all that is contained within it.

The Khwarenah

Before we leave the Avesta to consider the religion of the Achaemenian kings, a few words must be said about a concept that plays an important part in all phases of the Zoroastrian religion. This is the *khwarenah*. This word was, until Professor Sir Harold Bailey subjected it to a searching critical treatment,[13] almost invariably translated as 'glory', and in *Yasht* 19 which is devoted to the *khwarenah*, this translation is not inappropriate. Bailey, however, demonstrated that its basic meaning must be 'welfare, well-being' or 'fortune'. The 'kingly glory' which Yima lost, and over which his successors were to fight, is the *fortuna regia*, something akin to the Arabic *baraka*, the royal 'touch', which makes a king a king. Once Yima lost his royal *khwarenah* he automatically ceased to be a king. Thus the royal *khwarenah* may correctly be translated as 'glory' because a king's *fortuna* is *eo ipso gloriosa*. Similarly the 'glory, or fortune which cannot be seized', which is the prerogative of the whole Iranian nation[14] could not be captured by Frañrasyan (Afrāsyāb) because he was no Iranian. For once the Pahlavi translation of this word is impeccable: it is rendered as *khwēshkārī* which literally means 'own-work'. As every man has his Fravashi, so does he also have his *khwarenah*, his *fortuna* or destiny, but it is not destiny in the sense of a predetermined fate, but that for which you are created, your own perfection, your final cause. You can be false to your destiny as Yima was in one of the legends concerning him, and you thereby become separated from your *khwarenah* which is more intimately yourself than your own soul for it pre-exists you.[15] More specifically the *khwarenah* is the fulfilment of God's purpose, for 'the Creator created his creation for action, and specified for each individual creature his own sphere of action. Any action that contributes to the natural development (*ravākīh*) of a creature is the *khwarenah* of that creature.'[16] The *khwarenah* of an individual is the job that God has set him to do on this earth, God's purpose for him here and now: for Zoroastrianism in all its phases is a religion that fully accepts this life here and now, as it also accepts a stratified society divided into the broad classes of priests, warriors, peasants, and artisans. Each class has its own *khwarenah*, its own job to do and no one else's. Thus it was not possible for an artisan to become a peasant, a peasant a warrior, or a warrior a priest; this could only be effected by obtaining a decree from the Great King himself,[17] and in any case it was considered both unnatural and undesirable. 'A man should do himself [the work that is peculiarly] his. If he fails to do so, no one else can do it for him.'[18] Each man has his own individual *khwarenah*, and to this he must cling, for it is the instrument of his salvation. The *khwarenah* is not a kind of mystic nimbus as some would have us believe, it is *work* in fulfilment of your final cause.

'The Creator created his creation for action (work), and creatures are the Creator's agents. Their work can only develop satisfactorily by obtaining a right view (*bavandak-mēnītārīh*) of their *khwarenah*, that is, by doing their own job. By making a success of one's own job one furthers the Creator's work and thereby conforms to his will and pleasure; but by neglecting one's job out of conceit one frustrates that *khwarenah* which is the Creator's work, fails to conform to his will, and suffers thereby.'[19]

But it is not only individuals who have their individual *khwarenah*, their individual jobs to perform; each household, village, county, province, and country has a *khwarenah* in common, a communal duty which is yet individual to each. And above these national aspirations there is the *khwarenah* of the whole world, of all the 'seven climes' which must strive together to remove the obstacles that stand in the way of the common destiny,[20] and since all *khwarenah* is from God,[21] it instinctively seeks to return to God.[22]

And not only is the earth animated and activated by this buoyant drive towards fulfilment, which the *khwarenah* represents, the heavens too are girt with the *khwarenah* of the Good Religion which acts as an impregnable bastion beyond which it is not permitted to the Evil One to advance.[23] This, the heavenly *khwarenah*, is indeed 'glory', for it functions 'in a pure state' among the heavenly lights and is never obstructed or thwarted by the malice of the Adversary. The *khwarenah* of the Good Religion does its 'own work' by hemming the powers of evil in, while on earth it works untiringly towards the bringing about of the *Frashkart*, the 'Making Excellent' or final Rehabilitation when evil will be for ever deprived of actuality. The Religion is regarded as being identical with wisdom, or rather with reason (*khrat*), and it is this that protects man's *khwarenah* from the onslaughts of Āz, the demon of gluttony, lust, and concupiscence, who would destroy it.[24]

That *khwarenah* should so long have been translated as 'glory' is comprehensible, for the 'royal fortune' is identical with a blazing fire,[25] whereas all *khwarenah* is said to derive from the Endless Light.[26] Material light is said to emanate from it[27] and the moon stores it up and then distributes it to the sub-lunary world.[28] Similarly the *khwarenah* of the Prophet Zoroaster descended in the likeness of fire before he was born, and was visible for three days and nights.[29] Yet the essence of the *khwarenah* is not that it partakes of the glory of light, but that it is the 'agent' through which the Creator works out the salvation of his creation; for 'its proper function is to save and bring about salvation, to ennoble and to cause to be ennobled every entity which possesses it by means of each entity's own *khwarenah* and what is proper to it. . . . It is the omniscient and omnipotent Creator Ohrmazd who reunites it to what is properly its own—both in individual cases [when each individual *khwarenah* is reunited] to its particular seed and body, and universally, at the time of the "Making Excellent" [when the universal *khwarenah* will be reunited] to the architects of that

"Making Excellent"; . . . and again at the Final Body [when the *khwarenah* is reunited] to the whole of material existence.'[30]

The *khwarenah*, then, can best be described as the final cause of every single creature, every organized group of creatures, and of creation as a whole. It is the priesthood of the priest, the kingship of the king, the craft of the craftsman, and the valour of the warrior: it is the humanity of man and the godhead of God who is its creator. But it is more than this: it is these qualities in action, and not only in action but also in purposeful action through friendship, companionship, and mutual consultation,[31] which will inevitably lead to the 'Making Excellent' of God's stricken creation and to the Final Body, which is the restoration of the true humanity of man. By the onslaught of Evil and the concupiscence that accompanies it man is separated from his *khwarenah*, what he is, is separated from what he ought to be. At the 'Making Excellent' all *is* what it ought to be, and the universal *khwarenah* thereby finds its fulfilment in what is indeed 'glory'.

CHAPTER SEVEN

ACHAEMENIDS AND MAGI

Primitive and 'Catholic' Zoroastrianism—The God of Darius the Great—The 'Zoroastrianism' of Darius—The Daiva-Inscription of Xerxes—Xerxes' 'Un-Zoroastrian' Acts—Artaxerxes II and III—The Magi—Zoroaster and the Magi—Magavan—Popular Religion in Western Iran—Zoroastrianism and the Popular Cults—The Religion Described by Strabo—Decline and Fall of 'Catholic' Zoroastrianism

HITHERTO we have been exclusively concerned with the religion of the Avesta, that is, with the religion that developed after Zoroaster's death in the eastern part of what was to become the Persian Empire. In the Avesta plenty of place-names occur,[1] but there is no mention of any place west of Rhages which was approximately on the site of the modern Tehran; it is, then, certain that the Avestan religion not only began but also developed in Eastern Iranian lands. For the development of Iranian religion in the West we have to rely on the inscriptions of the Achaemenian kings and the Greek accounts of the Iranian religion, particularly Herodotus. There are probably no two problems in Zoroastrian studies more vexed than that of the religion of the Achaemenian kings and that of the part played by the Magi in the development of Zoroastrianism. Yet both Darius and Xerxes have left us inscriptions which give us a pretty clear idea of what their religion was, and the problem, therefore, really boils down to this: What do *we*, in fact, mean by Zoroastrianism?

Primitive and 'Catholic' Zoroastrianism

We have seen that the Zoroastrians themselves used four terms to define their religion: *ahura-tkaēsha*, 'holding to the doctrine of Ahura or the *ahuras*'; *vīdaēva*, 'opposed to the *daēvas*'; *zarathushtri*, 'follower of Zoroaster'; and *māzdayasni*, 'worshipper of Mazdāh'. The last term became standardized as the official designation of the religion. The Achaemenian kings, from the time of Darius at least, were certainly *ahura-tkaēsha* and *māzdayasni*, for they were worshippers of Ahura Mazdāh, and neither Darius nor Xerxes mentions any other god by name. Xerxes was certainly *vīdaēva*, for he seems to have proscribed the cult of the *daēvas* throughout the Empire. All that is in doubt, then, is whether they were also *zarathushtri*, confessed disciples of the Prophet Zoroaster. The fact that none of the inscriptions mentions Zoroaster by name

154

proves absolutely nothing, for even the Indian Emperor Aśoka, a devout Buddhist if ever there was one, mentions the Buddha only once.

Moreover, we can now be certain that primitive Zoroastrianism differed very widely from the later 'catholic' variety, and the change is so marked that we cannot help feeling that the Prophet's original teaching was radically altered in order to fall more in line with the popular religion of the Iranian masses owing to considerable pressure from above, and this can only have been exercised by the Achaemenian kings themselves. Of only one fact can we be reasonably certain, and that is that during the reign of Artaxerxes I, round about 441 BC,[2] the calendar of the Persian Empire was reformed and that in this reformed calendar the months were named after the leading deities of 'catholic' Zoroastrianism. Hence it would seem reasonably certain that from Artaxerxes I (465–25 BC) on, the official religion of the Empire was 'catholic' Zoroastrianism of the later Avesta, whereas Xerxes' edict proscribing the worship of the *daēvas* makes it probable that he too followed, in some respects at least, the teachings of Zoroaster.

The God of Darius the Great

The god of the Achaemenian house, at least from the time of Darius, was Ahura Mazdāh, spelt in one word in the inscriptions which, in this respect, differ from the *Gāthās* where the two component parts—*Ahura* and *Mazdāh*—still appear in separation. This Gāthic usage has led us to believe that the god Ahura Mazdāh, the Wise Lord, was Zoroaster's own invention, and, if that is so, Darius' exclusive devotion to this deity would mean that that monarch followed the teaching of the Prophet to the extent at least that he worshipped the Prophet's god and acknowledged him alone as creator and Lord. For whether he was consciously a Zoroastrian or not, Darius was every bit as much a monotheist as was Zoroaster himself. Bearing in mind that Darius' inscriptions were hewn out of the rock for mainly political reasons, it is surprising how much space he devotes to his personal religion.

Darius does not attribute the fact that he is king to any merit of his own. 'By the will of Ahura Mazdāh am I king,' he says. 'On me did Ahura Mazdāh bestow the kingdom.'[3] Ahura Mazdāh 'created me and made me king'.[4] 'Such was Ahura Mazdāh's will; he chose me a man, out of the whole earth and made me king of the whole earth. I worshipped Ahura Mazdāh and he brought me aid. What I was commanded to do, that he made easy for me. Whatever I did, I did in accordance with his will.'[5] Just as Zoroaster had recognized the existence of other *ahuras* or 'lords' besides the Wise Lord who alone is creator, so did Darius recognize the existence of other gods besides his own 'Wise Lord': he calls them 'the other gods who exist',[6] but they are not considered to be of sufficient importance to be invoked or even mentioned by name. Again like Zoroaster, Darius does not feel himself to be a stranger to his God: 'to me,' he says, 'Ahura Mazdāh was a friend.'[7] Like Zoroaster's God, too, Darius' God is the creator of heaven and earth. 'A great god is Ahura Mazdāh who created this earth, who created yonder sky, who created man, who created happiness for man, who made Darius king, one king among many, one ruler among many.'[8]

Darius' great inscription at Bīsitūn is an account of the rebellions he put down throughout the Empire, and it is significant that he equates rebellion with the Lie. The rebels lie in that they claim to be kings, when in fact they are no such thing. 'Lying', then, means much the same for Darius as it did for Zoroaster: it is a violent onslaught against the established order as well as an offence against Truth. The order of Ahura Mazdāh is based on rectitude, peace, and prosperity, and it is his intention for man that he should prosper and be happy in a peaceful society. So Darius prays to him and 'all the gods' to keep enemy hoards, famine, and the Lie away from the Empire.[9] The source from which these evils proceed is not mentioned but it is certainly not God, for he makes only 'what is excellent on this earth';[10] he does not originate evil. True, he chastises those who oppose or conceal the truth,[11] but this is no more than the manifestation of his justice. He is the source of all good things, both physical and moral, and Darius sees all his good qualities as deriving from God. It is through God's grace that he is a 'friend of Truth (*rāsta*), not of falsehood',[12] and it is God who bestows on him wisdom and virtue and the ability to control his impulses by his mind; and here Darius uses the word *manah*[13] in very much the same way as Zoroaster might have spoken of his own *vohu manah*, the 'good mind'. Both spiritual and material gifts are in the hand of God, and Darius is grateful for both, for it is thanks to him that he excels at horsemanship and is expert at handling both bow and spear.

The 'Zoroastrianism' of Darius

Darius' religion, then, agrees with that of Zoroaster in that it recognizes Ahura Mazdāh as the supreme Lord, 'great, the greatest of the gods',[14] but does not deny the existence of other gods. Ahura Mazdāh is the creator of heaven and earth and of man; and he is man's friend so long as he holds to the Truth. He protects from evil,[15] for his will is that man should be happy and at peace. He is the author of Righteousness or Truth and of all legally constituted authority, and man, on his side, is required to follow the straight path and to fight untruth wherever it may be found. 'Do not leave the straight (*rāsta*) path,' Darius admonishes his subjects, 'and do not rebel.'[16] Similarly the Zoroastrian liturgy ends with the words: 'One is the path of Truth, the paths of others are no paths.'[17]

In its bare essentials, then, the religion of Darius is very closely akin to that of Zoroaster. The supreme God is the same and has the same name, there is the same insistence on Truth and Righteousness, and the same diagnosis of evil as being the manifestation of the Lie. Of course the emphasis differs in the two cases. For Darius the Lie manifests itself as rebellion against the royal authority, but the royal authority itself is in the gift of the Wise Lord, and rebellion against the King amounts to rebellion against God. For Zoroaster the Lie manifests itself primarily in the rejection of his prophetic mission, in violence and in injustice; but in both cases the Lie is basically the same concept: it is the violation of a divinely appointed order of Truth, incorporated in the one case in the Prophet, in the other in the King. The dualism between Truth and the Lie is as sharply etched in Darius' inscriptions as it is in the *Gāthās* of Zoroaster, except that for Darius the field is narrower: he sees this cosmic conflict only as it is manifested in his own Empire, whereas Zoroaster sees it both in the political and economic sphere and as a universally valid cosmic principle. The pattern of thought that underlies Darius' inscriptions is that of primitive Zoroastrianism. The fact that he neither mentions the Destructive Spirit nor any of the Bounteous Immortals by name and that his terminology is not that of the *Gāthās* and that there is no reference to Zoroaster himself, can scarcely be advanced as a serious argument that he was ignorant of the Zoroastrian reform. His exclusive devotion to Ahura Mazdāh, his constant emphasis on the opposition that exists between Truth and the Lie, and his acknowledgement of Ahura Mazdāh as the creator of heaven and earth, show that he was familiar with the main tenets of primitive Zoroastrianism. He does not show himself familiar with the more abstruse aspects of Zoroaster's teaching, and this is scarcely surprising since his teaching as it was propounded in the western half of the Persian Empire may well have been in a simplified form; and, as we have seen, the Bounteous Immortals, which scholars have too long regarded as being an essential feature of primitive Zoroastrianism, were very soon relegated to a position of exalted irrelevance. In Darius' inscriptions—except for the 'Kingdom'—they are never mentioned by name; but *Asha*, the Truth, is clearly present in Darius' *rāsta*, 'Right' or 'Truth', and *Vohu Manah*, the 'Good Mind', is as clearly the same mind present to the King, by which he fights down his own impulsiveness. For the King the 'Kingdom' is, of course, his own kingdom, the Persian Empire; but this kingdom is only his because the Wise Lord has bestowed it on him; he holds it from him on trust. And since in the last analysis it is God's, he must promulgate God's law of Truth and Righteousness and Right-Mindedness within it—and in practice this means that he must repress all manifestations of the Lie, all haughty attempts to wrest God's earthly kingdom from the hands into which God has entrusted it. Darius would thus appear to have accepted the vital core of Zoroaster's teaching without thereby supporting any form of organized Zoroastrianism, if indeed such organized forms existed at the time. He does not boast, as the Sassanian kings were later to do, of his pious foundations; he boasts only of his own moral stature which he sees as the gift of God. Darius speaks to us in the spirit of Zoroaster in a way that no so-called Zoroastrian text does except the *Gāthās* themselves. This much must, I think, be conceded. Whether or not we should take the further step and declare that he was a 'Zoroastrian' is a matter of how we wish to define our terms. It is a waste of time.

Yet though Darius adhered to the essential Zoroastrian beliefs, he did nothing to destroy any national cult. We are told that he restored the places of worship that the usurper Gaumāta, the Magian, had destroyed,[18] and in this he shows himself to be totally lacking in the prophetic intolerance of Zoroaster; but this is simply because God had made him king, and the King's first duty is to repress hostile armies. His interpretation of the scope of the Lie is a king's, not a priest's or a prophet's. For Zoroaster kingship and prophecy were interconnected, but Darius, as King, regarded the pacification and reconstruction of his Empire as his first duty. In an empire that was, in any case, only partly Iranian, he was not prepared to interfere with traditional religion. This is not merely his private interpretation of the duties of the king of kings: it is God's will. 'When Ahura Mazdāh saw that this earth was in turmoil, he bestowed it on me. He made me king. I am King. By the will of Ahura Mazdāh I restored it to its [proper] state.'[19] God's will for this earth is not turmoil, but peace, prosperity, and good government. 'Much that was ill done,' the Great King declares, 'I made good. The provinces were in turmoil and one man slew another. By the will of Ahura Mazdāh I brought it about that one man should not slay another. Each man [was to be] in his own place. My law do they fear, so that the stronger does not smite the weak.'[20] In this respect, too, Darius conforms to a trend that runs through the whole history of Zoroastrianism—by rebuilding, by constructive and productive work he pleases God because by so doing he imitates God's own creative activity. Truth is productive, the Lie destroys.

The Daiva-Inscription of Xerxes

So much, then, can we deduce about Darius' religious policy from his inscriptions. His son, Xerxes, left no comparable evidence of the quality of his personal religion, but one inscription which only came to light in the nineteen-thirties, shows that he had a religious policy of his own. Like his father he was a worshipper of Ahura Mazdāh, but not to the exclusion of other gods, and, again like his father, he acknowledged him to be creator of heaven and earth, of man and of man's happiness. In addition, however, he tells us that whereas previously the *daēvas* had been worshipped within the Empire, this must stop. This is what he says:

'Within these provinces there were places where previously the *daivas* had been worshipped. Then by the will of Ahura Mazdāh I uprooted that cult of the *daivas*[21], and I made a proclamation [saying]: "The *daivas* shall not be worshipped." Where the *daivas* had previously been worshipped, there did I worship Ahura Mazdāh in accordance with Truth and using the proper rite. Much else that was ill done did I make good. All that I did, I did by the will of Ahura Mazdāh. Ahura Mazdāh brought me aid until I finished my work. O thou who shalt come after me, if thou wouldst be happy when alive and blessed when dead, have respect for the law which Ahura Mazdāh has established, and worship Ahura Mazdāh in accordance with Truth and using the proper rite. The man who has respect for the law which Ahura Mazdāh has established and who worships Ahura Mazdāh in accordance with Truth and using the proper rite, may he be both happy when alive and blessed when dead.'[22]

The *daivas* mentioned in the inscription can scarcely be other than the *daēvas* whom Zoroaster so vigorously attacks in the *Gāthās*, a class of Indo-Iranian deity which had come to be associated with violence. This does not necessarily mean that Xerxes was a professed Zoroastrian, for it is perfectly possible that there were communities before Zoroaster which did not worship the *daēvas*, nor does the 'law which Ahura Mazdāh has established' necessarily mean his revelation to Zoroaster, for in the Avesta there are two laws—the law against the *daēvas* and the law of Zoroaster[23]—and it is quite possible, as we have already seen, that Zoroaster was born into a community in which the *daēvas* were no longer worshipped.[24] On the other hand, the command to worship Ahura Mazdāh 'in accordance with Truth and using the proper rite' must refer to some kind of already existing orthodoxy which made Truth (*arta* = Avestan *asha*) central in the worship of Ahura Mazdāh; and such a form of worship can scarcely have been any other than that of the Zoroastrians. The use of the word *artāvan* (= Avestan *ashavan*) to refer to the state of the blessed dead confirms this, for it is commonly so used in the later Zoroastrian texts and on the Sassanian inscriptions. It is not used by Darius when he speaks of the happiness the righteous dead were supposed to enjoy; he merely says: 'Whoso shall worship Ahura Mazdāh so long as he has strength, may he enjoy happiness both when alive and when he is dead.'[25] The terminology is not yet Zoroastrian; with Xerxes it is. It can then be assumed that during the reign of Xerxes Zoroastrianism became almost a state cult.

Xerxes' 'Un-Zoroastrian' Acts

But what sort of Zoroastrianism? Xerxes, like his father, did not deny the existence of gods other than Ahura Mazdāh, but, again like his father, he does not bother to mention them by name. Yet Herodotus reports religious acts performed by Xerxes which do not seem compatible with the practice of the Zoroastrian religion as commonly understood. He is said to have lashed the Hellespont in a fit of pique,[26] and scholars have thought that this was scarcely compatible with the reverence of the waters that is so typical of the Zoroastrians. Again he is said to have sacrificed a thousand oxen to 'Ilian Athene', while the Magi, who seem to have been fully in control of religious affairs during his reign, sacrificed white horses on the river Strymon[27] and also offered sacrifice to the Winds, 'Thetis', and the 'Nereids'.[28] Herodotus even accuses the Persians—though not the Magi or the King himself—of human sacrifice.[29] Yet none of this is very surprising if our own account of the development of Zoroastrianism is at all correct. Zoroaster *may* have condemned animal sacrifice out of hand; on the other hand he may have condemned only a specific form of it. We do not know. But we do know that the Zoroastrian liturgy as preserved in the *Yasna* included the sacrifice of a bull or cow and the ritual consumption of the Haoma juice, possibly replaced by wine in Western Iran. The performance of animal sacrifice, then, both by Xerxes and by the Magi, so far from being surprising, is precisely what one would expect. Similarly his chastisement of the Hellespont (of which he is in any case said to have repented) does not necessarily conflict with the Zoroastrian reverence for water, for Xerxes upbraids it as *bitter* water, and we learn from one of the later Zoroastrian texts that when the Destructive Spirit defiled the waters, he made them brackish.[30] There is, then, no reason at all why Xerxes should not chastise a form of water that had been contaminated by the Devil. Again, there is nothing surprising in his or the Magi's sacrificing to the Winds, 'Athene', 'Thetis', or the 'Nereids', for Xerxes himself mentions 'gods' other than Ahura Mazdāh; and if the form of Zoroastrianism he professed was rather 'catholic' than 'primitive', as we would expect it to be, he would almost certainly honour the 'Winds', that is, Vayu, who, as patron of the warrior caste, would be a most potent ally in battle. 'Athene' and 'Thetis' would be hellenizations of the Iranian goddess Anāhitā, and the 'Nereids' may well represent the *ahurānīs*, the 'wives of Ahura Mazdāh', whom we met in the *Gāthā* of the Seven Chapters and who are the waters. There is, then, nothing in Xerxes' behaviour as reported by Herodotus that conflicts with the 'catholic' Zoroastrianism we have studied in the later Avestan texts. In spirit Xerxes is further removed from Zoroaster than was his father, but he seems to have consciously adhered to the later and admittedly distorted form of the Prophet's religion as interpreted to him by the Magi.

Artaxerxes II and III

Xerxes is the last of the Achaemenian kings to have left us any considerable legacy of inscriptions. After him only Artaxerxes II and III need to be mentioned, and they for no other reason than that they mention Mithra and Anāhitā by name in addition to Ahura Mazdāh, and that Artaxerxes II on one occasion invokes the protection of Mithra alone.[31] By this time 'catholic' Zoroastrianism had probably captured not only the royal house but also the bulk of western Iran.

The Magi

The acceptance of Zoroastrianism in the western half of the Persian Empire, its propagation, and its transformation into something quite unlike the Prophet's original message, seems to have been the work of the Magi who enjoyed a monopoly of religious affairs not only in their native Media but also in Persis and the whole western half of the Achaemenian Empire. There are few subjects on which scholars have differed more than on what part the Magi played in the dissemination of Zoroastrianism. For Moulton,[32] whose zeal for the Prophet burned a little too brightly, the Magi were the villains of the piece, and they were not even allowed to belong to either the Aryan or the Semitic race, so repulsive did their peculiar doctrines appear to him to be. For Messina, on the other hand, it was the Magi themselves who were the true heirs of Zoroaster and who alone faithfully transmitted his doctrines.[33] That scholars can differ so widely can only be attributed to a rather one-sided reading of the available sources. Moulton's view bases itself mainly on Herodotus, while Messina reaches a perhaps too favourable view of these strange people by discounting the reliability of Herodotus' sources. Throughout antiquity the Magi were notorious for two things: they did not bury their dead, but exposed them to be devoured by vultures and wild animals, and they considered incestuous marriages to be exceptionally meritorious.

'The Magi,' says Herodotus, 'are a very peculiar race, different entirely from the Egyptian priests, and indeed from all other men whatsoever. The Egyptian priests make it a point of religion not to kill any live animals except those which they offer in sacrifice. The Magi, on the contrary, kill animals of all kinds with their own hands, excepting dogs and men. They even seem to take a delight in the employment, and kill, as readily as they do other animals, ants and snakes, and such-like flying and creeping things. However, since this has always been their custom, let them keep to it.'[34]

This custom of the Magi which Herodotus found so peculiar is, in fact, typical of later Zoroastrianism, particularly the *Vidēvdāt*. The slaying of noxious beasts, the exposure of the dead, which according to Herodotus, the Magi practised openly,[35] and incestuous marriages are all attested of the Magi in our Greek sources, and they are also typical of the latest stratum of the Avesta. It is, then, fair to conclude that it was the Magi who were responsible for the drawing up of the *Vidēvdāt*, the 'law against the *daēvas*'; and this would go a long way to account for the appalling grammatical confusion that characterizes that not very admirable work. What hand they had in the compilation of the rest of the Avesta, however, is less certain, though it is unlikely that they had any direct share in the compilation of the great *Yashts* which, on the whole, adhere to grammatical rule. It cannot therefore be legitimately argued that because the Achaemenian kings were buried and not exposed, they cannot have been Zoroastrians, since we do not know how the Zoroastrians disposed of their dead until they came into contact with the Magi. All we know is that they not only came into contact with them but were also deeply influenced by them. One can, perhaps, go a little further than this, for the extraordinary zest with which the Magi are alleged to have killed 'with their own hands' flying and creeping things, can scarcely be accounted for except on the supposition that they thought such creatures to be the handiwork of an evil power. It is they, then, who would be responsible for the cut-and-dried division of creation into two mutually antagonistic halves—the creatures of the Holy Spirit on the one hand and the creatures of the Destructive Spirit on the other. Thus they can be regarded as the true authors of that rigid dualism that was to characterize the Zoroastrianism of a later period, but which is only implicit in the *Gāthās* of Zoroaster.

According to Herodotus[36] the Magi were one of six Median tribes, though Messina and many other scholars prefer to see in them a caste. Certainly, if they were ever a tribe, they were also very much more than that, since they made themselves indispensable at any form of religious ceremony, whether Zoroastrian or otherwise. Their presence was necessary even to the rite described by Plutarch in which an offering was made to Ahriman[37] and which must therefore be regarded as a sacrifice performed by the worshippers of the *daēvas*. It would be quite wrong to suppose that the Magi represented any kind of orthodoxy, for we sometimes find them officiating at sacrifices, and sometimes we are told that they execrate sacrifice as such[38] or that they merely stand by while others offer sacrifice.[39] Their position would seem to correspond to that of the Levites among the Jews or, even more closely, to that of the Brāhmans in India : they were a hereditary caste entrusted with the supervision of the national religion, whatever form it might take and in whatever part of the Empire it might be practised. How they attained to this privileged position remains quite obscure, but there seems to be no doubt that their functions passed from father to son right up to the Muslim conquest and after.[40]

Zoroaster and the Magi

It was Messina's contention that the Magi were the original followers of Zoroaster; and this view deserves serious consideration, though there are obvious objections to it. First, the word for 'Magus' (Avestan *mōgu*) occurs only once in the Avesta, and this would be surprising if the Magi were responsible for the final redaction of that scripture. Secondly, Herodotus says that they were a Median tribe, and it can no longer be seriously maintained that the Avesta was a product of Media. From the whole of Herodotus' history, however, and from all subsequent accounts of them, it is quite clear that the Magi were in fact a sacerdotal *caste* whose ethnic origin is never again so much as mentioned. We hear of Magi not only in Persis, Parthia, Bactria, Chorasmia, Aria, Media, and among the Sakas,[41] but also in non-Iranian lands like Arabia, Ethiopia, and Egypt.[42] Their influence was also widespread throughout Asia Minor. It is, therefore, quite likely that the sacerdotal caste of the Magi was distinct from the Median tribe of the same name.

Magavan

The Old Persian form of the word rendered into Greek as *magos* is *magu*. In the *Gāthās* we meet with a noun *maga* and an adjective formed from it *magavan*; and it is quite possible that the Old Persian *magu* is an adjectival derivative from this same word *maga* with a different suffix. *Maga* can scarcely be separated from the Vedic *magha* (together with its adjective *maghavan*) meaning 'riches' or 'gift'. Messina, taking each passage in which the word occurs separately, has shown that 'gift' makes good sense in all the contexts. *Maga*, however, must have been a semi-technical term meaning God's 'gift' of the Good Religion to Zoroaster. The Pahlavi translators, for once, bear this out, for they translate the word as 'purity' or 'pure goodness'. In this they were probably following a live tradition, for when they simply do not know the meaning of an Avestan word they content themselves with a near-transliteration. Moreover, the adjectival form of the word in the form *maghvand* survives in Pahlavi and seems to mean something like 'adorning'.[43] In the *Gāthās* the word seems to mean both the teaching of Zoroaster and the community that accepted that teaching, but there is no reason to suppose that the western Iranian form *magu* (Magus) has exactly the same meaning despite the fact that in the Greek sources Zoroaster himself appears as a Magus and that he was claimed as such by the Magi who had emigrated outside Iran. Herodotus, however, knows nothing of Zoroaster and speaks of the Magi as officiating at religious ceremonies that seem to have little in common with Zoroastrianism in any form we know or indeed with the religion of the Achaemenian kings.

According to Porphyry[44] the word 'Magus' means 'one who is wise in the things of God and serves the divine', and there is plenty of evidence to support this view. The Magi were considered to be philosophers, they were the teachers of the Achaemenian kings, they were the best of the Persians and strove to lead a holy life, and so on.[45] The 'Magus', then, would be the man possessed of *maga*—the man who enjoys God's 'gift' or 'grace'; and he is in receipt of this 'gift' simply by virtue of belonging to the priestly caste. We have an exactly parallel case in India where the Brāhmans who constitute the hereditary priesthood are sacrosanct simply because they inherit the *brahman* or 'sacred power' of which their caste is the vehicle. So it would seem that both the western Magi and the *magavans* of Zoroaster's community were members of a sacerdotal caste, but that they differed in this, that the Magi claimed priestly functions throughout the Empire and in association with all cults, while Zoroaster's *magavans* derived their authority solely from what they considered to be a direct irruption of the divine in the person of Zoroaster. At some stage the Zoroastrian priesthood must have made contact with the Magi known to the West, and the latter then adopted the name of 'Zoroastrian' and transformed Zoroaster himself into a Magus, though they may have meant no more by that term than a 'holy man'. That some of the Magi became profoundly influenced by Chaldaean astrology in the course of their migration to the West, and that they were commonly accused of 'magic' (i.e. the art peculiar to a Magus) and sorcery, has little or nothing to

do with the religious situation in Iran. It can be assumed that even the
'worshippers of the *daēvas*' and the 'followers of the Lie' had Magi
of their own, but their authority would not have been accepted by any
Zoroastrian. It is fairly clear that during the early Achaemenian period
the Magi gained control of Zoroastrianism in the West, for as early as
Plato[46] Zoroaster is spoken of as a Magus. Thus Zoroastrianism fell
under the influence of a hereditary priestly caste that ministered to the
spiritual needs of not only the Zoroastrians but also the entire Iranian
nation. What the specific contribution of the Magi to Zoroastrianism
was is largely a matter of guesswork and need not detain us for long.

It does, however, seem fairly certain that it was the Magi who were
responsible for introducing three new elements into Zoroastrianism—
the exposure of the dead to be devoured by vultures and dogs, the
practice of incestuous marriages, and the extension of the dualist view
of the world to material things and particularly the animal kingdom.
It is not to be supposed, however, that with the conversion of a majority
of the Magi and of the royal family itself to Zoroastrianism anything
like religious uniformity was produced within the Persian Empire, for
the type of religion described by Herodotus differs considerably from
Zoroastrianism as we know it and probably reflects a more primitive
and popular form of religion.

Popular Religion in Western Iran

'The customs which I know the Persians to observe [writes Herodotus] are
the following. They have no images of the gods, no temples or altars, and
consider the use of them a sign of folly. This comes, I think, from their not
believing the gods to have the same nature with men, as the Greeks imagine.
Their wont, however, is to ascend the summits of the loftiest mountains, and
there to offer sacrifice to Zeus, which is the name they give to the whole
circuit of the firmament. They likewise offer to the sun and moon, to the
earth, to fire, to water, and to the winds. These are the only gods whose
worship has come down to them from ancient times. At a later period they
began the worship of Urania, which they borrowed from the Arabians and
Assyrians. Mylitta is the name by which the Assyrians know this goddess
whom the Arabians call Alilat, and the Persians Mitra.[47]

'To these gods the Persians offer sacrifice in the following manner: they
raise no altar, light no fire, pour no libations; there is no sound of the flute,
no putting on of chaplets, no consecrated barley-cake; but the man who
wishes to sacrifice brings his victim to a spot of ground which is pure from
pollution, and there calls upon the name of the god to whom he intends to
offer. It is usual to have the turban encircled with a wreath, most commonly
of myrtle. The sacrificer is not allowed to pray for blessings on himself alone,
but he prays for the welfare of the king, and of the whole Persian people,

among whom he is of necessity included. He cuts the victim in pieces, and having boiled the flesh, he lays it out upon the tenderest herbage that he can find, trefoil especially. When all is ready, one of the Magi comes forward and chants a theogony, for such the Persians allege the chant to be. It is not lawful to offer sacrifice unless there is a Magus present. After waiting a short time the sacrificer carries the flesh of the victim away with him, and makes whatever use of it he may please. . . .

'Next to prowess in arms, it is regarded as the greatest proof of manly excellence to be the father of many sons. Every year the king sends rich gifts to the man who can show the largest number: for they hold that number is strength. Their sons are carefully instructed from their fifth to their twentieth year in three things alone—to ride, to draw the bow, and to speak the truth. . . .

'They hold it unlawful to talk of anything which it is unlawful to do. The most disgraceful thing in the world, they think, is to tell a lie; the next worst, to owe a debt: because, among other reasons, the debtor is obliged to tell lies. If a Persian has the leprosy he is not allowed to enter into a city, or to have any dealings with other Persians; he must, they say, have sinned against the sun. . . . They never defile a river with the secretions of their bodies, nor even wash their hands in one; nor will they allow others to do so, as they have a great reverence for rivers. . . .

'Thus much I can declare of the Persians with entire certainty, from my own actual knowledge. There is another custom which is spoken of with reserve, and not openly, concerning their dead. It is said that the body of a male Persian is never buried, until it has been torn either by a dog or a bird of prey. That the Magi have this custom is beyond a doubt, for they practise it without any concealment.'[48]

Much of this is familiar and is pan-Iranian, such as the veneration of the natural elements—fire, water, wind, and earth—and of the sun and moon. Herodotus is, of course, mistaken in supposing that the Iranian goddess of the sky was Mithra. His mistake, however, shows that his informant was well acquainted with both Mithra and Anāhitā, both of whom are for the first time mentioned in the inscriptions of Artaxerxes II. The 'whole circuit of the firmament' which Herodotus identifies with Zeus may either be the ancient Ahura, the 'Lord' *par excellence*, or the Ahura Mazdāh of the Seven Chapters. The sacrifice Herodotus describes, however, differs from any known Zoroastrian rite, for he explicitly states that they light no fire and pour no libations, whereas the Zoroastrian rite must, from the beginning, have been associated with the sacred fire, and libations have a vital part to play in the Avestan ritual. The laying of flesh on tender herbage, however, would point to an ancient Indo-Iranian usage, for this type of sacrifice is found in the *Veda*, and the Avesta itself speaks of the *barsom* or bundle of twigs which the priest holds in his hands, as being *strewn*, thereby indicating an earlier usage when the twigs were laid out on the ground. That a Magus had to be present at this sacrifice shows either that all the Magi were not Zoroastrians or that, though Zoroastrians, they were quite happy to officiate at non-Zoroastrian ceremonies.

The sacrifice described by Herodotus bears a curious resemblance to the sacrifice of Mashyē and Mashyānē which we have had occasion to discuss above. According to Herodotus the sacrificer carries the flesh of the sacrificial animal away with him and does with it whatever he likes, and Strabo explicitly states that no portion of it is given to the gods, since 'the deity needs the soul of the victim and nothing more'. [49] Similarly Mashyē and Mashyānē give only a portion of the victim to the gods and the fire, and this the gods deem to be an act of ingratitude. Such practices, moreover, are condemned in the Avesta itself, for in the *Yasna* the sacrificial bull indignantly complains of the man who is stingy enough to keep all the sacrificial flesh for himself and his family, and in any case the jaws, the tongue, and the left eye should be reserved for Haoma. [50] Perhaps it was this practice of withholding the sacrificial meat from the gods that constituted the sin of Yima 'who gave to our people portions of [the flesh of] the ox to eat'. If this is so, then it is perfectly possible that the rite described by Herodotus was that of the still-surviving *daēva*-worshippers.

The extreme veneration for water which Herodotus describes, though quite typical of the *Gāthā* of the Seven Chapters and the later Avesta, is foreign to the primitive Zoroastrianism of the *Gāthās* proper where the only element that is explicitly venerated is fire.

Zoroastrianism and the Popular Cults
The bulk of the people of Western Iran at the time of Herodotus would not seem to have been greatly influenced by any recognizable form of Zoroastrianism and only a portion of the Magi would seem to have adhered to the new cult. Moreover, when the new Zoroastrian calendar was introduced by Artaxerxes I, the form of Zoroastrianism adopted was the 'catholic' Zoroastrianism of the later Avesta, and even after Xerxes had proscribed the worship of the *daēvas*, it would seem that the people were allowed the widest latitude of cult and were no doubt free to carry on traditional forms of worship so long as they did not invoke the *daēvas* by name. Zoroastrianism by this time must have become fully polytheistic, and Artaxerxes II was only following the popular trend when he associated Mithra and Anāhitā with the Wise Lord. There must, however, have been a party within the Zoroastrian community which regarded the strict dualism between Truth and the Lie, the Holy Spirit and the Destructive Spirit, as being the essence of

the Prophet's message. Otherwise the re-emergence of this strictly dualist form of Zoroastrianism some six centuries after the collapse of the Achaemenian Empire could not be readily explained. There must have been a zealous minority that busied itself with defining what they considered the Prophet's true message to be; there must have been an 'orthodox' party within the 'Church'. This minority, concerned now with theology no less than with ritual, would be found among the Magi, and it is, in fact, to the Magi that Aristotle and other early Greek writers attribute the fully dualist doctrine of two independent principles —Oromasdes and Areimanios.[51] Further, the founder of the Magian order was now said to be Zoroaster himself. The fall of the Achaemenian Empire, however, must have been disastrous for the Zoroastrian religion, and the fact that the Magi were able to retain as much of it as they did and restore it in a form that was not too strikingly different from the Prophet's original message after the lapse of some 600 years proves their devotion to his memory. It is, indeed, true to say that the Zoroastrian orthodoxy of the Sassanian period is nearer to the spirit of Zoroaster than is the thinly disguised polytheism of the *Yashts*. Mithra and Anāhitā were to make great conquests in non-Iranian lands, but in the reformed Zoroastrianism which was inaugurated in the second Persian Empire, their wings were severely clipped, and they were never again allowed to usurp a position of near-equality with the Wise Lord. They became, again, as they had originally been for the Prophet, largely irrelevant figures, archangels at best, but not comparable in any way to the Creator. As the 'gods' receded into the background, the dualism between Creator and Destroyer, the Wise Lord and the Destructive Spirit, Ohrmazd and Ahriman as they came to be called, became ever more sharply emphasized, and this was in the spirit of the Prophet himself, not of his epigones who so radically altered his religion during the Achaemenian period.

According to one of the Pahlavi books the fall of the Achaemenids resulted in a dearth of properly qualified religious teachers, and heresy of every kind was rife.[52] This would account for the great variety of views attributed to the Magi by the Greek and Latin sources. There was no longer any Xerxes to punish those who continued to worship the *daēvas*, and though a minority might cling to their own orthodoxy, the civil power was for long not in Iranian hands, and even the Parthians seem to have cared little for the Prophet's faith.

The Religion Described by Strabo
Of the classical accounts of the Iranian religion after Herodotus, Strabo's is the most important because it shows how Iranian religion

in general was approximating more and more to the type of Zoroastrianism we know from the Avesta and the Pahlavi books. It is true that Strabo distinguishes separate fire and water sacrifices among the Magians, but this is not surprising, for the *Yasna* as we have it today would seem to be composed of one main sacrifice which must originally have included the slaying of a sacrificial bull as well as the ritual immolation of the Haoma, and of a subsidiary rite which follows the recitation of the *Gāthās* and which is mainly concerned with the propitiation of the waters. Both the sacrifices described by Strabo reflect genuine Zoroastrian practices. He describes how only dry wood may be used, how the fire may only be fanned, not blown upon, and how anyone impious enough to defile the fire with dead matter or dung was put to death. All this is consonant with the extreme care Zoroastrians have always taken not to defile their most sacred element, and Parsee priests to this day wear a cloth over the nose and mouth to prevent them blowing on the fire. Again, in the water sacrifice the Magi are said to have held a bundle of rods, a practice among the Zoroastrians that still survives. In Cappadocia, where the Magi were numerous, he notes other peculiarities which tally nicely with genuine Zoroastrian practice. The Magian priests are called *pyraithoi*, 'fire-priests', an exact translation of the Avestan *athaurvan*. Moreover, they did not kill the sacrificial victim with a knife but by striking it with a log of wood on the forehead—a custom that we meet with again in the Pahlavi books.[53] Sacrifices are no longer celebrated in the open air as they were in Herodotus' time, but in a fire-temple 'in the middle of which is an altar with a great deal of ashes on it; there the Magi guard a fire which is never allowed to go out. They enter these [temples] by day and chant for almost an hour in front of the fire, holding a bundle of rods, wearing felt head-gear which falls down on both sides so that the cheek-pieces cover the lips'.[54] All this might be said of the present-day Zoroastrians and it is strange that Strabo should report this rite as taking place in Cappadocia rather than in Persis.

Decline and Fall of 'Catholic' Zoroastrianism

In the first part of this book we have attempted to give an account of Zoroastrianism as it developed before and during the Achaemenian period, and we have seen that the Prophet's message became increasingly adulterated, probably as a result of political pressures. Yet, however much Darius' religious opinions may have approximated to those of the Prophet, and however zealous Xerxes may have been in his suppression of the cult of the *daēvas*, neither is remembered in the later Zoroastrian tradition, nor, for that matter, is Artaxerxes I who introduced a Zoroastrian calendar. This can surely only mean that the Zoroastrian reformers of the early Sassanian period did not look back on the Achaemenian dynasty with any favour: indeed, they did not so much as remember the names of the ancient kings, and speak only of 'Darius, son of Darius', by whom they presumably mean Darius III who allegedly 'commanded that two copies of all the Avesta and *Zand* should be written even as Zoroaster had received them from Ohrmazd, and that one should be preserved in the Royal Treasury and one in the National Archives'.[55] This total ignorance of the greatest Empire it has fallen to the lot of an imperial race to rule displayed by the theologians of the later Empire can only mean that the 'orthodox' never regarded the Achaemenian period as being a particularly glorious one for the Zoroastrian religion. It must have been regarded as a period of laxness and compromise in which the message of the Prophet had become obscured, and the Good Religion had come to terms with much that was not good. Thus while King Vishtāspa who befriended the Prophet and all his other associates are remembered, the far greater glories of the house of Achaemenes are totally forgotten. If they were Zoroastrians, then their Zoroastrianism was not of a kind that appealed to their successors. The antipathy of the later Zoroastrians towards the polytheism of the *Yashts* in which the Wise Lord suffers the humiliation of having to worship other gods and is incapable of preserving his own handiwork without the all-powerful aid of the external souls of men, is illustrated by the fact that no Pahlavi translation of the *Yashts* survives. This excessive aggrandisement of created spirits was not regarded as being consonant with the majesty of God, and the *Yashts*— with the notable exception of those addressed to Sraosha and Haoma— were quietly allowed to fall into disuse. During the period of the later Avesta, Zoroastrianism, the only prophetic religion ever produced by the Aryan race, very nearly lapsed right back into being a nature religion pure and simple, and was only revived in something approaching its original form by the royal protection of a self-consciously Persian dynasty, which sought to impose unity on its racially heterogeneous Empire through religious uniformity.

Of all the great religions of the world Zoroastrianism was the least well served. Zoroaster himself has every right to the title he claimed: he was a prophet and his claim to be such deserves to be taken as seriously as is that of Moses or Muhammad; but his successors never fully understood his message, nor had they a living and authentic tradition to guide them. During the Achaemenian period and after, they seem to have indulged in a liberalism and an indifferentism that was wholly at variance with the Prophet's spirit while, in the Sassanian period, they went to the other extreme and tried to impose a strict orthodoxy which few could tolerate. Moreover, they interpreted the Prophet's message so dualistically that their God was made to appear very much less than all-powerful and all-wise. Reasonable as so absolute a dualism might appear from a purely intellectual point of view, it had neither the appeal of a real monotheism nor had it any mystical element with which to nourish its inner life.

The *Gāthās* of Zoroaster, despite our relative ignorance of the language in which they are written and despite the difficulty of the Prophet's own thought, do make an impact: they have a direct and urgent message to convey: they are spiritually alive. The later Avesta, and particularly the *Yashts*, has its moments of freshness and beauty, but it neither fascinates nor awes, while the *Vidēvdāt*, the latest production of the Avestan age, shows no spiritual life at all, only a futile legalistic dualism which, if it had ever been put into practice, would have tried the patience of even the most credulous. The productions of the Sassanian and post-Sassanian age are little better: they neither inspire nor please. One is tempted to say that all that was vital in Zoroaster's message passed into Christianity through the Jewish exiles, whereas all that was less than essential was codified and pigeon-holed by the Sassanian theologians so that it died of sheer inanition.

In the long run the fall of the Sassanian dynasty had a far more lasting effect on Iran's destinies than did the fall of the far greater house of Achaemenes, for it not only smashed Zoroastrianism as a national power, but also destroyed it as a cultural influence: for the Muhammadan conquest resulted in the re-emergence from the ruins of defeat of a culture not at all Zoroastrian but wholly Muslim in content, which was to make Iran for the first time a cultural as well as a political power of the first magnitude. Islam did not succeed in Iran simply because it was the religion of the conqueror; it succeeded because Zoroastrianism, in its reformed as much as in its catholic form, had been tried and found wanting. All this does not detract one whit from the stature of the Iranian Prophet himself, who remains one of the greatest religious geniuses of all time. It merely shows how political vicissitudes can strangle the life out of even a great religion with a vital message for man, and turn it into something wholly different from what the founder had intended. Also it must be said that Zoroastrianism lacked what all other religions have had—a living and continuous tradition. When the religion was revived under the Sassanians, it must have become lamentably apparent to the reformers that they could, in fact, make nothing of their own sacred texts and had to rely, very much more than the modern scholar has to do, on mere guesswork. It is impossible to revive a religion once the well-springs of the original revelation have been allowed to dry up, and once the sacred language itself has become so sacred that it is no longer understood even by those who set themselves up as its official interpreters.

Part II

TWILIGHT

CHAPTER EIGHT

IN SEARCH OF AN ORTHODOXY

Revival of Zoroastrianism by the Sassanians—In Search of an Orthodoxy—Three Sects—The 'Mazdean' Dualists—The 'Monotheists'—The Zurvanites—Zurvanism Predominant in the Third Century AD—The Eclecticism of Shāpūr I—The High Priest Kartēr and the 'Zandīks'—Āturpāt and the 'Fatalists'—The Zurvanism of Yezdigird II and his Grand Vizier—The Synthesis of Khusraw I—Study of Indian and Greek Works—The Second Decline and Final Fall of Zoroastrianism

Revival of Zoroastrianism by the Sassanians

FROM the fall of the Achaemenian Empire until the advent of the Sassanian dynasty in AD 226 the fortunes of Zoroastrianism are wholly unclear. During the Seleucid period which followed on the overthrow of the Achaemenian Empire a deliberate attempt was made to fuse the Iranian and Hellenistic cultures, and some cross-fertilization certainly took place. Iranian deities were identified with what were considered to be their Greek equivalents, and on the great monument set up by Antiochus I of Commagene at Boghaz Köy in Eastern Anatolia the equations Zeus-Oromasdes, Apollo-Mithras-Helios-Hermes, and Artagnes (Verethraghna)-Heracles-Ares are found. This tendency was not reversed by the Parthians who, though Iranian by race, never seem to have sought to establish a centralized Empire or to revive the ancient Iranian religion as a means of consolidating their power. It is only with the emergence of the Sassanian dynasty from Persis proper in AD 226 that Zoroastrianism once again arises as a power in the Iranian lands. The story of the restoration of the 'Good Religion' after its long eclipse is told in the *Dēnkart*, though only the later developments recorded there can be regarded as fully historical. The account is, however, of sufficient interest to deserve quotation in full:

'Dārāy, son of Dārāy (sc. Darius III) commanded that two copies of all the Avesta and *Zand* (commentary) should be written down, even as Zoroaster had received them from Ohrmazd (Ahura Mazdāh), and that one should be preserved in the Royal Treasury and one in the National Archives.

'Valakhsh (Vologeses), the Arsacid, commanded that a memorandum be sent to the provinces [instructing them] to preserve, in the state in which they had been found in [each] province, whatever of the Avesta and *Zand* had come to light and was genuine, and also any teaching deriving from it which, although scattered owing to the chaos and disruption that Alexander

175

had brought in his wake and the pillage and looting of the Macedonians in the kingdom of Iran, either survived in writing or was preserved in an authoritative oral tradition.

'His Majesty, the king of kings, Ardashīr, son of Pāpak, following Tansar as his religious authority, commanded all those scattered teachings to be brought to the Court. Tansar set about his business, selected one [version] and left the rest out of the canon : and he issued this decree : "The interpretation of all the teachings from the Religion of the worshippers of Mazdāh is our responsibility : for now there is no lack of certain knowledge concerning them."

'The king of kings, Shāpūr, son of Ardashīr, further collected those writings from the Religion which were dispersed throughout India, the Byzantine Empire and other lands, and which treated of medicine, astronomy, movement, time, space, substance, creation, becoming, passing away, qualitative change, logic, and other arts and sciences. These he added to the Avesta and commanded that a fair copy of all of them be deposited in the Royal Treasury : and he examined the possibility of basing every form of academic discipline (? *argastān*) on the Religion of the worshippers of Mazdāh.

'The king of kings, Shāpūr, son of Ohrmazd (Shapur II), summoned men from all lands to examine and study all doctrines so that all cause for dispute might be removed. After Āturpāt had been vindicated by the consistency of his argument against all the other representatives of the different sects, doctrines, and schools, he issued a declaration to this effect : "Now that we have seen the Religion upon earth, we shall leave no one to his false religion and we shall be exceeding zealous." And so did he do.

'His present Majesty, the king of kings, Khusraw (Chosroes I), son of Kavāt, after he had put down irreligion and heresy with the greatest vindictiveness according to the revelation of the Religion in the matter of all heresy, greatly strengthened the system of the four castes and encouraged precise argumentation, and in a diet of the provinces he issued the following declaration : "The truth of the Religion of the worshippers of Mazdāh has been recognized. Intelligent men can with confidence establish it in the world by discussion. But effective and progressive propaganda should be based not so much on discussion as on pure thoughts, words, and deeds, the inspiration of the Good Spirit, and the worship of God (*yazdān*) paid in absolute conformity to the Word. What the chief Magi of Ohrmazd have proclaimed, do we proclaim ; for among us they have been shown to possess spiritual insight. And we have asked and continue to ask of them the fullest exposition of doctrine both in the matter of spiritual insight and in its practical application on earth, and for this we give thanks to God. Fortunately for the good government of the country, the realm of Iran has gone forward relying on the doctrine of the Religion of the worshippers of Mazdāh, that is, the synthesis of the accumulated knowledge of those who have gone before us throughout the whole of this central clime. We have no dispute with those who have other convictions, for we [ourselves] possess so much both in the Avestan language through pure oral tradition and in written records, in books and memoranda, and in the vulgar idiom by way of exegesis—in short the whole original wisdom of the Religion of the worshippers of Mazdāh. Whereas we have recognized that, in so far as all dubious doctrines foreign to the Religion of worshippers of Mazdāh reach this place from all over the world, further examination and study prove that to absorb and publish knowledge foreign to the Religion of the worshippers of Mazdāh does not contribute to the welfare and prosperity of our subjects as much as one religious leader who has examined much and pondered much in his recital [of the liturgy]; with high intent and in concert with the perspicacious, most noble, most honourable, most good Magian men, we do hereby decree that the Avesta and *Zand* be studied zealously and ever afresh so that what is acquired therefrom may worthily increase and fertilize the knowledge of our subjects. Those who tell our subjects either that it is not possible to acquire, or that it is possible to acquire in its entirety, knowledge of the Creator, the mystery of spiritual beings, and the nature of the Creator's creation, are to be deemed men of insufficient intellect and freethinkers. Those who say that it is possible to understand reality through the revelation of the Religion and by analogy, are to be deemed researchers [after truth]. Those who expound [this doctrine] clearly are to be deemed wise and versed in the Religion. And since the root of all knowledge is the doctrine of the Religion, both in its spiritual power and through its manifestation here on earth, a man [who speaks in this cause] speaks wisely, even if he derives the doctrine from no Avestan revelation. So he should be esteemed as [speaking] in accordance with the revelation of the Religion, the function of which is to give instruction to the sons of men." '[1]

In Search of an Orthodoxy

From the whole of the above document it is abundantly clear that from the very beginning of their dynasty the Sassanian kings were profoundly interested in the restoration of the 'Religion of the worshippers of Mazdāh', the national religion that had Ahura Mazdāh, or Ohrmazd as he was now called, as its god; for the Sassanians, who, like the Achaemenids, originated in the province of Persis or Pārs as it was now called, reacted violently against the racial and religious syncretism that had characterized former regimes. Their approach both to politics and to religion was nationalistic. There were exceptions, of course: Shāpūr I, for instance, was at one time seriously interested in the new religion proclaimed by Mānī, the founder of the Manichees, and Kavāt very nearly brought the Empire to a premature end by his infatuation with the personality and doctrine of the heretic Mazdak. But these exceptions, for once, prove the rule; for these kings, unlike the Parthians, were interested in religion as such, they were no indifferentists or crude '*politiques*'. Apart from these purely religious aberrations, the

Sassanian kings saw in Zoroastrianism the only answer to the rising dogmatisms of both Christianity and Manichaeanism. They came into power in the third Christian century, and they were thereby faced with a challenge which their 'irreligious' predecessors had not had to meet; for just as the Christian refusal to conform to the minimum requirements of Emperor-worship in Rome affronted the Roman authorities, so did this new and basically intolerant creed seem to threaten the imperial unity of the Iranians that the early Sassanian monarchs were consciously trying to impose. But whereas Rome had no rival dogmatism to oppose to the new religion, Sassanian Persia at least had the remnants of an ancient tradition of its own, and the Sassanian kings conceived it their duty gradually to rebuild the shattered edifice and make of it something that in doctrine and controversy could be squarely set against the newer systems. Sassanian Persia was in search of an orthodoxy.

According to the tradition preserved in the *Dēnkart*, efforts to reconstitute the lost Avesta were made even under the Parthians, but it remained for the new dynasty to reduce the scattered writings to a coherent corpus of doctrine. This would appear to have been undertaken by a priest called Tansar during the reign of the founder of the dynasty, and he seems to have arrogated to himself the sole right to interpret the reconstituted scriptures. From this time on concern with religious orthodoxy among the Zoroastrians themselves was very much in the air. It is, however, not at all easy to determine what this orthodoxy was before the time of Khusraw I, from whose definitive reform of the Zoroastrian faith the doctrines enshrined in the Pahlavi books as we have them today arose.

Three Sects

From the non-Zoroastrian sources it is clear that at least three distinct sects of Zoroastrians existed, of which only the most strictly dualist was finally triumphant. The differences between them resemble in some respects the early Christian controversies concerning the Nature and Person of Christ and the interpretation of the doctrine of the Holy Trinity: they seem to have been purely theological and did not affect the day-to-day life or the liturgy of the faithful. The crucial issue for the Zoroastrians was the origin of evil, and how far, if at all, the permission of evil might be attributed to God. The three different solutions propounded by the sects can all be seen as rival interpretations of the meaning of the Gāthic stanzas, *Yasna* 30.3–4, which must here be quoted again:

'In the beginning the two Spirits who are the well-endowed(?) twins were known as the one good, the other evil, in thought, word, and deed. Between them the wise chose rightly, not so the fools. And when these Spirits met, they established in the beginning life and death, that in the end the followers of the Lie should meet with the worst existence, but the followers of Truth with the Best Mind.'

On the lips of Zoroaster this probably meant that Ahura Mazdāh, the Wise Lord, had created two spirits from his own mind who were required to make their irremediable choice between good and evil at the beginning of time: *by their choices* they became the Holy Spirit and the Destructive Spirit, and this choice was so radical that the Holy Spirit could say to his enemy: 'Neither our thoughts, nor our teachings, nor our wills, nor our choices, nor our words, nor our deeds, nor our consciences, nor yet our souls agree.'[2] God, then, is the author of the two Spirits, the one of whom chooses good, the other evil. Since he is omniscient, he must have known that one of the Spirits would choose 'to do the worst things', and to that extent he permits evil. Zoroaster's God, however, was the Wise Lord who transcended the two Spirits, though he associates only with the Holy one, and utterly rejects the other. However, later Zoroastrianism, as we have seen, identified the Wise Lord completely with the Holy Spirit, and a new problem therefore arose. What was meant by the statement that the Holy Spirit (now merely another name for Ahura Mazdāh) and the Destructive Spirit were twins? Did this mean that they had a common parent, or did it mean that they were co-eternal principles? Alternatively, could one legitimately derive the Evil Principle from God himself?

The 'Mazdean' dualists

The second alternative was that adopted by the orthodoxy of the Pahlavi books which was, however, not accepted by the whole Zoroastrian community even after the overthrow of the Good Religion by Islam. The great Muhammadan theologian Al-Ghazālī, writing at the beginning of the twelfth century, quotes this fully dualist doctrine as being typical of the Magi, and says of them that:

'They worship absolute light which comprises all lights. They think that it is the Lord of the worlds, and that all good things are to be attributed to it. They see, however, that evil things exist in the world, and they will not allow them to be attributed to their Lord, wishing to keep him clean away from evil. So they conceive of a struggle between him and the darkness and attribute the [origin of the] universe to both light and darkness, which they sometimes call God and Ahriman.'[3]

This is an accurate description enough of the religion we find in the

Pahlavi books, all of which—even those which show deviationary tendencies—firmly take their stand on the 'two Principles'. So a Zoroastrian catechism which happens to have come down to us, only amplifies the position Ghazālī attributes to the 'dualists':

'This must I know without venturing to doubt: I came from spirit, nor was I [always] in the world. I was created, and have not [always] been. I belong to Ohrmazd, not to Ahriman; to the gods, not to the demons; to the good, not to the evil. I am a man, not a demon. I am a creature of Ohrmazd, not of Ahriman. . . . I must firmly believe that there are two principles, one the Creator, and the other the Destroyer. It is the Creator, Ohrmazd, who is all goodness and all light, and the accursed Destroyer, Ahriman, who is all evil, full of death, a liar and a deceiver.'[4]

The 'Monotheists'

This is the position of orthodoxy as it developed in the last religious crisis of the Sassanian period, the final restatement of a categorical dualism which seems to have resulted from the religious reforms of Khusraw I—these reforms themselves being necessitated by the religious anarchy provoked by the Mazdakite heresy of the previous reign. Yet this was not the only form of Zoroastrianism known to non-Zoroastrian writers; for another Muhammadan writer, no less reliable than Ghazālī, attests a different version of the Zoroastrian solution of the problem of evil which is not dualistic at all. The Muslim heresiographer, Al-Baghdādī, who died in AD 1037, refers repeatedly to the Magians, but so far from attributing to them a categorical dualism, declares that they believed that God created Ahriman and that between them they manage the affairs of the world, God doing only what is good, and Ahriman what is evil.[5] This form of Zoroastrianism is attested elsewhere,[6] and Shahristānī, another Muslim heresiographer, goes so far as to say that this was the original doctrine of the Iranians which was supposed to have originated with Gayōmart, the first man in the Zoroastrian tradition.[7] The Zoroastrian texts, however, preserve no clear trace of this doctrine although it, too, can be legitimately inferred from the Gāthic passage quoted above.

Two sects of the Zoroastrians were recognized by the Muslims as 'people of the book' and thereby liable to the poll-tax in lieu of military service. This means that in Muslim eyes they were the recipients of a true revelation comparable to that of the Jews and Christians, and were considered orthodox by their own religious authorities as opposed to other sects which, though they called themselves 'Magians', were not so recognized.[8] These were the Zurvāniyya and the Maskhiyya. Of the first we shall have much more to say later, and we will only allow the second to detain us for a moment. Baghdādī, who is again our source for this information, does not directly mention the strict dualists at all, and he can then scarcely be referring to them when he speaks of the *Maskhiyya*. The word literally means 'Transformationists', and presumably refers to the sect which attributes the origin of Ahriman, the Devil, to God—the transforming, then, of something in the good Principle—an 'evil thought' according to Shahristānī—into its opposite, evil. This sect, which claimed immense antiquity, is only attested in Muslim sources, but there can be little doubt that it existed, for theirs is a view to which the modern Parsees are again reverting. Since, however, there is no clear trace of it in the Pahlavi books, it is quite possible that it was what the Zoroastrians told their Muslim masters they believed in order to be accepted by them as true monotheists. In any case there is no evidence that they ever had any influence in Sassanian times.

The Zurvanites

The case of the *Zurvāniyya* or Zurvanites, as they are usually called in English, is quite different and vastly more complicated; for it is this form of Zoroastrianism, of which only the vaguest traces exist in the Pahlavi books, that is attacked by both Christian and Manichaean apologists who wrote during the Sassanian period. It has, then, sometimes been inferred that Zurvanism was the dominant form of Zoroastrianism during the whole of that period. This, however, is to over-simplify the issue.

Zurvanism differs from the two forms of Sassanian Zoroastrianism we have so far considered in that it introduces a third character into the cosmic drama in addition to Ohrmazd and Ahriman: this is the *Zrvan Akarana* (Pahlavi *Zurvān i Akanārak*) or 'Infinite Time' of the Avesta. The Zurvanite solution of the problem of evil is again based on *Yasna* 30.3–4, which it interprets literally. There it is unequivocally stated that the Holy Spirit and the Destructive Spirit were twins; and, if they are twins, then they must surely have a parent. Who, then, was this parent? We know that in the *Gāthās* Ohrmazd, that is, Ahura Mazdāh, himself was said to be the father of the Holy Spirit and therefore, presumably, of the Destructive Spirit too. But for the later Zoroastrianism, Ohrmazd and the Holy Spirit were identical; and it was therefore necessary to find a parent for Ohrmazd himself, for he had now become one of the 'twins'. As early as the *Gāthā* of the Seven Chapters, Ohrmazd had been identified with light and, it is fair to assume, Ahriman with darkness, and later they were assigned their respective spheres, the one on high in endless light, the other below in endless darkness. Thus each limited the other: neither transcended space and time. To the religious consciousness a limited God—limited by space if not by time—can never be wholly satisfying. The Zurvanites, then, would seem to have invented a myth out of *Yasna* 30.3–4 (in which the two Spirits are spoken of as twins) according to which the parent of the finite Spirits was the Infinite—infinite space as well as infinite time. This would appear to be the origin of the Zurvanite myth which makes Zurvān or Infinite Time the original principle from which light and darkness, good and evil, Ohrmazd and Ahriman, proceed. This is borne out by the earliest reference we have to this myth in a Greek source; for according to Eudemus of Rhodes, a disciple of Aristotle, the Magi and all the Aryan race:

'call the whole intelligible and unitary universe either Space or Time from which a good god and an evil demon were separated out or, according to others, light and darkness before these. Both parties, however, suppose that this dual constitution of the higher [powers] is subsequent to and differentiated out of undifferentiated being (*physis*). One [of these higher powers] is ruled by Ohrmazd, the other by Ahriman.'[9]

This is the earliest account of the Zurvanite myth that has come down to us, and there is no serious reason to doubt that its attribution to Aristotle's pupil is authentic[10] since it has not yet assumed the stereotyped form we find in the later sources. In this case we may be certain that the two views concerning the origin of evil were both current in the fourth century BC, for Aristotle himself mentions the view of later orthodoxy according to which there are two principles, a good spirit and an evil one, one of which is called Zeus or Oromasdes (Ohrmazd), and the other Hades or Areimanios (Ahriman).[11]

In its original form, then, the myth would seem to say no more than that infinite Time-Space originated the two 'principles' of light and darkness, Ohrmazd and Ahriman. It is a theological speculation on *Yasna* 30.3–4 designed to show just how the good and evil powers can be twins; and infinite Time-Space is chosen as the ultimate source of all things simply because it alone is infinite, God having already ceased to be so. The choice was, indeed, a natural one, since the liturgy itself was heavily concerned with the veneration of units of time and space and culminates in a final invocation of both Infinite Time and 'Space which follows its own law'.[12] By the time the Sassanian dynasty was founded, both strict dualism and the Zurvanite modification of it were fully alive.

Thus, though it is evident that the Sassanian kings were vitally interested in finding a Zoroastrian orthodoxy which could meet the

Christians and later the Manichees on their own ground, they would seem from the beginning to have been faced with a choice between two theological trends within Zoroastrianism itself, each of which claimed to be orthodox; and it is not without interest to see how the trends alternated during the Sassanian period.

Zurvanism Predominant in the Third Century AD

It would appear that when the dynasty succeeded in ousting the Parthian Arsacids in AD 226, the Zurvanite form of the Good Religion was in the ascendant. This seems to be certain from the evidence supplied by the Manichees. Mānī began his mission in AD 242 during the reign of the second of the Sassanians, Shāpūr I, with whom he had an interview in Susiana,[13] and he had high hopes of converting that monarch to the new faith. With this aim in mind he dedicated the only work he wrote in Persian, the *Shāhpuhragān*, to him. At first he met with the royal favour, spent much time in the royal suite, and was given full liberty to preach his religion wherever he wished. Mānī too was a dualist, but his dualism was of a radically different order from that of the Zoroastrians. The latter conceived of evil as a *spiritual* principle, either as the Lie or, more personally, as Ahriman, the Destructive Spirit; matter they regarded as the creation of Ohrmazd and as such holy—and in its most simple forms—as fire, water, earth and wind—they worshipped it as divine; they tended fire and water with elaborate ceremony and deep reverence because they were in very truth *gēteh amahraspandān*, 'Bounteous Immortals of this earth'.[14] Throughout their whole motley history they did not falter on this point; they reverenced the natural world because it was a reflection of the supernatural, and because it was God's creation. Mānī's dualism provided a sharp contrast to this this-worldly interpretation of the universe. Though a Parthian nobleman by birth his roots were in Gnosticism, not in Iran. His dualism was not a dualism between an abstract principle of good and an abstract principle of evil, but between light which he identified with spirit and darkness which he identified with matter. He knew full well that his doctrine cut at the roots of everything that Zoroastrianism stood for, but he was an extremely clever propagandist and knew that the particular brand of Gnostic pill he had to offer could only be made palatable to the Iranians if it were sugared over with an Iranian terminology. So, for each of the deities and demons which proliferated in his system in luxuriant profusion he found an Iranian equivalent. The two systems had this, at least, in common: they conceived of good in terms of light, and evil in terms of darkness. But it was on what constituted moral good and moral evil that they so profoundly differed. In both systems, however, the good God was symbolized by light, and this light was regarded as dwelling on high, far removed from the realm of darkness. The Manichaean Father of Greatness or Father of Light was indeed so nearly identical with the Zoroastrian Ohrmazd that one would be astonished indeed if Mānī had not called him Ohrmazd in his Persian writings. Yet he did not; he called him Zurvān. This is all the more astonishing in that the Zurvān of the Zurvanite myth cannot be exclusively associated with light in that he gives birth to both light and darkness, Ohrmazd and Ahriman. This amounts to proof, it would seem, that in the first half of the third century at least it was Zurvān, not Ohrmazd, who was regarded as the supreme deity in Zoroastrianism. The revival of Zoroastrianism under the first two Sassanian monarchs would, then, seem to have been a revival of that religion in its Zurvanite manifestation. This would certainly seem to be true of Shāpūr I, who himself inclined towards Manichaeanism, though it is much more doubtful in the case of his predecessor, Ardashīr I, for the Pahlavi books, from which practically all trace of Zurvanism has been eliminated, reverence him and his high priest Tansar as the founding fathers of the Zoroastrian revival.

The Eclecticism of Shāpūr I

Politically both Ardashīr and Shāpūr were interested in finding a religion which would solder together the heterogeneous nationalities that went to make up their Empire. For Ardashīr no alternative presented itself except Zoroastrianism in one or other of its dominant forms; but with the arrival of Mānī on the scene with a brand-new religion that claimed to be the fulfilment not only of Zoroastrianism, but also of Christianity and Buddhism as well, Shāpūr was presented with an attractive alternative and for a time was tempted by its unifying possibilities. Could the various religions represented in his Empire be persuaded to accept this new faith which claimed not only to fulfil all previous dispensations, but also to restore them to their pristine purity? Shāpūr was at first inclined to think so. He was, however, reckoning without taking into account his own high priest, Kartēr, who had no intention of allowing the new religion to interfere with his own plans for making Zoroastrianism the sole tolerated religion of the entire Empire. The persecution of the Manichees, in all probability, did not begin in Shāpūr's reign, but at least he was weaned away from the Manichaean allegiance and persuaded to carry on the work of reconstructing Zoroastrianism which his father had begun. His contribution to this process was, however, rather different from that of the other kings cited in the *Dēnkart* passage we quoted at the beginning of this chapter, for while both Ardashīr and Shāpūr II threw the full weight of the royal authority into the scales of one individual teacher who was almost certainly a straight dualist, and whereas Khusraw I put the seal of his approval on the decisions reached by the principal Magians in conclave, Shāpūr I, so far from narrowing the scope of renascent Zoroastrianism, sought to incorporate into it elements from other cultures. He:

'collected those writings from the Religion which were dispersed throughout India, the Byzantine Empire, and other lands and which treated of medicine, astronomy, movement, time, space, substance, creation, becoming, passing away, qualitative change, logic, and other arts and sciences. These he added to the Avesta . . . and he examined the possibility of basing every form of academic discipline on the Religion of the worshippers of Mazdāh.'

His political aim, then, and the method he thought best to achieve it, remained the same: finding that Manichaeanism was meeting with too tough an opposition from the Zoroastrian clergy, he decided to add to the Avesta a whole corpus of philosophical and scientific matter both from the Eastern Roman Empire and from India. Whether or not this included works attributed to Zoroaster by the Greeks it is impossible to say. The Pahlavi books, however, in so far as they are philosophical, show an unmistakable Aristotelian influence, and one case at least of direct borrowing from an Indian source seems certain. Again, however, we cannot be certain whether this dates from the time of Shāpūr or Khusraw I.

The mention of time and space in the catalogue of the topics which Shāpūr is said to have introduced from abroad is interesting, for, as we have seen, in the earliest reference we have to the Zurvanite myth, it is Time or Space which is regarded as being the first undifferentiated principle from which light and darkness, good and evil proceed. This, of course, rather adds to the confusion of the picture, for we do find speculations about the nature of time and space in the Pahlavi books which seem to be Hellenistic in origin and perhaps quite unconnected with the Zurvanite myth as such. We shall try to clarify this when we come back to tackle the Zurvanite problem as a whole. For the moment we must be content to say that Shāpūr I expanded the sacred canon by adding much philosophical material that was not Iranian at all, and that the form of Zoroastrianism he adhered to was Zurvanite rather than Mazdean (as we will call the pure dualism of orthodoxy); otherwise Mānī's adoption of the name 'Zurvān' to represent his own 'Father of Greatness' would be incomprehensible.

The High Priest Kartēr and the 'Zandīks'

The death of Shāpūr left the religious field open to his fanatical high priest Kartēr. A long and detailed inscription of this man, which was first published in 1940,[15] brought to light a major religious and political personality who had hitherto been unknown except as the inquisitor who did Mānī to death.[16] From this inscription it appears that he was the principal agent in the Zoroastrian revival that took place in the first century of Sassanian rule. Under him Zoroastrianism appears for the first time as a fanatical and persecuting religion. The list of the sects persecuted, however, shows how justified the early Sassanian kings were in seeking a unifying force that would weld their Empire together, for not only do we find Jews, Christians, Manichees, and Mandaeans (*Nāsōrāyē*) mentioned, but also Buddhists and Brahmans; all these Kartēr claims to have chastised. Zoroastrianism was actively enforced under the Magian hierarchy, the last vestiges of *daēva*-worship were uprooted and the worshippers of the *daēvas* were brought back to the true religion. Every effort was made too to extirpate all non-Zoroastrian religions, including the 'Zandīks' who were probably Zurvanite materialists,[17] and, what is more, strict uniformity was to be the rule within the Zoroastrian Church itself. 'Heretics and apostates(?),' Kartēr tells us, 'who were within the Magian community, were spared for the religion of the worshippers of Mazdāh and the rites of the gods but not for [the spread of] propaganda: I chastised and upbraided them and improved them.'[18] Uniformity of belief was, then, certainly enforced, and the probability is that this unity was along strictly dualist and Mazdean lines. Kartēr's policy must then be seen as a reaction, under a series of weak kings, against the personal religious policy of Shāpūr.

Shāpūr had tried to broaden the basis of Zoroastrianism so as to include much purely secular material derived from foreign sources, and the speculation on time and space, etc., which the *Dēnkart* mentions may well have brought into Zoroastrianism doctrines which were at variance with its basic beliefs. Among these was probably a form of materialism which derived everything from Infinite Time—a heresy attacked by the Muslims no less than by the Zoroastrians[19]—and which denied the existence of both heaven and hell, and of rewards and punishments. These are the doctrines which Kartēr, in his inscriptions, repeatedly and fervently upholds, and the inference is that they had formerly been denied by persons calling themselves Zoroastrians. These would be the Zandīks[20] of the inscription—those who follow their own interpretation (*zand*) of the Avesta. It is a moot point whether such persons may legitimately be termed 'Zurvanites', and we will have to return to this later, but in so far as they derive all things from Infinite Time (*Zurvān*), they may aptly be called 'Zurvanite materialists'. These were among the people persecuted by Kartēr.

Āturpāt and the 'Fatalists'

Kartēr did not, however, succeed in stamping out heresy altogether; for further action had to be taken during the reign of Shāpūr II (AD 307–379), and this time there can be no doubt that the orthodoxy upheld was of a strictly dualist kind, for the hero of this particular drama is the high priest Āturpāt, son of Mahraspand, to whom the Pahlavi books look back as to the very embodiment of orthodoxy. Āturpāt submitted himself to the ordeal by molten metal and emerged from it victorious 'during his controversy with all manner of sectarians and heretics. He triumphed over the greatest of the heretics among them, who were also called "fatalists".'[21]

Zoroastrianism, as proclaimed by the Prophet, was essentially the religion of free will, and even the Destructive Spirit, Ahriman, is evil not by nature but by choice. It is true that very soon this freedom was taken from him, and he became an evil *substance* incapable of change, but freedom of will was at least left to the creatures of Ohrmazd. With the rise of Zurvanism, however, fate took on a menacing importance, and man became a puppet in its hands. This was a direct challenge to a doctrine that was central to the Prophet's own teaching, and it was to vindicate this that Āturpāt submitted to the ordeal. Thus while Kartēr condemned a form of materialism associated with Zurvān or Infinite Time, Āturpāt vanquished the fatalists who saw in Zurvān as *finite* Time the absolute master of man's fate. Both doctrines ran directly counter not only to the Mazdean dualist orthodoxy but also to the teaching of the Prophet himself. The one denied the existence of rewards and punishments on which the Prophet had laid such immense stress, the other denied man's free will and thus subjected him to rewards and punishments for deeds he had no choice but to do.

The Zurvanism of Yezdigird II and his Grand Vizier

Zurvanism, however, was far from dead and seems to have been consciously revived by one of the great Sassanian Grand Viziers, Mihr-Narsē, who continued in office during the three reigns of Yezdigird I, Bahrām V, and Yezdigird II. It was, however, only during the reign of the last that he seems to have embarked on a career of religious proselytism in which the particular object of his attention was Christian Armenia. Now the Armenian historian, Elishē Vardapet, a contemporary of Yezdigird II, tells us that, in his efforts to convert the

Armenians by peaceful methods, he issued a decree demanding the adherence of the Armenians to the Good Religion, accompanying it with a digest of the religion they were supposed to adhere to. There is no good reason to doubt the authenticity of this digest since of the many sources that retail the Zurvanite myth in its classical form, Elishē is, with his fellow-Armenian, Eznik of Kolb, the oldest—and his testimony is supported by the Christian martyrs, Ādhur-Hormizd and Anāhīdh, who were put to death during Yezdigird's reign.[22] The digest is, in fact, the Zurvanite myth relating the birth of Ohrmazd and Ahriman from Zurvān.[23]

There is, however, further evidence that Mihr-Narsē was a Zurvanite for he named his eldest son Zurvāndāt, that is either 'created by Zurvān' or 'one who follows the law of Zurvān', and he was duly elevated to the rank of high priest during the reign of Bahrām V. To name one's *eldest* son after Zurvān would, of course, imply a particular reverence for that deity; but this of itself would not amount to proof that Mihr-Narsē was a Zurvanite. This Zurvāndāt, however, is mentioned in the Pahlavi books—and in no complimentary terms; for whereas Mazdak, the Communist prophet who so nearly gained control of the Empire under Khusraw I's predecessor Kavāt, whom he had converted, is described as the 'apostate' *par excellence*, Zurvāndāt is described as the 'tyrant' or 'heretic' (*sāstār*) *par excellence*. In another Pahlavi work Mihr-Narsē himself whom, from other sources, we know to have been a most efficient and upright administrator, is said to have been received into a position of trust(?) by Yezdigird II because he was a sinner! It would, then, seem certain that during the reign of Yezdigird II Zurvanism was the official religion of the Empire.[24] The Zurvanism of Yezdigird and Mihr-Narsē, however, must be distinguished both from the Zurvanite materialism which Kartēr combated and from the fatalism over which Āturpāt triumphed. The variety propagated by Mihr-Narsē may be described as 'classical' Zurvanism: it taught that Zurvān, a highly personalized and mythologized Infinite Time, was the father of Ohrmazd and Ahriman. This doctrine was probably proscribed during the reign of Khusraw I since it has entirely disappeared from the Pahlavi books.

The Synthesis of Khusraw I

Khusraw I succeeded to the throne at a time of particular unrest. A new religion preached by a 'prophet' Mazdak, among the most notorious and revolutionary of whose tenets was the communization of wealth and women, had won the favour of the former monarch, Kavāt, whereas, it can be assumed, the Zurvanism propagated under

Yezdigird II still received the official sanction of the Magian hierarchy. Khusraw celebrated his accession to power by tricking Mazdak into a gruesome death and by a general massacre of his followers. Within the Zoroastrian Church he re-established the dualist orthodoxy of Āturpāt and vested full authority in the Magian hierarchy. 'He united the people of his realm in the religion of the Magians, and forbade them discussion, divergence of opinion, and controversy in the affairs of state'.[25] Khusraw, however, realized that if Zoroastrianism were to survive, it was not enough simply to impose it by force. If it were to compete intellectually with its rivals, it would have to equip itself with the philosophical weapons which they used. Khusraw, therefore, took a personal interest in Greek philosophy and granted asylum at his court to seven philosophers from Athens who had fled the Byzantine Empire when the schools of philosophy were closed.[26] In this respect Khusraw sought to combine the syncretistic approach of Shāpūr I with the rigid dualist orthodoxy sponsored by Shāpūr II. He regarded Zoroastrianism as the specifically national religion to which Iran owed its greatness, but it must no longer be a religion that was not prepared to learn from others; it represented the 'synthesis of accumulated knowledge of those who had gone before'. This synthesis he regarded as being now capacious enough to stand its own ground against all comers. This rather surprising self-confidence is reflected in the large tolerance he accorded to Christianity—a tolerance, however, that did not permit them to make further converts.

Study of Indian and Greek Works
It was during Khusraw's reign too that Indian works were translated into Persian, and both Indian and Greek learning were treated with respect. These foreign writings, we read:

'have recently been arranged by scholars, for they were brought from foreign countries: they have been considered and studied, nor have they been neglected or slightingly received on account of their inferiority and foreign name. It happened, indeed, that with the growth of knowledge they became more highly esteemed, and they did not suffer on account of the outlandish names attached to the books. No single book or volume was discovered which contained in its entirety all the science and learning [contained] in [other] books and volumes, but each [school] carried out research on the basis of its own original book or volume.'[27]

From this and other evidence it would appear that Khusraw, though he insisted on doctrinal uniformity within the Zoroastrian Church itself, nevertheless encouraged a rational approach to religion as such; and this seems to have been accepted by the Magian hierarchy who, considering the problem of evil to be at the very heart of religion, thought their own dualist solution was alone philosophically tenable. This encouragement of a philosophical and rationalistic approach to Zoroastrianism may well have spelt the ruin of Zurvanism whose solution of the problem of evil could satisfy no one. 'Analogy', that is a philosophical approach to religion, was henceforward to have its place in Zoroastrianism; revelation and reason were seen not as antagonistic, but as complementary, and the study of the sacred literature was given new encouragement.

This encouragement, however, came too late; for although the actual performance of the liturgy, which included the recitation of the *Gāthās*, had been handed down from Magian father to Magian son throughout the dark years that intervened between the fall of the first and the rise of the second Persian Empire, the faithful repetition of the word had been accompanied by no complementary understanding of the sense. The Magi of Khusraw's time no longer understood the meaning of the words the Prophet had uttered, and it is indeed possible that it was only then that they committed them to writing, for Khusraw himself speaks of the Avesta as being 'orally' handed down; he does not speak of it as a book. Sassanian Zoroastrianism, then, as finally reformed, had no secure scriptural basis from which to build up its doctrines. The purely scriptural portions of the Pahlavi books are thus composed largely of bits and pieces of mythological matter of very varying merit, whereas it is the purely speculative portions that alone succeed in holding our attention. We search them in vain for any sign of an exalted spirituality.

The Second Decline and Final Fall of Zoroastrianism

Khusraw I's was the last great reign of the Sassanian epoch, and little need be said of the last reigns of the dynasty. Suffice it to say that what vitality the Zoroastrian religion may have possessed in the early days of revival and reform, it must have lost in the years that followed Khusraw's death. The extent of this degeneration is illustrated by the fact that after the Iranian Empire had been overthrown by the Muhammadan conqueror, Zoroastrianism, itself an essentially national Iranian religion, was not able to capture resurgent Iranian nationalism when it finally asserted itself against the Arab. Neither the early Iranian dynasties nor the writer of Iran's national epic were Zoroastrians. Firdausī, indeed, was a pious Shī'a Muhammadan, and we look in vain through the pages of the epic of Zoroastrian Iran for anything that might enlighten us on the religion its heroes practised. Zoroastrianism, with all the vicissitudes that marked its long history, is presented to us in a uniformly pietistic and respectably monotheistic garb: Zurvanites and dualist Mazdeans might never have existed. Though the decline of the Good Religion after the Muslim conquest was not as rapid as is sometimes supposed, and though the Pahlavi books as we have them today were only written down in the ninth century or after, Zoroastrianism was already a dying thing when the Muslims finally administered the *coup de grâce*; and the sad fact remains that Iran only emerged as a powerful cultural as well as political power when she repudiated her own national religion which she owed to her own prophet, Zoroaster.

Yet, despite all this, the Sassanian period represents the high-water mark of Zoroastrianism. The impetus that led to its revival and to its adoption as the imperial cult was largely nationalistic, and herein lay its principal weakness. Much of the later Avesta concerned itself with Iranian national folklore, and the gods that had come to be invoked alongside Ahura Mazdāh were Iranian national gods who could only make an appeal to a pagan society. The Sassanian theologians seem to have been aware of this, for, despite the Zurvanite heresy, they restored Ahura Mazdāh or Ohrmazd to his ancient eminence; he became once again the supreme creator and conserver of all that is good. On the other hand the importance that Mithra, Anāhitā, and the other gods had lost was gained by Ahriman, the Devil. Ohrmazd, it is true, no longer had any serious rival on his own side, but his position *vis-à-vis* his eternal enemy was very much weaker than it had ever been in the Prophet's mind. This was almost as true of the Zurvanite scheme of things as it was of the Mazdean, for though, in both systems, the triumph of the good was theoretically assured, the dark twin displayed in Zurvanism an intelligence not granted to him in the orthodox system, which might have been deemed to weigh strongly in his favour.

The Zurvanite question itself must have weakened the Zoroastrian propaganda effort against both Christians and Manichees considerably; for though it is not difficult to discover at what periods 'pure' Mazdeanism was predominant and at what periods Zurvanism held sway, it is unlikely that either ever entirely prevailed, and Zoroastrianism was therefore unable at any time to present a united front against its rivals. True, the difference between the two schools of thought was purely theological, but since the theological point at issue concerned the nature of God, and the nature and origin of evil, any divergence here would invalidate the claim of Zoroastrianism to be a *revealed* religion. Things had changed very much since Achaemenian times. Zoroastrianism, which owed what authority it possessed to Zoroaster's claim to be the chosen Prophet of God, had not only to face the prophetic claims of Jewry, but had also to cope with two new and militantly proselytizing religions—Christianity and Manichaeanism, both of which claimed to be divine revelations. At the beginning of the Sassanian period not only was the Good Religion in a state of extreme disarray, it had also become so cluttered up with its own pagan heritage that the Prophet's message was all but smothered. The Sassanian theologians were genuinely concerned with rediscovering the teaching of the Prophet, and, no doubt, both Zurvanites and Mazdeans regarded themselves as authentic exegetes of the Prophet's teaching. Both parties failed in the long run because they lost sight of the transcendent majesty of God which was central in Zoroaster's thought. The Mazdean dualists consciously accepted this: they accepted a finite God who creates, not because it is his good pleasure to do so, but because he has to interpose a barrier between himself and the Enemy he knows will attack him. The strength of their position, they thought, lay in its rationality. The Zurvanite compromise, however, was from every point of view unsatisfactory; for in seeking to re-establish the unity of the godhead, they produced a god who was neither omnipotent, omniscient, nor good—a god who, as we shall very soon see, suffered from a failure of nerve. Religiously unsatisfying as Mazdean dualism may have been, it was, even so, a good deal better and a good deal more sensible than the setting up, over and above the principles of good and evil, of a first cause that was so uncertain of itself that it unwittingly gave birth to the Devil.

From our available sources it is quite impossible to say how bitter the battle between dualists and Zurvanites was, but the repeated attacks of the dualists against Zurvanism in all its forms throughout the Sassanian period would seem to show an awareness on their part that the whole core of what they considered to be the Prophet's message was being nibbled away. Zurvanite materialism, which Kartēr had combated, denied the basic Zoroastrian doctrines of heaven and hell, rewards and punishments. Zurvanite fatalism did away with man's free will and the choice that the Prophet demanded that he should make between good and evil; whereas mythological Zurvanism reduced Zoroaster's God, the Wise Lord, to the status of an originated being. All three heresies were successively attacked during the Sassanian period, and all three would seem to have enjoyed royal patronage for a short time, the first under Shāpūr I (AD 241–272), the second shortly before the accession of Shāpūr II and during the early decades of his reign (AD 309–379), and the third during and after the reign of Yezdigird II (AD 438–457). Yet, despite the efforts of Khusraw I, the heresy was never finally scotched, and faint traces of it can still be found in the Pahlavi books.

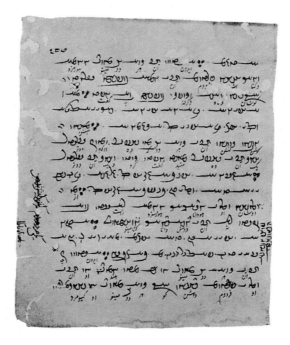

1a, b

Two pages from the oldest extant manuscript of the *Avesta*: the Avestan text of each line is followed by a translation in Pahlavi. These two pages tell of the encounter of the Primordial twins (*p.* 42)

2

The symbol of the 'great god' Ahura Mazdāh used by the Achaemenian kings: this particularly well-preserved example is from Darius' palace at Persepolis (*pp.* 155–8)

3

The tomb of Cyrus the Great (died 529 BC) at Pasargadae, now a solitary monument on the vast plain

DARIUS THE GREAT

4, 5

Darius (*c.* 549–485 BC) receives the homage of the defeated 'kings'. He faces the god Ahura Mazdāh, to whose aid he attributes his victory (*pp.* 155–8). (*Below*) Close by this relief is Darius' great inscription, describing his suppression of rebellions throughout the Empire. The inscription is in three versions: Persian, Elamite and Accadian. These carvings are high up on the rock of Bīsitūn (*p.* 20)

6

Darius leaves the Council Chamber at Persepolis. One of his attendants carries the royal parasol while the other holds a fly-whisk in one hand and a towel in the other. The symbol of Ahura Mazdāh can be seen suspended above the king

7

Detail of the head of Darius from the carvings at Bīsitūn

8

King Darius enthroned, Persepolis, holding a sceptre and a
lotus symbolizing royalty: behind him stands his son and
heir, Xerxes. They are receiving a high court dignitary in
audience, while the air is perfumed by incense burners

9

The tomb of Darius at Naqsh-i Rustam: the relief shows the
king worshipping Ahura Mazdāh in front of a fire altar

SPLENDOUR OF PERSEPOLIS

10-11

A general view of the palace at Persepolis. Darius I constructed the huge terraces on which the palace stands, using stone hewn from the hills above. To the right is Xerxes' Hall of a Hundred Columns, once roofed with timber. The city itself stood on the plain below. (*Below*) Detail of the palace

12

(*Right*) Detail of Xerxes' Hall of a
Hundred Columns

13

Part of the great frieze at Persepolis,
representing Median and Persian
rulers. The latter are wearing fluted
tiaras

THE EMPEROR XERXES

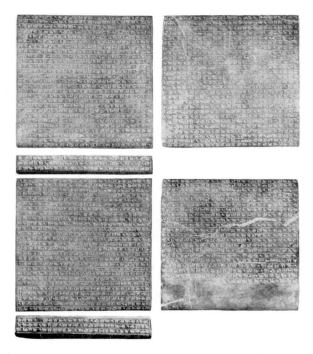

14

The *Daiva* inscription of Xerxes (died 465 BC), discovered at Persepolis (*p.* 159)

15

The tomb of one of the Achaemenian kings, probably Xerxes, in the hills above Persepolis. The king is shown in prayer before Ahura Mazdāh, opposite a small fire altar

ACHAEMENIAN FIRE TEMPLES

16-17

Ruins of Achaemenian fire temples:
at Bishāpūr and (*below*) at Naqsh-i
Rustam, commonly known as the
Ka'ba of Zoroaster

18

Artaxerxes I giving audience, from the portico of the Hall of a Hundred Columns. It was he who introduced the Zoroastrian calendar (*p.* 155)

19

Zāl, the father of the traditional Iranian hero Rustam, is tested in his religious knowledge by the Magi, who are questioning him: a later Islamic manuscript (*pp.* 240–2)

EXTINCTION OF THE FIRST EMPIRE

20-21

The battle of the Issus in 333 BC between Alexander the Great and Darius III brought the first Persian Empire to an end: a Roman mosaic at Pompeii. (*Below*) A later Islamic miniaturist's interpretation of the same battle

22-23

The rival commanders: Darius the Persian and (*below*) Alexander the Macedonian

THE WORSHIP OF MITHRAS

24

Antiochus I of Commagene faces the god Mithra. The religion of Commagene was a Hellenized form of Iranian paganism, the Iranian gods being identified with their nearest Greek equivalents. In this way Mithra was identified with Apollo, Hermes and the sun (*p.* 175)

25-26

(*Below left*) *Deus Arimanius*, 'the god Ahriman': the lion-headed deity in Mithraism is probably a version of the Iranian Ahriman. He holds the keys that unlock the door to Heaven. (*Below right*) The signs of the Zodiac on his body and the fact that he is standing on the globe of the world show that the lion-headed god was regarded as the 'Prince of this World' from whom the initiate sought escape (*pp.* 129–30)

27

Mithras slays the bull, thereby renewing the fertility of the earth and bringing immortality to his followers. The dog and the snake (representing good and evil creation) dispute the blood of the sacrificial victim, while the scorpion in attacking the bull's scrotum seeks to stifle life at its source (*p.* 130)

28

In this statue of Mithras' sacrifice the blood of the bull is identified with the new corn. As usual, Mithras is flanked by two torchbearers, Cautes and Cautopates, who are miniature doubles of himself (*pp.* 141–3)

THE SASSANIAN EMPIRE

29

Anāhitā, goddess of the waters, is also a goddess of fertility (*pp.* 145–6)

30

(*Below*) A rock-relief at Naqsh-i Rustam shows the investiture of the founder of the Sassanian Empire, Ardashīr I, by the god Ohrmazd (the newer form of the ancient name Ahura Mazdāh), who is represented in human shape. Ardashīr revived Zoroastrianism after its six hundred year eclipse (*p.* 176)

31

The captive Roman emperor Valerian kneels before Shāpūr I. Shāpūr was responsible, too, for the introduction of fresh ideas into sacred Zoroastrian literature, and favoured the prophet Mānī, founder of the Manichaean religion (*pp.* 184–5)

32

Under the Sassanians the god Ohrmazd was represented in human form, rather than in the winged, symbolic form of the Achaemenians: a detail from a relief at Shāpūr showing the investiture of Bahrām I by the god

33

After the death of Shāpūr I, the High Priest, Kartēr, put Mānī to death (AD 242) and restored orthodox dualism in place of the innovations probably introduced by Shāpūr (p. 186)

34

Part of the great inscription of Kartēr, carved beside him (p. 186)

35

Yezdigird II (AD 438–457) seems to have favoured the Zurvanite form of Zoroastrianism. His Vizier, Mihr-Narsēh, was as fervent in his espousal of this cause as Kartēr was in opposing it (reproduced twice actual size) (*pp.* 187–8)

36

The Sassanians, too, built fire temples: ruins at Shāpūr

37

The imperial palace of Khusraw II at Ctesiphon: Muhammad is said to have sent an emissary to this last great Sassanian monarch, bidding the Great King submit to the new faith. His refusal led to the collapse of the second Persian Empire and its state religion, Zoroastrianism

ZOROASTRIANISM AS SEEN BY ISLAM

38

With the coming of Islam Zoroastrian legends became distorted and much of their meaning lost. A Muslim version of the story of Mashyē and Mashyānē: Ahriman here appears as an old man, tempting the first human beings with an apple. This *motif* is not Zoroastrian but borrowed from the story of Adam and Eve (*p.* 267)

39

Jamshid, the modern form of the Avestan *Yima Khshaēta*, "bright Yima", is sawn in two (*p.* 139)

40

Gushtāsp, the later version of th
Avestan Vishtāspa (Zoroaster's roya
patron), entertains the legenda
King Isfandiyār. In the *Persian Ep*
by Firdausi historical fact is mixe
up with legend but the conversion
Vishtāspa (*p.* 133) by Zoroaster
remembered: the figure behind th
King's throne is probably intende
to be Zoroaster

41

In the Muhammadan period Khus
raw I became the ideal of Irania
kingship. His justice was proverbi
as was the wisdom of his Vizie
Buzarj-mihr. As the picture show
his justice was not always tempere
by mercy

THE PARSEE COMMUNITY

42

Priests officiating in a Parsee temple in Bombay. The fire altar is on the right. The cloth covering the priests' faces was observed by the Greek traveller Megasthenes (quoted by Strabo) (*p.* 169)

43

In this 'Tower of Silence' in Bombay the bodies of the dead are exposed to be eaten by vultures. This mode of the disposal of the dead was probably introduced into Zoroastrianism by the Magi (*pp.* 161–5)

44-45

Modern Zoroastrian ceremonies: the marriage service and
(*below*) the *Naojote*, or initation of the child into full member-
ship of the Parsee community

CHAPTER NINE

THE VARIETIES OF ZURVANISM

The Pahlavi Books—Priestly Brothers: Mānushchihr and Zātspram—The Influx of Greek and Indian Ideas—The 'Zandīks' and 'Dahrīs'—'Classical' and Materialist Zurvanism—The Zandīk Ontology and Metaphysics—Mēnōk and Gētēh—Creative Evolution—The Dualist Interpretation of Evolution—A Zurvanite View of Evolution—The Three Types of Zurvanism— Zurvanite Fatalism—'Classical' Zurvanism—The Zurvanite Myth—Zurvān and the Pact between Ohrmazd and Ahriman

The Pahlavi Books

THE Pahlavi books, which were in the main written in the ninth century AD, some three centuries after the fall of the Sassanian Empire and the extinction of the Zoroastrian religion as the official creed of the Iranian peoples, remain our principal source for the Zoroastrianism of the Sassanian period. They do not, however, give us any clear picture of the theological development and the gradual crystallization of the orthodox dualist position that must have taken place during this period. No hint is allowed to appear in them that throughout its silver age Zoroastrian dualism was carrying on a running fight with the Zurvanite heresy in one form or another. That such a fight did go on can only be discovered from the inscriptions and from the Christian and Manichaean polemics directed against the Zoroastrians. What the exact nature of this heresy was, is, then, extremely difficult to determine. Traces of it, however, survive in the Pahlavi books themselves, and one 'Zurvanite' treatise written in New Persian in the thirteenth century, incongruously known to us as the '*Ulamā-yi Islam*', 'The Doctors of Islam', still survives.

Of the Pahlavi books themselves by far the most important from the theological point of view is the *Dēnkart*, a corpus of religious knowledge that runs into nearly a thousand printed pages. The first two books and part of the third are no longer extant, but what remains of the third book is our most important source of Zoroastrian theology and religious science—for the Zoroastrians claimed that the full religious revelation contained in the Good Religion held the keys of the physical as well as the spiritual universe: it was an all-embracing 'gnosis' or 'science'. Of the remaining Pahlavi books two contain passages that are at least 'semi'-Zurvanite in tendency. These are the *Mēnōk i Khrat*, 'The Spirit of Wisdom', and the *Selections of Zātspram*. The first of these is an imaginary dialogue between a wise man and personified Wisdom. In places it shows a tendency towards fatalism which is foreign to Zoroastrian orthodoxy.

Priestly Brothers: Mānushchihr and Zātspram

In the ninth century, it would appear, the religious life and thought of the Zoroastrian community was dominated by two brothers, both of whom were high priests. The one was Mānushchihr, High Priest of Shīrāz and Kirmān, the other Zātspram, High Priest of Sirkān. Both brothers have left treatises dealing with the central doctrines of Zoroastrianism, and it is clear from Mānushchihr's own *Epistles*, which are directed explicitly against his brother's innovations in the matter of purificatory rites, that he regarded him as little better than a Manichee. 'You should know,' Mānushchihr writes to his brother, 'that were you to speak in the assembly of the Tughazghaz, you would find few to contradict you.'[1] The Tughazghaz were not only a Turkish tribe, which was bad enough; they were also Manichees, which was very much worse. This was a serious accusation, and it is apparent from Zātspram's own writings that the charge was not baseless. Zātspram is Zurvanite to the extent that he at least recognized Zurvān, for him a highly personalized Infinite Time, as a principle independent of both Ohrmazd and Ahriman and as, in some sense, the arbiter between them. He was the last protagonist of a once powerful heresy; but the heresy is already a much diluted version of the original, for Zātspram dare no longer affirm that Ohrmazd and Ahriman are originated beings deriving from Infinite Time which alone is uncreated.

If Zātspram can be regarded as the last of the Zurvanites, Mānushchihr saw himself as the very embodiment of orthodoxy, and his major work, the *Dātastān i Dēnīk*, 'The Religious Norm', can be regarded as an authoritative statement of orthodoxy. Equally orthodox in the dualist sense is the *Shkand-Gumānīk Vichār*, an 'Analytical Treatise for the Dispelling of Doubts', by a certain Mardān-Farrukh who also flourished in the ninth century. This is in some ways the most interesting of all the Zoroastrian books since it presents a philosophical justification of Zoroastrian dualism in a more or less coherent form; and it further contains a detailed critique of the monotheistic creeds, Islam, Judaism, and Christianity as well as an attack on Zoroastrianism's dualistic rival, Manichaeanism.

Of the remaining Pahlavi books only the so-called *Bundahishn* need detain us. *Bundahishn* means 'original creation', and this indeed is one of the topics with which the book deals. Apart from this, however, it deals, somewhat cursorily, with a wide variety of topics ranging from Ahriman's attack on the good creation and the resurrection of the dead on the one hand to a discussion on the nature of plants, animals, etc., on the other.

The Influx of Greek and Indian Ideas

Such, then, are the main sources on which we must rely for our information on the Zoroastrianism of the Sassanian period. The 'orthodoxy' they reflect is that imposed on the Zoroastrian Church by Khusraw I. It is, however, not to be supposed that that monarch had eliminated all questionable doctrine from the corpus of writing in the Pahlavi tongue which constituted the Sassanian Avesta. This corpus, which probably bore little relation to what of the original Avesta had survived in the Avestan language, had already been heavily adulterated with extraneous material, and this material, once it had become embedded in it, passed off as having divine sanction. Shāpūr I, it will be recollected, had 'collected those writings from the Religion which were dispersed throughout India, the Byzantine Empire, and other lands, and which treated of medicine, astronomy, movement, time, space, substance, creation, becoming, passing away, qualitative change, logic, and other arts and sciences. These he added to the Avesta and commanded that a fair copy of all of them be deposited in the Royal Treasury; and he examined the possibility of basing every form of academic discipline on the Religion of the worshippers of Mazdāh.'[2]

Little is known of what 'writings from the Religion' can possibly have been circulating in India, but it is clear from the *Dēnkart* and the *Shkand-Gumānīk Vichār* that Aristotelian philosophy had been adopted into the main stream of Zoroastrianism, and that this philosophy, on occasion, took on some very queer forms. We know from our Greek sources that some very curious works circulated under Zoroaster's name in the Hellenistic world, and that Zoroaster was supposed to have been the preceptor of Pythagoras whom he allegedly met in Babylon;[3] and it can therefore be surmised that works circulating under Zoroaster's name might contain Pythagorean ideas. That this may have been so will come out in the sequel.

Dualist orthodoxy was first proclaimed by Kartēr shortly after the death of Shāpūr I, and in reasserting what he considered to be the principles of traditional dualism as against all watering-down of this 'true' doctrine, he singled out for attack not only the non-Iranian religions, but also the Zandīks. Who, precisely, were these Zandīks?

The 'Zandīks' and 'Dahrīs'

In Muhammadan times the word *Zandīk* (in its Arabicized form *Zindīq*) continued to be used to indicate two classes of people who had only this in common, that they were recognized by neither Muslims, Christians, Jews, nor Zoroastrians, and that they were regarded by the Muslims as being particularly pernicious heretics, the shedding of whose blood was lawful. The two classes of heretic which the term covered were the Manichees on the one hand, and those materialists who believed in the eternity of the world and denied that there was a creator on the other. According to the Arab historian Mas'ūdī, the term was first used during the reign of Bahrām I who—with the intervention of a reign lasting only one year—followed on Shāpūr I, that is to say, when the High Priest Kartēr was at the height of his power. The term *Zandīk* was coined to denote all those who based their teaching on the *Zand* or 'commentary' on the Avesta rather than on the Avesta itself. The term was used both of the Manichees and of all those 'who believed in the eternity of the world and denied that it had been originated'.[4] In later times these two different types of Zandīks were differentiated, the Manichees being usually referred to simply as 'dualists', and the materialists as *Dahrīs*,—*dahr* being the Arabic word for 'time'. The roots of both sects are, however, in Sassanian Persia, and long antedate the Muhammadan era.

The great Muhammadan theologian, Al-Ghazālī, classifies the various philosophical schools into Dahrīs, naturalists, and theists. Of the Dahrīs he says:

'The first school, the Dahrīs, are one of the oldest sects. They deny the existence of a creator and disposer who is omniscient and omnipotent. They think that the world has always existed of itself and as it [now] is, without a creator; and that animals have always sprung from seed and seed from animals. So has it [always] been, and so will it be forever. These are the Zandīks.'[5]

The Zandīks mentioned in Kartēr's great inscription, therefore, probably included both Manichees and materialists, and the 'commentary' or '*Zand*' that at least the latter followed was probably to be found in those writings deriving from the Byzantine world which treated of movement, time, space, etc., and which were incorporated into the Avesta by Shāpūr I. In the Zoroastrian writings themselves these Dahrīs or Zandīks, who are equated with the Sophists,[6] were felt to be un-Iranian.[7] They must have constituted a hellenizing party which still claimed to be Zoroastrian, and which could defend its orthodoxy by saying that it was following authentic teachings of Zoroaster which, though lost in their original form when Persepolis was sacked by Alexander, had miraculously survived in a Greek translation;[8] these translations had now been restored to their rightful place in the canon of the Avesta by the action of the king of kings.

Al-Jīlī, one of the later Muhammadan mystics, tells us that these same Dahrīs refrained from all acts of worship because, believing in the eternity of Time, they venerated it as God in his essence, as pure potentiality, and not as an actual creator.[9] Jīlī, then, would have it that, beneath the materialism of the Dahrīs, there was a mystical element of pure contemplation of the Godhead in its essence; and, as we come to examine some of the more abstruse texts of the *Dēnkart*, we shall perhaps be disposed to agree with him. From the side of orthodox dualist Zoroastrianism, Mardān-Farrukh attacks the Dahrīs, but makes no allowance for any mystical element there may have been in their beliefs. For him they are out-and-out materialists.

'Different [from the atheists proper],' he says, 'are the atheists called Dahrīs. They give up their religious duties and make no effort to practise virtue: [rather] they indulge in endless discussion. . . . They believe that Infinite Time is the first Principle of this world and of all the various changes and [re-]groupings to which its members and organs are subject as well as of the mutual opposition that exists between them and of their fusion with one another. [They believe too] that virtue goes unrewarded, that there is no punishment for sin, that heaven and hell do not exist, and that there is no one who has charge of [the rewarding of] virtue and [the punishment of] sin. [They believe too] that all things are material and that the spiritual does not exist.'[10]

These were the 'Zandīks' or 'Dahrīs' whom Kartēr persecuted. This seems certain because Kartēr makes a point of affirming the very doctrines that the Zandīks deny. In no uncertain terms he bids the passer-by to remember that 'heaven exists and hell exists, and whoso is virtuous will go to heaven, and whoso is vicious will be cast into hell'.[11] Since the Zandīks saw in Infinite Time the one ultimate and changeless principle from which all else proceeds, they must be considered as Zurvanite materialists. Their doctrines were almost certainly derived from those 'scientific' works which Shāpūr I had incorporated into the Avesta from Byzantium and India. Indeed, the idea that Time is the source of all things is perhaps derived from India rather than from the Hellenistic world. Already in the *Maitrī* Upanishad (*c.* 500 BC?) we find Time identified with the supreme principle; and Time has two forms, the 'timeless', which is without parts, the eternal 'now', and time which is divisible into parts as it is normally understood: the first is 'Time without form', the second the 'form' of Time.

From Time do contingent beings flow forth,
From Time too do they advance to growth;
In Time too do they return home.[12]

Time, for the Indians, was not simply time as we understand it. As the Infinite it is the raw material, the *materia prima*, of all contingent being. As Being it is the source of all becoming: it is Infinite Time-Space and it becomes embodied in the universe, and 'this embodied Time is the ocean of creatures'[13]. Ideas not unlike these reappear in the *Dēnkart*, and efforts, often not very successful, were made to adjust them to the exigencies of a dualist theology.

It would seem certain that at the time of this influx of Greek and Indian ideas into Sassanian Zoroastrianism, Zurvanism in its mythological form already existed; otherwise Mānī's choice of Zurvān rather than Ohrmazd to represent his own 'Father of Greatness' would be inexplicable. Zurvān, then, already conceived of as infinite Time-Space, the whole intelligible universe from whom a good and an evil daemon proceed, or who gives birth to light and darkness before these[14] —Zurvān, already referred to in the Avesta as the 'Infinite'—must inevitably have coalesced with the more abstract concept of infinite Time-Space as primal matter, the ultimate source of all things, which the Iranians probably derived from India, and which they combined with the Aristotelian key concepts of matter and form, potentiality and actuality.

'Classical' and Materialist Zurvanism
The two types of Zurvanism, however, were originally quite distinct and derived from quite different sources. Mythological Zurvanism starts as an attempt to explain what Zoroaster could have possibly meant when he said that the Holy and Destructive Spirits were twins. It picks on the Infinite (Time or Space) as being the only possible 'Absolute' from which the twins could proceed: it is the source of the good in the one and the evil of the other, of light and of darkness in which they respectively have their beings. It elevates Zurvān or Infinite Time to the status of father of the spirits of good and evil, the father of light and darkness. It thereby makes Ohrmazd, now identified with Zoroaster's Holy Spirit, subordinate to Zurvān—Zurvān himself remaining a shadowy figure over against which the cosmic drama plays itself out.

Materialist Zurvanism, the religion of the Zandīks, however, is quite different from this. Its leading idea, namely, that infinite Time-Space which is itself without form, though the source of all that has form, is probably of Indian origin, but the philosophical development of the idea is worked out along Aristotelian lines. The whole thing, as the *Dēnkart* says, is un-Iranian. Both types of Zurvanism, however, present a direct challenge to the orthodox dualism, and both challenge it where it is weakest—in its conception of a godhead which, though perfectly good, is nonetheless limited by a positive power of evil. Zurvanism brings a new dimension into Zoroastrianism—the dimension of an eternity which is not simply infinite duration, but a condition that is beyond space and time, and which, being itself a state of perfect rest, must also be the source from which all movement and all action proceed. Orthodoxy tried to wrestle with this problem and offered not one but many solutions. The result was that in the end their rigid dualism gave way to an unsure 'trialism' in which there were not two principles only, but three—Ohrmazd, the good God, Ahriman, the Devil, and a neutral principle of primal matter, infinite Time-Space which is beyond good and evil and possessed of neither intelligence nor will.

As we have had occasion to say time and time again, Zoroaster's God creates *ex nihilo*—he thinks the world into existence. In the words of another prophet he says: 'Be,' and it is. Both the Greeks and the Indians, however, accepted it as axiomatic that nothing can arise out of nothing. Either, then, God emanates both the intelligible and sensible orders from himself, or he gives form to an eternally existing primal matter. It was the latter view that predominated in Sassanian orthodoxy, and we find it explicitly stated that 'no form can be brought into being from not-being, nor can it be made to return thither'.[15] Creation is no longer a philosophically respectable idea: the Prophet's insight had been forgotten, and the Sassanian theologians became the victims of two alien philosophies which had no roots in Iran.

For, since the initiative of Shāpūr I, orthodoxy was in no position utterly to reject the new philosophy which had been grafted on to the restored Avesta; it could only seek to combine it with its own dualism as best it could. It is quite true that under Shāpūr II, Āturpāt, son of Mahraspand, once that he had defeated his rivals, did his utmost to re-establish a more simple dualist belief in which the purely philosophical element was minimized; for, to judge from the extant sayings attributed to him, his emphasis was primarily on practical morality, and it would seem that only under Khusraw I was a balance struck between faith and reason. Khusraw certainly regarded faith in the revealed texts as being primary, but he also demanded that faith should be substantiated by reason. Should the two appear to conflict, then the decision rested with the authority of the college of Magi; they would have to decide how the various portions of the reconstituted Pahlavi Avesta, which presumably still contained the foreign material introduced by Shāpūr I, were to be interpreted and how they were to be reconciled.

The Zandīk Ontology and Metaphysics

What the Zandīks appear to have done was to single out those passages from the 'Avesta' and Zand which suited their purposes, and to have ignored the ancient traditional doctrines altogether. This would be all the easier for them to do in that there never seems to have been any clear dividing-line between what was 'Avesta', that is, the 'received text' of revelation, and what was Zand or 'commentary',[16] the two together being known to the Muslims indifferently as the Avestā u Zand or the Zand u Avestā which was later to appear in European languages as Zend-Avesta. These Zandīks or Zurvanite materialists, in fact, wholly denied three Zoroastrian dogmas, that is, the existence of a good God and an Evil Spirit, the freedom of the human will to choose between good and evil, and the rewarding and punishment of individual souls according to their good and evil deeds. Moreover, they also believed that 'all things are material and that the spiritual does not exist'.

Mēnōk and Gētēh

The Pahlavi words for 'spiritual' and 'material' are, in this context, mēnōk and gētēh, and they derive from the Avestan words mainyu and gaēthya. Mainyu derives from the same root as Latin mens and our own mind: it is what thinks, chooses, and wills—what distinguishes the purely spiritual gods as well as man from all the rest of creation. Gaēthya derives from a root gay-, jay-, meaning 'to live'; it means anything that is possessed of physical life, and since all material things were regarded by the Zoroastrians of the 'catholic' period as being in some sense alive, gaēthya came to mean 'material'. The two words, then, corresponded exactly to what is called 'spiritual' and 'material' in other Near Eastern religions.

With the introduction of Aristotelian terminology, however, these simple religious concepts became confused. 'Matter', for Aristotle, was of itself so nebulous a concept that it could hardly be said to exist at all until it received 'form'. Thus the classic pair of opposites is, for him, not matter and spirit, but matter and form. It is true that the Iranians found suitable words other than mēnōk and gētēh to express these ideas,[17] but they re-defined mēnōk and gētēh in accordance with Aristotelian principles. Because the mēnōk or spiritual side of man which included mind, will, and consciousness, was regarded as being immaterial, the word was re-defined as meaning a single, uncompounded substance without parts, invisible and intangible;[18] and because Aristotle's 'matter' was also invisible and intangible, 'matter' in its primary unformed state was also described as *mēnōk*.[19] Thus there are three forms of *mēnōk* existence, the two *mēnōks* or 'Spirits' of orthodox theology, neither of which is the *material* cause of the material and physical world, and a third *mēnōk*, which is the totally unformed primal matter of Aristotelian philosophy, the unseen source of all material things. The Armenian historian, Eznik of Kolb, noticed this discrepancy and pointed out that the Zoroastrians were divided into sects, and that among them there were some who admitted two principles only while others accepted three.[20] In fact, even the fully orthodox account of the creation admits the existence of a third entity between Ohrmazd who dwells on high in the light and Ahriman who prowls below in the darkness: this entity is the Void, otherwise called Vay; and 'Vay' is simply the Pahlavi form of the ancient god Vayu used now to mean the 'atmosphere' that separates the heavenly lights above from the infernal darkness below. To this mythological account of the creation we shall have to return once we have considered the various philosophical interpretations of creation preserved in the *Dēnkart*. Some of these come perilously near to the position of the Zandīks or materialist Zurvanites.

Creative Evolution

Mēnōk, we learn, used in the quite new sense of invisible and intangible primal matter, is uncompounded,[21] and devoid of parts;[22] it is called *ras*, the 'wheel'.[23] The 'wheel' seems rather an odd name to apply to what Aristotle would have called 'primal matter' and calls for some explanation. It is, however, the word used elsewhere for the 'wheel' of heaven, the heavenly sphere in which the whole material creation is contained. This 'heavenly sphere' or firmament is thought of as comprising the whole material creation; it is the macrocosm in the image of which man, the microcosm, is made; it is the universe as it is when fully formed, the 'world' or *gētēh*.

Matter, however, can neither be created nor destroyed; hence, primal matter, which is one, devoid of parts, and lacking all form, is also called *ras*, the 'wheel'. Itself eternal, it is the source of all becoming.[24] It is infinite Time-Space, the *Zrvan Akarana* mentioned in the Avesta. Space is the pre-condition of matter, and Time is its eternity, and without infinite Time-Space there could have been no creation.[25] The word 'creation', of course, implies a creator and in most of the cosmological passages in the *Dēnkart* Ohrmazd appears as the creator who fashions forth his creation from primal matter; he gives form to the formless Time-Space continuum. There are, however, two passages in which no reference at all is made to a creator;[26] the whole process of creation is represented as an automatic process of 'becoming' from a unitary, infinite and eternal Time-Space. Time-Space is the primal 'matter' from which all 'becoming' proceeds. 'Becoming' is perhaps not the best translation of the word *bavishn* which seems to stand for a state of indeterminate being from which the whole evolutionary process starts, for it is also called the 'seed' and the 'seed of seeds'. Even so it is posterior to Time-Space and originates from it. The whole process of evolution from primal matter (Time-Space) to the fully developed universe is seen as taking place in four stages. These are called 'becoming', the 'process of becoming', the 'stabilization of becoming', and finally the 'world', *gētēh*. This scheme of things, which makes no mention of a creator God is, of course, wholly un-Zoroastrian; it is a purely materialistic and mechanistic interpretation of the universe, yet it lays claim to scriptural authority, for it uses the phrase 'as is said in the Religion'. This 'Religion' is obviously not the Avesta as we know it; it can only refer to the Graeco-Indian writings imported into the Sassanian Avesta by Shāpūr.

This fourfold scheme of evolution, however, whatever its source, is repeated again and again in the *Dēnkart*, and efforts are made to fit it into a strictly dualist framework. The three stages that precede the emergence of the fully differentiated cosmos—becoming, the process of becoming, and the stabilization of becoming—are elsewhere equated respectively with two of the four 'natural properties', the hot and the moist; with the four elements (fire, air, water, and earth); and with organic life as manifested in animals and men. Again, 'becoming', that is, the hot and the moist, is called 'primal matter', 'unformed and the origin of all material forms'; the 'process of becoming', that is, the four elements, is 'mediary matter' or 'potential form', while the 'stabilization of becoming', defined as 'form detached from matter', is 'ultimate matter'.[27]

To make confusion worse confounded the 'process of becoming' is also called the 'first form' and the 'stabilization of becoming' the 'second form', while living creatures are termed the 'third form'.[28] 'Matter' and 'form' are, of course, basic to Aristotle's philosophy, but in the *Dēnkart* the author rarely seems to understand what the terms mean and uses them in an exceedingly arbitrary way. The terminology is Aristotelian, but the evolutionary cosmogony we meet with seems to be peculiar to the *Dēnkart*. In substance it would seem to be nearer to Indian thought and particularly to the *Maitrī* Upanishad, which also distinguishes three stages in the evolutionary process, than it is to Aristotle.

The two passages from the *Dēnkart* from which we have drawn these curious evolutionary ideas are thus almost indistinguishable from the mechanistic materialism of the Zandīks, for they are concerned exclusively with the development of the material world, and say nothing at all about spirit. Only in the last sentence of each is any reference made to good and evil. 'From the world (*gētēh*),' we read, '[proceed] specific things and persons together with their respective operations, or, as the Religion says: "From the world proceeded that which grew together within both the two Spirits—righteousness and unrighteousness." '29 This, presumably, is a concession to traditional orthodoxy, but it is a strange one; for, though it mentions the 'two Spirits', that is, Ohrmazd and Ahriman (though not a word was said of them in what went before), it implies that good and evil, righteousness and unrighteousness, too, proceed *naturally* from the now fully differentiated and individuated material 'world'. We are moving in a circle of ideas in which Ohrmazd and Ahriman find no natural place.

The Dualist Interpretation of Evolution

Now, in Greek physics the four primary properties are the hot, the cold, the moist, and the dry; yet the stage called 'becoming' in our texts is equated with the hot and the moist only. Why, one wonders, should this be? The reason can only be that, in the Iranian tradition, Ohrmazd was identified with the hot and the moist, Ahriman with the cold and the dry, for 'the substance of Ohrmazd is hot and moist, bright, sweet-smelling, and light',30 while that of Ahriman is 'cold and dry, heavy, dark, and stinking'.31 So, when orthodoxy attempted to adapt the purely physical account of the evolution of the universe which they imported from Byzantium or India to their own way of thinking, they excised the cold and the dry from the group of the natural properties because they were considered to constitute the substance of Ahriman—and the material world is created by Ohrmazd, not by Ahriman. Further, of the four elements it is the air which is hot and moist according to Aristotle,32 and the air or wind is identical with the ancient god Vayu who, in the orthodox cosmology, has become the Void which separates the kingdom of light from the kingdom of darkness; and this Void is the raw material from which Ohrmazd forms the material universe.

The *Dēnkart* is by no means a consistent whole; least of all is it so in its description of the origins of the universe. Because this is so, we are able to register the modifications that a purely mechanistic and atheistic doctrine which was incongruously grafted on to the Avesta, underwent at the hands of the orthodox. The fourfold evolutionary scheme is accepted, but it is no longer an automatic process. It is controlled and directed by Ohrmazd. The re-definition of *mēnōk* as meaning not only the traditional 'spirit, intellect, and will', but also all that is beyond the physical senses, that is, primal matter as understood by Aristotle, is accepted; but the world no longer proceeds automatically from this primal matter which is the Time-Space continuum, but is formed by Ohrmazd in the same way that a diadem is fashioned out of gold by a goldsmith, or a spade out of iron by an iron-founder.[33] *Ras*, that is, primal matter and the embodiment of Time-Space, now appears as the 'implement' which Ohrmazd wields against his eternal enemy. The material world was drawn forth from the unseen 'to strive against the author of disorderly movement (*ōshtāpāk*), that is, to repel the Adversary of creation; and this has as its corollary an eternal increase in well-being. This is what it was created for. . . . No action undertaken by any material creature exists which is not aimed at the repulse of the author of disorderly movement.'[34] Creation, then, is God's reasoned reaction against the attack he foresees must come from the opposing side. The evolutionary process is now no longer a purely automatic process of development inherent in the very nature of matter. The 'seed' or first origin of the material world is now not *from* the *ras* or Time-Space continuum: it results 'from the creative activity of the Creator *through the instrumentality of* the power of Time-Space (*ras*)'.[35] Time-Space is thus the instrument which God uses to bring his enemy into the open. What is more, eternal Time-Space is now identified not simply with primal matter but with the Endless Light which is Ohrmazd's eternal habitat; and creation, in its various stages, is thus seen as an ever-diminishing reflection of the divine light.[36]

A Zurvanite View of Evolution

Similar ideas are developed on more strictly dualist lines in another passage in the *Dēnkart*.[37] Here the *mēnōk* or invisible world in general is described as being single and uncompounded; but within this unity, it appears, the basic polarity of light and darkness is latently present, and this polarity also includes the polarity of life and death. Through God's creative activity, creation emerges from its pristine unity into a multiplicity of compound beings, 'visible and tangible', and these again will return to their source. The original unity, however, becomes differentiated into the four natural properties of hot, moist, cold, and dry—the hot and the moist being the principle of life, and the cold and the dry being the principle of death; and it is the mere fact that the hot and the moist are *naturally* alive that enables them to develop in material form. The cold and the dry are sterile by nature and cannot develop any living organism. What appear to be physical manifestations of evil and were traditionally so in earlier Zoroastrianism—wolves, serpents, and heretics, for example—are rather physical manifestations of the original light possessed by an evil spirit: they are the garments put on by the demons. Now, this would appear to be almost exactly the theory of creation which Eudemus of Rhodes attributed to the Magi; for, according to him, the Magi called the whole intelligible universe (which is a unity) Space or Time, and from this unity either a good god and evil demon proceeded, or light and darkness before these. Similarly, in our *Dēnkart* passage the *mēnōk*, defined as 'uncompounded' (*a-ham-būt*), 'single' (*ēvtāk*), 'invisible and intangible', divides into the *mēnōk* of light and that of darkness, the first being the principle of life and the second of death. Light, life, hot and moist we know to be of the substance of Ohrmazd, and darkness, death, cold and dry are no less of the substance of Ahriman. Both, then, according to this account, proceed from the single, undifferentiated *mēnōk* which we have encountered elsewhere as the *ras*, primal matter or Space-Time. The dualism between the two opposing Spirits is there all right, but it is a dualism that proceeds from a primal unity. This is the Zurvanite heresy in philosophical disguise.

The Three Types of Zurvanism

We have seen that three types of Zurvanism were combated in Sassanian times. First there were the Zandīks, Zurvanite materialists who derived all creation from infinite Space-Time, who denied heaven and hell, did not believe in rewards and punishments, and did not admit the existence of the spiritual world. With these we are now familiar. Secondly there were the straight fatalists, and lastly the Zurvanites proper who regarded Infinite Time, in its personification as the god Zurvān, as being the father of the twin Spirits of good and evil, Ohrmazd and Ahriman.

Zurvanite Fatalism

Both the orthodox and the Zurvanite heretics regarded creation as being a limitation of infinite space and infinite time. Primal matter is reduced to an orderly cosmos, and this is the embodiment of limited time and space. Thus the cosmos is a living organism bounded by the heavenly sphere which, being itself limited time-space, controls all that is within it, for it is the soul of the world.[38] All that takes place in the twelve thousand years which is the life-span allotted to this material creation, is, then, controlled by the sphere, and by the twelve constellations and the seven planets that inhabit it. Human destiny, then, must be in the hands of these astral powers. This was the second

Zurvanite heresy—astrological fatalism—and it, too, ran directly counter to the Prophet's clear affirmation of the absolute freedom of the human will. Like all things, however, in this state of mixture of good and evil, the luminaries are divided between the good god and his enemy: the constellations or Signs of the Zodiac are on the side of Ohrmazd, whereas the planets are literally the spawn of Satan.[39] Whatever good Ohrmazd transmits to his creatures through the constellations risks being intercepted by the malevolence of the planets and being re-distributed unjustly.

'The twelve Signs of the Zodiac . . . are the twelve commanders on the side of Ohrmazd, and the seven planets are said to be the seven commanders on the side of Ahriman. And the seven planets oppress all creation and deliver it over to death and all manner of evil: for the twelve Signs of the Zodiac and the seven planets rule the fate of the world and direct it.'[40]

Of the Pahlavi books that have come down to us it is the *Menōk i Khrat* that shows the most pronounced fatalist tendencies. The orthodox themselves did not deny that one's earthly condition was ruled by fate; what they did deny was that fate could affect moral action on which man's ultimate salvation or damnation depended; these rested squarely in man's own hands. In places the *Menōk i Khrat* comes perilously near to denying this. Fate not only determines one's earthly lot, but also one's character.

'Though [one be armed] with the valour and strength of wisdom and knowledge, yet it is not possible to strive against fate. For once a thing is fated and comes true, whether for good or the reverse, the wise man goes astray in his work, and the man of wrong knowledge becomes clever at his work; the coward becomes brave, and the brave man becomes cowardly; the energetic man becomes a sluggard, and the sluggard energetic: for, for everything that has been fated, a fit occasion arises which sweeps away all other things.[41] [So too] when fate helps a slothful, wrong-minded, and evil man, his sloth becomes like energy, and his wrong-mindedness like wisdom, and his evil like good: and when fate opposes a wise, decent, and good man, his wisdom is turned to unwisdom and foolishness, his decency to wrong-mindedness; and his knowledge, manliness, and decency appear of no account.'[42]

Such were the views of the Zurvanite fatalists against which the High Priest Āturpāt, son of Mahraspand, struggled during the reign of Shāpūr II; but though he won his battle and saved the doctrine of free will for Zoroastrianism, fatalism, in the long run, triumphed over its rival; for, with the coming of Islam to Iran, it found a ready ally, and Firdausī himself, who did more than any other man to revive the glories of their Zoroastrian past in the minds of his fellow-countrymen, paints a picture of Zoroastrianism that in no way reflects the spirit of hopeful free enterprise that is characteristic of all phases of that religion; rather he shows us a universe inexorably ruled by an ineluctable fate, subject to the revolving heavens and a pitiless Time in which all man's striving and all his heroism crumble away to dust.

'Classical' Zurvanism

Zurvanism proper, it would appear, did not receive official sanction until the reign of Yezdigird II, although it must have existed as early as the fourth century BC as the testimony of Eudemus shows. It was a heresy which, unlike the Zurvanite materialism we have discussed, originally owed nothing to the foreign accretions introduced by Shāpūr I. It was genuinely Iranian and Zoroastrian in that it sought to clarify the enigma of the twin Spirits which Zoroaster had left unresolved. If the Holy and Destructive Spirits, or Ohrmazd and Ahriman, as they had now become, were indeed twins, then they must have had a father; and this father, according to the Zurvanites, was Zurvān, the Zrvan Akarana of the Avesta, Infinite Time personified.

The myth of the two primeval twins who are born of Infinite Time is only attested in non-Zoroastrian and anti-Zoroastrian sources: only the late 'Ulamā-yi Islām[43] among the Zoroastrian sources preserves it in a modified form. Among the Pahlavi books Zurvān appears as a god, and not simply as the principle of Infinite Time, in both Zātspram and the Mēnōk i Khrat; he is also given a brief notice in the Bundahishn catalogue of deities. In the Dēnkart he never appears under his own name, but is simply referred to as 'infinite time' (zamān i akanārak).

The Zurvanite Myth

The myth is preserved in a number of Christian sources[44] which differ but little among themselves, and the purport of it is roughly as follows:

When nothing existed at all, neither heaven nor earth, the great god Zurvān alone existed, whose name means 'fate' or 'fortune'. He offered sacrifice for a thousand years that perchance he might have a son who should be called Ohrmazd and who would create heaven and earth. At the end of this period of a thousand years he began to ponder and said to himself: 'What use is this sacrifice that I am offering, and will I really have a son called Ohrmazd, or am I taking all this trouble in vain?' And no sooner had this thought occurred to him than both Ohrmazd and Ahriman were conceived—Ohrmazd because of the sacrifice he had offered, and Ahriman because of his doubt. When he realized that there were two sons in the womb, he made a vow saying: 'Whichever of the two shall come to me first, him will I make king.' Ohrmazd was apprised of his father's thought and revealed it to Ahriman. When Ahriman heard this, he ripped the womb open, emerged, and advanced towards his father. Zurvān, seeing him, asked him: 'Who art thou?' And he replied: 'I am thy son, Ohrmazd.' And Zurvān said: 'My son is light and fragrant, but thou art dark and stinking.' And he wept most bitterly. And as they were talking together, Ohrmazd was born in his turn, light and fragrant; and Zurvān, seeing him, knew that it was his son Ohrmazd for whom he had offered sacrifice. Taking the *barsom* twigs he held in his hands with which he had been sacrificing, he gave them to Ohrmazd and said: 'Up till now it is I who have offered thee sacrifice; from now on shalt thou sacrifice to me.' But even as Zurvān handed the sacrificial twigs to Ohrmazd, Ahriman drew near and said to him: 'Didst thou not vow that whichever of thy sons should come to thee first, to him wouldst thou give the kingdom?' And Zurvān said to him: 'O false and wicked one, the kingdom shall be granted thee for nine thousand years, but Ohrmazd have I made a king above thee, and after nine thousand years he will reign and will do everything according to his good pleasure.' And Ohrmazd created the heavens and the earth and all things that are beautiful and good; but Ahriman created the demons and all that is evil and perverse. Ohrmazd created riches, Ahriman poverty.

This is the Zurvanite myth in its crudest form, and it is strange that this myth, which was regarded by both Christians and Manichees as being typical of the Zoroastrian religion, is mentioned only once in the whole of the Pahlavi books. This one mention occurs in a passage in the *Dēnkart* which purports to be a commentary on *Yasna* 30.3, the very passage in which the Prophet speaks of the Holy and Destructive Spirits as twins. Even the Sassanian theologians, ignorant though they were of the sacred tongue in which the Avesta was written, must have known that this was the only possible interpretation of the stanza in question, for it is quite one of the clearest in the *Gāthās*. Their resolution of the dilemma was ingenious, if disingenuous. It so happens that the Avestan word *eresh* occurs in this stanza; and though they knew that this word meant 'rightly' and usually so translate it, they preferred on this occasion to feign ignorance and translated it with the Pahlavi word *arish*, which is one of the names of the demon of envy; and so it was possible for the author of the *Dēnkart* to represent the offensive doctrine as being the invention of the demons! The whole thing is passed off as being 'a proclamation of the Demon of Envy to mankind that Ohrmazd and Ahriman were two brothers in one womb'.[45] So was the Zurvanite heresy dismissed as being the invention of devilry.

What is rather strange, however, is that though we know of the struggle waged by Kartēr against the Zandīks and of Āturpāt's vindication of his own orthodoxy as against the fatalists, we have no direct reference in the Pahlavi books or elsewhere to any official condemnation of mythological Zurvanism as such. This would lead us to suppose that the question was never entirely resolved; and in the *Mēnōk i Khrat* and in Zātspram we do still find references to Zurvān which seem to presuppose at least his co-eternity with Ohrmazd and Ahriman. Thus in the former we read that Ohrmazd fashioned his creation from his own light 'with the blessing of the Infinite Zurvān, for the Infinite Zurvān is unageing and deathless; he knows neither pain nor decay nor corruption; he has no rival, nor can he ever be put aside or deprived of his sovereignty in his proper sphere'.[46] And again it is by the agency of Infinite Time that Ohrmazd and Ahriman enter into a solemn pact by which they limit the time in which they will do battle together for nine thousand years,[47] this nine thousand years of warfare corresponding to the nine thousand years of earthly sovereignty allotted to Ahriman by Zurvān in the fully Zurvanite version of the myth.

Zurvān and the Pact between Ohrmazd and Ahriman
This pact is also mentioned by Zātspram; and his introduction of the figure of Zurvān into the cosmic drama is even odder. Zātspram starts with the classical dualist account of the creation—Ohrmazd is above in the light, and Ahriman below in the darkness, and between them is the Void. Yet when Ohrmazd begins to fashion forth his creation, he has to beg Time to aid him, for all things have need of Time; and once he has completed his creation, he is quite unable to set it in motion, for Time alone has the power to do this; and it is Zurvān-Time again who settles the terms of the pact between the two Spirits.

'Pondering on the end, [Zurvān] delivered to Ahriman an implement [fashioned] from the very substance of darkness, mingled with the power of Zurvān, as it were a treaty, resembling coal(?), black and ashen. And as he handed it to him he said: "By means of these weapons, Āz (Concupiscence) will devour that which is thine, and she herself shall starve, if at the end of nine thousand years thou hast not accomplished that which thou didst threaten—to demolish the pact, to demolish Time." '[48]

It is true that neither text even hints that Zurvān is the father of Ohrmazd and Ahriman, or that the two Spirits are twins (Zātspram even going so far as to affirm his belief in the two *Principles* through the lips of Zurvān!), yet it is Zurvān to whom Ohrmazd has to appeal for help, it is he who settles the terms of the combat, and he again who arms Ahriman with the one weapon which is certain to destroy him. No Pahlavi text, indeed, ever speaks of Zurvān's paternity of Ohrmazd and Ahriman, but they all agree that Zurvān-Time is co-eternal with them. Zurvanism, indeed, appears to have started simply as an attempt to make sense of *Yasna* 30.3 in which the two Spirits appear as twins, and to provide them with a father. Under Shāpūr I the situation is complicated by the fact that the Zandīks—Zurvanite materialists—jettisoned the whole of the ancient tradition and sought to explain the universe as emerging from an undifferentiated One—Infinite Time, which is at the same time Infinite Space and undifferentiated matter. Both doctrines were finally rejected by the orthodox, but orthodoxy itself remained unaffected by neither, and the efforts that it made to assimilate what was assimilable in these two strands of Zurvanism will be occupying our attention in the following chapters.

CHAPTER TEN

CLASSICAL ZURVANISM

Zurvān, the One and the Many—Zurvān's Doubt—Ohrmazd and Ahriman in Mythological Zurvanism—Main Differences between Zurvanism and Orthodoxy—Aberrant Versions of the Zurvanite Myth—The Sect of Gayōmart—The Four Elements and their Prototypes—Infinite and Finite—Emergence of the Finite from the Infinite—The Emergence of Consciousness and the Genesis of Evil—The Changelessness of Created Being—Āz, the Weapon of Concupiscence— The 'Endless Form' or Macrocosm—The Zurvanite and the Manichaean Āz—Āz, a Borrowing from Buddhism?—Essential 'Zoroastrianism' of classical Zurvanism—The Gender and Sex of Āz—The Wickedness of the Female—The Defection of Woman to Ahriman—The Defilement of Man by Woman

Zurvān, the One and the Many

'I do not think that any sensible person will give credence to this idiotic doctrine, or look [favourably] on this feeble and idle religion. Yet perhaps it is a mystery of what is figured in the mind. But whoso knows the Lord Most High in his glory and majesty will not assent to such nonsense, nor lend his ears to these absurdities.'[1]

So does the Muhammadan heresiographer, Shahristānī, dismiss the Zurvanite myth, a version of which he has just retailed. Certainly as an explanation of the origin of the universe it is childish, and it is for this reason, presumably, that it is always this myth that the Christian apologists seize upon when they are attacking the Zoroastrians. 'Yet,' as Shahristānī says, 'perhaps it is a mystery of what is figured in the mind.' A mystery it certainly is—the perennial mystery with which all religions are at some stage confronted—the relationship between the infinite and the finite, the unchanging, impassive One, and the ever-changing, striving, and active many. For the religion of the Hindus this is the only worthwhile religious quest—how to arrive at the One behind the manifold; and it is quite probable that Zurvanite speculation owes a great deal to India here. Zoroaster was a prophet and, as such, concerned with life as lived in this world; his God was a living god who spoke to him face to face, an active god and the creator of all things. His heaven, too, was no condition of timeless bliss, but an endless prolongation of life as lived on this earth, though purified of all taint of sin and all trace of sorrow. He was vitally concerned with the fact of evil, but did not seek to explain its origin. His followers, however, drifted into a fully dualist position which inevitably limited their God and made him less than infinite and less than omnipotent. Zurvanism, even in its crudest form, is an attempt to arrive at a principle which is an all-inclusive One, changeless in essence, yet the source of all change. The Muhammadan poet, Jalāl al-Dīn Rūmī, has some beautiful lines on the mystery of creation:

> David said: 'O King, since thou hadst no need of us,
> Say, then, what wisdom was there in creating the two worlds?'
> God said to him: 'O temporal man, I was a hidden treasure,
> And desired that that treasure of loving-kindness and bounty should be revealed.'[2]

This too was the dilemma of the infinite Zurvān. Zurvān-Time alone stands in need of nothing, yet all else needs him. The very 'being of all things has need of Time. Without Time one can do nothing that is or was or shall be. Time has need of none of these for anything.'[3] So even Ohrmazd, God, the Creator, must ask Time's aid when he contemplates the act of creation, for he too *needs* Time,[4] since without time action of any kind is impossible: were there no time, there would be no creation.

Zurvān's Doubt

In purely mythological passages the archaic word *Zurvān* is usually used to represent the god, rather than the ordinary Persian word for 'time', *zamān*. The term *Zurvān*, however, is also used to mean the 'Infinite' or 'unqualifiable Absolute' as such.[5] The mythological god, then, must be seen as the centre of the 'mystery' through which the unqualifiable One originates multiplicity. In the Zurvanite myth, Zurvān, like Rūmī's God, desires 'that that treasure of loving-kindness and bounty should be revealed'. The latent and potential wishes to become manifest and actual: he wishes to have 'a son whose name should be Ohrmazd and who would create heaven and earth and all that in them is'. Zurvān, however, does not create out of any superfluity of being, for at the core of his being there is a latent defect of which he knows nothing. In the myth this is symbolized by his doubt: he sacrifices for a thousand years, and then doubts whether his sacrifice will have any effect. The sacrifice, as in Indian mythology, is also creative and results in the birth of Ohrmazd who is also the 'Bounteous Spirit' or, more literally, the 'Spirit who brings increase', while the doubt, the Absolute's failure of nerve at the very moment when the creator is about to issue forth from him, produces the principle of evil. The 'Fall' in Zurvanism does not originate with man, it results from an imperfection, an unsureness of self, in the very heart of God. The 'One' has given birth to the 'Two', and 'in duality is evil'.[6] The whole purpose of the cosmic drama which is about to unfold is to restore the shattered unity, but this cannot be done by trying to re-integrate the Devil into the Absolute: it can only be done by eliminating him altogether. Ahriman, the Devil, is the concretization of God's own imperfection, his failure of nerve; and if God is ever to become perfect, he must become fully identified with Ohrmazd who personifies his essential wisdom, goodness, and light. God *qua* the Infinite is the source of good and evil; but God *qua* creator of heaven and earth proceeds from the Infinite and is absolutely good. The Godhead is divided and can only be restored by the total destruction of evil, when, with the abolition of finite Time, the Infinite and the Good will for the first time be wholly one.

Ohrmazd and Ahriman in Mythological Zurvanism

All this is to be found in the *Dēnkart*. It represents an assimilation by orthodoxy of certain Zurvanite ideas. There are, however, features in Zurvanism which are wholly incompatible with the orthodoxy of Sassanian times. The Ohrmazd of the Pahlavi books is omnipotent in the sense that he can do anything that is possible. 'His power,' indeed, 'in so far as it is confined to the possible, *is* limited, but in the sphere of the infinite (*abrīn*) it is limitless.'[7] This means that in so far as he is identical with the Infinite, every potentiality is latent within him, but in so far as he acts in time, he can only do what is possible. He cannot, for instance, change the evil nature of Ahriman into good, for Ahriman, according to the orthodox, is an evil *substance*, and a substance is, by definition,[8] something that can never change. In the Zurvanism presented to us by the non-Zoroastrian sources, however, Ohrmazd is neither omnipotent nor omniscient: he is not even capable of looking after his own interests. Thus he gratuitously reveals to Ahriman the secret that whichever of the twins will first present himself to their father, Zurvān, will receive the kingdom. Again, after creating heaven and earth, he can think of no way of illuminating them and has to be instructed on how to do this by a demon who is a renegade from Ahriman's camp.[9] Similarly, Ahriman who is an evil substance for the orthodox, is, for the Zurvanites, evil by choice. He *chooses* the sinister weapon offered to him by Zurvān, 'like unto fire, blazing, harassing all creatures, that hath the very substance of concupiscence (Āz)', and himself boasts that ' "it is not that I cannot create anything good, but that I will not." And that he might give effect to his words, he created the peacock.'[10] This is a genuine, and a fundamental, difference between Zurvanism and orthodoxy, and a Christian convert from Zoroastrianism can thus taunt his inquisitors with these words:

'Should we, then, try to please Ahriman who, according to what you yourselves say, appears wise, knowing, and mighty from his works, just as Ohrmazd appears weak and stupid, for he could create nothing till he had learnt from the disciples of Ahriman.'[11]

In asserting that the twin Spirits were good and evil by choice the Zurvanites were nearer Zoroaster's own views than were the latter-day orthodox, but in attributing less than omnipotence and omniscience to Ohrmazd they stray very far indeed from the path that he had traced. Moreover, in the Zurvanite mythology Ahriman is granted far more power to do harm in this world than the orthodox would concede. Zurvān had promised to make the first of the twins which came before him king, and, because his essential nature is rectitude,[12] he cannot go back on his word. Ahriman, then, becomes Prince of this World for nine thousand years, whereas Ohrmazd reigns only in heaven above him. The orthodox are more optimistic, for during the nine thousand years in which good and evil are mingled together and strive with each other in this world 'three thousand years will pass entirely according to the will of Ohrmazd, three thousand years in mixture will pass according to the will of both Ohrmazd and Ahriman, and in the last battle the Destructive Spirit will be made powerless and [Ohrmazd] himself will save creation from aggression.'[13]

Main Differences between Zurvanism and Orthodoxy

Thus, apart from the all-important question of origins, orthodoxy and Zurvanism differ in three main respects. In Zurvanism, first, the twin Spirits are good and evil by choice rather than in substance. Secondly, Ohrmazd is neither omnipotent nor omniscient, whereas for orthodoxy he is both, limited though he is by the opposite principle. Thirdly, in Zurvanism Ahriman not only displays the signs of a lively intelligence, but also enjoys the undisputed sovereignty of this world for nine thousand years, whereas for orthodoxy it is his slowness in knowledge and wrong-mindedness, his sheer stupidity, that, despite his aggressive power and lust for destruction, finally brings about his ruin.

The question of origins divides the two parties less sharply, for while the orthodox flatly deny that 'Ohrmazd and Ahriman were two brothers in one womb', they would perhaps not have objected to some such formula as this: Ohrmazd and Ahriman co-exist from all eternity in Infinite Time, but their respective good and evil natures become manifested and actualized only when Infinite Time which knows neither past, present, nor future,[14] passes into finite time; at the end, finite time will be reabsorbed into the Infinite, and with the cessation of finite time Ahriman will be finally and totally incapacitated, whereas

Ohrmazd and all his creation will pass again into a state of pure timelessness which is eternal rest and eternal bliss.

Aberrant Versions of the Zurvanite Myth

Before we pass on to this philosophical synthesis, however, we must say something of some variant forms of Zurvanism which have left traces in the Pahlavi books and are also attested in non-Zoroastrian writers. The starting point of the Zurvanite cosmology is closely akin to that of the cosmologies we find in the Upanishads in India. In the beginning is the undifferentiable One from which all duality and all pairs of opposites proceed. From it proceed not only light and darkness, good and evil, hot and cold, moist and dry, but also that most basic of all polarities—the polarity of male and female. Zurvān himself was originally bisexual; and his full name may well have been *Zurvān i Khwashkhwarrīk*, 'Zurvān whose *Khwarenah* or fortune is fair'; for a person of the name of *Khwashkhwarrīk* is once said to be the mother of Ohrmazd and Ahriman.[15] This, however, denotes no absolute differentiation of sex, for even those sources which speak of a *mother's* womb in which the twins are contained later speak of Zurvān as father *and* mother: as Zurvān he is father, as Khwashkhwarrīk he is mother.

In the *'Ulamā-yi-Islām*, Zurvān does not give birth to Ohrmazd and Ahriman directly. He first 'created fire and water, and when he had brought them together, Ohrmazd came into existence'.[16] Thus the first duality to emerge from the One was that of a male element, fire, and a female element, water; for fire is the male principle, water the female, and they are brother and sister, husband and wife.[17] Of the origin of Ahriman no more is said than that he was created by Zurvān.[18] The duality of good and evil is, then, secondary to the duality of sex. The same scheme of things appears in the account of Zoroastrianism attributed to Eudemus of Rhodes, in which Space or Time produces light and darkness first, Ohrmazd and Ahriman second; whereas Hippolytus tells us that according to Zoroaster there are two first principles, a male and a female. The male is light, the female dark, and the 'parts' of light are hot, dry, light, and swift, while the parts of darkness are cold, moist, heavy, and slow. 'The whole universe consists of these, the female and the male.'[19] So, too, the *Dēnkart*[20] tells us that 'all material becoming, ripening, and order proceed from the coming together in due proportion of water, the female, and fire, the male'. Hippolytus also tells us that Zoroaster considered that the universe had originated from two demons, the one celestial and the other terrestrial. The latter is water and has its source in the earth, while the former is fire mixed with air.

Water is the moist element *par excellence*, fire the hot,[21] the quality of cold being subsidiary in the case of water, that of dryness in that of fire. Ohrmazd, who is himself described as being 'hot and moist',[22] derives, then, from the primary qualities of the sacred elements, Ahriman who is 'cold and dry' proceeds from their secondary qualities. Ahriman, moreover, cannot create any material thing because cold and dryness are the qualities of death. Ohrmazd, on the other hand, can do so because his qualities are the qualities of life. So we find in the *Dēnkart* that the *mēnōk* or invisible and intangible principle of light and the *mēnōk* of darkness emerge from a single, uncompounded *mēnōk*[23] elsewhere identified with *ras*, the 'Wheel', itself identical with primal matter or infinite Space-Time. 'The *mēnōk* of light, because it has the properties of the hot and the moist, that is, the very nature of life, can evolve from a state of uncompounded *mēnōk* existence (*bavishn*) to a state of compounded existence which is material (*gētēh*) . . . while the *mēnōk* of darkness, because it is cold and dry, the [very] substance of death and meet for damnation, cannot develop into compounded existence or take on material form.'[24] This is pure Zurvanism in philosophical rather than mythological form. Ohrmazd and Ahriman, the Spirit of light and the Spirit of darkness, emerge from the simple, uncompounded One, the one taking on the qualities of heat and moisture which are the positive side of the elements, fire and water, and the source of life, the other receiving only the negative, cold and dryness, the ingredients of death. Seen in this light Ahriman is not only the source of death: he is the very substance of death—and what is dead cannot be said to be. Hence it is possible to say that *sub specie aeternitatis* 'Ahriman is not':[25] 'he was not eternally nor will he be'.[26]

This would appear to be a far cry from orthodoxy which maintained that both Ohrmazd and Ahriman are substances that exist from the beginning. Philosophically, however, it can be justified in this way: Ohrmazd is eternal being and therefore must exist *in actu*, not merely potentially. Ahriman, on the other hand, can only attain the semblance of being in finite time since in eternity he is not. His actualization depends on the nature of eternal being itself. This being is the simple, uncompounded One, in other words, Zurvān, who, as infinite Space-Time, contains all potentialities within him. Zurvān's doubt in the myth is the mythological representation of an essential flaw in the godhead: the birth of Ahriman represents the actualization of that flaw, and with the actualization of Ahriman, Time and Space too assume a finite form, for finite space and time are in a sense a lapse from the perfect state of infinitude; and it is therefore logical that Ahriman should be lord of the temporal world for as long as it lasts, and it is logical that Ohrmazd who, as eternal Being, is one with Zurvān, but who is greater than he in that he is also eternal Wisdom, should be separated out from him as soon as Zurvān's inherent defect makes itself manifest. This gives new meaning to the myth of Zurvān and also explains how two versions of it persisted side by side. For beside the myth of Zurvān and the twin Spirits that proceed from him we have that other story in which it is Ohrmazd, in this context, simply called *Yazdān*, 'God', who has an evil thought, that is to say, he considers the possibility of what it would be like to have an adversary,[27] and from this unworthy thought Ahriman, the Adversary, is actualized.

The Sect of Gayōmart

It is interesting to note that this sect should call itself the 'sect of Gayōmart', thereby claiming for itself an immemorial antiquity, for Gayōmart is the first man among the Zoroastrians. This, they claimed, was the original doctrine to which the Magi adhered before the coming of Zoroaster. They differ from the Zurvanites in this, that they wholly eliminate Zurvān-Time and have no preoccupations about the infinite. By claiming a revelation older than Zoroaster's they thereby dissociated themselves from the Prophet, and in this they may or may not have done rightly; for though we know that both the orthodox and that wing of the Zurvanites which considered itself to be orthodox, held the absolute goodness of Ohrmazd, the God they worshipped, to be fundamental to their faith, we do not know how far the Prophet would have gone with either party. It is not impossible that the 'sect of Gayōmart' more nearly represented the Prophet's own views, though he would have been shocked at the crude manner of their expression.

The Four Elements and their Prototypes

We have seen that Ohrmazd is identified with the hot and the moist in the natural order, Ahriman with the cold and the dry. Between them, then, they share the four natural properties recognized by Aristotle. The simple, undifferentiated One, then, from whom they proceed, must possess all four *in potentia*. Theodore bar Konai, a Christian writer of the seventh century, tells us that Zoroaster recognized four principles which resembled the four elements and whose names were Ashōqar, Frashōqar, Zarōqar, and Zurvān.[28] If this account is to be brought into relation with the semi-Zurvanite fragments preserved in the *Dēnkart*, then we would expect these four 'principles' to correspond to the four natural properties from which the elements proceed. The words *Ashōqar, Frashōqar,* and *Zarōqar* mean 'he who makes virile', 'he who makes excellent', and 'he who makes old', whereas the word *Zurvān* had in popular parlance come to mean 'old age'.[29] Ashōqar and Frashōqar, then, would represent the polarity of life, Zarōqar and Zurvān the polarity of death. In the Infinite they are no more than potentialities: in finite time they will be actualized as the hot and the moist, the Spirit of life, and the cold and the dry, the Spirit of death.

All that has occurred so far in the cosmic drama belongs to the order of nature (*chihr*). Sassanian Zoroastrianism, however, distinguishes two orders, the order of nature and the order of intellect and will (*akhw*): these correspond more or less exactly to the Avestan *mainyu* and *gaēthya*.[30] Time and space, whether infinite or finite, are of the order of nature and therefore unconcerned with human virtue and human wickedness. Ohrmazd, however, is not only eternal and infinite in time, he is also possessed of perfect wisdom. The Godhead, in its totality, is then infinite in time, infinite in space, and infinite in wisdom. We have seen how the Spirit of light and the Spirit of darkness proceed from the undifferentiated One, and how the first is life and the second death— life and death, of course, belonging to the order of nature, not to that of will. How, then, did the intellect develop out of the One?

Infinite and Finite
Before we attempt to answer this question, however, we must consider briefly the relationship between the infinite and the finite as this was understood by the Zoroastrians. The majority were content to say that the one developed out of the other or that Ohrmazd 'fashioned forth' finite Time from Infinite Time. Mardān-Farrukh, however, thought differently, for he was an extreme dualist and goes far beyond the *Dēnkart* in his eagerness to eliminate all trace of Zurvanism from the Zoroastrian faith. He admits, indeed, that there is such a thing as the infinite: both space and time are infinite, and nothing else. The infinite, moreover, is without parts, and it cannot, then, be the source of composite beings: there is no possible link between them. No finite thing, then, can have an infinite dimension, it can have no part in what he calls the Zurvānic substance. Moreover, the infinite is by definition incomprehensible, and so it cannot be comprehended even by God for 'if he were infinite, he would be unaware of it'. Both God and the Devil, Ohrmazd and Ahriman, then, are finite, for only so can God be said to understand and know his own being. All that can be said of the infinite is that it is 'that without which nothing from the first is. Nothing can exist without it or separate from it. But in so far as it is infinite, it cannot be understood.' Infinite Time-Space is an incomprehensible and uncomprehending mystery. To speculate on just how the finite

proceeds from it (which Mardān-Farrukh denies anyhow) is a pure waste of time.

'So what, pray,' he goes on to say, 'is the point of stupidly discussing something one does not know, of disputing and bandying words, and so deceiving the immature and those of immature intelligence? If one fatuously asserts that its essence is infinite and that its knowledge is infinite, and that with its infinite knowledge it knows that it is infinite, that is false and doubly false. . . . Knowledge can only be predicated of a thing that is within the scope of, and comprehensible to, the intellect,'[31]

and the infinite is therefore incomprehensible simply by the fact of its being infinite.

This radical treatment of the relationship of finite to infinite and the round assertion that Ohrmazd himself is finite, is peculiar to Mardān-Farrukh, and in this respect he deviates from the orthodox norm. The orthodox view of the limitation of space and time is that they are hewn out of a pre-existing infinite substance by God. For the *Dēnkart* the process is sometimes automatic, sometimes *pat dātār ābhurishn*, 'through the fashioning of the Creator'. The world is formed by God rather as a diadem is fashioned by a goldsmith out of gold.[32] Time-Space is thereby actualized as the universe of nature, while the actualization of the intellect, the faculty of knowing, develops simultaneously along parallel lines.

Emergence of the Finite from the Infinite

Time and Space 'on which the material world is [founded]'[33] are the indispensable prerequisites for the existence of the material universe. 'Knowledge' is an equally indispensable prerequisite for the existence both of the intelligent subject and an intelligible universe. We have seen how the material world in all its variety developed from the undifferentiated One or infinite Space. Such a development, however, presupposes the existence of finite time, and this too comes into being and progresses on similar lines. Finite time, moreover, is the prerequisite of action of any kind, whether 'natural' or 'voluntary'. 'Infinite Time', that is, timelessness, can be considered as action *in potentia*: and 'action *in potentia*' is also 'the original seed the Avestan name of which is *arshnōtachin* ('the seminal flow'); from this:

'through the Creator's fashioning it forth, [results] the [actual] performance of action with which coincides the entry of Time into action. From the performance of action [arises] the completion of action with which coincides the limit of finite time. The limit of finite time merges into Infinite Time the essence of which is eternity; and [this means that] at the Final Body what is associated with it cannot pass away.'[34]

In terms of time and action the evolution of the cosmos is thus seen to go through four phases:

	(a) Action	(b) Time
(1)	Action *in potentia.*	Infinite Time.
(2)	Action proper.	Time-in-action.
(3)	The completion of action.	The limit of finite time.
(4)	Return to the state of rest.[35]	Infinite Time.

The Emergence of Consciousness and the Genesis of Evil
So much, then, for the evolution of the world of nature—the material cosmos—from infinite Time-Space into a finite mode of existence, its passage from potency into act. What of the order of intellect and will? How does consciousness arise? The *Dēnkart* gives the answer, and it is so interesting that we must quote it in full:

Of knowledge (lit. 'the condition of being a knower') thus is it taught. By the Creator's marvellous power, in infinite Time and by its power knowledge came to know (the immutability of Ohrmazd's essence depends on Infinite Time). From this [act of knowing] resulted the rising up of the Aggressor, unwilled [by Ohrmazd], to destroy the essence [of Ohrmazd] (i.e. his immutability) and his attributes, by means of false speech. The immediate result of this was that [Ohrmazd]'s essence and attributes turned back [into themselves] in order to [come to] know their own ground. So much knowing was necessary for the Creator [himself] to rise up for the creative act. The first effect of this rising up was the Endless Light. From the Endless Light is the Spirit of Truth which derives from Wisdom (knowledge) because it has the potentiality of growing into the knowledge of all things. By knowing all things he has power to do all he wills. Thence creation and the Aggressor's defeat thereby, the return of creation to its proper sphere of action, and the eternal rule of Ohrmazd in perfect joy; for it is he who is the origin of good things, the source of good, the seed and potentiality (or power) of all that is good. All good creatures are from him as a first effect by creation or by emanation, as sheen is from shining, shining from brilliance, brilliance from light.'[36]

Ohrmazd, in this passage, is conceived of primarily as 'Wisdom', that is, the faculty of knowing. He is also immutable being in virtue of the fact that his habitat is Infinite Time, the Absolute. As Wisdom and the knowing faculty he is latent and potential only: he is not yet actualized. This groping awareness seeks an object outside itself, and, finding none, an object generates itself without God willing it, and this self-generated object is none other than Ahriman, the Aggressor, whose object now is to destroy God's essence which is his immutable being. He seeks to imprison the infinite in the finite, the eternal in the temporal,

God in the world. His aim is nothing less than to do away with un-
conditioned being.[37] Thus Ahriman originates in Ohrmazd's accession
to consciousness: in Jungian terminology, the dim dawn of consciousness from the unconscious engendered the 'shadow' or dark side of the
divine personality. The awakening of the divine consciousness in
Ohrmazd is the equivalent of Zurvān's doubt in the Zurvanite myth,
and this initial failure to reach full self-consciousness puts Ohrmazd
into mortal peril; he risks the loss of his very essence, eternal being
which he now sees to be identical with eternal knowing or eternal
Wisdom. Hence he makes an effort of total introspection—his 'essence
and attributes turned back [into themselves] in order to [come to] know
their own ground'. In order to eliminate the destructive element
engendered by incomplete knowledge Ohrmazd must first know himself
as he is: he must do what Mardān-Farrukh said no one, not even God,
could do—he must know himself as infinite and as possessed of infinite
knowledge, and this self-knowledge alone will enable him to 'rise up
for the creative act'. This saving knowledge engenders endless light, for
light, as always, is the symbol of spiritual illumination or insight.
This is the light of Wisdom which is proper to the nature of Ohrmazd,
that same Wisdom which 'descends from the light on to the earth and
by which [men] see and think well',[38] and this Wisdom is identical
with the Good Religion. From this Light of Wisdom proceeds the Spirit
of Truth which enables Ohrmazd to know all things as they are. By
knowing himself and knowing his Adversary too he knows he must
create or emanate the universe, if his Adversary is to be defeated; but
he also creates because he knows himself as good, and the 'definition
of goodness is that which of itself develops';[39] so God himself must
develop and 'grow into the knowledge of all things'.

The whole of this remarkable passage is Zurvanite rather than
Mazdean, first because the 'Endless Light' is here originated, not
eternal as it is in all the strictly orthodox texts, and secondly because
the divine personality is composed not of God, Time, Wisdom, and
Light (= Ohrmazd),[40] but of God, Time, potential Wisdom, and
Space, from which alone the Endless Light can originate; and all this
adds up not to Ohrmazd, but to Zurvān.[41]

The Changelessness of Created Being
From the One, then, finite time and finite space, which together add
up to the material world, are actualized in the order of nature,
consciousness, thought, and a sense of purpose in the order of intellect
and will. The conditions of creation are now fulfilled, and Ohrmazd
creates heaven and earth as his first line of defence against the

Aggressor. Finite time is destined to last twelve thousand years, at the end of which it merges again into its source which is the Infinite, and action merges into rest from which it sprang. But the universe created by Ohrmazd in all its infinite variety does not revert to its own source which is the undifferentiated One or primal matter. All creation is dependent on Infinite Time, and as such it must partake of eternity. So it can be confidently stated that 'those things which Ohrmazd created at the original creation do not change'.[42] For Ohrmazd, in creating finite beings to do battle with Ahriman, who can only exist and operate on the finite level, gives them an infinite dimension; and just as Time, Space, Wisdom, and Ohrmazd himself are eternal and immutable, so is all that he creates out of them. All the good creation, then, has an eternal substrate which will be realized at the end of time as eternal well-being and bliss.[43] This constitutes the 'Final Body'— the body of a universe renewed and perfected because finally purged of the malice and corruption of the Aggressor. This 'body' continues to exist in all its variety, and within it exist in harmony the resurrected bodies, now once again united to their souls, of all men reconstituted and transfigured. It is true that every material thing was elicited from the potentiality of matter and every spiritual thing from the potentiality of spirit, but in the end 'possessed of image and body (*adhvēnakōmand ut karpōmand*) they will be reunited to their souls, all undefiled, and together with their souls they will be made immortal, reconstituted as eternal beings in perfect bliss'.[44] The end of the cosmic drama, then, is not just a return to the *status quo ante*, a reversion to a state of pure undifferentiated being, it means rather that every separate creature has grown and developed to its highest capacity, it has become its final cause, the sum-total of all its good thoughts, words, and deeds, what the Iranians call its *khwarenah*, or *khwarr* as it is now called in Pahlavi. This glorious state it achieves on its own account certainly, but also in full union and harmony with the whole human race which itself is transfigured in the beatific vision of God. Life in Infinite Time is thus a life of union and communion both with God and with the whole of his creation now finally released from all the torments inflicted on it by the Fiend. He and his entire creation will be utterly destroyed. This constitutes the purpose of life for the Zoroastrian, whether he be, in his mythology and philosophy, an orthodox dualist or a Zurvanite.

We have seen how the *Dēnkart* tries to achieve a philosophical synthesis between orthodox dualism and Zurvanism, and how it seeks to identify Ohrmazd with Infinite Time, Ahriman with finite Time. Mythologically, however, the two wings of Zoroastrianism are not so easily reconciled.

Āz, the Weapon of Concupiscence

In Zātspram there is a very strange myth concerning Zurvān which we have already quoted, but which must be quoted again in our present context.

'Pondering on the end [Zurvān] delivered to Ahriman an implement [fashioned] from the very substance of darkness, mingled with the power of Zurvān, as it were a treaty, resembling coal (?), black and ashen. And as he handed it to him, he said: "By means of these weapons, Āz (Concupiscence) will devour that which is thine, and she herself shall starve, if at the end of nine thousand years thou hast not accomplished that which thou didst threaten, to demolish the pact, to demolish Time." ' [45]

Or in slightly different words we read:

'When first creation began to move, and Zurvān for the sake of movement brought that form, the black and ashen garment, to Ahriman, he made a treaty in this wise: "This is that implement like unto fire, blazing, harassing all creatures, that hath the very substance of Āz (Concupiscence). When the period of nine thousand years comes to an end, if thou hast not perfectly fulfilled that which thou didst threaten in the beginning, that thou wouldst bring all material existence to hate Ohrmazd and to love thee—and verily this is the belief in one Principle [only], that the Increaser and the Destroyer are the same—then by means of these weapons Āz will devour that which is thine, thy creation; and she herself will starve; for she will no longer obtain food from the creatures of Ohrmazd—like a frog that liveth in the water; so long as it defileth the water, it liveth by it, but when the water is withdrawn from it, it dieth, parched." ' [46]

This obviously forms part of the original Zurvanite myth and is preserved only by Zātspram who, as we have seen, had Zurvanite tendencies. Even he, however, will not go so far as to say that Zurvān was the father of Ohrmazd and Ahriman; he simply allows him to appear on the scene unexplained. It is, however, Zurvān who offers Ahriman the 'weapon of Concupiscence' by which he and his creation will be ultimately destroyed, and Ahriman chooses it of his own free will 'as his very essence'. [47] It would, then, be reasonable to suppose that Zurvān armed Ohrmazd with a similar weapon—a weapon that would ensure his victory over his enemy. Such a weapon we do find again and again mentioned in the Pahlavi texts, but in no case does Zurvān give it to Ohrmazd. The reason is, no doubt, that the authors of the Pahlavi books were unwilling to represent Ohrmazd as being in any way dependent on, or inferior to, Zurvān. So we find that the *Dēnkart* speaks of Ahriman's weapon being bestowed on him 'through Time from its decisive dispensation that orders aright', [48] but

223

in the case of Ohrmazd his weapon or robe was 'bestowed on him by *his own* dispensation through finite Time'. It would, then, seem to be abundantly clear that in the original legend both weapons or robes must have been in the gift of Zurvān-Time. In the *Bundahishn* an attempt is made to fit this episode into an orthodox dualist scheme of things. Thus, in the case of Ahriman, too, the sinister weapon which Ahriman chooses is no longer proffered to him by Zurvān: rather, 'from the material darkness which is his own essence the Destructive Spirit fashioned forth the body of his creation in the form of coal(?), black and ashen, worthy of the darkness, damned as the most sinful noxious beast.'[49] So too we learn of Ohrmazd that 'from his own essence which is material light he fashioned forth the form of his creatures—a form of fire—bright, white, round, and manifest afar.'[50] This is the dualist account of the affair. In the true Zurvanite version, however, it must have been Zurvān-Time who armed his two sons with their respective weapons, robes, or forms, which they, in their turn, chose of their own free will. This doctrine of the choice granted to the two Spirits the orthodox regarded as being heretical, and their own term for this type of Zurvanism appears to have been *Zōishīk*, 'belief in the free choice [of Ohrmazd and Ahriman]'.[51]

Zurvān-Time, then, in the Zurvanite account, will himself have armed the two Spirits with their respective weapons, and we shall now have to consider a little more carefully what these weapons were. We have seen that in the *Dēnkart* Ahriman is regarded as being an entirely spiritual being and that the matter with which evil spirits are clothed is borrowed from another source, and that this derives ultimately from infinite Space-Time, mythologically represented by Zurvān. The 'power of Zurvān', then, which the baleful weapon handed to Ahriman contains, is probably no more than materiality—in the case of Ahriman material darkness, in the case of Ohrmazd material light; these are the two physical weapons with which the two Spirits will fight.

The 'Endless Form' or Macrocosm

These weapons, however, also have a spiritual side: they have soul as well as body. Ohrmazd's weapon is called the 'Endless Form', and it is in fact the whole material creation contained within the circle of the sky. It was fashioned from the Endless Light, and it is twofold. On the one hand it contains the spiritual creation, on the other the material creation.

'In the spiritual creation the Spirit of the Power of the Word was contained; and in the material creation the Spirit of the Power of Nature was contained,

and it settled [in it]. The instrument which contains the spiritual creation
was made perfect, and the spiritual gods of the Word were separated out
from it, each for his own function, to perform those activities which were
necessary for the creation that was within the instrument. And within the
instrument which contains the material creation the marvellous Spirit of the
Power of Nature was united to the kingdom of the Spirit of the Power of
the Word through the will of the Creator.'[52]

Nature and spirit, that is, matter and spirit are thus united to form
the cosmos, and the cosmos is the 'Wheel', the heavenly sphere, the
embodiment of the finite Zurvān. As the Infinite, Zurvān is the father
of both Ohrmazd and Ahriman; as the finite he is the weapon of the
one as well as of the other. Thus the 'weapons' he gives his sons are
himself in finite form. All that is good in him he gives to Ohrmazd;
what is evil he gives to Ahriman, for Āz is not only concupiscence,
greed, and lust, it is also *Varan*,[53] which means not only sexual desire
but also religious doubt. Āz, then, in this myth, must represent Zurvān's
doubt—that essential imperfection which lurked deep down in the
godhead and, in the course of what perhaps we should call 'aeveternity',
took shape and materialized in the form of Ahriman. Zurvān expiates
his original sin by becoming embodied in the cosmos and suffering the
evil effects of his sin to work themselves out in his own body. In this
he, as macrocosm, prefigures the fate of each individual man; and
just as he controls human destinies, so does the collective consciousness
of mankind—the union of the Fravashis or external souls—control
him.[54]

The macrocosm, Zurvān's body, is ensouled by the Spirit of the
Power of the Word which appears to be identical with that Wisdom
which fosters and protects it.[55] Finite Space-Time, then, which is
Ohrmazd's 'creation' and the weapon he had received from Zurvān,
is animated and guided by Wisdom or reason. And just as Ohrmazd
received light and Wisdom from Zurvān, so did Ahriman receive
Āz-Concupiscence; and it is with this weapon that he attacks both the
'natural' or material side of Ohrmazd's creation and the 'spiritual' side,
the domain of intellect and will. Āz, as we have seen, comprises both
natural concupiscence and what the Marxists call 'incorrect thinking'.
Zātspram, however, who alone among our sources preserves the myth,
knows nothing of the latter; for him Āz is simply the instinctual side of
man. Her nature is threefold and consists of eating, sexual desire, 'and
yearning for whatever good thing one sees or hears'.[56] The *Dēnkart*,[57]
however, has a fuller account of the activities of this very considerable
demon. Man's 'humanity' is defined as a combination of life which he
has from nature and knowledge which is of the intellect and will. He

is by nature disposed to nourish his own body and to cultivate the religious knowledge which is ingrained in him and which spurs him on to virtue. Āz is the power that perverts both his natural and his voluntary drives. Heresy, then, and sensuality are both manifestations of Āz. Nature and will, and will and intellect, should all work together, but Āz seeks to drive a wedge between them. Her essential activity is 'disorderly motion' or 'disruption' (ōshtāp),[58] and the whole purpose of the creation of the world is to eliminate this element of instability with which Ahriman has armed himself.[59] Āz is the enemy both of the natural order (chihr) and of reason (khrat). As the enemy of the natural order and of life, she also causes death.

'In the mixed state life as a general rule is maintained in the body by the continuous working of the natural functions in the body; and this continuous working of the natural functions is up against the "natural" Āz. Āz, faced as she is by the natural functions, seeks to destroy them: she withholds Hurdāt and Amurdāt,[60] [that is to say,] she cuts off food and drink from the natural functions. Nature is the ally [of the body], Āz its enemy. When Hurdāt and Amurdāt, that is, food and drink, are cut off from the natural functions, the latter, deprived of any ally and being in the grip of Āz, are destroyed, and life can no longer be maintained in the body; and since this is so, the body is ripe for death.'[61]

Āz, then, the demon of concupiscence, is also the demon of death, and in this she is akin to the finite Zurvān of whose evil side she is indeed the earthly manifestation. For Zurvān, as father Time, is seen as the author of both life and death, and since it is death that invariably and inevitably extinguishes individual life, he is primarily thought of as death. In the Avesta, where he is still a very shadowy figure, he controls the path along which the souls of the dead must travel on their way to the Judgement. '[The souls of] wicked and righteous alike proceed along the paths created by Zurvān to the Bridge of the Requiter created by Mazdāh.'[62] In the Gāthās it is Ahriman who brings death into the world; in Zurvanism Zurvān arms Ahriman with Āz, the principle of death as well as of concupiscence, while he arms Ohrmazd with the material world which is his own body and which is destined for immortality once the curse of Āz has been expelled.

The Zurvanite and the Manichaean Āz
Āz is the principle of disorder that has invaded the natural order: she is excess and deficiency as opposed to the Mean.[63] But she would seem to be very much more than this; for basically she is desire—hunger and thirst on the one hand and sexual desire on the other. As such she is the very precondition of physical life as well as of physical death; and in this

226

she closely resembles her Manichaean namesake, for in the Manichaean texts $\bar{A}z$ is the Persian word used to translate the Greek *hyle*, 'matter'.

Zoroastrianism, however, even its Zurvanite manifestation, is very different from Manichaeanism. For the Manichees 'matter' and 'concupiscence' are interchangeable terms: they are both the 'disorderly motion that is in every existent thing'[64] and, as such, the principle that militates against eternal life. But in Zoroastrianism, whether Zurvanite or orthodox, matter and concupiscence are not by any means identical. On the contrary, matter itself is the vehicle of eternal life, and concupiscence is like an infection that attacks it from outside. Originally man was created without needs; he did not need to eat or drink, and in the last days he will return to this blessed independence and thereby break the power of $\bar{A}z$. This means that the material world will partake of spirit without for that reason ceasing to be material; and those who are born in the last days will be 'sweet-smelling, with but little darkness in them, spiritual in nature, without offspring, for they will not eat';[65] and Nature itself 'will be clad in spirit and intelligences will be more clearly grasped'.[66] This will mean the final annihilation of $\bar{A}z$ who as universal greed devours creation ever anew and who as sexuality recreates her portion for the morrow. Once men cease to eat and are 'clad in spirit', $\bar{A}z$ has no power over them, and 'since she will derive no power from the creatures of Ohrmazd, she will chide Ahriman who had appointed her captain of his commanders [saying] in her greed to the judge of creatures: "Satisfy me, satiate me, for I derive nor food nor strength from the creatures of Ohrmazd." '[67] Then at the command of Ahriman she devours all the demons except only Ahriman himself. This is the final crisis: Ahriman is now left alone and finds himself pitted not only against his eternal adversary, Ohrmazd, but also against the very weapon he had chosen when it was offered to him by his father, Zurvān. This weapon now turns on him in fury and threatens to devour him, for there is nothing else left for her to devour. Ahriman, at bay, rather than submit to this final horror, turns in desperation to his ancient enemy, Ohrmazd, and makes his first and last appeal to his goodness to save him. Ohrmazd, rather than see him succumb to her 'who comprises [all] evil',[68] himself administers the *coup de grâce*, while Sraosha is left to finish off $\bar{A}z$.[69] In what appears to be the true Zurvanite account, however, the destruction of $\bar{A}z$ falls not to Sraosha, but to the infinite Zurvān himself accompanied by the Genius of the Law and Fate.[70] This is only as it should be, for it represents the final conquest of Zurvān's original doubt. By doubting he was himself responsible for originating the principle of darkness and evil, and by offering Ahriman that 'implement [fashioned] from the very substance of darkness, mingled with the power of Zurvān, as it were a treaty, resembling coal(?), black and ashen', he divests himself of the 'concupiscence' that is still within him, and thereby assures the ultimate annihilation of his unwanted son through the instrumentality of the weapon he had himself chosen.

All this is, indeed, a long way removed from Manichaeanism, but there are, as in Manichaeanism, distinctly Buddhistic overtones, for not only are the spiritual worlds of Ohrmazd and Ahriman at war with each other, but the temporal and eternal orders also seem to be mutually contrasted and opposed. Ohrmazd's original creation was wholly static, 'without thought, without movement, intangible',[71] and it is only the disorderly movement (ōshtāp) that is Āz that sets the temporal process going. The temporal process is the Buddhist samsāra, the ebb and flow of physical life regarded by the Buddhists as being evil simply because it is impermanent and therefore void of lasting value. In Zurvanism, Infinite Time represents eternal and timeless existence and this is the realm of Ohrmazd; finite Time is temporal existence as lived on earth, subject to birth and death, coming to be and passing away, and it is not only the kingdom of Ahriman, but also the very food on which the demon Āz thrives. Yet finite Time is not evil of itself; it is the locus of evil and the food by which it lives. When it 'dies' by being reabsorbed into the Infinite, evil, like a cancer whose life is sustained by the thing it kills, must itself perish with it. The world-process, then, is God's struggle to rescue temporal, conditioned existence from the very powers which seem to make its continuance possible—hunger and thirst and sexual desire. The result, however, is not the escape of the individual or of the universe into a featureless and timeless Nirvāna, but the subsuming of the material world into spirit in which time merges back into the timeless; but the timeless is now no longer the simple, undifferentiated One from which all existent things originally issued forth, but a timeless world in which all created things share in the plenitude of their khwarr, their consummated personality finally delivered from the toils of concupiscence. Ahriman had foolishly threatened to 'demolish the pact, to demolish time', and by this he meant that he would put an end to eternal existence as such and drag all creation down to a purely temporal and therefore mortal level, thereby depriving men for ever of any hope of immortal life; but in the end he himself is vanquished by Āz, the seed of corruption he was fool enough to choose as his weapon against the radiant creation of Ohrmazd. Ohrmazd, on the other hand, once his enemies are annihilated, elevates the whole material creation into the spiritual order, and there the perfection that each created thing has as it issues from the hand of God is restored to it at the final Rehabilitation, the *Frashkart* or 'Making Excellent' when everything that was excellent in time will be excellent in eternity.

Āz—a Borrowing from Buddhism?

Yet different though the goals of Buddhism and the Zurvanism deducible from the Pahlavi books may be, the demon Āz is a Buddhist rather than a Zoroastrian idea; there is no trace of it in the Avesta.[72] In Buddhism, on the other hand, the root cause of the chain of conditioned existence is *avidyā*, 'ignorance', and its principal manifestation is *trshnā*, 'thirst', which means the desire for continued existence in time —intellectual error, then, manifesting itself in concupiscence. The Zoroastrian Āz, too, is both 'ignorance' and 'thirst', both 'wrong-mindedness' and concupiscence; she attacks man both in his body and in his mind. To the body she ultimately brings death, and, in the sphere of responsible human activity, she seeks to drive a wedge between intellect and will.[73] In this she is identical with Akōman, the Evil Mind.[74]

God's weapon is the embodied Zurvān, finite time operating in finite space, the *khwarr* of the whole world; Ahriman's is Āz and Āz thus attacks both the macrocosm, the embodied Zurvān, and the microcosm, man; she is the arch-enemy of both nature and reason. 'During the period of the Aggressor's operation in this world man is tainted with concupiscence whose object is to destroy his *khwarr*,' that is, to divert him from the end for which he was created. Reason, on the other hand, 'was created by the Creator to protect his *khwarr* from concupiscence. Concupiscence is the vice most akin to desire, and a limit [must be set] to desire. Once desire for wealth and power is gratified, concupiscence will be greatly strengthened and reason gravely impaired in [its function of] protecting the *khwarr* from concupiscence.'[75] Concupiscence, then, tries to divorce man's natural desires from the control of reason: as such it is 'self-will', 'wrong-mindedness', and 'heresy'; it leads astray, unsettles, and deceives.[76] In short it is 'ignorance' of the right order of things on the intellectual plane, gluttony, lust, and avarice on the material. It is the transposition of the Buddhist *avidyā* and *trshnā* into a Zoroastrian scheme of things. But the Zoroastrian version of what constitutes 'ignorance' is very different from the Buddhist; it is in no sense a cosmic principle inherent in the very nature of the transitory world, it is simply the failure to recognize the right order of things; it is a deviation from the Aristotelian Mean which the Zoroastrians interpreted as meaning the orderly arrangement of a cosmos created by God. If the idea is originally Buddhistic, the working out of it is thoroughly Zoroastrian.

Essential 'Zoroastrianism' of classical Zurvanism

What remains of Zurvanism in the Pahlavi books is orthodox to this extent, that the goal of creation remains the same as for the orthodox dualists; it is the final expulsion of evil, that is, disorder in all its forms, from the universe, and the transfiguration of the material creation into a 'spiritual' form of existence in which neither death nor wrong thinking will have any place. In the terminology of the Zurvanite myth it means that Zurvān whose doubt engendered Ahriman will, by himself taking on material form, in the end be freed from doubt and all imperfection for ever and ever. Zātspram, too, in his apocalyptic vision of the end, says: 'There will be seen by night in the atmosphere a form of fire in the shape of a man, conceived by the spiritual powers, riding as it were a fiery horse, and fearful [to behold]: and all will be freed from doubt.'[77]

Perhaps the fiery horseman is nothing less than that original 'form of fire, bright, white, round, and manifest afar', with which, in the beginning, Zurvān armed his beloved son, Ohrmazd. Perhaps it is the finite Zurvān himself, the totality of created being, riding back, purified from all doubt and unlawful desire, into the Infinite from which he originally proceeded.

The Gender and Sex of Āz

In its teleology Zurvanism does not seem to differ appreciably from orthodoxy, but there was nonetheless an un-Iranian and Gnostic current within Zurvanism which sought to identify the typically Zoroastrian polarity of good and evil with the more basic polarity of male and female.

Throughout this chapter we have spoken of the demon Āz as 'she'. Middle Persian, however, has no means of distinguishing gender, and there is nothing in the Pahlavi texts themselves to show to what gender this particular demon belongs. In the Avesta, it is true, there is a demon Āzi of masculine gender who extinguishes the fire at night,[78] who is the opponent of the sacrificial milk and fat[79] and of the *khwarenah*;[80] his stock epithet is *daēvō-dāta*, 'created by the demons' or 'following the law of the demons'. It is also true that the Āz of the Pahlavi books has the same stock epithet and that it also assails the *khwarenah* or *khwarr*. But here the resemblance ends, for nowhere does it appear that the Āzi of the Avesta is specifically the demon of greed, and this is the basic characteristic of the later Āz.

The demon Āz, however, as it appears in Zātspram, is closely akin to the Manichaean demon of the same name. In the Persian Manichaean texts, as we have seen, Āz corresponds to the *hyle* of the Greeks—matter not at all in the Aristotelian sense, but in the typically Manichaean sense of 'disorderly motion'. For the Manichees, indeed, 'disorderly motion' was inseparable from everything that exists in space and time, whereas, for the Zoroastrians, it was something imported from outside. The Manichees, however, in attaching Zoroastrian names to their own concepts, did try to make the correspondence as exact as possible. Thus it is not surprising that they should have chosen Āz to represent the totality of the realm of matter which is, for them, through and through evil since, in Manichaean eyes, matter and concupiscence are interchangeable terms.

The Manichaean Āz, however, is feminine: she is the 'mother of all the demons'.[81] It is, then, reasonable to suppose that the Zoroastrian demon was also feminine as the Manichees would scarcely choose a male Zoroastrian demon to fulfil the role of the 'mother of the demons'. Moreover, were it not for the fact that they needed a female entity to represent the totality of evil, they could scarcely have failed to pick on Ahriman for this part.

The Wickedness of the Female

The equation of light with the male principle and of darkness with the female crops up all over the world and has been made much of by C. G. Jung in his psychology of the archetypes. It is, however, a thoroughly un-Iranian idea, yet we do find it cropping up both in the Christian accounts of Zurvanism and in the Pahlavi texts themselves. Hippolytus, as we have seen, said of Zoroaster that he believed the whole universe to have developed from a primal father and mother, the first of whom was light and the second darkness. Similarly we saw that in the Pahlavi texts fire and water were spoken of as male and female, brother and sister, husband and wife, and that from their union proceeded 'all becoming, ripening, and order'.[82] The same is true of the Zurvanite treatise, the *Ulamā-yi Islām*. Water, moreover, is the dark element, and what is dark is generally evil. Water, however, had from the days of the *Gāthā* of the Seven Chapters been regarded as holy and was venerated as such throughout the whole chequered history of Zoroastrianism. Zurvanism, however, is not fully explicable as a purely Iranian phenomenon, and it should not surprise us to find what seem to be un-Iranian ideas in it. Thus a Christian convert from Zoroastrianism tells us that water, though created by Ohrmazd, deserted him for Ahriman.[83] These Zurvanites were not prepared to go so far as to say that water was evil in itself; it only chose evil just as Ahriman himself had done.

The Defection of Woman to Ahriman

On the origins of woman the Pahlavi books are extraordinarily reticent. The Bounteous Immortals who have become fully personalized in the Pahlavi books are all male except Ārmaiti, Right-mindedness, who is identified with Mother Earth. On Ahriman's side there is a mysterious figure Jēh, the Whore. Both the *Bundahishn* and the Christian Syriac writer, Theodore bar Konai, give accounts of the activities of this lady, but whereas the *Bundahishn* speaks of her as the 'whore', Theodore speaks of her as simply 'woman'. She too, like water, deserts her creator, Ohrmazd, for his enemy, Ahriman. Theodore describes the behaviour of the first women in these words:

'After Ohrmazd had given women to righteous men, they fled and went over to Satan; and when Ohrmazd provided righteous men with peace and happiness, Satan provided women too with happiness. As Satan had allowed the women to ask for anything they wanted, Ohrmazd feared that they might ask to have intercourse with the righteous men and that these might suffer damage thereby. Seeking to avoid this, he created the god Narsēh, [a youth] of fifteen years of age. And he put him, naked as he was, behind Satan so that the women should see him, desire him, and ask Satan for him. The women lifted their hands up towards Satan and said: "Satan, our father, give us the god Narsēh as a gift." '84

The *Bundahishn* account differs from Theodore's in some respects. There is one Righteous Man only, Gayōmart, the progenitor of the human race; and there is one woman only, Jēh, the whore, whose origins are left wholly unexplained. Moreover, Theodore seems to have imported the god Narsēh from a similar Manichaean myth, for he is wholly absent from the *Bundahishn* account.

In Zoroastrianism man is God's supreme creation, designed to play the foremost part in the destruction of Ahriman and the Lie. So holy was he that the mere sight of him caused Ahriman to faint, so hopeless did he now consider the struggle to be.

'When the Destructive Spirit saw that he himself and the demons were powerless on account of the Righteous Man, he swooned away. For three thousand years he lay in a swoon. And as he lay thus unconscious, the demons with monstrous heads cried out one by one [saying]: "Arise, O our father, for we would join a battle from which Ohrmazd and the Bounteous Immortals will suffer straitness and misery." And one by one they minutely related their own evil deeds. But the accursed Destructive Spirit was not comforted, nor did he arise out of his swoon for fear of the Righteous Man;

till the accursed Whore came after the three thousand years had run their course, and she cried out [saying]: "Arise, O our father, for in the battle [to come] I shall let loose so much affliction on the Righteous Man and the toiling Bull that, because of my deeds, they will not be fit to live. I shall take away their dignity (*khwarr*): I shall afflict the water, I shall afflict the earth, I shall afflict the fire, I shall afflict the plants, I shall afflict all the creation which Ohrmazd has created." And she related her evil deeds so minutely that the Destructive Spirit was comforted, leapt up out of his swoon, and kissed the head of the Whore; and that pollution called menstruation appeared on the Whore. And the Destructive Spirit cried out to the demon Whore: "Whatsoever is thy desire, that do thou ask, that I may give it thee." Then Ohrmazd in his omniscience knew that at that time the Destructive Spirit could give whatever the demon Whore asked and that there would be great profit to him thereby. (The appearance of the body of the Destructive Spirit was in the form of a frog.) And [Ohrmazd] showed one like unto a young man of fifteen years of age to the demon Whore; and the demon Whore fastened her thoughts on him. And the demon Whore cried out to the Destructive Spirit [saying]: "Give me desire for man that I may seat him in the house as my lord." But the Destructive Spirit cried out unto her [saying]: "I do not bid thee ask for anything, for thou knowest [only] to ask for what is profitless and bad." But the time had passed when he could have refused to give what she asked.'[85]

Now the Pahlavi word for 'whore' means etymologically no more than 'one who bears children' and must originally have meant simply a 'woman', and this presumably is what she originally was in mythology too. There is, moreover, another curious resemblance to Theodore bar Konai's account. Unlike the other demons the Whore does not seem to have been with Ahriman from the beginning: she came to him 'after three thousand years'. So it would seem that in this very unorthodox account of the creation Ohrmazd provided Gayōmart with a consort and that the pair of them existed side by side for three thousand years without making contact of any kind; and it was only after the full three thousand years had run their course that the woman, understandably bored, decided to seek adventure elsewhere. Undeterred by the unpleasing form Ahriman had elected to assume just then, she attached herself to him, and by submitting to his kiss became irremediably defiled. As if this were not enough, she then proceeded to 'join herself [to the Destructive Spirit]. For the defilement of females she joined herself to him, that she might defile females; and the females, because they were defiled, might defile the males; and [the males] would turn aside from their proper work.'[86]

The Defilement of Man by Woman

Apart from the three passages we have quoted we know nothing more of the 'Whore', and we are never told the end of the story. Since, however, the Whore is the 'most grievous adversary of the Righteous Man', and since, merely by recounting the harm she can do to him, she could arouse Ahriman from the stupor into which the mere sight of the Righteous Man had cast him, and since her aim is to defile the male through the already defiled female, the end of the affair can scarcely be in doubt: she forced the Righteous Man into union with her. Only so can it be explained how Ohrmazd 'knew that at that time the Destructive Spirit could give whatever the demon Whore asked and that there would be great profit to him (Ohrmazd) thereby'. It was his intention all along that, despite the woman's perverse behaviour, the two sexes should be united so that the human race could increase and multiply. With this end in mind he exhibited to her a 'young man of fifteen years of age'. The stratagem worked, for the woman immediately demanded of Ahriman that he give her the 'desire for man', which, it would appear, Ohrmazd had not himself been able to supply. The balance of advantage was now with Ohrmazd. It is true that Ahriman had succeeded in defiling woman and that she in her turn would defile man, but, in compensation for this, it was now assured that woman would be subjected to man for ever and that—what was much more important—she would enable the Righteous Man to propagate his race.

We have seen that one of the characteristics of Zurvanism is that it does, on occasion, represent Ohrmazd as being rather less than all-wise and all-powerful. It is therefore somewhat surprising to read in an otherwise orthodox book like the *Bundahishn* that he himself confesses that, think as he might, he could find no other way of ensuring the survival of the human male except by creating 'woman whose adversary is the whore species'. And so he laments:

'I created thee, O thou whose adversary is the whore species, and thou wast created with a mouth close to the buttocks, and coition seems to thee even as the taste of the sweetest food to the mouth; and thou art a helper to me, for from thee is man born; but thou dost grieve me who am Ohrmazd. But had I found another vessel from which to make man, never would I have created thee, whose adversary is the whore species. But I sought in the waters and in the earth, in plants and cattle, in the highest mountains and deep valleys, but I did not find a vessel from which righteous man might proceed except woman whose adversary is the whore.'[87]

This, again, has a Zurvanite flavour about it, for Ohrmazd, the all-mighty and all-wise, confesses that he is neither. In order to multiply the males of the human race who fight his battle against Ahriman, he can think of nothing better to do than to create woman, despite the fact that she causes him pain. This attribution of a certain naïveté to Ohrmazd combined with an almost horrified aversion to all that is female seems to be typical of Zurvanism. The female is represented as having a fatal propensity to evil, for both water and woman herself, though created by Ohrmazd, desert him and take the Devil's part.

This Gnostic element in Zurvanism, however, which equates the female with evil, is peripheral, but it is nonetheless there; and it is this, no doubt, that induced the High Priest Mānushchihr to say that his brother, Zātspram, would find few to gainsay him among the Manichees.[88] Zātspram, indeed, stands nearest to the Zurvanites of all our extant Pahlavi sources, and it is he, more than anyone else, who raises Āz-concupiscence to an almost Manichaean eminence in the hierarchy of evil. For him, at least, we cannot help feeling, Āz was, as she was for the Manichees, not just one female among many, but the 'mother of all the demons'.

CHAPTER ELEVEN

ZURVĀN

The Sevenfold Zurvān—Macrocosm and Microcosm—Zurvān, the God of Fate—The God of Death—The God of the Resurrection—The Fatalism of Firdausī's Epic—The Orthodox Attitude to Fate—Man's Response to Fate—Orthodoxy's Reaction to the Three Types of Zurvanism

ZURVANISM proper differs from orthodoxy in that it posits a principle prior to the two Spirits of light and darkness, good and evil—the principle of Infinite Time. There is no evidence that it made any difference to the cult or that any particular reverence was paid to Zurvān as a god. Indeed, there would be singularly little point in doing so, for as the Infinite he is incomprehensible, and as finite Time he is a Fate that cannot be deflected, a law that cannot be altered. Before we leave him to study a little more closely the theology of the orthodox, let us try to see just what kind of god he was.

The Sevenfold Zurvān

'Zurvān has seven faces, and on each face three eyes,' we read.[1] He is a sevenfold god, and each of the seven aspects of his complex nature has three facets. As Infinite Time his three aspects are infinite space, infinite wisdom, and infinite power, that is, an infinite potentiality of initiating contingent beings, whether good or evil. He is passionless and indifferent, 'unageing and deathless; he knows neither pain nor decay nor corruption; he has no rival, nor can he ever be put aside or deprived of his sovereignty in his proper sphere.'[2] He has neither 'pleasure nor pain from the evil of Ahriman or the goodness of Ohrmazd'.[3]

As finite Time he is primarily 'he who makes virile, he who makes excellent, and he who makes old'. Alternatively, the order of the attributes is altered and he becomes 'he who makes virile, he who makes old, and he who makes excellent'. As such he is the god of life and death, presiding over the birth, maturity, and death of the body. As *Frashōqar*, 'he who makes excellent,' he is both the god who brings creatures to maturity and the author of the *Frashkart*, the 'Making Excellent' or final Rehabilitation at the end of time. When he is thought of in this role, the epithet *frashōqar*, 'he who makes excellent' appears at the end of the series.[4]

236

Seen simply as Infinite Time, his aspects are finite Time, the course of fate, and the year. As Order, his aspects are the god Mithra, the Spirit of Right Order (*dātastān*), and Fate; and as Fate itself he is also the actual decree or moment of destiny, the decisive moment at which what is fated comes to pass, and the fixed decision. On the earth he represents the social order, and he is therefore the three great social orders of priests, warriors, and husbandmen. He is also the author of good and evil: he is the Cherisher, the Adversary, and he who has command of both. Thus the sevenfold Zurvān's functions can be tabulated thus:

ZURVĀN

Being: (Time), Space, Wisdom, Power.
Becoming: he who makes virile, he who makes excellent, he who makes old.
Order: Mithra, Order, Fate.
Time: Finite Time, the course of fate, the year.
Fate: the decree, the decisive moment, the fixed decision.
Good and Evil: the Cherisher, the Adversary, the One who has command of both.
Social Order: priests, warriors, and husbandmen.[5]

Macrocosm and Microcosm

As finite space as well as finite Time Zurvān is embodied in the macrocosm, and man, the microcosm, is made in his image, the parts of man corresponding in every respect to the parts of the universe *in toto*. Thus, the seven constituents of the material world which themselves correspond to the seven Bounteous Immortals—fire, water, earth, metals, plants, animals, and man—correspond to the marrow, blood, veins, sinews, bones, flesh, and hair of man. The four elements in the macrocosm correspond to the breath, blood, bile, and phlegm in man; and just as the world is controlled and kept in working order by the elements of fire and air, so is man's body controlled and directed by his Fravashi or external soul working in close co-operation with his vital spirit. In the world this vital spirit which maintains the macrocosm as a living unit is Vay(u), the atmospheric wind, in exactly the same way as breath keeps the human body alive. In man it is the soul (*ruvān*) which guides the body and gives it consciousness; so too is the world guided by the world-soul, which is nothing less than the heavenly sphere.[6] The heavenly sphere, then, is not only the body of Zurvān, but also his soul. And Zurvān is sick in soul.

Zurvān, the God of Fate

He is sick in soul because he doubted; and this sickness reflects itself in the heavenly sphere, for it contains not only the twelve Signs of the Zodiac which pour out abundance on to the earth, but also the seven planets which intercept the good gifts of the Zodiac and divert them to people and purposes for which they were never intended. Thus, the embodied Zurvān is the god of fate, and because he himself must work out his own salvation in finite time and gradually wear away the residue of his sin which is still very much with him, he is willy-nilly the dispenser of good and bad fortune alike. As macrocosm he is subject, like the microcosm, man, to the depredations of Ahriman; and as man is afflicted by disease and sin, so is the poise of the macrocosm upset by the disorderly motion of the planets; and this disorderly motion accounts for the evil lot on earth that man is sometimes fated to endure.

'All the welfare and adversity that come to man and other creatures come through the Seven and the Twelve. The twelve Signs of the Zodiac . . . are the twelve commanders on the side of Ohrmazd; and the seven planets are said to be the seven commanders on the side of Ahriman. And the seven planets oppress all creation and deliver it over to death and all manner of evil: for the twelve Signs of the Zodiac and the seven planets rule the fate of the world and direct it.'[7]

The orderly functioning of the universe is the responsibility of the Zodiac just as man's ordered moral activity is directed by the Good Mind indwelling him. The planets, on the other hand, originated by Ahriman, are likened to the Evil Mind in man; and just as the Evil Mind seeks to drive a wedge between man's intellect and will, so do the planets seek to bring about disarray in the heavenly sphere, the soul of the world.[8]

The Zoroastrians turned the planets into demons because their irregular motion could not be explained. When, however, they came into contact with the Babylonians, they learnt the 'science' of astrology, and this attributed different influences to the different planets. Some, like Saturn and Mars, were inauspicious; others, like Jupiter and Venus, auspicious. How was this to be explained? In the Zoroastrian scheme of things the planets who accompany Ahriman in his invasion of the material world, each choose a specific constellation as their opponent. Thus Jupiter is matched against the Great Bear, Venus against Scorpio. In their case their opponents prove more than a match for them and force them to do whatever they wish. The reverse, however, is true of Saturn and Mars, who, proving stronger than their chosen opponents, are free to do more or less what they like.[9]

The God of Death
Zurvān, as finite Time and Fate, is neither good nor evil: he is 'dyed'

238

with both.[10] Being the embodied universe he is the *locus* of good and evil, just as man's body is the *locus* of sin as well as of virtue. As a deity, rather than as an abstract concept, Zurvān, being also fate, is primarily thought of as the god of death, and as such he is:

'mightier than both creations—the creation of Ohrmazd and that of the Destructive Spirit. Time understands action and order. Time understands more than those who understand. Time is better informed than the well-informed; for through Time must the decision be made. By Time are houses overturned—doom is through Time—and things graven shattered. From him no single mortal man escapes, not though he fly above, not though he dig a pit below and settle therein, not though he hide beneath a well of cold waters.'[11]

Time is synonymous with death; and even in the Avesta the paths of Time are the paths the soul must traverse on its way from death to the Judgement.[12]

The inevitability of death and man's helplessness before it is a constant undercurrent of much that is greatest in Persian poetry, and this thoroughly pessimistic and almost morbid strand in the Persian national tradition must ultimately go back to that Zurvanite fatalism over which Āturpāt, son of Mahraspand, gained his all too ephemeral victory. Typical of this dreary preoccupation with a banal subject is this: 'As to him whose eye Time has sewn up, his back is seized upon and will never rise again; pain comes upon his heart so that it beats no more; his hand is broken so that it grows no more; and his foot is broken so that it walks no more. The stars come upon him, and he goes not out another time; fate comes upon him and he cannot drive it off.'[13]

The God of the Resurrection

Death is the lot of all men, and in this respect the fate of the macrocosm is no different from that of the microcosm. The world is born, grows old, and dies; but the death of the world is only the prelude to its transfiguration at the *Frashkart*, the 'Making Excellent' of existence when finite Time rejoins the Infinite, and when the Final Body, which is the material creation renewed, sets in. Zurvanism, so long as it remains within its Zoroastrian context, is no more pessimistic than is orthodoxy, for Zurvān is not only *Zarōqar*, 'he who brings old age', but also *Frashōqar*, 'he who brings about the *Frashkart*' itself. The 'fatalists', then, against whom Āturpāt strove, were not the same as the 'classical' Zurvanites who saw in Zurvān the father of Ohrmazd and Ahriman.

239

The Fatalism of Firdausī's Epic

Firdausī, in his great epic, has little to tell us about Zoroastrianism proper. His whole poem, however, is pervaded with an atmosphere of fatalistic gloom which he may well have inherited from the 'fatalists' of the Sassanian period. These may either have been genuine Zoroastrians who merely extended the sphere of fate from man's purely material lot to his moral action, men like the author of the *Mēnōk i Khrat* whose pessimism we have had occasion to note above; or they may have been, like the Zandīks or Dahrīs, men who derived all things from Infinite Time and who took no cognizance of either Ohrmazd or Ahriman. That such a sect existed can be inferred from a passage in Firdausī which contains what looks very like a Magian catechism. Zāl, the father of the great Iranian hero Rustam, is summoned by the king to appear before the Magian hierarchy, and he is required to answer a whole series of riddles: he is being submitted to an examination in religious knowledge. The first question they put to him is this: 'What are those twelve noble cypresses which grow majestic and luxuriant, and each one shoots forth thirty boughs which neither wax nor wane?'

These, Zāl replies, are the twelve new moons that occur in every year, and their branches are the days of the month, for 'such is the revolution of Time'.

The second Magus now puts his question: 'Two horses, precious and fleet of foot, are galloping, the one [black] as a lake of pitch, the other lustrous as white crystal. On they hasten, but never do they catch each other up.' 'Both,' says Zāl, 'the white and the black are Time, and they are hot on each other's heels. These are night and day, ever passing on, which count every moment of the heavenly sphere above us. They do not catch each other up as they gallop on, running like the quarry before the hounds.'

Next he is questioned about 'those thirty horsemen passing in review before the king—one was lost; but if thou lookest aright all thirty are back again when thou dost number them.' These, Zāl sees, must again represent the numbering of the new moons, and the one that appears to be missing is the day on which the moon wholly disappears. Next comes a question concerning a 'meadow full of greenery and streams. A man with a great sharp scythe strides insolently towards the meadow. Moist and dry he mows down, and if thou make supplication he will not hear thee.' Zāl has no difficulty in finding the answer to this one, for:

'this is the woodcutter Time, and we are like the grass. All one to him are grandson and grandsire, he takes account of neither old nor young. He hunts whatever prey comes his way. Such is the nature and composition of the world that save for death no mother bore a son. We enter in at one door and pass out of another: Time counts our every breath.'

Next he is again questioned about

'two lofty cypresses [shaken] like reeds in a stormy sea. On these a bird has made its home: at dusk it perches on the one, at dawn on the other. When it flies from the one, its foliage withers, and when it alights on the other, it gives out a scent of musk. Of these two one is ever fresh, but the leaves and fruit of the other are all withered up.'

These, Zāl sees, are the 'two arms of the lofty sphere through which we rejoice and through which we are grieved. . . . The flying bird is the sun from which the world has hope and of which it is afraid'.

The last question has a more sombre note:

'In a mountainous country I came upon a massive fortress. Wise men left that citadel and settled on the plain in a thorny place. They built buildings reaching high up to the moon: some became menials, others men of high estate. Suddenly an earthquake arose and all their lands and habitations clean disappeared. Necessity brought them [back] to the citadel and brought them long forebodings. These words hide a mystery. Seek, and speak up plainly before the lords.'

Zāl is not confounded and answers:

'The citadel in a mountainous country is the House of Eternity and the Place of Reckoning. The thorny place is this transitory abode which is at once pleasure and treasure and grief and pain. It counts the breath you breathe, it gives increase and carries it away. Wind and earthquake arise and bring grief and lamentation on the world. [The fruits of] all our toiling must be left behind in this thorny place and we must pass on to the citadel. Another will taste of [the fruits of] our toil, but he [again] must leave them and pass on. So has it ever been from the beginning, so it is, and so will it ever be. If our provision is a fair repute, our soul will be honoured on the other side; but if we practise wantonness (*āz*) and twist and turn, [all] will become manifest when we pass beyond life. Though our palace outstrip Saturn, nothing but a winding-sheet will be our portion. When brick and earth are heaped upon us, then will there be every reason for fear and care and anguish.'[14]

The whole tone of this passage is totally unlike anything we have yet come across in Zoroastrianism. The buoyant optimism of that religion has given way to the total scepticism of despair, yet the terminology used shows that Firdausī is drawing on a genuine Iranian tradition. The House of Eternity (*sarāy-i dirang*) is plainly the realm of Infinite Time whose essence is 'eternal duration (*drang*) undivided into past and future'.[15] Similarly the 'two arms of the lofty sphere through which we rejoice and through which we are grieved' correspond to that same sphere which is the body of Zurvān and which contains both the Signs of the Zodiac—the source of well-being—and the planets—the oppressors of man—the good sphere 'which gives [good things] in abundance', and the evil sphere 'which gives them sparingly'.[16] Further, the two horses, the black and the white, which are night and day, remind us of the light and the darkness from which, according to Eudemus of Rhodes, the twin Spirits proceeded and which were themselves the first emanation of the ultimate Unity called alternatively 'Time' or 'Space'.

Again, the preoccupation with the days, the months, and the years displayed by Firdausī's Magi takes us right back to the Avesta with its curious veneration of the divisions of time. Firdausī, then, is drawing on genuine Iranian material, but he suppresses the Zoroastrian message of hope which proclaims that though this world is transitory and subject to decay and though its balance has been upset by the disorderly motion brought into it by Ahriman and the demons, this will in the end all be made right; the whole will be redeemed and 'made excellent' in eternity. Of this there is no hint in Firdausī. The House of Eternity is the kind of place you leave to try your fortune in a world you know to be full of thorns, and it is the kind of place that only an earthquake will make you return to and then only with 'long foreboding'. It is implied that virtue will be rewarded and wantonness exposed, but there is no hint of what the reward will be. The House of Eternity is devoid of joy; it is a 'massive fortress' more like a beleaguered city than the traditional 'garden' of paradise. It is the very symbol of hopelessness. Such may well have been the gloomy vision not only of the fatalists but of the Zandīks too, who believed in neither heaven nor hell, God nor the Devil, but only in an impersonal and inscrutable Infinite Time from which a senseless and uncomprehending world proceeds and into which it is reabsorbed.

Zurvanism, then, would seem to have sheltered two quite distinct aberrations within its fold, the one equating the female principle with evil, the other assigning all power to fate and thereby making all action and all resolve futile. Fatalism was perhaps the gravest threat against which Zoroastrianism had to fight, for it sought to undermine the rock of the unfettered freedom of the human will on which the Iranian Prophet's religion was founded. It is now time to consider what the orthodox had to say on this thorny question of fate and free will.

The Orthodox Attitude to Fate

Fatalism in its extreme form, of which the passage we have just cited from Firdausī is a good example, probably entered into Zoroastrianism from Babylonian astrology. It was challenged and overcome by Āturpāt, son of Mahraspand, during the reign of Shāpūr II. His views on this subject may then be taken as authoritative.

'It is said that Āturpāt, son of Mahraspand, divided the things of this world into twenty-five parts: five [he assigned] to fate, five to [human] action, five to nature, five to character, and five to heredity. Life, wife, children, sovereignty, and property are chiefly through fate. Salvation and damnation, and the qualities that make a [good] priest, warrior, or husbandman are chiefly through action. Eating, walking, going in to one's wife, sleeping, and satisfying the needs of nature are chiefly through nature. Worthiness, friendship, goodness, generosity, and rectitude are chiefly through character. Intelligence, understanding, body, stature, and appearance are chiefly through heredity.'[17]

Thus the operation of fate is restricted to a bare minimum; it controls only the material side of life, your family life, the social position you occupy, and your income. The major virtues are 'through character', and that means, presumably, that there are natural tendencies towards virtue and its opposite in each man, and that his natural endowment of virtue is therefore variable. This will mean that the quest for salvation will be easier for some than it is for others, and that men, in this respect, are not born equal. Yet the chance of salvation is there for all to take, and no man is damned through anyone's fault but his own. Salvation and damnation result from our actions and the free will that initiates them. The semi-Zurvanite *Mēnōk i Khrat*, as we have seen, had allotted to fate a sinister power to change a man's character; it could make the wise foolish, the brave cowardly, and the energetic sluggish; but this is untypical, for we read elsewhere that 'sloth is to be attributed to action, not to fate';[18] and even the *Mēnōk i Khrat* nowhere suggests that the future destiny of the soul can be conditioned by fate. True, one man's material lot on earth may be very different from another's, and this may affect his conduct, but in the long run this cannot influence his final spiritual state.

'In his kindly care for his creatures Ohrmazd the Lord distributes all good things to good and bad alike; but when they do not arrive equally, it is due to the violence of Ahriman and the demons and to the theft of them by the seven planets. The soul in the spiritual world is made to receive its deserts in accordance with its deeds because each man is damned [only] on account of the deeds which he himself has done.'[19]

Fate and effort on man's part each had its proper part to play in the general scheme of things. Contentment with one's lot is a cardinal Zoroastrian virtue, but being content with one's lot is very different from attributing one's moral shortcomings to a blind and pitiless fate as Firdausī so often does in his epic. As so often, Zoroastrian orthodoxy comes down on the side of sanity. Misfortune must be cheerfully borne as a temporary affliction inflicted by the demons; it cannot last for ever because the demons who are the authors of it are themselves doomed to destruction.

What is fated, is fated in the beginning, and cannot normally be changed. Even so the powers of good can initiate special dispensations in favour of the just, but only on a spiritual, not on a material plane 'because the accursed Ahriman makes this a pretext to rob the good and worthy of wealth and all other material prosperity through the power of the seven planets, and to bestow it chiefly on the evil and unworthy'.[20]

This is in the nature of things in this world so long as it exists in a mixed state, and human action is powerless to ward off the blows of fortune, but efforts exerted in a good cause bear their fruit in the next world. 'One cannot appropriate by effort such good things as have not been fated; but such as have been fated always come when an effort is made. But effort, if it is not favoured by Time, is fruitless on earth, but later, in the spiritual world, it comes to our aid and increases in the balance.'[21]

Misfortune, then, though initiated by the malice of the seven planets, indirectly stimulates man to further effort, or at least it should do so, for 'fate and action are like body and vital spirit. The body without the vital spirit is a useless carcase, and the vital spirit without the body is an impalpable wind. But when they are fused together, they are powerful and exceedingly beneficial.'[22]

Man's Response to Fate
The right attitude towards fate and human endeavour is even better formulated in the so-called *Epistle of Tansar* which was probably written in the reign of Khusraw I.

'Know for certain that whoso neglects to make efforts and puts his trust in fate and destiny, makes himself contemptible, and whosoever continually exerts himself and makes efforts but denies fate and destiny, is a fool and puffed up with pride. The wise man must find the mean between effort and fate, and not be content with [only] one of them. For fate and effort are like two bales of a traveller's baggage on the back of a mule. If one of them is heavier and the other lighter, the load will fall to the ground, and the back of the mule will be broken, and the traveller will suffer embarrassment, and will not reach his destination. But if both bales are equal, the traveller will not need to worry, the mule will be comfortable, and both will arrive at their destination.'[23]

Orthodoxy, then, does not deny fate but restricts the field over which it has control. It cannot affect man's ultimate destiny nor can it cheat him of his salvation; it is rather a testing of a man's character, and the right attitude towards it is one of philosophic acceptance. The manner of this acceptance is again referred to by Āturpāt, son of Mahraspand, in a saying that was reputedly among his last words. He bids his hearers to be contented in adversity and patient in disaster. They should not put their trust in the life of this world, but rather in good works, for 'the good man's works are his advocate and an evil man's [works] are his accuser'. Moreover, there are six good reasons for accepting misfortune with a good grace.

'There is no misfortune that has befallen me, Āturpāt, son of Mahraspand, from which I have [not] derived six kinds of comfort. First, when a misfortune [befell me], I was thankful that it was no worse. Secondly, when a misfortune fell not upon my soul but upon my body, [I was thankful,] for it seemed to me better that it should befall the body rather than the soul. Thirdly, [I was thankful] that of all the misfortunes that are due to me one [at least] had passed. Fourthly, I was thankful that I was so good a man that the accursed and damnable Ahriman and the demons should bring misfortune on my body on account of my goodness. Fifthly, [I was thankful] that since whoever commits an evil deed will be made to suffer for it either in his own person or in that of his children, it was I myself who paid the price, not my children. Sixthly, I was thankful that since all the harm that the accursed Ahriman and his demons can do to the creatures of Ohrmazd is limited, any misfortune that befalls me will be a loss to his treasury, and he will not be able to inflict it a second time on some other good man.'[24]

In this saying of Āturpāt's we meet with a principle that seems to be held in common by both orthodoxy and 'classical' Zurvanism, namely, that the evil that Ahriman does must ultimately turn out to the advantage of Ohrmazd and his creation. And just as in this passage Ahriman is the ultimate loser, so too, in the Zurvanite account of woman's defection from Ohrmazd to Ahriman, the net result is good, for she is definitively subjected to man and an unfailing supply of male progeny is assured. In both wings of Zoroastrianism, despite the occasional insights the Zurvanites ascribed to him, Ahriman is in the long run defeated by his own stupidity.

The reformed Zoroastrianism of the Sassanian period was the result of a conscious attempt of the secular and religious authorities to find a religion that was at once national and rational and which would be able to weld the Iranian nation into a unity. This unity was constantly threatened by the recrudescence of Zurvanism in one of its three forms. It would, however, be wrong to suppose that reformed Zoroastrianism was entirely a matter of political expediency, for at the time when the Sassanians ousted the Arsacids as the ruling house of Iran, Zoroastrianism was still a living faith. It is true that it had been dealt a shattering blow by Alexander and that its organization had been disrupted, but there must have remained a substantial remnant that had preserved the basic teachings of Zoroaster. This remnant called itself the *Pōryutkēshān*, 'followers of the ancient faith', and the Zurvanites in their various forms must therefore have been regarded as innovators.

Orthodoxy's Reaction to the Three Types of Zurvanism

We have attempted to distinguish between three distinct sects which considered Time to be the source of all things—the Zurvanite materialists or Zandīks, the fatalists, and the 'classical' Zurvanites who elevated Zurvān to a supreme ontological position as being the father of Ohrmazd and Ahriman. It should not, however, be supposed that the three sects did not overlap. Even so, classical Zurvanism must be distinguished from Zurvanite materialism in that it not only admits the existence of Ohrmazd and Ahriman, but also lays very nearly as much stress on the duality of good and evil as does orthodoxy; and in this it remains true to the spirit of the Prophet's teaching and to his whole attitude to religion. Zurvanite materialism, on the other hand, which almost certainly derived from India or Greece, jettisoned everything that had for centuries been characteristic of Zoroastrianism— free will, rewards and punishments, heaven and hell, Ohrmazd and Ahriman themselves. It was thoroughly un-Zoroastrian in that it no longer thought in ethical terms; it was quite literally the dialectical materialism of its day. Fatalism was its natural offshoot; but whereas an unethical materialism was never likely to find acceptance within the Zoroastrian fold—although there is at least one passage in the *Dēnkart* which seems to be purely materialist—fatalism could be combined either with classical Zurvanism or with orthodoxy. From the point of view of orthodoxy, then, it was a more subtle poison; for whereas the question of whether God and the Devil were independent substances or had proceeded from the womb of a morally neutral Time might be a most serious theological issue, it need not necessarily run counter to the essential Zoroastrian dogmas of free will, rewards and punishments and so on. By identifying Time with fate, however, and making all human and divine activity dependent on it, the fatalists divested not only Ahriman but also Ohrmazd of all effective power. In Zāl's reply to the Magi, which is nothing if not fatalist, there is a faint reference to rewards and punishments, but that is all that survives of the old religion. Otherwise Time, both in the 'House of Eternity' and in this 'transitory abode', is in complete and awful control of the human situation. This kind of fatalism and Zoroastrian orthodoxy stand poles apart: the assumptions from which they start are totally different. So it was that Zurvanite materialism and fatalism were both officially condemned. Classical Zurvanism was in a different case. The myth of the genesis of Ohrmazd and Ahriman from Time could be incorporated into orthodoxy in philosophical if not in mythological terms. This done, there remained very little of real importance that separated the two parties. Even the question of the origin and nature of woman does not seem to have stirred up any partisan feeling, for the myth of the Primal Whore occurs both in a Zurvanite context and in the Pahlavi books. The only difference is that whereas in the Zurvanite account it is woman as such who deserts Ohrmazd for Ahriman, in the *Bundahishn* she is disguised as the 'whore'. Moreover, once mentioned she is promptly forgotten; and the human race is represented as arising not from her union with the Righteous Man, but from the emission of the latter's seed into Mother Earth out of which he had himself been formed. From the earth, too, the first human *couple* would also arise who, through their offspring, would carry Ohrmazd's fight against Ahriman and the Lie to a victorious conclusion.

CHAPTER TWELVE

OHRMAZD AND AHRIMAN

The Orthodox Cosmogony—Finite and Infinite in the Orthodox Account—The Nature of God—The First Creation—Ahriman's Reaction—The Weapons of Ohrmazd and Ahriman—The Limiting of Time—The Perdurance of Ohrmazd's Creation—Ohrmazd's Instrument, the Endless Form—Ahriman's Instrument, Concupiscence—Zurvanite Origin of these 'Instruments'—Creation of Truth and Falsehood—Ohrmazd's Offer of Peace—Ahriman Laid Low—Creation of the Bounteous Immortals and their Demonic Counterparts—The Material Creation—The Heavenly Sphere or Macrocosm—A Variation Derived from India—Man the Microcosm—Man's Fravashis Consent to Descend to Earth—Ahriman's Revival and Assault against the Material World—The Fall of Man

The Orthodox Cosmogony

'Ohrmazd was on high in omniscience and goodness: for Infinite Time he was ever in the light. That light is the Space and place of Ohrmazd: some call it the Endless Light. Omniscience and goodness are the totality of Ohrmazd: some call them the Religion. The interpretation of both is the same. That totality is [also] Infinite Time, for Ohrmazd, and the Space, Religion, and Time of Ohrmazd were and are and ever shall be.

'Ahriman, slow in knowledge, whose will is to smite, was deep down in the darkness: [he was] and is, yet will not be. The will to smite is his all, and darkness is his place: some call it the Endless Darkness.

'Between them was the Void: some call it Vay in which the two Spirits mingle.'[1]

So does the *Bundahishn* describe the original state of existence. Zātspram, more succinctly, simply says: 'The light was above and the darkness beneath; and between them was the Void. Ohrmazd in the light and Ahriman in the darkness.'[2]

This is the orthodox dualist position. From the beginning light and darkness exist, the one extending infinitely in an upward direction, the other in a downward one. Between them is the Void which, presumably, is extended *ad infinitum* on either side. Thus Ohrmazd is spatially limited but unlimited in time, for he will vanquish Ahriman and live on for ever. Ahriman is limited both spatially and temporally, for it is his destiny to be destroyed. Neither in the *Bundahishn* nor in Zātspram is there any conception of 'Infinite Time' as a state of being exempt from duration. The *Bundahishn* is literalist in the extreme.

Finite and Infinite in the Orthodox Account

'Concerning the finite and the infinite: the heights which are called the Endless Light (since they have no end) and the depths which are the Endless Darkness, these are the infinite. On the border both are finite since between them is the Void, and there is no contact between the two. Again both Spirits in themselves are finite. Further . . . everything that is within the knowledge of Ohrmazd is finite; that is, he knows the norm that exists between the two Spirits until the creation of Ohrmazd shall rule supreme at the Final Body for ever and ever: that is the infinite. At that time when the Final Body comes to pass, the creation of Ahriman will be destroyed: that again is the finite.'[3]

Thus Ohrmazd, though described as omniscient, is nevertheless not so; he knows only what will take place in finite time and finite space; he cannot know more, that is, he cannot know the infinite, for the infinite is of its nature incomprehensible.[4] Neither before the creation of finite time nor after its cessation, then, can God know his infinite nature. This problem which was squarely faced by Mardān-Farrukh, does not seem to have been understood by the author of the *Bundahishn* since for him Infinite Time means not an eternal, timeless state of being, but an infinite time sequence—time without beginning and time without end.

The Nature of God

The divine personality is made up of Ohrmazd himself and the 'Space, Religion, and Time of Ohrmazd'. These constitute the four hypostases of the one God: they are Ohrmazd and the 'three creators who have one name: one is Space, one Religion, and one Time: they have always existed.'[5] Space, however, in an orthodox context, commonly means the Endless Light, while 'Religion' is itself identical with the divine omniscience or Wisdom.[6] The divine personality, then, comprises Infinite Time, Light, Wisdom, and lastly Ohrmazd himself, the active creator-God.

The First Creation

Ohrmazd, in his omniscience, knows of the existence of Ahriman and of the inevitability of an attack from that quarter. As an initial precaution, then, he creates within the Void an 'instrument' called the 'Endless Form' which derives from the Endless Light and is the raw material of creation. This Endless Form corresponds to the weapon which, in the Zurvanite version of the same story, Zurvān gives to Ohrmazd. It is the 'form of his creatures—a form of fire, bright, white, round, and manifest afar'.[7] For three thousand years this 'form' is

249

'without thought, without movement, intangible, in a moist state like semen'.[8] It is the source from which all creation proceeds, it is the 'Wheel' or heavenly sphere,[9] elsewhere described as the body of Time,[10] it is the sky,[11] and it is macrocosmic man.[12] From it all creation proceeds.

'The creation of Ohrmazd was fostered spiritually in such wise that it remained without thought, without movement, intangible, in a moist state like semen. After this moist state came mixture like [that of] semen and blood; after mixture came conception, like a foetus; after conception came diffusion, such as hands and feet; after diffusion came hollowing—eyes, ears, and mouth; after hollowing came movement when it came forward to the light. Even now on earth do men in this wise grow together in their mother's womb, and are born and bred. Ohrmazd by the act of creation is both father and mother to creation: for in that he nurtured creation in unseen (*mēnōk*) form, he acted as a mother, and in that he created it in material form, he acted as a father.'[13]

Ohrmazd, in this passage, is, like Zurvān, bisexual: he is both father and mother of his creation, and his son is the heavenly sphere which is itself the macrocosm and finite space. The roles are reversed, for now it is no longer Zurvān who is father and mother of Ohrmazd; Ohrmazd is father and mother of Zurvān as finite space and macrocosmic man.

Ahriman's Reaction
The whole cosmic process from the original creation to the final Rehabilitation lasts twelve thousand years, the duration of finite time, corresponding to the twelve Signs of the Zodiac in the heavens.[14] During the first three thousand years Ahriman becomes aware of the existence of Ohrmazd. He 'beheld a point of light, and, because it was of a different substance from himself, he strove to attain it; and his desire for it waxed so mightily that [it was as great as his desire] for the darkness.'[15] 'Seeing valour and supremacy superior to his own, he fled back to the darkness and fashioned many demons—a creation destructive and meet for battle.'[16] Ohrmazd, meanwhile, had created or given birth to the Endless Form or raw material of the physical cosmos which as yet neither moved nor thought nor could be touched.

These first three thousand years of the cosmic cycle are spent by the two Spirits in the creation or rather gradual manifestation of their respective creations. Of the last nine thousand years 'three thousand would pass entirely according to the will of Ohrmazd, three thousand years in mixture would pass according to the will of both Ohrmazd and Ahriman, and in the last battle the Destructive Spirit would be made powerless, and [Ohrmazd] himself would save creation from aggression.'[17] Thus there is a period, in what we have previously called aeveternity, at the beginning of which Ahriman becomes aware of the existence of Ohrmazd, in the middle of which both Spirits prepare their respective creations, and at the end of which Ahriman delivers his first assault.

The Weapons of Ohrmazd and Ahriman

Of the first three thousand years when the two Spirits are arming themselves the shorter version of the *Bundahishn* merely says: 'In unseen (or "ideal", *mēnōk*) form he fashioned forth such creation as was needful for his instrument.' In the longer version usually known as the *Greater Bundahishn*, however, there is a long passage dealing first with the creation of finite time and secondly with the nature of the 'instruments' of both Ohrmazd and Ahriman. In our account of classical Zurvanism we concluded that these two 'instruments' or 'weapons' were handed by Zurvān to his two sons, Ohrmazd and Ahriman, although the transfer is only attested in our texts in the case of the latter. In the *Bundahishn* we meet with these identical instruments, but they are said to be fashioned forth by the rival Spirits from their own essences which are light and darkness respectively. In the orthodox account this corresponds to the making finite of space.

The Limiting of Time

Similarly with Time. Just as the instruments of Ohrmazd and Ahriman are concretizations or manifestations of their own essences, so is finite time the concretization, manifestation, and limiting of Infinite Time. So:

'Time of the long Dominion (finite Time) was the first creature that [Ohrmazd] fashioned forth. . . . From the Infinite it was fashioned finite; for from the original creation when creation was created until the consummation when the Destructive Spirit will be made powerless there is a term of twelve thousand years which is finite. Then it mingles with and returns to the Infinite so that the creation of Ohrmazd too shall be eternally with Ohrmazd in purity.'[18]

Infinite Time, whether in orthodoxy or in classical Zurvanism, is a principle independent of both Ohrmazd and Ahriman. It is also Infinite Space, and the heavenly sphere, that is, finite space, derives from it;[19] but though independent of the two Spirits, in its two aspects it is akin to both. As Infinite Being it is associated with Ohrmazd, and as finite it helps Ahriman, only to destroy him in the end; it 'is a good helper and right orderer of both'.[20]

251

The Perdurance of Ohrmazd's Creation

The limitation of Time is Ohrmazd's first creative act, for he saw that if Ahriman were to be destroyed, he would have to be lured out of eternity, actualized in finite time, and forced into the open. For all eternity he had been a latent canker in the divine unconscious, and it is only when God became conscious of this canker that he could become conscious of himself, and with the dawn of this consciousness of his own eternal essence, he realized that such a canker not only existed, but also stood over against him as a separate and implacably hostile principle. This principle, however, did not share his own eternity and could be utterly destroyed; and the only means of doing this was to create. True, the other principle might incapacitate what he created for a while, but he could not utterly destroy it since all that issues from the hand of the Eternal must share in his eternity.

'So from Infinite Time he fashioned and made Time of the long Dominion whom some call finite Time. From Time of the long Dominion he brought forth permanence that the works of Ohrmazd might not pass away. From permanence unease became manifest, that is, there should be no ease for the demons. From unease the course of fate, the idea of changelessness, became manifest, that is, those things which Ohrmazd had created at the original creation, would not change. From the idea of changelessness a perfect will [to create material] creation became manifest, the concord of the righteous creation.'[21]

Infinite Time, though limited for a space, remains infinite and eternal none the less. Ohrmazd participates in its infinite aspect, Ahriman in its finite aspect; so Ohrmazd projects his own eternity on to his own creation which, of necessity, he has to create in time: 'the works of Ohrmazd will not pass away'. Meanwhile Ahriman too had become conscious of himself and of his own nature which is the 'will to smite' and the 'substance of envy'. Simultaneously he became aware of the light of Ohrmazd, and, consumed by a wild desire to spoil what he secretly admired, he resolved to destroy it. His tragedy was that he could not but admit that Ohrmazd and what he had created were superior to himself and his own creation. 'He beheld the creation of Ohrmazd and it seemed good to him—a creation most profound, victorious, informed of all: and he revered the creation of Ohrmazd.'[22] Realizing obscurely that what Ohrmazd had created could never pass away and that his own pandemonium must inevitably perish, he was filled with anxiety and unease—there would never be any ease or rest for him and his demons. Ahriman's sudden unsureness of himself and Ohrmazd's complete confidence that what he himself creates will not ultimately be destroyed, together settled the 'course of fate', and this in turn confirmed that 'those things which Ohrmazd had created at the original creation would not change'. This is not to deny that they change in form; it simply means that they do not change in essence with the passage of time because their essences are beyond the reach of Ahriman. 'What does not depart from its personal essence (avē-īh) with the passage of finite time is the thing in itself [which remains] beyond the reach of the Adversary.'[23] This must refer to the *khwarr* of each man, each community, and the whole human race, all of whose essences will be reunited with their perishable accidents at the final Rehabilitation. Seeing this Ohrmazd wills the material creation into existence—he wills the 'concord of the righteous creation', for he knows that the Resurrection will be brought about 'by the co-ordination of all the actions of all mankind which [will come to] believe in the religion of the worshippers of Mazdāh',[24] as much as by the disunion, lack of method, and stupidity of the opposing camp.

Ohrmazd's Instrument, the Endless Form

The limitation of Time thus reveals the perdurance of Ohrmazd's creation and the final destruction of Ahriman's. We saw earlier that Ohrmazd 'fashioned forth such creation as was needful for his instrument in unseen form'. This instrument we now learn is Vay(u), the Void that separates his own kingdom from that of Ahriman, 'for when he created creation, Vay was the instrument he needed for the deed.'[25] The Void, then, or space between the two kingdoms which is limited by them on the upper and lower sides but infinitely extended in the two lateral directions, pre-exists creation, and Ohrmazd utilizes it for his own purposes. From the Endless Light which is his own physical essence he creates the Endless Form or macrocosm. This Endless Form is made up of three ingredients: first, 'from his own essence which is material light he fashioned forth the form of his creatures—a form of fire—bright, white, round, and manifest afar'. From the Void, here identified with 'power' or 'Time', he fashioned forth the 'form of Vay', that is, the primal matter of the macrocosm. Thirdly, he created the 'essence of the gods, fair (orderly) movement, that spiritual property by which he made his own body better'. Ohrmazd's Endless Form, then, is made up of his light; it is material because it is made out of Space and Time; and it is governed by a natural order.

Ahriman's Instrument, Concupiscence

Ahriman, on his side:

'From the material darkness which is his own essence fashioned forth the body of his creation in the form of coal(?), black and ashen, worthy of the

253

darkness, damned as the most sinful noxious beast. From material self-will he fashioned forth concupiscence (*varan*). . . . Next he created the essence of the demons, evil (disorderly) movement, that spiritual property from which destruction came to the creatures of Ohrmazd. For he created a creation by which he made his own body more evil that [in the end] he might be powerless.'[26]

The 'form', then, that Ahriman opposes to Ohrmazd's Endless Form is, like his, threefold: it is composed of his own darkness, of concupiscence, and of disorder which finally leads to his own undoing. That light should be opposed to darkness and order to disorder is readily understood. What, however, is far less clear is what is meant by the contrast between 'self-will' and the Void or Space-Time on the one hand, and what amounts to much the same thing, that of concupiscence and the 'form of Vay', that is, the material cosmos, on the other. In what way can matter and concupiscence be said to be opposites?

Zurvanite Origin of these 'Instruments'

Now we have seen that the Manichaeans define matter as a 'disorderly motion in everything that exists', and that the word *Āz*, 'concupiscence', is regularly used to denote 'matter' in the Manichaean texts written in Persian. The Zoroastrians, however, held a diametrically opposite view: matter was intrinsically good because created by Ohrmazd, and this was thought to be proved by the natural law that governs it. What ran counter to the natural law, like the irregular courses of the planets, must, then, be an importation from outside. 'Concupiscence' or disorderly motion, so far from being an inherent property of matter, was, on the contrary, its eternal antagonist, as was light to darkness, order to disorder.

In Zurvanism it is Zurvān who arms Ahriman with the weapon 'that hath the very substance of Āz', but in the orthodox account Ahriman evolves it from his own *khwat-dōshakīh*, his 'self-will' or selfishness. The Zurvanite version is almost certainly prior to the orthodox since, though the contrast between matter and concupiscence is comprehensible as being the Zoroastrian's natural reaction against the Gnostic and Buddhist condemnation of matter as essentially evil, the contrast between substantial self-will on the one hand and power and Time on the other is not. It can only be understood against the background of the Zurvanite myth in which Zurvān is not only infinite Time-Space, but also the god who doubted whether he really would have a son, Ohrmazd, who would create heaven and earth, and who, by doubting, gave birth to Ahriman. The doubt, then, concerned the very possibility of a material world coming into existence, and once it is itself materialized in a finite mode of existence, it is only natural that it should become the implacable enemy of the material world, the possibility of whose existence it had denied: hence it must seek to destroy it. Āz-concupiscence is the materialization of that doubt, for Āz is not only concupiscence but also wrong-mindedness, self-will, and heresy—what leads astray, unsettles, and deceives[27]—in a word she is intellectual pride. So it is only natural that the primordial doubt, made manifest in Āz, should attack both the natural order and the intelligible order which give meaning and direction to the sensible one.[28]

Creation of Truth and Falsehood

So far the twin Spirits have created their respective material 'forms'— 'material' in this context referring to the natural order rather than that of intellect and will. They now turn their attention to the sphere of intellect, and Ahriman from the Endless Darkness creates Lying Speech, 'and from Lying Speech the harmfulness of the Destructive Spirit became manifest.' Ohrmazd, on his side, created True Speech from the material light; 'and from True Speech the productiveness of the Creator was revealed.'[29]

It is significant that Ahriman's 'lying speech' is said to precede the 'true speech' of Ohrmazd; but this is just what we would expect by analogy with both the Zurvanite myth and the *Dēnkart* passage we analysed above. In the myth it is the doubt that originates Ahriman, it is Ahriman who issues first from the womb, and it is Ahriman who utters a 'lying speech' to his father Zurvān before Ohrmazd has a chance to utter the truth; he lies to Zurvān by saying that he is Ohrmazd when Ohrmazd is as yet unborn. Similarly in the *Dēnkart* passage we saw that Ohrmazd's passage from an unconscious to a conscious state resulted in a state of semi-consciousness—'he came to know', but had no object on which to concentrate his knowledge. From this uneasy half-knowledge Ahriman arose, intent from the beginning on destroying Ohrmazd precisely by *false speech*.

In the *Dēnkart* Ohrmazd's reaction to Ahriman's lying speech is to turn his energies inward on to himself in order that he may come to know his own essence as it is, and in himself he finds the truth. So too, in the *Bundahishn*, he creates true speech from the light, which is his 'material' essence, and this truth he utters in the form of the *Ahuna Vairya* prayer, the matrix of the whole grand structure of the Good Religion, and 'through it the creation and end of the world are revealed'.

255

Ohrmazd's Offer of Peace

These central sections of the first chapter of the *Bundahishn* which are lacking in the shorter version, are an esoteric interpretation of what happened in those mysterious three thousand years in which existence hovered on the brink between eternity and finite time, the period when, dimly at first, but ever more clearly in the sequel, the shape of good and evil came to be defined. The popular account given in the first part of the chapter is much simpler. As we have seen, there was a first encounter between the two Spirits in which Ahriman, 'seeing valour and supremacy superior to his own, fled back to the darkness and fashioned many demons, a creation destructive and meet for battle.' 'And when Ohrmazd beheld the creation of the Destructive Spirit, it seemed not good to him—a frightful, putrid, bad, and evil creation : and he revered it not.'

By now Ohrmazd had become aware of himself not only as light, wisdom, and power, but also as goodness and mercy; so, though he knew that there could in the long run be no compromise, he offered peace to Ahriman and invited him to co-operate with him in his creation so that he too could share in eternal life and become 'deathless and unageing, knowing neither corruption nor decay'. Ahriman, however, will not and cannot be cajoled out of his wickedness, for his very essence is aggression and envy. 'I will not bring aid to thy creation nor will I give it praise,' he says, 'but I will destroy thee and thy creation for ever and ever. I shall incline all thy creatures to hatred of thee and love of me.' For Ahriman, ill-informed as ever, did not and could not believe that Ohrmazd's offer was genuine; he thought that his rival offered him peace out of weakness.

This dialogue would seem to have been uttered at the end of the first three thousand year period, for Ohrmazd now decides that, since battle is now inevitable, time must be set in motion, for were it to continue to hover between the eternal and the temporal 'the struggle and the mixture would be everlasting, and Ahriman could settle in the mixed state of creation and take it to himself'. 'And Ohrmazd said: "Fix a time, that by this pact we may extend the battle for nine thousand years." For he knew that by fixing a time in this wise the Destructive Spirit would be made powerless. Then the Destructive Spirit, not seeing the end, agreed to that treaty.'

Ahriman Laid Low

The battle now begins and the initiative is with Ohrmazd, for he immediately chants the *Ahuna Vairya* prayer, thereby setting the Good Religion off on its triumphant though chequered career. In chanting it he revealed in a blinding flash to Ahriman 'his own final victory, the powerlessness of the Destructive Spirit, the destruction of the demons, the Resurrection, the Final Body, and the freedom of [all] creation from aggression for ever and ever'.[30] Ahriman, on hearing the appalling doom that was to overtake himself and his creation, swooned, lost consciousness, and reeled back into the bottomless darkness. There he lay, as it were dead, for a full three thousand years.

With the chanting of the *Ahura Vairya* time passes finally out of aeveternity in the shape of the 'Spirit of the Year', and by means of it both creations are set in motion; and the full splendour of all that Ohrmazd had done in those first three thousand years stands revealed.

The central section of the first chapter of the *Bundahishn* which we discussed above dealt with Ohrmazd's 'Endless Form' and the corresponding 'form' produced by Ahriman. Both these forms belong to the sphere of matter or nature, not to that of intellect and will: they belong to the natural not the moral order, for the 'essence of the gods' mentioned as the third constituent of the Endless Form is described as 'fair (orderly) motion', that is, the regular operation of natural law. This function is now rather incongruously associated with Vahuman, the Good Mind, whom we first met in the *Gāthās*.

Creation of the Bounteous Immortals and their Demonic Counterparts
The central portion of the *Bundahishn*, not present in the shorter version, has almost certainly been introduced from another source, but even so it does not necessarily conflict with the conclusion of the chapter, for this too is concerned with the material creation rather than with the spiritual. The creation of the Bounteous Immortals and the other deities is simply catalogued without any sort of comment except in the case of the Good Mind. This entity 'with whom the Good Religion dwelt', is fashioned from the 'fair (orderly) movement of material light' and himself gives movement to the creation of Ohrmazd.[31] The Good Mind, then, here fulfils the function of Zurvān-Time in Zātspram,[32] and Akōman, the 'Evil Mind of the lying word' that of Āz-concupiscence. Once again it is stressed that whereas the Bounteous Immortals were created solely by Ohrmazd, the material creation was created 'with the aid of Vay of the long Dominion', that is, finite Time-Space-matter, for 'when he fashioned forth Vay of the long Dominion, it too was an instrument and needful for the act of creation'.[33] With all this we are already familiar.

The Material Creation
Just as there are six Bounteous Immortals of whom Ohrmazd himself

is the seventh, so are there six material creations to which Ohrmazd adds himself as the seventh. These are the sky, water, the earth, plants, cattle, and man. This is the classical order in which material things were created, but it does not correspond to the classical correspondences between the Bounteous Immortals and the material creations we discussed in the first part of this book,[34] though these duly reappear in the third chapter of the *Bundahishn*. The sky, for one thing, has no counterpart among the Bounteous Immortals, whereas the metals, the counterpart of the Kingdom, and, much more strangely, fire, the counterpart of Truth, do not appear among the original six creations at all. This is all the more strange in that the Avestan passage on which this grading of material existence is based[35] does include fire. The two series would, then, seem to go back to different traditions, and both are quite distinct from, and irreconcilable with, the theory of the development of the cosmos through four stages of becoming, the last of which is organic life.[36]

The Heavenly Sphere or Macrocosm

The 'sky' in the *Bundahishn* is simply another word for *ras* or *spihr*, the heavenly sphere, from which all creation is said to proceed; it is the macrocosm and the body of Zurvān-Time, and from it Ohrmazd creates all his creation; it is the end-form of the Endless Form,[37] and contains within it all other creations just as the human body contains all the bodily organs.[38] But it is more than this: it is the fortress, prison-house, or trap in which Ahriman will be imprisoned and ensnared.

'First [Ohrmazd] created the sky, bright and manifest, its ends exceeding far apart, in the form of an egg, of shining metal that is the substance of steel, male. The top of it reached to the Endless Light, and all creation was created within the sky—like a castle or fortress in which every weapon that is needed for the battle is stored, or like a house in which all things remain.'[39]

Yet the heavenly sphere is not only a fortress, it is a rational and living being, like its Maker, intelligent and productive.

'Like a husbandman the Spirit of the Sky thinks, speaks, acts, knows, produces much, discerns. And it received durability as a bulwark against the Destructive Spirit that he might not be suffered to return [to whence he came]. Like a valiant warrior who dons his armour that fearlessly he may return victorious from the battle, so does the Spirit of the Sky wear the [material] sky.'[40]

The sky or heavenly sphere is the prototype of man and its predicament is the same. Its first duty is, like the husbandman, to promote increase, but in this it is constantly thwarted by the enemy who has invaded its body from outside. It is, then, no longer fighting an external enemy, but a physical and moral disease within itself. The Devil is in its own body, and its body is his prison. The Spirit of the Sky is, then, not only a warrior who goes out to battle against an external foe, he is also the gaoler of that same foe within him.

A Variation Derived from India

Elsewhere[41] we find another account of how the six grades of creation proceed from the heavenly sphere, here once again called an 'instrument'. Again it is 'like a flame of fire, pure in light' and fashioned from the Endless Light; and from it all creation proceeds. It is an intelligent being in the form of a man, cosmic Man, the macrocosm and creation can only come into existence by means of the sacrificial dismembering of this first prototype of the human race. The sky is fashioned from its head, the earth from its feet, water from its tears, plants from its hair, the Bull from its right hand, while man, that is the first man, Gayōmart, was conceived by the seed of the cosmic Man falling into the earth which had itself been fashioned from his feet.[42] In this strange account of the world's origin which has no parallel in any other Zoroastrian text, we cannot fail to see a direct borrowing from India where, since the composition of the so-called *Purushasūkta*[43] in the tenth book of the *Rig-Veda*, the sacrifice of a cosmic man and the formation of the universe from his dismembered limbs not only forms a constant mythological theme, but also provides the mythological foundation on which the great sacrifices described in the post-Rigvedic literature are built up. In the *Purushasūkta* not only are various natural phenomena born from the different parts of his body, but also 'his mouth was the Brāhman, his two arms were made the warrior, his two thighs the *Vaiśya* (husbandman), and from his two feet the *Sūdra* (servant class) was born.' Mardān-Farrukh produces a precise parallel to this, and it is interesting that he actually uses the word 'microcosm' (*gēhān i kōtak* = 'small world') to describe man. 'In the microcosm which is man these four [social] classes appear as a similitude: the priests correspond to the head, the warriors to the hands, the husbandmen to the belly, and the artisans to the feet.'[44]

This seems to be a clear case of direct borrowing from an Indian source, whereas the use of the Persian equivalent for 'micro-cosmos' shows how dependent the Iranians were in their philosophical terminology on the Greeks.

Man the Microcosm

Although all the material world derives from the heavenly sphere and constitutes its body, man alone is its image, each part of his body corresponding to an analogous part of the universe contained within the sphere. His skin corresponds to the sky, his flesh to the earth, his bones to the mountains, his veins to the rivers, his blood to water, his stomach to the sea, his hair to the plants, the 'substance' of the body to metals, his inborn reason to the human race itself because it alone gives rationality to the universe, and his acquired reason to cattle.[45] All this seems very far-fetched, and a similar account in the *Dēnkart*[46] is quite different in detail, while Zātspram[47] compares the various parts of man to the seven planets, following an astrological rather than a genuinely Zoroastrian tradition, for the planets, as we know, were anathema to the Zoroastrians.

In Mānushchihr's *Dātastān i Dēnīk*[48] or 'Religious Norm', macrocosm (the Endless Form) and microcosm are brought intimately together— the one dwells within the other; but whereas the macrocosm was created 'without thought, without movement, intangible' and only developed these qualities later, Gayōmart, the microcosm and first man, from the beginning 'thinks upon perfect Righteousness'.[49] This is why mankind in the macrocosm is compared to innate reason in the microcosm.

'The Lord of all, Ohrmazd, fashioned forth the Endless Form[50] from the Endless Light. Its creaturely existence (*dām*) was of Ohrmazd and its light was that of fire which does not burn. Bright it was like a flame, productive like the fertile earth. And within the Endless Form he created man who is called the [small] world.[51] For three thousand years he neither moved nor ate, nor slept, nor spoke, but thought upon perfect Righteousness, which is the true Religion and pure praise of the Creator's will.'

Gayōmart can be, and is, destroyed by Ahriman when he finally attacks the material world, but the macrocosm, being the totality of material existence, cannot be, for 'the Endless Form is exempt from the passage of Time'.[52] The macrocosm, which is itself controlled by the totality of the Fravashis or external souls of all righteous creatures, is the 'weapon' or 'instrument' with which Ohrmazd finally lays his Adversary low. Individual men may and do perish, but the totality of mankind ever increases and multiplies until its strength is great enough to expel Ahriman from the good creation for ever. Ahriman knows that man is his principal enemy, and it was not for nothing that the mere sight of Gayōmart, the 'Righteous Man', caused him to faint away and lie prostrate for three thousand years: and in the creation of woman, too,

Ohrmazd had outwitted him, for though woman was perverse enough to take refuge with Ahriman and to allow herself to be defiled by him, yet this too would in the end work out to the advantage of Ohrmazd; for defiled though she was, she alone could bring it about that at no time would the earth lack human males to do battle with Ahriman and the Lie. 'Never from the time of creation until the Rehabilitation in purity has this earth been devoid of men, nor will it ever be; and the Destructive Spirit, not being good, cannot understand this will to succeed.'[53]

Man's Fravashis Consent to Descend to Earth

Ohrmazd, on his side, does nothing selfish in creating man as his principal bastion against the Devil. Souls and Fravashis are created free; they are in no wise compelled to go down to earth to lead the battle against the powers of darkness. If they do go, they will go of their own free choice. So:

'He took counsel with the consciousnesses and Fravashis of men and infused omniscient wisdom into them, saying: "Which seemeth more profitable to you, whether that I should fashion you forth in material form and that you should strive incarnate with the Lie and destroy it, and that we should resurrect you in the end, whole and immortal, and recreate you in material form, and that you should eternally be immortal, unageing, and without enemies; or that you should forever be preserved from the Aggressor?" And the Fravashis of men saw by that omniscient wisdom that they would suffer evil from the Lie and Ahriman in the world, but because, at the end, at the Final Body, they would be resurrected free from the enmity of the Adversary, whole and immortal for ever and ever, they agreed to go down into the material world.'[54]

Ahriman's Revival and Assault against the Material World

Ahriman, it will be remembered, had been prostrated into his primeval darkness by the original recital of the *Ahuna Vairya* prayer which, in its twenty-one words, contained in germ the whole revelation of the Good Religion and the twenty-one *Nasks* of which it was made up. This, in turn, had revealed to him his own annihilation and the total destruction of all that he had created. Only the demon Whore was able to revive him. Her words, however, inspired him with a frenzied energy. The initiative had passed to him; he took the offensive, and launched an attack of devastating fury.

His first objective was the sky which contained the whole of the good creation.

'Then the Destructive Spirit rose up together with his demons and his

weapons to attack the lights. For he had seen the sky when it appeared to him in its spiritual form before it was created in corporeal shape. In envious desire he rushed upon it . . . and dragged it down into the Void. . . . Like a serpent he darted forward, trampled on as much of the sky as was beneath the earth, and rended it. In the month of Fravartīn on the day of Ohrmazd at midday he started to invade. And the sky shrank from him in terror even as a ewe shrinks from a wolf.'[55]
'Burning and blazing he fell upon it.'[56]
'Then he fell upon the waters which . . . are established below the earth; and he bored a hole in the middle of the earth and entered in thereby. He fell upon the plants, and he fell upon the Bull and Gayōmart; and then he fell upon the fire in the likeness of a fly. All creation did he assail. At midday did he trample on all the world and make it as dark as darkest night. The sky that is beneath the earth and that which is above he blanketed in darkness; and the Spirit of the Sky said to the Destructive Spirit: "[Till] the end of Time must I mount guard over thee and not suffer thee to escape." '[57]

Ahriman has gained his first objective: he has broken into the body of creation, he has pierced the sky and installed himself in the very heart of Ohrmazd's master-weapon, the 'Endless Form', with which he had sought to keep him at bay. 'Burning and blazing' he will turn the pure light of Ohrmazd—the 'form of his creatures—a form of fire—bright, white, round, and manifest afar', 'whose light is that of fire which does not burn' into a smoking and scorching inferno. But it is not only the material light that he obscures, but also the pure light of the spirit, the light of Wisdom and the contemplative intellect which he clouds over with that 'implement like unto fire, blazing, harassing all creatures, that hath the very substance of concupiscence'.

Moreover, his perforation of the sky gives him access to all the good creatures that Ohrmazd had created within it; the outer rampart has fallen and the whole earthly kingdom is surely his:

'And upon the water he brought brackishness . . . and upon the earth he let loose reptiles in corporeal form—and they copulated one with another—reptiles biting and poisonous—serpent and scorpion, venomous lizard, tortoise and frog, so that not so much as a needle's point on [the whole] earth remained free from creeping things. . . . And upon the plants he brought so much poison that in a moment they dried up.'[58]

Of the whole material creation there remain now only the Primal Bull and Primal Man who stand between the Destructive Spirit and total victory. But these are Ohrmazd's supreme achievements, for they are the earthly replicas of the two great luminaries that give light to the earth by day and by night—the Bull 'white and lustrous like the

moon'[59] and the Man 'shining like the sun'.[60] If the world was to be
secured from the creeping darkness that was upon it, then these earthly
luminaries must at all costs be saved, for were the lamp of their life to
be extinguished, there would be no more growth or increase or forward
drive left in the material world; and with the realm of matter in his
hands the Fiend could then turn his attention to his final objective which
is to wipe out and eliminate for ever not only the good creation, but
also its source and origin, Ohrmazd, the Spirit who is Bounteous and
Holy, the author of light and the giver of life. With this prize within
his grasp, the Fiend redoubles his efforts, and flanked by concupiscence
and want, bane and pain, disease and lust and sloth, he hurls himself
upon the hapless Bull:

'He let loose upon the Bull and Gayōmart concupiscence and want, bane
and pain, disease and lust and sloth. [But] before he fell upon the Bull
Ohrmazd had given him healing hemp to eat . . . and rubbed it on his eyes,
so that he might suffer less from the smiting and the wickedness and the
torture. In a moment his strength gave out and sickness overcame him;
but the pain passed from him, and straightway he died. . . .

'And before [the Destructive Spirit] fell upon Gayōmart, Ohrmazd
cast sleep upon him [lasting] as long as it takes to say a short prayer; for
Ohrmazd created sleep in the form of a youth of fifteen years of age, bright
and tall. And when Gayōmart awoke from his sleep, he beheld a world as
dark as night, and on [the whole face of] the earth there was not so much as
a needle's point that remained free from the crawling of creeping things.
The heavenly sphere began to turn and the sun and moon to move; and
the world was all amazed(?) at the thundering of gigantic demons as they
struggled with the stars.

'Then the Destructive Spirit thought: "All the creatures of Ohrmazd
have I deprived of power save [only] Gayōmart." And he let loose upon
Gayōmart the Loosener of Bones[61] and a thousand [other] demons that
deal out death, but because of a decree of Time they found no means of
slaying him; for it is said that at the beginning of creation when the
Destructive Spirit [first] turned to aggression, Time extended the life and
reign of Gayōmart for thirty years, so that Gayōmart lived for thirty years
after the assault was unleashed. . . .

'Then he fell upon the fire, and mingled with it darkness and smoke;
and the seven planets, together with many a demon ally, mingled with the
heavenly sphere to do battle with the Signs of the Zodiac. All creation did
he befoul, and it was as if [a pall of] smoke rose up from fire [burning]
everywhere.'[62]

The Fall of Man

Ahriman has achieved his highest power: he has forced open the
'Endless Form', pierced through the waters under the earth, and the

earth itself. Water, earth, and plants, all are defiled and parched. Neither the 'lone-created Bull' nor the 'Righteous Man' who had held him at bay for three thousand years, has been able to withstand him; his dearest henchmen, the planets, whom he produced by committing sodomy on his own person,[63] have now broken through into the empyrean and will henceforth pervert destiny itself by diverting to evil uses the good things God had willed for men. This is the moment of Ahriman's triumph, and he knows it. Exulting in his strength and the ruin he has wrought, he cries out in triumph:

'Perfect is my victory: for I have rent the sky, I have befouled it with murk and darkness, I have made it my stronghold. I have befouled the waters, pierced open the earth and defiled it with darkness. I have dried up the plants, and brought death to the Bull, sickness to Gayōmart. Against the stars have I set up the planets, fraught with darkness. I have seized the kingdom. On the side of Ohrmazd none remains to do battle except only man; and man, isolated and alone, what can he do?'[64]

Nothing: for, after thirty years when Time's decree runs out, he too must die. This is the total triumph of death: the material creation has failed.

CHAPTER THIRTEEN

MAN

Ahriman Imprisoned in the Material World—The Re-creation of Plant and Animal Life and of Man : Man's Second Fall—Soul and Body—Body, Vital Spirit, Soul, Image, and External Soul—The Fravashi or External Soul—Essential Goodness of Man—The Soul's Free Will—Soul and Reason—Relationship of Soul to Body—Concupiscence, the Enemy of Soul and Body Alike—The Interconnexion of Bodily Health and Virtue—Primacy of Spirit over Matter—Moderation in All Things—Self-love the Foundation of All Love—The Solidarity of Mankind—The Indwelling of the Good Mind—Contemplation and Action

'OHRMAZD the Lord is the most patient; for, for nine thousand years he sees Ahriman inflict misery on his own creatures, yet he does not smite him except with justice and patience.'[1]

Because he is patient and just, Ohrmazd's reaction to Ahriman's invasion of the material creation seems to be slow. It is, however, carefully planned. Though Ahriman had boasted that the kingdom was his and that all his enemy's creation had been annihilated, he was very soon to discover that he had been trapped.

Ahriman Imprisoned in the Material World

'For when he entered the sky, the Spirit of the Sky, like a valiant[2] warrior clad in iron mail (the sky itself is made of iron) cried out[3] to Ahriman with a loud and awful voice: "Now that thou hast entered in, I will not let thee go . . . until Ohrmazd raises up another fortress round the sky, yet stronger [than am I]; and it shall be called the "Consciousness of the Righteous".

'And the Fravashis of the Righteous, warriors [all], were [then] drawn up all round that fortress, mounted on horses, and spears in hand. Like hair on the head [were they, so close did they stand together]. They are like gaolers who guard a prison from outside, nor do they suffer their enemy hemmed inside to come out.'[4]

Ohrmazd's plan, then, is not to overcome Ahriman by a frontal attack, but to ensnare him in the material world and to use his own destructive instincts against himself. Ahriman is like a beast caught in a trap, and his struggles to break free only succeed in progressively weakening him until he reaches the stage of utter exhaustion, whereas it is Ohrmazd who has set the trap and impassively watches the beast destroy himself.

'He is like the owner of a garden or a skilled gardener whose garden harmful and destructive beasts and birds would ruin by spoiling the fruit on the trees. The skilled gardener, to save himself trouble and to keep these harmful beasts out of the garden, devises tools with which to capture them—gins, and snares, and bird-traps, so that when the beast sees the trap and longs[5] to approach, not knowing what it is, he is caught in it. Of course, when the beast falls into the trap, [he is caught] not because the trap has of itself any superior merit, but because its maker has. The man who owns the garden and who devised the trap knows full well just how great the beast's strength is and how long [it can hold out]. All the strength of the beast's body is used up in its struggles, and by trampling on the snare and rending it, by worrying it and fighting with it, it [only succeeds in] exhausting itself. Since its strength is [now] insufficient, its fighting spirit collapses and it is reduced to powerlessness. Then the skilled gardener, having achieved his objective . . . ejects the beast from the trap. The beast's substance indeed remains, but its faculties can no longer be actualized. [The gardener then] returns his trap and snare to his armoury where, without having suffered any hurt himself, he will refit it.

'So the Creator Ohrmazd, the saviour of his creatures and the orderer of creation, by his reduction to powerlessness of the Evil Principle, [can be likened to a gardener] who protects his garden from what harms it. The harmful beast which ruins the garden is the accursed Ahriman who harries and assails [all] creatures. The good trap is the sky in which the good creatures [of Ohrmazd] are guests and in which the Destructive Spirit and his abortions are held captive. The gin or snare which prevents the beast from getting its own way, is the Time in which the struggle with Ahriman, his powers and weapons takes place, [that is], Time of the long Dominion. By his very struggles in the trap and snare the beast's power is brought to nothing.'[6]

Ahriman, then, is trapped, and all his efforts to find a way back to his native darkness are of no avail. He is not only hemmed in by the sky which girdles the macrocosm: outside this there is an even stronger bastion to oppose him, and that is the group consciousness of the whole human race, a united spiritual front in which each man yet to be born is represented by his pre-existent external soul or Fravashi; this is the impregnable fortress into which the Evil One can never penetrate. Meanwhile, however, the material world has been reduced to a desert. Human, animal, and plant life is extinct and the waters are dried up. To remedy the immediate emergency Ohrmazd deluges the earth with rain. The seas and rivers come to life and the plants begin to grow.

The Re-creation of Plant and Animal Life and of Man:
Man's Second Fall
Now when the Bull succumbed to Ahriman and died, a miracle occurred; for from his various members all manner of plant life came

into being, from his marrow sesame and from his blood the fruit of the
vine. His seed was borne up to the moon, purified in its light and
brought back to earth again; and from this seed not only did all manner
of cattle proceed but every species of animal life[7] except only noxious
beasts, reptiles, and harmful insects. Gayōmart too had passed away,
but, as he died, his seed was carried up to the sun and purified in its
light; one-third of it was returned to earth where it lay buried for forty
years. After forty years the first human couple, Mashyē and Mashyānē,
the Iranian Adam and Eve, grew up from the earth in the form of a
rhubarb plant. 'It was as if their hands were clapped to their ears, and
they were joined the one to the other, joined in limb and form. And
over the twain hovered their *khwarr*.'[8] From plant form they grew into
human form and were separated out from each other, a male and a
female. But their world was a very different place from the world into
which Gayōmart had been born, for though the powers of evil were now
to some extent under control, they were still very active. So Ohrmazd
warned them, saying: 'Ye are human beings, the father [and mother]
of the world: do your work in accordance with righteous order and
right-mindedness. Think, speak, and do what is good. Worship not the
demons.' Thus warned, they confessed that Ohrmazd was the creator
of 'water, the earth, plants, cattle, sun, moon, and stars, and of all
fertile things'. But temptation was soon to come their way and very
quickly did they succumb to it; for 'the Aggressor assailed their minds
and corrupted them, and they cried out: "The Destructive Spirit
created water, the earth, plants, and other things." When they uttered
this first lie which ruined them, they spoke in accordance with the will
of the demons. This first joy did the Destructive Spirit have of them
and make his own. And for this lie both were damned, and their souls
[shall remain] in hell till the Final Body.'[9]

Man's original sin, then, in Zoroastrianism is seen not so much as an
act of disobedience as an error of judgement: he mistakes the Devil for
the Creator, the root sin against dualism, to think that 'the increaser
and the destroyer are the same'.[10] From this moment everything went
wrong. They instituted a form of sacrifice that was not pleasing to the
gods and offended them thereby. Nevertheless, they grew in worldly
wisdom, learning how to clothe themselves, how to weave cloth, carve
wood, and smelt iron. This common toil, however, brought them
neither peace nor trust in each other: 'They became wickedly jealous
of each other, attacked each other, struck and rent each other, and
ripped out each other's hair.'[11] Seeing this the demons took heart and
demanded worship of them 'that their envy might subside', and worship
them they did.

Man and woman were created by Ohrmazd for the propagation of the human race, yet so corrupt had they already become and so unconscious of their destiny that for fifty years they had no intercourse with each other; and when at last they did and a pair of twins was born to them, so brutalized had they become that the mother devoured the one and the father the other. 'Then Ohrmazd took away the sweetness of children from them so that their children might survive.'[12] Such were the unpromising beginnings of the human race.

Soul and Body

What, however, is the constitution of man himself? We have seen that when our first parents were growing out of the ground, their *khwarr* hovered over them. This *khwarr* is the final cause of each man: it is what God intends him to be and it pre-exists his physical birth, then 'it is put into the body of him for whom it was created, for man's own-work was fashioned [first] and the body was created for the performance of [each man's] individual work. This means that the soul was created first, then the body. The soul directs [each man's] proper work within the body.'[13] Though the soul is formally identified with the *khwarr* only a few lines later, there is a real distinction between the two. The *khwarr*, as we have seen,[14] originally meant 'good things, good fortune' or 'prosperity'. Applied to the world of spirit it means 'spiritual excellence', almost exactly what is meant by the 'talents' of Christ's parable. The soul is the directing faculty in man, and it must therefore see to it that the *khwarr* or talents entrusted to it are not misused but allowed to grow to the limit of their capacity; for in this respect, too, Zoroastrianism is the religion of growth, increase, fulfilment, and prosperity, the religion of creative evolution. The growth in virtue of the individual is seen as part of the growth of the whole community: it is part of the *patvandishn i ō Frashkart*, the 'continuous evolution towards the Making Excellent', a continuous growth of the whole of humanity into the plenitude of the perfection planned for it by God. 'The consummation of [all] things is increase—from one thing, many things.'[15] 'Increase and multiply' is the basic Zoroastrian message, not only by propagating the human race, but also by developing to the utmost both individual talent and all spiritual good. However, this is to anticipate.

Man distinguishes himself from the beasts in that he is not merely a product of nature (*chihr*), he has also a moral dimension in that he is possessed of intellect and will (*akhw*). 'According to the divine dispensation it is nature that looks after the material side of man, and will that directs his spiritual side. So it is that life which depends on nature and knowledge which has its seat in the intellect and will [between them] constitute the humanity of man.'[16] This distinction between natural man and *homo sapiens* is basic to Zoroastrian thought; but the dualism is not unbridgeable as it is between the two Spirits. It is rather a duality in unity, and though the soul survives at death, this does not mean that man himself survives; for he is by nature a composite being, and once his constituent parts are sundered, none of them, not even the soul, which is the guiding principle, can claim to be the whole man. Until the soul is once again united with the body, there can be no question of a fully human immortality.

Body, Vital Spirit, Soul, Image, and External Soul
Man, however, is not just a simple compound of body and soul; there are other elements that need to be considered. According to the *Bundahishn* 'man was fashioned in five parts—body, vital spirit, soul, image, and external soul. The body is the material [part]; the vital spirit that which is connected with the wind—the inhaling and exhaling of breath; soul is that which, together with consciousness, hears, sees, speaks, and knows in the body; the "image" is that which is situated in the station of the sun; the external soul is that which is in the presence of Ohrmazd the Lord; and it was created in this wise because during the period of the assault of the Aggressor men die, and their body rejoins the earth, their spirit the wind, their image the sun, their soul the external soul so that the demons cannot destroy the soul.'[17]

Thus man was believed to possess no less than five souls, (i) the vital spirit (*jān*), (ii) the soul proper which operates through consciousness, (iii) consciousness itself, (iv) the 'image', and (v) the external soul (*fravahr* = Avestan *fravashi*). The 'image' (*adhvēnak*) which has its abode in the station of the sun corresponds roughly to the Platonic 'form', but this concept is brought into relation with Iranian mythology according to which man has a solar origin just as the animals have a lunar one.[18] The Pahlavi words *adhvēnak* and *karp*, meaning 'image' and 'form' respectively, however, are probably direct translations of the Greek *eidos*, 'form, image'. The vital spirit gives life to the body,[19] and when it leaves it, the body dies. There remain the soul proper and the Fravashi.

The Fravashi or External Soul
The Fravashis, as we have seen, play an important part in the Avesta,[20] one of the longest *Yashts* being dedicated to them. It is not at all clear what their original function was, but two functions stand out: first they are warrior spirits, secondly they are concerned with fertility and the preservation of life. The same dual purpose can be observed in the

Pahlavi books. As we have seen, they are likened to warriors ranged round the fortress of the sky, 'mounted on horses, spears in hand'; they form an impregnable bastion that makes it impossible for Ahriman to break loose from the material world into the lights above. Further, the *Bundahishn* tells us that it was they who, of their own free will, chose to go down to earth to do battle with the Lie. The *Dēnkart* and Zātspram, however, regard the Fravashi as being quite distinct from the soul proper and confine its activities to the natural order, not to the order of intellect and will. 'The soul and the Fravashi differ from each other in that the soul is possessed of will, and its actions depend on will, whereas the Fravashi belongs to nature and its actions are natural.'[21] The explanation of this would appear to be that the Fravashi is naturally good and incorruptible: it is beyond the reach of Ahriman and the demons. Only the soul can be damned, just as only the body can die by being separated from the vital spirit which continues to live on as air. The Fravashi, on the other hand, 'having the nature of fire, quickens the wind, and by quickening the wind it brings the body to life.'[22] The soul, once embodied, uses consciousness to give sight and the other senses to the body, and it uses the body as its instrument. Bodily death means inevitably the separation of body and soul; but it does not necessarily mean that the soul is separated from the Fravashi and consciousness. If it is saved, this union apparently continues,[23] but if it is damned, it is damned alone and is followed by neither Fravashi nor consciousness.[24]

Essential Goodness of Man

Man was created completely good, immortal in body and soul. Death and damnation, and disease and sin, which are the causes of death and damnation, were brought into the material world by Ahriman; they are not natural to it. Human nature, however, as it now is, has a divine, a diabolic, and a purely animal[25] side, just as reality itself is divided between Ohrmazd, Ahriman, and the morally neutral Void that lies between them. Divine beings or 'gods' are good spirits endowed with wisdom or reason, demons are evil spirits ruled by concupiscence or wrong-mindedness (*varan*). Both spirits are present in man, the divine which is living, deathless, and wise, and the diabolical which is living, but destined for an evil death. Salvation means to become like the gods, damnation is to be assimilated to the demonic.[26] All this, however, applies only to the soul. During its brief sojourn in the body it may be likened to a householder in his house or to a knight upon his horse.

'In the body of man there are four principal agents—soul, vital spirit, Fravashi, and consciousness. The soul, which consists of intellect and will, is lord over the body as a householder is over his house or a knight over his horse; it directs the body as well as vital spirit, consciousness, Fravashi, and the spirit (*vākhsh*) that is within it (i.e. reason). These[27] are the instruments of the soul.

'Vital spirit is [from] the wind and is brought to life by the natural activity of its Fravashi. Being alive, it preserves life in the body, just as does the householder's private physician or the knight's trainer. When it is separated from the body, the body dies, just as when the [central] pillar of a house breaks, the house collapses.

'The Fravashi maintains the natural functions of the body and nurtures them, just as a foreman or manciple [maintains] the householder's house or a groom the knight's horse. When it is separated from the body, the body is weakened and remains inactive, just as a house falls into ruin if the [necessary] repairs are not attended to.

'Consciousness keeps the householder's house lighted and guides the knight's horse: it enables the householder to see inside the house and the knight [to see] upon his horse, just as the sun illumines the world and a lamp[28] illumines the house. When it is separated from the body, the soul suffers misery within the body, and the body, though still alive, is deprived of sense.

'The soul, then, armed as it is with Fravashi, consciousness, vital spirit, and body, has no excuse [but to perform] the individual task to perform which it was sent [on to this earth]: and this task is to struggle with the Lie till it vanquish it, even as a knight, equipped with his horse, smites and vanquishes his enemies. And the enemies of the soul and the enemies of its instruments too are creatures of the Lie, created[29] to destroy creation— concupiscence (*āz*), heresy (*varan*), anger, vengefulness, disrepute, and envy, which fall upon the body to do battle with[30] body and soul, to destroy them, or keep them away from the battle so that, once the soul is vanquished, all the other creatures of the good who struggle [against the Lie] may be destroyed and put out of action. The commander of the army[31] and the leader in battle is the soul.'[32]

The Soul's Free Will

The soul, then, is God's most powerful ally against his Adversary, and it controls the psychic functions as well as the body; these are no more than instruments given to it with which it must fight him. With the slaying of Gayōmart, Ahriman brought physical death into the world; but his soul he could not slay. He can, however, deceive the soul and bring upon it all the torments of the damned in hell; he can torture it unhindered till the final Resurrection when all is made anew, and this is his dearest desire; for 'all creatures are mirrored in man who is the material symbol (*dakhshak*) of Ohrmazd'.[33] So when the Evil One 'robs a man of life and wife and child and all the good things of this world, he does not think that he has done him any harm; but when he robs him of his soul alone and ruins it, then he considers that he has done him a perfect injury.'[34]

The soul, however, is free and therefore responsible to its maker: man is free and the master of his own destiny; he is an 'incarnate lord'. He is master both of himself and of all created things on earth; but his status as 'incarnate lord' he owes primarily to a misunderstanding of an Avestan text, for in Pahlavi the Avestan words *ahu- astvant-* ('material existence') become *akhw i astōmand,* and the first of these Pahlavi words can mean 'existence' or 'intellect and will' (the primary characteristic of the soul), or lastly 'lord'. So, thanks to a felicitous pun, the soul is elevated to the rank of a king.

'In the material world man [alone] is possessed of free will. His Avestan name is *akhw i astōmand* which means "incarnate lord".'[35] The proof that man is possessed of free will and is master of himself is that he can impose his will on other creatures which cannot master their own desires as man can; none of these has the power to control any other as man has the power to control them. The fact that man is incarnate distinguishes him from the spiritual gods, because these are lords but not incarnate. The Creator Ohrmazd is the creator of free will, and free will means man's mastery[36] of his desires. [Men] are free to accept or not to accept virtue or sin. The reason why the Creator created man with a free will, and not a mere automaton[37], was that he [thereby] secured his own army by giving him the command over it[38] and the power inherent in the command, so that by means of this power he would obtain the overwhelming strength [required] for the defeat of the Lie's entire army, for the destruction of [Ahriman?][39] together with the Lie, and their banishment from among the creatures of Ohrmazd.'[40]

'Man,' then, 'is the commander-in-chief of the entire material creation'[41] in its battle against the powers of evil, because he alone is possessed of free will; and, being free and able to control himself, he is able to control all other creatures. Because the soul is the lord of the body and the total man the lord or king of creation, so is kingship itself sanctified along with the whole hierarchy of delegated monarchical authority. 'The headship of a household, or village-community,[42] or province, or the Empire (*kishvar*), is of the creative dispensation of the beneficent, omniscient, omnipotent Lord, just as is [man's lordship] over his own body.'[43]

Soul and Reason

Yet the human soul, though it is the king of its body, the senses, and the intellectual faculties, is itself subject to higher powers. Man's essence is the *akhw*, his intellect and will, but these must be subject to 'discriminative wisdom or reason' (*khrat*) and to free will seen as a gift of God: the first is the secular ruler of the soul, the second its religious authority.[44] Man, then, is designed by God to use his free will in accordance with sound reason which is inborn in him, and just as the essence of man is his free will and his intellect, so is the essence of these, when united with the body, 'clear vision,' the faculty by which man may gain an intellectual insight into the nature of spiritual realities. This can only be achieved by uniting the mind with innate wisdom, that is, with the Good Mind of God himself which draws the soul on like a magnet, and by eschewing concupiscence and the other vices that impair the health of the soul.

'The essence of man's intellect and will, even when in the body, is clear vision, and man can [only] achieve wisdom right up to the degree of spiritual insight by following the teachings of traditional wisdom and by firmly cleaving with the mind to the teachings of innate reason.[45] The wisdom that is more excellent than any other is the Zoroastrian (*māzdēsn*) religion adorned as it is with wisdom. The close co-operation of mind and will (*akhw*) is [brought about] by freeing the mind from sin and purifying it with virtue, by holding aloof from concupiscence, envy, heresy, disrepute, vengefulness, and other sins, and from the Lie which seeks to subdue the will to its yoke. Purification by virtue means that the will is entirely indwelt (*mēhmānīh*) by virtue and by the Good Mind which draws the will on and the other powers [that indwell it].'[46]

Relationship of Soul to Body
The soul, then, was created to do battle with the powers of darkness, for only by the elimination of these could God and his creation be secure; but it was also created for final beatitude in which intellect and will, which together form the soul's essence, would combine in contemplation of spiritual reality. This cannot happen, however, until the Lie is annihilated for ever, for in this present state of the world which is already corrupted, concupiscence never tires of fighting against the soul and the innate reason that indwells it as well as against the body and its physical health, and it fights with the twin weapons of wrong-mindedness and sensuality.

'The soul, as it is in itself, is the faculty of knowing united to will. United to the body which is of like substance to itself, its instrument or garment, it is [the total] man who, in his pure condition, is sinless.[47] In the state consequent on the Aggressor's invasion called the "mixed state", the soul (*akhw*) whose knowledge comes to it by sense-perception, as well as the will, comes into opposition with concupiscence (*varan*) because the body's genius (*vākhsh*) is conjoined to a dark genius which is of another substance. Sense-perception may lead either to a virtuous frame of mind or to sin. If, however, a man chooses the easy way and is indolent,[48] he will fall away from virtue; the bright substance of his soul will be harmed by his sinful deeds and driven out from on high, its virtue sullied.[49] This means that because of the heaviness [of its sins] it falls right down to hell, the lair of the Lie. In the end when the divine powers triumph and the power of the Lie is smashed, it is brought up from hell in accordance with the Creator's will. By the cleansing it receives from the spirits in charge of purification it is made pure of the harmfulness of sin, and once again it puts on its garment, the body, which is of like substance to itself, cleansed as it will be from the pollution of the Aggressor. Then it will enjoy the plenitude of bliss, uninterrupted for ever and ever.'[50]

This passage, which is directly aimed against the Manichees, is intended to show how soul and body form the closest possible unity, each playing its part against the spiritual or unseen power of the Lie. The body is the instrument or garment of the soul, just as the macrocosm is the body of the spiritual power that inhabits it, 'be it Power or be it Time.'[51] The soul acts through the body as it is bound to do, since action for which man was created[52] can scarcely be conceived of except in material terms. The body, moreover, is not made of the substance of palpable darkness as the Manichaeans hold, but is of like substance to the soul, fragrant by nature, but rendered evil-smelling by the hold that concupiscence has upon it.[53] Moreover, the body is as necessary to the soul as clothing is to the body; and if it is disgraceful for a man to go about naked,[54] how much more disgraceful must it be for the soul to appear before its Maker unclothed? It is, then, only seemly that the soul should be resurrected in the last days clad in a new and glorious body. The Lie, on its side, knows that its surest weapon is to bring disruption into the total personality of man, to upset the balance between right reason and free will, and to dash the soul's weapon, the body, from its hand.

'The struggle of the Lie is with man's essence which is his soul and with the soul's weapon and garment which is the body. . . . [It strives] to annihilate man's essence and his weapon and instrument, to defile them, and by grievously polluting man's essence, weapon, and instrument, and by driving a wedge between them, to separate them and destroy their union.'[55]

In its insistence on the essential unity of body and soul Zoroastrianism allies itself with the Judaic religions as against the Indian and Gnostic view that soul and body are so radically different as to constitute two different worlds. It would be untrue to say that Zoroastrianism was unconcerned with the soul's condition as an entity that transcends time, for the speculations of the *Dēnkart* concerning the nature of the infinite and the finite and the relationship between the two have to do with precisely this; but, in sharp contrast to both Indian and Gnostic speculation, it refuses to consider the eternal apart from the temporal, the spiritual apart from the material, the soul apart from the body, or the individual apart from the totality of mankind. Existence starts as a duality, it ends as a unity. The whole point of creation is to eliminate the principle of destruction and negation, and this can only be done by increase and yet more increase, creatures multiplying everywhere, with man as chieftain, king, and guide, until the whole creation, working in total harmony and concord, finally deals the death-blow to the principle of disunion which had existed from the beginning. So it is that while individuals may fall by the wayside and sink for a while into the pit of hell, they cannot stay there for all eternity; for salvation must and will be total. And as mankind was created one and undifferentiated in Gayōmart, so will it be resurrected one and whole—yet no longer a single being, but a unity in diversity in which each individual value, each individual *khwarr*, will contribute to the total *khwarr* created by God; for 'each individual creature can only preserve its own *khwarr* by loving, praising, and thanking the Creator's *khwarr* in all purity.'[56]

Soul and body are likened to horseman and horse; and this time the soul is identified with reason (*khrat*).

'The essence of man is reason[57] which holds sway in the body over the will. It sustains the will and impels it forward to specific objectives, restrains it [from others], and manages it. It is like a horseman who drives his horse on or restrains it[58] with the bridle, controlling it with his thighs. Reason is this powerful essence,[59] and reason's helpmate is the will by which it saves itself and conquers the Adversary. . . . So is it victorious like the valiant horseman who spurs on his horse to attack the enemy and restrains it when he would avoid him. The will of the man bereft of his essential reason becomes unstable[60] because of his foolishness; [he procures] harm only for himself, benefit for his adversary, like a bad horseman whom his adversary lures[61] to his death by [making use of] his own horse.'[62]

Concupiscence, the Enemy of Soul and Body Alike

The essence of man is his soul, but the body is the soul's garment which it puts aside at death but will take up again at the time of the Resurrection. The soul again consists of intellect and will, and reason or wisdom is or should be the guiding principle of both. The soul is by nature sinless because it is created by God: sin, like disease and death, attacks it from outside. This outside principle is either referred to by the general terms of 'Adversary' or 'Aggressor' or, more specifically as *āz* or *varan*, 'concupiscence,' both in the sense of bodily sensuality (lust, greed, avarice, etc.) and of intellectual licentiousness (heresy, wrong-mindedness, etc.);[63] for concupiscence not only attacks the body, but also perverts the mind; and it is the duty of every Zoroastrian both to preserve and increase his own bodily and mental health and to look after that of others as well as to promote the growth of all God's material creatures. Man is expected not only to do his own job dutifully and efficiently, but also to enjoy himself to the utmost limit, and by enjoying himself to radiate joy over his fellow-creatures. Bodily pleasure is not regarded as being in any way incompatible with the soul's salvation. After all, the body is your weapon with which you fight the enemy, and it would be stupid not to keep it bright and keen: it is your horse which carries you into battle, and nobody in their senses ever went to war on a half-starved horse.

The Interconnexion of Bodily Health and Virtue
Zoroastrianism is the religion of plenty, of seemliness, and of common sense. It abhors asceticism, and the ascetic virtues so highly prized in India find no place in it. Man is by nature endowed with six cardinal virtues—right reason (*khrat*), temperance (*khēm*), modesty, honesty (*mithr*), gratitude, and hope;[64] and the man who exhibits these virtues to the highest degree may be described as a 'superman' (*apartom martōm*). The man, however, who has the least share in them must be considered 'sub-human' (*nitom martōm*), while the man who lacks them entirely is 'devoid of humanity' or simply 'inhuman' (*amartōm*). The vices opposed to the six cardinal virtues are concupiscence, deceitfulness, arrogance, acquisitiveness (*nērōk-hanbārīh*), and despair. The possession of such characteristics makes a man a devil, whereas the man in whom there is an uneasy mixture of the cardinal virtues and vices is half devil and half man. The really good man, however, must in addition be healthy, happy, contented, at peace with the world; he must prosper and develop both in body and in soul.

'That man [only] is good who is consistently good, who enjoys bodily health, is master of his own body, does not fret about his daily bread, is at peace with his household, and who [develops and] increases his talents and the good things which are his (*khwarr*). That man is consistently good who always enjoys himself. The man who enjoys bodily health [also] enjoys health of soul. The man who is master of his own body is he who has expelled the Lie from his body. The man who does not fret about his daily bread is he who is content with whatever comes his way. The man who is at peace with his household is he who well maintains the fires, water, cattle, and men over whom he exercises authority. The man who [develops and] increases his talents and the good things that are his, is he who does his own job.

'The evil man [on the other hand] is he who is consistently evil, who is sick in body, who is not master of his own body, who frets about his daily bread, is not at peace with his household, who neglects his talents and the good things that are his. That man is consistently evil [who is always] miserable. The man who is sick in body is he who is [also] sick in soul. The man who is not master of his own body is he in whose body the Lie is violently active. The man who frets about his daily bread is he who is dissatisfied with whatever comes his way. The man who is not at peace with his household is he who ill maintains the fires, water, cattle, and men over whom he exercises authority. The man who neglects his talents and the good things that are his, is the man who does not do his own job.'[65]

For the Zoroastrians body and soul were so closely linked that it seemed to them that bodily sickness must denote sickness of soul. Happiness and pleasure are the natural state of man, and unhappiness is regarded as being an infliction imported into the material world by the Lie. Suffering, whether purgative or otherwise, has no part in the Zoroastrian scheme of things: it is restrictive, and what restricts is necessarily evil. Enjoyment is the natural ambience of the body, for 'the body naturally wants material prosperity, gracious living (*ārādhishn*), wit, display, music, and pleasure'.[66] All these things in themselves are good because they are natural to kings and approved by sound religion. Moreover, just as body and soul are the two facets of the one man, so do material prosperity and spiritual progress hang together; and 'one should make strenuous efforts to promote prosperity and affluence as well as righteousness and virtue, for this world is linked with the next, and the next world is linked with this'.[67]

Wisdom or reason, which is the highest good, is itself linked with happiness, and 'the sign of wisdom is this—peace, restraint in speech, a glad heart, friendship with the good, and generosity'.[68] All this, no doubt, sounds very materialistic, but Zoroastrianism in all its phases *is* a materialist religion in that it sees the material world as the concrete expression of the spiritual: the one emerges from the other and depends on it, and both have a perennial value. The final Rehabilitation of existence at the end of time means not only the complete annihilation of the Lie, but also the re-creation in the realm of pure goodness of the whole cosmos in matter and in spirit, in body and in soul. The apparent hedonism of the reformed Zoroastrian ethic is the logical result of the Prophet's own teaching as well as the healthy reaction of integral and integrated men against the anti-materialist fanaticism of the Manichees and those Christians who, forgetful of the fact that their God assumed a human body and all the transient matter that goes to make it up, vied with the Manichees in a futile and selfish asceticism.

Primacy of Spirit over Matter

Zoroastrianism is neither this-worldly nor other-worldly: it is both-worldly. But always the primacy is given to the other world, the world of unseen spirit, out of which this world of visible matter is born. For over and against those passages which equate virtue with pleasure, and righteousness with prosperity, we find others which warn us against a one-sided devotion to earthly prosperity at the expense of spiritual health. This world, after all, is transient because it has been corrupted by Ahriman and the Lie; you cannot put your trust in it, and must wait for its final reconstitution at the end of time. So the good things of this world are likened to a 'cloud that comes on a freezing day and does not linger on any mountain-top'.[69] All our earthly prosperity must, in the long run, be left behind except only righteousness which it is legitimate to hoard;[70] and:

'when the lusts of the body come upon you and make you itch for honour and prosperity more than is consistent with moderation, then your best antidote is to counter it by considering the transient nature of the body and of material things. And you should think things over [and say to yourself]: "Just think; I said that I wanted this much honour and prosperity. Well, what would be the use of them, as I should have to let them go, or they would go [of their own accord]. Since this is so, I shall not go on with it, so as not to suffer the pain of letting them go or of their going [of their own accord]." '[71]

The golden rule is that one should interest oneself in the things of this world only to the extent that they do not interfere with the things of the next;[72] and it is the sign of a wise man that 'he always bears in mind the end of the world'.[73] Āturpāt, son of Mahraspand, himself, though the confessed enemy of the fatalists, warns against placing any reliance on this transient world:

'You should not attach any value to the world, nor should you account it as anything, yet you should not abandon it. You should not attach any value to it because whatever is fated is bound to happen; and you should not account it as anything because it is transient and you will have to leave it; and you should not abandon it because spirit can only be won through the material world.'[74]

It is the last sentence that is peculiarly and typically Zoroastrian: depressed though one may well be at the transience of the world, one must realize nonetheless that life on earth is the necessary prelude to the life of the spirit in heaven, and this again is no more than a prelude to the resurrection life in which body and soul are once again united.

Moderation in All Things

It is true that Zoroastrianism sees an intimate link between worldly prosperity and spiritual progress, yet passages are even so not lacking which extol the virtue of poverty accepted with contentment. Worldly goods should not be sought after for themselves, nor should one aim at possessing more than what is moderate, and in no case should pre-occupation with this world be allowed to interfere with one's spiritual health: 'worldly goods in excess of the mean should be abandoned'.[75] In principle Zoroastrianism was bitterly opposed to asceticism as being a blasphemy against life; but we do read of holy men who retired to the mountains to lead a life of solitude and who gave up the world much as a Christian hermit would do; and it was, apparently, not considered inapposite for such a one to say: 'Consider your worldly goods as dust blown about on the plain.'[76] Poverty itself is occasionally extolled, for the virtuous poor, simply by being deprived of their earthly reward, are the more certain of receiving their heavenly recompense; for on the day of reckoning even those who were the poorest on earth will wish that they had been yet 'poorer so that the reckoning would be less [strict] and things would have been easier'.[77]

Zoroastrianism, however, like Islam, only praises poverty in its less characteristic moments, for its whole ethos is one of productivity, of giving *and* receiving, and of growth—growth in virtue on the one hand and growth in wealth on the other; and it is doubtful whether any other religion could define man's 'perfect desire' as being a 'desire to amass worldly goods as much as to further righteousness thereby'.[78] Instinctively, Zoroastrianism turns its back on asceticism in any form. Its occasional lapses from the ideal of fulfilment are due to the fact that all religions are forced at some time or other to take account not only of man's natural hankering after self-fulfilment, but also of his apparently quite irrational desire for self-denial. In this respect Indian and Iranian religion complement each other; the Indians make self-denial the cornerstone of all their religious thinking, the Iranians think only of self-fulfilment; and individual self-fulfilment is seen as part of the universal self-fulfilment of the cosmos and of God himself, who, originally limited by a rival principle, must expand and grow so that, by destroying the power of negation that limits him, he may in very deed become all in all.

Self-love the Foundation of All Love

So far from denying self, man should make self-love the well-spring of his actions. Self-love is implanted in every man and leads to the love of others; self-denial, on the other hand, which means hatred of self, can only lead to hatred of others. It is of Ahriman, not of Ohrmazd. For 'Ohrmazd asks of man that whatever he does he should do for himself . . . while Ahriman asks him not to do it for himself'.[79] This is regarded as being pure common sense; for however much you may prate about self-sacrifice and self-denial, the fact remains that selfless action is itself ultimately selfish and directed at the salvation of one's own soul. 'The man does not exist who does anything except for himself, whether it be righteous or unrighteous; for whatever a man undertakes, he either increases or restricts his soul [thereby]. In any case [what one does] one does for one's own soul. So we should be very insistent with all men that they desire good for their own souls, not[80] evil.'[81]

Knowledge of self leads to love of self, whereas indifference to self leads to hatred of self, and this in turn leads to self-injury. Self-injury again involves an affront against God, and this in turn will mean that one forfeits the divine protection.[82] Love of self and of one's children is natural to man, and it is only by developing this natural love that a man can grow to love his fellows; he will bear no ill-will to anyone, but will wish all men well; knowing trouble himself, he will wish to spare his fellow-men pain.[83] Happiness is not something you can enjoy on your own, it is a communal activity in which all men are called to share.

The Solidarity of Mankind

'Since the Creator Ohrmazd created creation from one substance, he caused man to be born of one father, so that creation, being of one substance, one thing should sustain, provide for, and help another, and men, being born of one father should esteem each other as their own selves. Like affectionate brothers they should do good to each other and ward off evil from each other.'[84] Thus unity is natural to man just as it is unnatural to the demons. The demons can only unite in a common aggression against man, and after each single act of aggression they return to their native discord 'which is the substance of evil'.[85] The union of the whole of mankind in brotherly love will spell the final defeat of the Lie.

'When mankind achieves union firmly based on mutual love, the demons will lose all hope of [ever again] being able to harm man, nor will they be able to change their own disunion into union. At the final Rehabilitation the whole of mankind will be firmly and unchangeably linked in mutual love, and this will mean that the demons will utterly despair of ever being able to harm man again. They will be annihilated and prevented from ever again coming together to take counsel with each other and plotting any new aggression against the creatures of Ohrmazd. Then there will be a universal joy for the whole of creation for all eternity; and fear will be no more.'[86]

The solidarity of the human race which will ultimately defeat the Lie, will be achieved under the aegis of the Zoroastrian religion which, at the end of time, all will confess; united they will march behind Saoshyans, the saviour to whom Ohrmazd entrusts the final resurrection.[87]

The unity of mankind, then, in mutual love, will spell defeat for the Lie and usher in the renewal of all things. This unity, however, is only a reflection of the divine unity; and man, in achieving his own total integration, must also be integrated in God; and God, to be loved, must be known, and he can only be known through the true Religion of Zoroaster which alone confesses him to be all-good.[88] By knowing God one draws near to him and sees him with no veil before the spiritual eye.[89] The faculty that enables man to know God as he is, to love him, and to see him, is his innate reason, for 'innate reason, grounded on goodness,[90] is the Creator's greatest messenger to the material world. By means of it men come to know the Creator, and see God as he really is, and the Devil as he really is, truth as it is and falsehood as it is, benefit as it is and harm as it is'.[91] The Zoroastrian religion alone can do this, for it alone, among all the religions of the world, acknowledges God as all-good and devoid of evil in any form. God's goodness is the truth, and it is also man's good and his joy.

The Indwelling of the Good Mind

The reformed Zoroastrianism of the Sassanian period has indeed moved a long way from the original message of the *Gāthās*. The Bounteous Immortals now appear as fully personalized archangels or simply as moral excellences. The only exception is the Good Mind. In discussing the *Gāthās* we saw that the Good Mind was the agency through which the Prophet communed with his God. In reformed Zoroastrianism this idea is not lost sight of, and the Good Mind becomes identified with man's innate reason. So too the Evil Mind is identified with concupiscence (*varan*, in this context perhaps better translated as 'heresy'). The Good Mind indwelling man is the source of virtue as the Evil Mind is of sin. 'The Good Mind is reason created in man by the Creator to lead him to virtue, salvation, benefit, and pleasure; the Evil Mind is concupiscence in man [which leads] him to sin, damnation, harm, and misery.'[92]

By the indwelling of the Good Mind the soul's eye is opened to see spiritual things.

'The source (*mātagh*) of wisdom can be defined as what opens the soul's eye to seeing those things the soul [alone] can see, just as the source of light can be defined as what opens the bodily eye to things that are visible to it. Wisdom in the wise man shows in his perfect control over his own will, his training of his character, his ever-increasing cultivation of the virtues, his good deeds, righteousness, and good repute among men. His nature is to bring increase to the world of righteousness. The source of wisdom is the Creator who is essential wisdom, and it is he who bestows it upon his creatures who themselves receive it through their own faculties. The Good Spirit who is the Good Mind it is who tends it and causes it to grow. The greatness of it all lies in this, that whoever is visited by the source of this divine wisdom, is exalted to the likeness of the Creator as a [physical] object is made like the source of light by being lighted up, and a man is made like the highest source of all righteous things by righteousness. . . .

'The source of wrong-mindedness can be defined as what closes the soul's eye to the vision of those things the soul [alone] can see, just as the source of darkness can be defined as what closes the bodily eye to things that should be visible to it. Wrong-mindedness in the wrong-minded man shows in his inability to control his will, his ruining of his own character,[93] his productiveness of vice, his sinfulness, wickedness, and ill-repute among men. His nature is to destroy the world of righteousness. Its source is essential wrong-mindedness which creates confusion (lit. "mixture", *gumēchakīh*) in the Creator's creation. It is generally that man who receives it who is unable to control his own will, is wrong-minded, and infatuated. The Evil Spirit which is the Evil Mind it is which cultivates and increases it. The grievousness of it all lies in this, that whoever is polluted by wrong-mindedness which stems from the Lie comes to resemble the demons and the Lie to the extent that his conduct is blameworthy.'[94]

Contemplation and Action

Innate reason is the inner eye by which the spiritual world is discerned; it must be indwelt by the Good Mind[95] if one is to grow in moral stature. The presence of the Good Mind in the soul gives it a sweet fragrance, whereas the Evil Mind brings stench upon it.[96] This indwelling of the Good Mind is by no means the privilege of the contemplative; it shows itself only in action, in the acquisition of the virtues, and above all in getting on with your own job. By the operation of the Good Mind one can become like God—and the Zoroastrian God is good and productive of good, and he has the biggest 'job' of all—to defeat and annihilate Ahriman and all his hordes, and so to bring his whole creation to the eternal bliss which is its destiny. So:

'among men who pursue good fortune (*khwarr*) and protect themselves from misfortune, the most characteristic is he who exerts himself most in the performance of his own allotted task; and just as God (*yazdān*) exerts himself most in the performance of his task, so among men he who exerts himself most at his task by being what he is, shares in the attributes and activity of God and is closest to God in the scale of value.'[97]

Thus despite occasional lapses into a mild other-worldliness Zoroastrianism sees man as God's protagonist in this world in the battle against the Lie. Any withdrawal from the world is, then, a betrayal of God; for man was created for the work he has to do, not vice versa. His allotted task, his *khwarr*, pre-exists him, and he must do it to the best of his ability. He must both cultivate the moral virtues of which truth and generosity rank highest and promote material prosperity as well. He is here to fight the Lie both on a spiritual and a material level, but fight he must. Only so can he draw near to God, who is himself the Spirit of Increase. He has the duty to develop his moral character, but he also has the duty to be happy; for by being happy he resembles God, misery being characteristic of the demons. Further, he must see himself not merely as an individual, but as a part of humanity as a whole, part of God's army striving to vanquish evil; he must see himself as part of an irresistible movement which is destined to rout out the last vestige of evil and to grow into the plenitude of life, that is, the 'Making Excellent' or final Rehabilitation of all things: 'he is the most perfect of material creatures, a fighter and a general in the battle'.[98]

CHAPTER FOURTEEN

THE RELIGION AND THE KING

The Interconnexion of the Zoroastrian Religion and the Sassanian Empire—The Doctrine of the Mean—The Mean as Cosmic Principle—The Mean as the Treaty between Ohrmazd and Ahriman—The Mean, the Essence of Reason—Virtue, the Mean between Contrary Vices— Wisdom or Reason in Man and God—Wisdom as Creative Principle—Ahriman's Lack of Wisdom and Reason—Concupiscence, the Misuse of Reason and Desire—Man's Khwarr (Khwarenah) and Concupiscence—The Good Religion in Essence and Manifestation—Religion and Royalty—The Function of Royalty—Royalty the Material Complement of the Good Religion—The Virtues of Kings—Royalty the Bond between God and Man

The Interconnexion of the Zoroastrian Religion and the Sassanian Empire

THE Zoroastrians regarded their religion as being the Word of God, the expression of the divine Mind which is the divine Wisdom. So the Religion and Wisdom are interchangeable terms.[1] The Religion, however, is rarely conceived of in the abstract—it is seen as God's Word operating on earth within a definite social structure; and this structure is the social hierarchy of the Sassanian Empire in which each man is allotted his due place. So close was the link between the Zoroastrian religion and the Sassanian Empire that the collapse of the one meant the downfall of the other. The founder of the dynasty who was the first to revive and reform the ancient faith is quoted as saying: 'Religion and kingship are two brothers, and neither can dispense with the other. Religion is the foundation of kingship, and kingship protects religion. For whatever lacks a foundation must perish, and whatever lacks a protector disappears.'[2]

In the event, with the collapse of the Iranian secular power the Zoroastrian religion all but disappeared. In a striking and typical passage Mardān-Farrukh compares the Religion to a great tree.

'[Ohrmazd] created the Religion which is omniscience like a mighty tree with one trunk, two great boughs, three branches, four off-branches, and five roots. The one trunk is the mean, the two great boughs are action and abstention, the three branches are good thoughts, good words, and good deeds. The four off-branches are the four religious castes by which both the Religion and secular life are maintained, [namely], the priesthood, the warrior caste, the caste of husbandmen, and the caste of artisans. The five roots are the five degrees in the government hierarchy whose names in religion are *mānpat* (householder), *vīspat* (village headman), *zandpat* (tribal chieftain), *dēhpat* (provincial governor), and *Zarathushtrōtom* (the highest religious authority and representative of Zoroaster on earth). [Over and above these] is another, the Chief of all chiefs, that is, the King of kings, the governor of the whole world.

'And in the microcosm which is man [four things] are seen to correspond to the four earthly castes, the head to priesthood, the hands to the warrior caste, the belly to the caste of the husbandmen, and the feet to the caste of the artisans. So too the four virtues indwelling man, that is, temperance, fortitude, reason, and energy. Priesthood corresponds to temperance, for temperance is the highest duty of the priests, and through temperance they do not commit sin for very shame and fear. The warrior caste corresponds to fortitude, for fortitude is the sovereign adornment of warriors; it is explained [as meaning] innate manliness. Reason corresponds to the caste of the husbandmen, for the function of reason is the tilling of the soil and the promotion of a continuous evolution towards the final Rehabilitation. Energy corresponds to the caste of the artisans, for it is the greatest stimulant of their trade. All these various functions [are based] on the one trunk of righteousness and the mean [and are] opposed to the Lie and its instruments, which are their opposites.'[3]

From this passage it will be seen how closely the Zoroastrian religion is identified with the social order, for the very roots of the great tree which is the Religion, are the five grades of civil authority which had already been prominent in the Avesta. From these roots the trunk of the tree, here called the mean, arises and from it spring not only the purely religious duties of 'doing and abstaining', that is, obeying the divine commands and prohibitions, and the duty to think good thoughts, speak good words, and do good deeds, but also the social organization of society into the four great classes of priests, warriors, husbandmen, and artisans.

As we have seen, each individual man is here on earth to do his own job and no one else's, and his own job will necessarily be dictated to him by his class. The social organism is, then, co-terminous with the Good Religion, and the two cannot be separated. Prosperity and virtue are thereby seen as two facets of an essentially unitary system, the spiritual and material sides of the good creation, the whole being subordinate to the good government of the King of kings. The whole structure is summed up in the 'mean', which is a just equipoise between excess and deficiency; it is also righteousness or truth, and as such is identical with the ancient Indo-Iranian concept of asha/rta as opposed to the Lie, of which Zoroaster himself had made so much. Thus the two key concepts of Zoroaster's own preaching, the Good Mind and Truth, are preserved under different names in the reformed Zoroastrian-ism of the Sassanian period: they have become Wisdom and the Mean. Both are identical with the Religion itself.

The Doctrine of the Mean

The mean, indeed, is said to be the essence of the Religion,[4] the Law of God,[5] and the Sacred Word.[6] The mean is of God, excess and deficiency of the Devil; both manifest themselves in both orders, the spiritual and the material. In the material order the mean manifests itself as health, excess and deficiency as sickness; in the spiritual order the mean consists in virtue, while excess and deficiency appear as the vices opposed or akin to particular virtues.[7] The mean, again, is 'right-mindedness'[8] (*bavandak-mēnishnīh*, the Pahlavi translation of the Avestan *Ārmaiti*, who, as we have seen, is one of the Bounteous Immortals). And again it is the foundation of good government,[9] the equivalent of yet another Bounteous Immortal, Khshathra Vairya, the Desirable Kingdom. The mean, then, in the theology of reformed Zoroastrianism, is not only regarded as the trunk from which the whole tree of Religion springs; it has also taken over the functions not of one or two only of the Bounteous Immortals, but of all of them. As Wisdom it is also the Good Mind; of its very nature it is Righteousness or Truth; it is Right-Mindedness; as good government it is the Kingdom; as health it is Wholeness; and as the treaty between Ohrmazd and Ahriman it is the earnest of Immortality.[10] It can, then, be said to sum up the whole of the good creation;[11] it is the very principle of goodness.

The Mean as Cosmic Principle

The idea of the mean as being the principle of virtue is, of course, Aristotelian and must be a direct borrowing from Greece. Yet the Zoroastrians developed it along their own lines and even raised it to the rank of a cosmic principle, identical with the Word of God—the principle in which the whole cosmos of the good coheres, by which it is ruled, and through which it wins salvation from the twin 'lies' of excess and deficiency. So attractive did the Zoroastrians find the Aristotelian conception that they claimed it as typically their own. 'Iran has always commended the mean and censured excess and deficiency. In the Byzantine Empire the philosophers, in India the sages, and elsewhere the specialists have in general commended the man whose argument showed subtlety, but the Kingdom of Iran has approved [only] the [truly] wise.'[12]

The Mean as the Treaty between Ohrmazd and Ahriman

The Pahlavi word *patmān*, however, which is used for 'the mean', also has the sense of 'treaty'. More specifically it is the treaty between Ohrmazd and Ahriman according to which they would do battle with each other for nine thousand years, and:

'this too did Ohrmazd know in his omniscience, that of those nine thousand years three thousand would pass entirely according to the will of Ohrmazd, three thousand in mixture would pass according to the will of both Ohrmazd and Ahriman, and that in the last battle the Destructive Spirit would be made powerless and that he himself would save creation from aggression.'[13]

The 'treaty', then, is identical with finite Time, and, in the last resort, guarantees the immortality of the whole of the good creation. The limitation of time makes action possible, and the mean is the norm of righteous action. Ahriman, 'not seeing the end,' had accepted the treaty; for the treaty is at the same time Ohrmazd's whole grand structure of time-space, the principle of which is immutable law; and once Ahriman introduces lawlessness and disorder into this perfectly constructed machine, it can do no more than reduce its efficiency for a short time, only to be ground to pieces in the end. Once he has accepted the pact, however, Ahriman realizes his great mistake, and he immediately tries to do away with the thing; for he now knows that this treaty, which is at the same time the divine order of existence, must in the end destroy him. So, according to one legend, he swallows it outright, and it is left to Yima, who has the habit of turning up in the most improbable contexts, to retrieve it from the Satanic maw.[14]

The Mean, the Essence of Reason
In the *Dēnkart* the *patmān* is thought of not so much as the treaty between Ohrmazd and Ahriman as the mean between excess and deficiency. The mean is identical with wisdom or reason (*khrat*) while excess and deficiency are the two facets of concupiscence. Wisdom or reason is Ohrmazd's spiritual weapon, whereas concupiscence, in the sense of wrong-mindedness or heresy, is the spiritual weapon of Ahriman. In the *Dēnkart* the treaty or mean is spared the indignity of being swallowed by Ahriman and is merely abducted into hell by the demons. The passage is worth quoting in full, for it shows how closely the Zoroastrians identified wisdom or reason with orderliness, and both with the mean. Evil is concupiscence, disorder, and deviation from the divine norm: it is 'disorderly motion' (*ōshtāp*).[15]

'The usefulness of every action and every thing is from the mean. [This usefulness] is destroyed and made of no effect by excess and deficiency. The mean is controlled by [man's] innate reason which is [in fact] the mean [itself as created] by the Creator in his creatures. Deviation from the norm (*yut-dātastān*) can be described as excess and deficiency [which together constitute] diabolical concupiscence, the opposite of innate reason. Whenever innate reason, which is of divine provenance, predominates over diabolical concupiscence, then the mean and natural law (*dātastān*) will triumph among men, excess and deficiency will be weakened, and creation will prosper. Among men it is the king (*dahyupat*) who is pre-eminently endowed by the Creator with innate reason so that he can vanquish that most contumacious of all "lies", concupiscence, thereby, and so stimulate the innate reason that is in [all] men which tends to be dissipated by concupiscence, by energetically promoting their welfare and by providing them with good government. Only so will men's [minds] be open to the counsels of that reason that is innate in them; natural law and the mean will be current among them, and creation will be well governed.

'Before Yima succeeded to the throne, thanks to the depredations of the demons, kings were sadly deficient in innate reason and much swayed by concupiscence. The mean, which is of innate reason and of God, was so dissipated by excess and deficiency which are of concupiscence and the Devil, that men had become like beasts. Yielding to the debased counsels which fell upon their ears and utterly overcome by excess and deficiency, they had become estranged from the mean in matters of conduct, food, alms, property and so on. The world was reft asunder. For since it is clear that any diminution of divine reason which is innate in man, must result in the predominance of diabolical concupiscence and in the disappearance from the world of the mean and natural law which depend on innate reason, men were the more possessed by injustice, [the fruit] of excess and deficiency, [that is,] concupiscence, and the world was reduced to a wilderness and [terribly] disorganized.

'Yima came to power by the will and bidding of the Creator. First he deprived the demons of their sovereignty over men and saved divine innate reason from diabolical concupiscence which knows no path. He thought out how he could save the mean (which is of God) and innate reason from excess and deficiency, that is, diabolical concupiscence, so that there should be order, seemliness, and prosperity on earth. [This was to be achieved] by weakening the demons and depriving them of their sovereignty over men, by increasing once again innate reason which is divine, by the defeat of diabolic excess and deficiency, and by causing the mean and natural law which are of innate reason, to shine brightly. . . .

'By the Creator's great supernatural power and glory (*khwarr*) he was lifted up bodily and descended into hell; and for thirteen years he wandered in hell in the form of a demon, devising weapons with which to vanquish the demons, so that their sovereignty over men might be broken. By marvellous and subtle means he was conveyed up from the demons; and he smote and vanquished them with the weapon [he had devised], deprived them of their sovereignty over men, and drove them away. Thus was diabolic concupiscence deprived of its sway over men, and excess and deficiency [which stem] from it, diminished; innate reason, which is of God, was increased among men, and the mean and the natural law which are of innate reason, were made to triumph throughout creation—for by these does the creation of Ohrmazd achieve immortality, and by these is it restored.'[16]

288

God's law for man, then, is the mean, which is both a cosmic concept, natural law, and the standard of moral conduct on earth. Deviation from this norm is described as *varan* or *āz*, 'concupiscence', and this means both inordinate indulgence in bodily pleasures and the wrong use of reason, that is, heresy. Yima, it will be observed, who had been so roundly condemned by the Prophet Zoroaster, is here not only completely rehabilitated, but also made responsible for the liberation of man from the tyranny of the demons. He is the first in a succession of heroes who prepare the way for the final Rehabilitation; he breaks the power of the demons just as Zoroaster himself was later to deprive them of their bodily substance. Here he is the ideal king just as Zoroaster was the ideal prophet. For the world to be redeemed, however, it is necessary that Religion and royalty should combine in one person; and this will only come to pass at the end of time in the person of the Saoshyans, the saviour who will make all things new.[17] Both the Good Religion and the royal power co-operate in the preservation of the mean against excess and deficiency. The Good Religion, indeed, in the sense that it is the Zoroastrian 'Church' on earth, is the concrete expression of the mean; it *is* the mean, for 'the religion of Ohrmazd consists of one word—the mean: that of Ahriman consists of two words—excess and deficiency'.[18]

Virtue, the Mean between Contrary Vices

The mean is both the natural law by which the physical world is regulated, and the moral law which should be the guide of all man's actions. Each virtue is considered to be the medial point between two contrary vices, but of those two vices the one is directly opposed to the virtue concerned, whereas the other is akin to it. Thus true knowledge is directly opposed to wrong knowledge, but is akin to sensuality, for sensuality is the misuse of sense-perception which must be an element in true knowledge. Courage is opposed to feebleness, but akin to anger; desire is opposed to procrastination, but akin to lust, and so on.[19] Each virtue, then, is seen as the mean between the vice that is its contrary and the vice that is an exaggeration of itself; and to preserve the true mean it is important that one should not fall into the kindred vice when seeking to eliminate the contrary one. Courage must not be allowed to degenerate into anger, desire into lust, thrift into stinginess, modesty into cowardice, and so on.[20]

Many of the virtues themselves appear to be opposites, but they ultimately converge into each other. Thus courage and even-mindedness may appear to be opposites, but they must ultimately join each other in harmony; and the same is true of desire and circumspection, endeavour and contentment, comporting oneself as a free man and obeying the law, magnanimity and humility, thrift and generosity, religious obedience and a reasoned faith. The balance between these competing virtues must be kept, and neither must be allowed to slip into its kindred vice.[21]

Wisdom or Reason in Man and God

The mean, then, is as much the golden rule for ethical conduct as it is a cosmic principle. In both its aspects it is regarded as being the offspring or embodiment of reason or wisdom (*khrat*), and wisdom forms part of the divine personality.[22] In the Pahlavi texts it corresponds almost exactly to the Good Mind of the *Gāthās*: it is both God's uncreated wisdom and wisdom infused into the minds of men, by which they are *naturally* able to distinguish good from evil. The exact nuance the word takes on depends very much on the context in which it appears. In the *Mēnōk i Khrat* ('Book of the Spirit of Wisdom') *khrat* must be translated as 'wisdom', since it is the power through which the creation and preservation of the universe is brought about; but in the *Dēnkart* the word is practically always best translated as 'reason' or even 'common sense'. Semantically it is an almost exact equivalent of the Greek *nous* which also contains the two poles of 'wisdom' and 'common sense'. In the sense of 'wisdom' it is also the Logos of God by which he creates and sustains the universe and which is the source of revelation. In a memorable passage the Spirit of Wisdom makes himself known as the creative principle in God.

Wisdom as Creative Principle

'From the beginning was I, who am innate Wisdom among spiritual and material beings, with Ohrmazd; and the Creator Ohrmazd fashioned and made, sustains and rules all spiritual and material creatures, the gods and all the rest of creation, through the power and valour, knowledge and awareness (*kār-ākāsīh*) of innate Wisdom. And at the final Rehabilitation Ahriman and his abortions will most surely be smitten and wiped out by the power of Wisdom. Saoshyans, Kay Khusraw, and [all] those [others] who bring about the Resurrection and the Final Body, will surely bring it about by the power of Wisdom and with its aid.

'It is through Wisdom that knowledge, worldly experience, education, the learning of all arts and sciences, and every form of secular activity exist [at all]. Surely it is through Wisdom's power and protection that the souls of the righteous are saved from hell and attain unto heaven and the House of Song. Through the power of Wisdom again do men on earth seek a good life and pleasure, a good name and all good things.

'Is it not through the power of Wisdom and through its far-flung bounty and mighty strength that the seed of men, pack-animals, kine, small cattle, and all the other creatures of Ohrmazd the Lord is deposited in the womb and maintained there, yet they do not die of hunger and thirst? [Through Wisdom again] they are nourished in the womb, their limbs are made to grow and to reach maturity.

'Surely it is through Wisdom that the earth is [thus] established, the waters mingle with the earth, the plants are made to grow and prosper, that all manner of colours, scents, tastes, and pleasures come to be and are widely diffused.

'Surely it is through the power of Wisdom that Mount Alburz is made to encircle the earth, that the seven climes of the earth and the sky were shown forth, that the sun and the moon and the twelve Signs of the Zodiac pursue their course above Mount Alburz, that the six *Gāsānbār* times and the five *Fravartīkān* times [were allotted their place in the days and years], and that the heavens of good thoughts, good words, and good deeds, the perfect House of Song where all is bliss, and the passage-way [that all] spiritual and material beings [must traverse, which is] the Bridge of the Requiter, received their due place.

'Is it not through the power of Wisdom that the crystalline clouds raise up the waters from the sea, establish them in the sky, and rain them down upon the earth, drop upon drop, in all due order? [Is it not through the power of Wisdom too that] a man knows the creation of Ohrmazd from [the creation of] Ahriman, [that he knows] the nature of heaven and hell, the merciful goodness of Ohrmazd and the Bounteous Immortals and all the gods to their own creatures, and the death-dealing aggression of Ahriman and the demons against the creatures of Ohrmazd?

'Surely it is through the most perfect instrumentality of Wisdom that the Good Religion of the worshippers of Mazdāh is proclaimed and taught among material creatures, that the material bodies of the demons were broken and made to vanish from the sight of men. By Wisdom's power [again] will Iran go to battle against the non-Iranian lands, and Ahriman and the demons will be struck down.

'By the power of Wisdom will the waters that lie hidden beneath the earth be brought up to the light of day and made to minister to the dignity, prosperity, well-being, comfort, and pleasure of men, pack-animals, kine, and small cattle; and by its power will [all] the ills and sicknesses of men, pack-animals, kine, small cattle, and [all] other animals be recognized, drugs and medicines [devised to overcome them], and health and ease established [in their place].'[23]

In this passage from the *Mēnōk i Khrat* Wisdom is clearly conceived of as the creative Word of God; it is the power through which God thinks creation into existence. This doctrine, however, though implicit in the other Pahlavi texts, is nowhere else so plainly affirmed. Rather, Wisdom or reason is regarded as being that which God and man have in common, God by nature and man by special creation or infusion. It corresponds exactly to the Good Mind of Zoroaster and is, indeed, formally identified with it.[24] As such it is created in man, and its fruits are virtue and salvation on the spiritual plane, prosperity and pleasure on the material.[25] It is the source of all true knowledge as true knowledge is the source of law.[26] In the orthodox dualism its diabolic adversary is concupiscence. This basic polarity is stressed time and time again, and corresponds to the opposition of Truth and the Lie in the *Gāthās*. Wisdom-reason is the source of all good, concupiscence-unreason the fountain-head from which all evil flows. From the one proceeds right knowledge (*dānākīh*), from the other wrong-mindedness (*dushākāsīh*); and from right knowledge proceeds order and justice, from wrong-mindedness, disorder and injustice. In the Pahlavi books there is a distinct shift of emphasis from the moral to the intellectual plane. All evil proceeds from 'concupiscence', which is fundamentally the abuse of the intellect, a failure to diagnose reality as it is; and this failure to assess reality can only lead to disorder and defeat. Ohrmazd is omniscient because he understands things as they are; Ahriman is 'wrong-minded' because he harbours absurd illusions about the nature of Ohrmazd and his creation—he believes that they can be finally separated and individually destroyed. His whole nature is 'disorderly motion'—chaotic movement on the physical plane, chaotic thought on the mental.

Ahriman's Lack of Wisdom and Reason

The Pahlavi books like to compare life on earth to a battle between two armies. Ahriman is doomed to failure not so much because he is the weaker party, for his assault troops prove devastatingly effective in the early stages of the war, as because his intelligence branch in all its ramifications is desperately inefficient. He can neither collect intelligence that bears any relation to the facts, nor can he collate it, nor can he assess it. His appraisal of the enemy's dispositions is therefore totally false, and his operations branch is therefore again and again taken by surprise; before he knows where he is, he finds himself totally encircled by two walls of steel from which he cannot escape—the wall constituted by the sky which encompasses the physical universe, and the even more formidable rampart beyond it, which is made up of the united consciousness of mankind. Had he had the slightest idea of what ordered and intelligent creation was, he would never have attacked. In the event he is defeated by his own stupidity. Ohrmazd's very name means 'productivity' and 'right-mindedness', Ahriman's 'aggression' and 'wrong knowledge'; and so 'the greater one's knowledge is, so much the greater will one's ability to remain in control and to bring about increase be; the more wrong one's apperceptions are, the greater will one's subjection to the control of others and one's need of others be. So too, among men, it is invariably the wise man who gets control over the wrong-minded, and the wrong-minded who falls under the control of the wise.'[27]

Yet though it is true that Ahriman's stupidity will be his ruin, he has the power to warp men's minds and make them stupid in their turn. Stupidity or wrong-mindedness in man consists in not recognizing the true nature of God by attributing evil to him and creativity to the Devil. This is characteristic of all religions with the sole exception of Zoroastrianism. Jews, Christians, Muhammadans, and even Hindus regard God as being the source of both good and evil, and this is *varan*—concupiscence and unreason.

Concupiscence, the Misuse of Reason and Desire

The Pahlavi word *varan* is a simple transcription of the Avestan *varena*, which means 'choice'. In Pahlavi, however, the meaning has completely changed; it has come to mean 'wrong choice', the misuse of the intellect, particularly in theological matters, and, like *āz*, it also means the misuse of legitimate desire, and more specifically, sexual desire. All religions other than Zoroastrianism are the fruits of Varan-concupiscence-unreason. One and all—with the single exception of Manichaeanism—they err in attributing evil to God; and Manichaeanism errs in an even more fundamental respect—it fails to recognize what constitutes good and what evil; it commits the dreadful blasphemy of considering God's adorable world to be constructed out of the bodies of the demons. All these wrong views or heresies are due to a misuse of reason; for it stands to reason from what we know of this visible world as it is, that no rational being destroys what he has created, leads astray those whom he has hitherto guided, or torments those whom he loves. Reason is natural to man in that it is a 'creation of the Creator in [all] creatures',[28] and God causes it to be born in man's soul.[29] It enables man 'to discriminate, to distinguish good from evil, and to do what is good and shun what is evil'.[30] If, then, God illumines man's soul with the light of reason, it is absurd to suppose that he would at the same time darken it with the fog of unreason and stupidity; hence the mere existence of unreason and heresy proves the existence of a separate principle.[31]

Reason is God's gift to his creatures—he 'chooses' it for them, for they are suited to it and thankful for it. It spurs them on to acquire more and more true knowledge, and this in turn causes innate reason to grow and translates itself into action. Reason translated into action reveals itself as virtue, and its fruits are deliverance from the Aggressor and the enjoyment of everlasting bliss. Right reason can be distinguished from wrong reason or 'concupiscence' in that a man recognizes it as being appropriate to his own nature and is therefore grateful for it. 'Concupiscence', whether understood as the misuse of legitimate desire or of right reason, is disturbing (ōshtāpāk)—it produces a feeling of anxiety; it impels a man to follow wrong doctrines which lead him to the neglect of virtue and an active striving in the pursuit of sin. Through his own fault and initiative, then, such a man puts himself in the power of his Enemy 'who drags and hurls him into misery abiding'. All this he owes to concupiscence, which he mistakenly and stupidly imagines to be part of his own nature,[32] oblivious of the fact that it has been injected into him from outside.

It is not clear whether the Zoroastrians regarded the sin incurred by man's first parents as being transmitted by heredity or not, or whether concupiscence is injected ever again into each new individual by a new and separate act of aggression on the part of Ahriman. However that may be, every man is provided with enough innate reason to enable him to save his soul.[33]

Man's Khwarr (Khwarenah) and Concupiscence
Man's *khwarr*, as we have seen, is his 'own-work', and his 'own-work' is to store up virtue on the one hand and to produce material prosperity on the other: it is to develop his talents to the limit. This noble pursuit is kept alive by reason, killed by concupiscence,[34] for reason and concupiscence are the *fons et origo* of the virtues and vices respectively.[35] The one manifests itself in liberality and peace, the other in avarice and strife,[36] the deadly foes of the common weal which is the *khwarr* in its collective aspect. Because reason is native to man, the only religion based on reason rather than on concupiscence, that is, Zoroastrianism, is natural to man. So:

'A man who is really himself is one whose thoughts, words, and deeds are [in accordance with] his soul (*akhw*). By adhering to the Good Religion he comes to adhere to the highest Lord (*akhw*), the Creator, Ohrmazd. Following the straight path of his own nature, he attains to his own plenitude of welfare, his own [appointed] place of overflowing joy. But the man who is not truly himself is he whose thoughts, words, and deeds are divorced from his soul.[37] He cleaves to concupiscence with which he has no kinship, and by cleaving to evil religions which are of concupiscence that has no path, he is dragged away to the Destructive Spirit and the Lie, and he lurches into a total misery that is none of his, and into a place full of torment.'[38]

294

The Good Religion in Essence and Manifestation

God is the source of wisdom and reason,[39] and wisdom and reason are identical with the Good Religion.[40] The Zoroastrian religion, then, is itself God's eternal Wisdom. Manifested, it is God's Word operating in finite space and time. At the beginning of time God pronounces the *Ahuna Vairya* prayer, the quintessence of the whole of revealed religion, and Ahriman is precipitated into the depths. With the coming of Zoroaster, however, the whole of the Religion is revealed in the shape of the Avesta which is the 'pure praise of God'[41] and 'all truth and justice'.[42] Translated from the spiritual world into this material world, it promotes the orderly development of the world[43] and its continued growth,[44] so that in the end it will be in a position to 'annihilate the Aggressor, to purify creation from all taint and opposition, and to bring about an everlasting plenitude of bliss'.[45]

In its extra-temporal essence, however, the Good Religion is identical with the Creator's Wisdom by which he creates and sustains the world, and by which he vanquishes the muddled-headedness of his Adversary, thereby restoring his own creation to a state of undiluted happiness. The divine omniscience, which the Good Religion is, manifests itself in universal justice, in the assignment to each creation of what is properly its own. The Religion's function is to heal creation from the wounds inflicted on it by Ahriman and the demons. It is, however, more than this, for all knowledge falls within its province, and it is therefore directly concerned with science. Its business is 'to recognize the forces [latent] in things and to make due use of them'. Having once found out how things work and what is wrong with them, it can eliminate the corruption brought upon them by Ahriman and heal them. Throughout the millennia that lead up to the Rehabilitation which is the consummation of the world, 'by knowing the forces [latent] in things and by making the best possible use of them, all creation will be completely healed from the [wounds inflicted on it by the] Aggressor, and the plenitude of everlasting joy will be brought into being'.[46]

In another passage true and false religion are contrasted. 'The essence of the Religion of Ohrmazd is right knowledge and its garment is goodness. It is controlled by justice. . . . The essence of the religion of Ahriman is wrong-mindedness, and its garment is heresy (*ahra-mōghīh*).'[47] Right knowledge consists in recognizing that 'the Creator is the source of all good and that no[48] evil proceeds from him. In this are [summed up] all the good things enjoyed by creatures from the original creation until the final Rehabilitation'.[49] To recognize God as absolutely good and the Devil as absolutely evil is the one sure way to salvation. 'When a man knows the Holy Spirit, he attains to him and wins through to heaven, and when a man knows the Destructive Spirit, he turns away from him, is saved from hell, and wins through to victory.'[50] This saving knowledge is the source of all good things both in this world and the next. It enables us to train our characters, to find the mean which is the source of justice, to think good thoughts, speak good words, and do good deeds. These, in turn, bring man welfare; and the welfare of man gives pleasure to the gods and dismays the demons; and 'through the joy of the gods and the discomfiture of the demons both the spiritual and material worlds flourish exceedingly', and this state of universal well-being brings about the Rehabilitation, the 'establishment of pure well-being in the entire creation'.[51]

The *Frashkart*—the 'Making Excellent' or final Rehabilitation—is often represented in the Pahlavi books in apocalyptic terms, as we shall see in our final chapter, but in the *Dēnkart* it is the natural culmination of the fructifying power of the Good Religion; it is the triumph of the positive forces of physical life allied to a positive morality of justice, generosity, and concord, over the bleak negation of physical death and the chaotic forces of injustice, avarice, and discord. One might almost say that it is the triumph of a free and socialized society co-operating to develop and exceed itself, over the forces of disruption, disunity, and war. The Good Religion can thus be seen as the religion of creative evolution, which culminates in the greatest possible growth of all and the elimination of all that militates against life and happiness. No wonder that the Zoroastrians could see nothing but evil in the non-Iranian religions which declared that the Creator and the Destroyer were the same!

The Good Religion, however, is not only synonymous with God's omniscience, it is also the expression of his will, and his will is that all men should be saved from the Adversary.[52] The Religion is, then, his principal instrument for bringing about his will on earth. This, however, can only be done with the co-operation of the royal power, for Ohrmazd unites in himself lordship and wisdom, and since man is the symbol of God on earth,[53] he cannot attain his true stature until royalty and religion are united in one person. This, however, is not to be until the millennium of Saoshyans, the eschatological 'saviour', sets in.

Religion and Royalty

Ideally the Religion and royalty are so intimately connected as to be inseparable: 'Religion is royalty, and royalty is the Religion,'[54] but this is only an ideal state of affairs, and the aphorism in any case needs qualifying. Certainly the royal power is constantly extolled in the

Dēnkart, but whereas the Religion, being the manifestation of God's essential wisdom, cannot be corrupted, royal power can, for power, divorced from wisdom, is characteristic of Ahriman, not of Ohrmazd. Religion is, or ought to be, the source from which the royal power springs, and royalty should consider its first duty to be the defence of the faith. This is wholly logical, for the duty of the royal power is to ensure the tranquillity of its subjects and to add to their prosperity; for Zoroastrianism, alone among the religions known to the Iranians, regarded productivity as being synonymous with virtue so far at least as the material world was concerned. Once the royal power is firmly based on the Good Religion, and the Religion is protected by the King, a just society will arise; 'the Empire will prosper, the common people will be freed from fear and enjoy a good life, science will advance, culture will be looked after, good manners will be further refined, and men will be generous, just, and grateful; many a virtue will they practise, and perfect will their goodness be'.[55] The Good Religion, indeed, gives its authoritative approval to the 'furtherance and refinement of legitimate prosperity, wit (*chāpukīh*), display, music, and [worldly] pleasure'.[56] All these are natural to kings, and the Good Religion is the foundation on which kingship is built.

The Function of Royalty

Royalty is concerned with the orderly and just government of the world, that is, the Persian Empire; religion is concerned both with this world and the next, with prosperity as well as with virtue. The King is 'grounded' in the Religion just as this world is grounded in the spiritual world, which is its exemplar (*namūnak*).[57] God is absolute lord of both worlds; the King is his representative on earth and, as such, may himself take the title of *bagh*, 'god'. 'The symbol of the Holy Spirit surely manifests itself on earth in [the person of] the good and righteous King, one whose will (*akhw*) is bent on increase, whose character is pure, whose desires for his subjects are good.'[58] Such a king is fulfilling his *khwarr* or true function, for sovereignty belongs to Ohrmazd; the King receives a portion of it, but in the end all sovereignty will return to its source, which is God.[59]

Royalty the Material Complement of the Good Religion

Man, as we have seen, is himself a king over his own body. As such, he too is a symbol of Ohrmazd on earth, but all men are mirrored in the King and derive their strength from him, and so it is from the King that all prosperity derives. Because this world is still subject to the malign influence of Ahriman and the demons, spirit and matter are not as closely associated as they were in the beginning and will be in the end; yet, even so, they collaborate harmoniously; they complement rather than oppose each other. The inter-connexion between the two worlds was fully explained to Yezdigird I by one Āturpāt, son of Zartusht, and these are the correspondences he established:

Matter	Spirit
Body	Soul
Wealth	Virtue
Honour	Righteous effort
Kingship	Religion
Generosity	Knowledge

The relationship of the royal power to the Religion, then, is that of body to soul, and just how each affects the other is further explained, the right relationship between the two being, of course, the mean.

'The material body achieves its full worth by the spiritual soul itself being blessed. The spiritual soul achieves blessedness by the instrumentality of the material body. Material wealth is respected only when it is accompanied by spiritual virtue. Spiritual virtue is won mainly through material wealth. Worldly honour becomes respectable only if one strives after spiritual righteousness. Striving after spiritual righteousness is increased by zeal for material honour. Earthly kingship is secured only on the basis of spiritual Religion, and spiritual Religion is propagated most successfully when it is allied with earthly kingship. Material generosity receives honour only when it is united to spiritual knowledge, and spiritual knowledge will show more practical results if allied with material generosity.'[60]

Similarly, on the obverse side, poverty reduces virtue, not being honoured among men impedes the quest for righteousness, just as the end of the Iranian monarchy stopped the propagation of the Good Religion, and schism within the Good Religion had hastened the end of the monarchy. This near-identity of Church and State which the Zoroastrians themselves admitted had been fatal to their religion once the Iranian monarchy collapsed, was nevertheless firmly embedded in their thought. The monarch was the symbol of Ohrmazd's universal sovereignty on earth, and the Religion was not only the symbol, but the manifested substance of the divine Wisdom. The Iranian state, then, was the earthly manifestation of the Godhead itself. In the last analysis, too, the ambitions of the monarchy and the Good Religion were the same. Ideally, the Persian Empire should include the whole world, and the King is therefore called *dahyupat i gēhān*,[61] the 'King of the world'. Similarly the Zoroastrian religion, though primarily and consciously of Iranian origin, did not regard itself as being for that reason narrowly nationalistic. 'The Creator, Ohrmazd,' a Christian polemist is told, 'did not send down this religion to the Iranian Empire only, he sent it to the whole world and to every nation.'[62] This, indeed, is the promise to which the Zoroastrians still looked forward even after the collapse of the Empire and the dismemberment of their religious organization; a day would come at the end of time when all men would be gathered together in the one true religion which alone denied all taint of evil to God, under the one King and Saviour, Saoshyans, Zoroaster's posthumous son, who was to be miraculously born from his seed, equally miraculously preserved. Ahriman might win many a battle yet, but final victory was already secure in Ohrmazd's hands.

This hope was possible for them because the Good Religion was the eternal Logos of God, and this could not perish. Ahriman's counter-creation was *aghdēnīh*, 'evil religion', and by this was meant both heresy within the Zoroastrian fold and other religions outside Zoroastrianism. Yet, despite the collapse of the Empire, no Zoroastrian could doubt that Truth must in the end triumph over the Lie. The question of the royal power was different, for, whereas the good king was the symbol of the divine sovereignty on earth, the wicked king or tyrant was rather that of Ahriman.[63]

The Virtues of Kings

If a king is to be a faithful image of God on earth, he must first of all be wise—he must be guided by reason. His job is first of all to protect his subjects; and the best way of doing this is not, of course, to consult the popular will, which would be folly, but to submit the general will to the royal will, the royal will to the royal reason, and this again to the divine reason which is made known in the Good Religion.[64]

The King is the centre on which his subjects converge; and it is therefore essential that he should be happy. For, just as it is the first duty of man to love himself so that he may extend his self-love to others, so is it not so much the duty as the very nature of a king to be happy; and the royal felicity cannot fail to extend in ever-widening ripples to his subjects. Thus, 'the principal characteristic of kings is pleasure . . . pleasure is consonant with kingship provided it is rooted in greatness. Pleasure rooted in greatness does not pass away'.[65] This is typical of the whole Zoroastrian ethos; the King is the centre of the universe, and the goal of the universe is happiness. Happiness is a good in itself, and without it the other virtues are sterile. Once again, however, it must be emphasized that the Zoroastrian exaltation of the pleasure principle is not just vulgar hedonism, for the texts stress time and again that material pleasure, if divorced from spiritual striving, is merely an excess; it is a departure from the mean and therefore of the Devil. But to suppress the pleasure principle or even to curb it unduly is to fall into the other extreme of deficiency, and this is the folly and the blasphemy of the Manichees and the Christians. The good king, on the other hand, will preserve the mean in all things:

'his *khwarr* (that is, in this case, his royalty) will indwell him, he will be a child of innate reason and justice; he will love prosperity, foster the royal power, offer fulsome praise [to the gods], extend his frontiers (*gēhān-frākhw-kar*), and cause his subjects to thrive. He is rooted in pleasure. Salvation is his fruit; and his generosity shines afar.'[66]

The good king, then, by training himself in wisdom, justice, legitimate pleasure, and luxury, extends his own virtue and prosperity to the whole Empire; and monarch and people should, thus, form one community, soldered together by contentment. This is, however, to reckon without Ahriman's deadly weapon of concupiscence, which lies in wait for kings no less than for the religious. Concupiscence, however, is formally opposed not only to reason, but also to the *khwarr* of all men—it beguiles them from what they ought to do. The King is the symbol of Ohrmazd in the material world; and concupiscence, in his case, will be not unreason and heresy which fall within the province of spirit, but greed, avarice, and lust. So:

'The worst of all kings is he who embraces an evil *khwarr*, who is a son of gluttony (*āz*), of lust that disturbs and has no path, and of injustice, [who is] the seed [and source] of penury, the weakener of his subjects, the murderer of royalty. He is rooted in sin; damnation, straitness, and misery abounding [are his fruit]. He draws in his frontiers (*gēhān tangēnītār*), weakens his allies, and strengthens his enemies.'[67]

Royalty the Bond between God and Man
The King, then, is not only in duty bound to protect the Good Religion and his subjects and to bring prosperity to the Empire; he should also extend his frontiers, thereby imposing a *pax iranica* on the whole world. In practice this policy failed, but to pursue it, as many of the Sassanian kings did, was logical enough; for the ultimate salvation of the world, and not only of Iran, depended on the Good Religion being accepted and practised by all mankind.

Of all the Sassanian kings none lived up to the ideal of kingship as outlined by the Zoroastrian priesthood except, perhaps, Khusraw I— Khusraw, 'the Just of Immortal Soul'. His memory is cherished to this day in Iran as the ideal king. The sayings attributed to him in the *Dēnkart* and elsewhere are therefore of some interest, particularly the first which interprets royalty as a bond between God and man. 'Let your thought transcend your own will (*akhw*) and pass on to the highest will and Lord (*akhw*) on earth, that is, the King acknowledged by the Religion, and let it pass on from him [too] to the highest Lord of all who is of the spirit, the Creator Ohrmazd.'[68]

The King is here seen almost as the mediator between God and man precisely because he is the King; for God is the universal sovereign of the two worlds and man is the sovereign of his own little world or microcosm—his body, mind, and emotions. Between them stands the King, the ruler of the whole material world by divine right. So, just as Christianity has its communion of saints, Zoroastrianism has its communion of kings.

Khusraw's other sayings are much what one would expect. Respect must be paid to the Good Religion, and heresy must be extirpated: hospitality must be offered to holy men, and the sacred fire must be duly tended: the King's law must be obeyed and enforced, and lastly, and not at all uncharacteristically, the King's subjects are bidden to afford all the aid they can to their kin, but to withhold it from foreigners and enemies. In the matter of the Religion itself the King requires his subjects to practise it 'according to the teaching and practice of the disciples of Āturpāt, son of Mahraspand'; and, lest the reader should feel that Sassanian Zoroastrianism is altogether too materialistic and too deeply committed to this world, let us, in conclusion, return to the rather more austere views of Āturpāt who, after all, ranked among the dualists as the very corner-stone of their orthodoxy.

'Do not regard this world as a [permanent] principle, for it has not long existed. Leave [all care for] the things of this world to God, and concern yourself [rather] with God's business, nothing doubting. [Then only] will the world be presented to you in a way that both your body and your soul will be perfected. Take to yourself personally the things of the spirit; for if you reject these, you will lose all worldly good. Make God a guest within your body; for if you make him a guest within your body, then you make him a guest within the whole material world.'[69]

CHAPTER FIFTEEN

THE END

The Soul's Fate at Death—The Nature of the Discarnate Soul—Heaven—Hell—The Frashkart or Final Rehabilitation—Ohrmazd's Master-plan for the Overthrow of Evil—The Three Phases of Ohrmazd's Plan—The Beginning of the End—The Destruction of Āz and Ahriman (Zurvanite Version)—The Meaning of Ahriman's Destruction—The Disintegration of Evil (Orthodox Version)—The Resurrection of the Body—The Role of Saoshyans and the Final Bull-Sacrifice—Purgation by Molten Metal—The 'Final Body' and Renewal of all Things—The Marriage of Matter and Spirit

ZOROASTRIANISM, like Christianity, lays great stress on individual salvation; yet the fate of the individual is ultimately seen in the context of the whole of the human race, and in Ohrmazd's plan the defeat of Ahriman also means the final release of all the souls of the damned from hell. In Sassanian Zoroastrianism there is no eternal damnation; no soul is eternally punished for the sins it has committed in time. The *Frashkart* or final Rehabilitation of all existence means literally the 'making excellent', and this means that evil in all its forms is finally destroyed. So not only are Ahriman and the demons who originate evil destroyed, but also the effects of evil, that is to say, the sufferings endured by the damned in hell. Before that joyful consummation comes to pass, however, each individual soul has to answer for itself and has to undergo an individual judgement after death. In this respect the Zoroastrianism of the Sassanian reform is true to the Prophet's message: each man must choose between good and evil and must bear the consequences of his choice. The judgement of the soul at death is still preserved in a fragment of the Avesta and frequently appears in the Pahlavi books. No book on Zoroastrianism would be complete without it, and we must, therefore, quote it in full.

The Soul's Fate at Death

'For three days and nights the soul sits beside the head-stone [of the slab on which] the body [is laid]. On the fourth day at dawn, accompanied by Sraosha, the blessed, the good Vay, mighty Vahrām (Verethraghna), and opposed by the Loosener of Bones, the evil Vay, and the demons Frēhzisht and Vizisht, and pursued by the malevolence of the evil-doer Wrath who bears a bloody spear, [the soul] will come to the Bridge of the Requiter, lofty and dreadful, for thither must saved and damned alike proceed. There does many an enemy lie in wait. [There will it have to face] the malevolence of Wrath who wields a bloody spear and the Loosener of Bones who swallows up all creatures and knows no sating, but Mithra, Sraosha, and Rashnu will mediate [on its behalf]; and just Rashnu will weigh [its deeds]. He lets his spiritual scales incline to neither side, neither for the saved nor yet for the damned, nor yet for kings and princes. Not for a hair's breath will he diverge, for he is no respecter [of persons]. He deals out impartial justice both to kings and princes and to the meanest of men.

'And when the soul of the saved passes over that bridge, the bridge appears to it to be one parasang broad; and the soul of the saved passes on accompanied by the blessed Sraosha. And his own good deeds come to meet him in the form of a maiden more beautiful and fair than any girl on earth. And the soul of the saved says: "Who art thou? for never did I see on earth a maiden more beautiful and fair than thee." Then will that form of a maiden make answer and say: "I am no maiden, but thine own good deeds, young sir, whose thoughts, words, deeds, and religion are all good. For when on earth thou didst see one who offered sacrifice to the demons, then didst thou sit [apart] and offer sacrifice to the gods. And when thou didst see a man commit violence and rapine, afflict good men and treat them with contumely, or hoard up goods wrongfully obtained, then didst thou refrain from visiting creatures with violence and rapine of thine own; [rather] wast thou considerate to good men; thou didst welcome them and offer them hospitality and give them alms, both to him who came from near and to him who came from afar. Thy wealth too didst thou store up in accordance with righteousness. And when thou didst see one who passed false judgement, taking bribes and bearing false witness, then didst thou sit thee down and speak witness right and true. I am thy good thoughts, good words, and good deeds which thou didst think and speak and do. For though I was venerable [from the first], thou hast made me yet more venerable; and though I was honourable [from the first], thou hast made me yet more honourable; and though I was endowed with dignity (*khwarr*), thou hast conferred on me yet greater dignity."

'And when [the soul] departs from thence, then is a fragrant breeze wafted towards it, more fragrant than any perfume. Then does the soul of the saved ask Sraosha: "What breeze is this the like of which in fragrance I never smelt on earth?" Then does the blessed Sraosha make answer to the soul of the saved [and say]: "This is a breeze from heaven; hence is it so fragrant."

'Then with its first step it treads [the heaven of] good thoughts, with its second [the heaven of] good words, with its third [the heaven of] good deeds; and with its fourth step it attains to the Endless Light where all is bliss. And all the gods and the Bounteous Immortals come to greet him and ask him how he has fared, [saying]: "How was thy passage from those transient, fearful worlds replete with evil to these worlds which do not pass away and in which there is no adversary, young sir, whose thoughts, words, deeds, and religion are good?"

'Then Ohrmazd the Lord says: "Ask him not how he has fared; for he has been separated from his beloved body and travelled on the fearful road."

303

Then do they serve him with the sweetest of foods, even the butter of early spring, so that the soul may take its ease after the three nights terror at the Bridge which the Loosener of Bones and the other demons brought upon him; and he is sat upon a throne everywhere adorned.

'For it is revealed that the sweetest of foods offered by the spiritual gods to a man or a woman after the parting of consciousness and body is the butter of early spring, and that they seat him on a throne everywhere adorned. And for ever and ever will he dwell in a plenitude of bliss together with the spiritual gods.

'But when the man who is damned dies, then for three days and nights does his soul hover near his head, weeping, [and saying]: "Whither shall I go? and in whom shall I now take refuge?" And during those three days and nights he sees with his eyes all the sins and wickedness that he committed on earth. On the fourth day the demon Vizarsh comes and binds the soul of the damned in most shameful wise, and, despite the opposition of the blessed Sraosha, drags it off to the Bridge of the Requiter. Then Rashnu, the Just, will unmask the soul of the damned as damned indeed.

'Then does the demon Vizarsh, eager in his wrath, seize upon the soul of the damned, smite it and despite it without pity. And the soul of the damned cries out with a loud voice, groans, and in supplication makes many a piteous plea; and desperate[1] will be his struggle. When all his struggling and his lamentations have proved of no avail, no help is proffered him by any of the gods nor yet by any of the demons, but the demon Vizarsh drags him off against his will to nethermost hell.

'Then a maiden who yet has no resemblance to a maiden comes to meet him. And the soul of the damned says to that ill-favoured wench: "Who art thou? for never have I seen an ill-favoured wench on earth more ill-favoured and hideous than thee." And in answer that ill-favoured wench says to him: "I am no girl, but I am thy deeds—hideous deeds—thy evil thoughts, evil words, evil deeds, and evil religion. For when on earth thou didst see one who offered sacrifice to the gods, then didst thou sit [apart] and offer sacrifice to the demons: demons and lies didst thou worship. And when thou didst see one who welcomed good men and offered them hospitality, and gave alms both to those who came from near and to those who came from far, then didst thou treat good men with contumely and show them dishonour; nor didst thou give them alms, but shuttest thy door [upon them]. And when thou didst see one who passed just judgement, or took no bribes, or bore true witness, or spoke up in righteousness, then didst thou sit down and pass false judgement, bear false witness, and speak unrighteously. I am thy evil thoughts, evil words, and evil deeds which thou didst think and speak and do. For though I was disreputable [at first], thou hast made me yet more disreputable; and though I was dishonourable [at first], thou hast made me yet more dishonourable; and though I sat [at first] among the unaware, thou hast made me yet more unaware."

'Then with the first step he goes to [the hell of] evil thoughts, with his second to [the hell of] evil words, and with his third to [the hell of] evil deeds.

And with his fourth step he lurches into the presence of the Destructive Spirit and the other demons. And the demons mock at him and hold him up to scorn [saying]: "What grieved thee in Ohrmazd the Lord, and the Bounteous Immortals, and in fragrant and delightful heaven, and what complaint hadst thou of them that thou shouldst come to see Ahriman, the demons, and murky hell? For we shall torment thee, nor shall we have any mercy on thee, and for a long time shalt thou suffer torment."

'Then will the Destructive Spirit cry out to the demons [saying]: "Ask not concerning him; for he has been separated from his beloved body and has come through that most evil passage-way. Serve him [rather] with the filthiest and most vile of foods, food produced in hell."

'Then they will bring him poison and venom, snakes and scorpions and other noxious reptiles [which thrive] in hell and give him thereof to eat. And until the Resurrection and the Final Body he must remain in hell suffering much torment and all manner of chastisement. And the food that for the most part he must eat there is rotten, as it were, and like unto blood.'[2]

The Nature of the Discarnate Soul

From this description of the soul's fate at death it can be seen that the Zoroastrian conception of the nature of the soul is rather materialistic; it has senses with which it sees, hears, touches, smells, and tastes, and it has the equivalent of physical organs, for it eats. Mānushchihr even goes so far as to describe the soul as the *mēnōk i tan*,[3] the 'unseen genius of the body'; it has the same senses as the body[4] through which it can enjoy the pleasures of paradise and suffer the torments of hell. In the three nights during which the soul awaits judgement, the soul of the virtuous man suffers punishment for the few sins it has committed and then passes on to paradise,[5] while the soul of the wicked man who, nevertheless, has some virtuous deeds on his credit side, is visited by the spirit of good thoughts on the first night, by the spirit of good words on the second, and by the spirit of good deeds on the third: these bring him some comfort and seek to console him,[6] but he has to go down to hell nonetheless.

Heaven and hell, however, are not the same for all: their joys and pains are strictly commensurate to the amount of virtue or sin a man has amassed during his earthly life.[7] In addition to heaven and hell there is another place to which the soul of the dead may go; this is called *Hamēstagān*, the 'place of the mixed', destined for those whose balance of virtue and sin is exactly equal.[8] This is situated between earth and the 'station of the stars', and the only pain the soul suffers there is from heat and cold.[9]

Heaven

Both heaven and hell are thought of in material terms and the pure contemplation of God is rarely mentioned. Mānushchihr almost goes out of his way to emphasize that the joys of heaven are exactly like the joys of earth except that there can be no real comparison between an infinite and a finite form of existence. The descriptions of heaven found in the Avesta must be considered simply as similitudes 'to give some idea of them to men still on earth';[10] for:

'the finite cannot be compared to the infinite, nor the transient to what is not transient, nor what is subject to diminution to what is not. This world is finite, transient, and subject to diminution, whereas the Endless Light is neither transient nor subject to diminution, and that Treasury of eternal Benefit is indestructible, and the bright House of Song is all joy with no admixture of pain.'[11]

Yet in his descriptions of heaven as it exists before the final Rehabilitation, Mānushchihr (and the other Pahlavi texts as well) seems to regard it as little more than a replica of this world from which all sin and all pain have been expelled. Moreover, it is very definitely a place, not a state. It is 'above' (and he uses no less than three words of identical meaning to emphasize this point), 'most brilliant, fragrant, pure and beautiful, most desirable and good, the place and abode of the gods. In it is all ease and pleasure, joy and bliss, a state of welfare greater and better than the greatest and highest welfare and pleasure on earth. In it there is neither need nor pain, nor misery, nor discomfort.'[12] The denizens of heaven are free from the fear of ever being hurt again.[13]

In addition to this the soul is said actually to see God. Ohrmazd gives him spiritual senses and he rejoices at what he sees.[14] Ohrmazd, however, is never thought of as having a human form, as the God of the Old Testament and the Allah of the Koran so frequently are; rather he is a pure light. Thus in the *Book of Artāy Virāf*, which describes the journeyings of that holy man throughout the different hells and his final emergence into the presence of the All Highest, we read that though Ohrmazd spake to him and though he heard his voice, he saw no physical form: 'When Ohrmazd spake in this manner, I was astonished; for I saw a light, but no body did I see. A voice I heard, and I knew that this was Ohrmazd.'[15]

The vision of God, however, is only one of the joys of heaven, though no doubt the greatest. After being introduced into the divine presence by the Good Mind[16] the newly-arrived soul is greeted by his friends, made welcome, and told of all the joys that await him.[17] Heavenly food, too, differs from our food on earth; for, on earth, we either eat because we are hungry and have to, or we eat for the pure pleasure of it: in heaven the pleasure motive is alone present.[18]

The soul will also enjoy the company of learned and pious friends and of wives who are fair and modest, devoted to their husbands and thrifty. There, too, will all the animal kingdom be—flocks and herds, wild animals, birds, and fish—fires and winds, shining metals, and water in rivers, springs, and wells. Trees, too, will there be, and luscious fruits, corn, and all manner of plants and flowers.[19] Yet this is only a similitude made to suit the finite mind, for the reality surpasses the description as much as the infinite surpasses the finite. Despite this qualification, however, it is clear that the Zoroastrians regarded heaven as being a perfect exemplar of this world in which personal relationships would subsist and sensuous pleasures would be enjoyed.

Hell

So, too, with hell. It lies deep down beneath the earth, 'is most dark and stinking, most fearful and thankless, most evil—the place and lair of the demons and lies.'[20] In it there is neither pleasure nor joy; all is stench and pollution, pain and punishment, affliction, suffering, misery, and discomfort—all this, too, to an infinite degree so that there can be no comparison with earthly pain; and whereas, on earth, the fear of some future evil is usually worse than the evil itself, in hell the reality far exceeds the dread.[21]

The most graphic description of hell is that given by Artāy Virāf who experienced it at first hand in a vision induced by hashish.

'And so I experienced cold and an icy wind, dryness and stench such as I had never experienced on earth nor yet heard of. And as I went on further I saw the ghastly deeps of hell; like a most fearful pit it led down to an even narrower and more terrifying place. Its darkness was so thick that it could be grasped with the hand. Its stench was such that whoever breathed it in must needs stagger(?), tremble, and fall. So narrow was it that none could stand up there. And all [who were there] thought, "I am alone"; and when only three days and nights have passed, they say: "Surely nine thousand years have passed by, yet they do not let me go." Even in the places where there are least noxious beasts, they are [piled up] as high as a mountain, and they tear, rend, and worry the souls of the damned in a way that would be unworthy of a dog.'[22]

Hell, then, is solitary confinement in a freezing and stinking darkness. It is laid out in three layers of descending gloom, situated in the north, between the underside of the earth and that part of the sky which is below the earth.[23] The sole companions of the damned are the demons that their own evil actions have engendered on earth, and these perpetually torment them. Despite the fact that these dead souls are fed on the most nauseating substances, they are never satisfied and always crave for more. Hell, however, is not a permanent state, nor is it considered possible that a man could be so wicked as to be incapable of repentance and of yearning for a virtuous state.[24] In hell the soul at last understands reality as it is, it understands the heartless wickedness of Ahriman who gloatingly mocks at his sufferings, and the total goodness of Ohrmazd whom he has betrayed. Hell, then, corresponds not so much to the Christian hell as to Purgatory. True, the sufferings of hell are not yet cathartic, but they are sufficient to awaken repentance, and this is enough to enable the soul to shake off its shackles when God's day of reckoning with the powers of evil comes; then the souls of the damned, the prisoners, will be strong enough to overcome their gaolers, the demons.[25] And then, at long last, when the final Rehabilitation comes to pass and the Lie is conquered, the souls of the damned will be made to pass through a river of molten metal, and this will purify them of all remaining taint of sin.[26] Sanctified they will join the souls of the saved and all will live in perfect harmony for evermore.

So much for the fate of the individual soul. Now it is time to consider the fate of humanity as a whole.

The Frashkart or Final Rehabilitation

The cosmic drama is seen as taking place in three stages—creation, the 'progress of religion', and the final Rehabilitation. The last—the *Frashkart* or 'Making Excellent'—is the end to which the whole of creation looks forward; it is regarded as being the inevitable consummation of a rational process initiated by God, and it is never supposed for one moment that there is any doubt that it will come to pass. The phrase used for this process is *patvandishn i ō Frashkart*, which can be translated as the 'continuous evolution towards the Rehabilitation'. Zoroastrianism differs from most other religions in that it sees reality as a spiritual disharmony: good and evil stand over against each other, irreconcilably opposed in a timeless eternity. Ohrmazd forces the issue by limiting Time and drawing Ahriman into battle, and his object is by these means to destroy the power of evil for ever. He knows that Ahriman cannot possibly win, for he represents only naked force; he is incapable of planning anything in advance and even of looking after his own interests. His attendant demons, moreover, are incapable of concerted action, since, of their nature, they are compounded of disorder, except only to combine in unnatural alliance against their arch-enemy, man. Ultimately he relies more on Ahriman's stupidity than upon his own strength to gain the final victory.

Ohrmazd's Master-plan for the Overthrow of Evil

Ohrmazd's plan, as we have seen, was to trap Ahriman within the cosmos and to allow him there to worry himself to pieces in his chaotic malevolence. The spiritual world of light and goodness is thus already sealed off from the powers of darkness, protected by the double rampart of the sky and the collective consciousness of all mankind, sometimes identified with the *khwarr* of the Good Religion.[27] Man, meanwhile, has agreed to fight out the good fight in the material world, and it is man who is thus the main agent in the defeat of the Evil One and his hateful minions. Man, however, was dealt two mortal blows when Ahriman slew his ancestor, Gayōmart: he was oppressed with the certainty of physical death, and, by being infected by the demonic bacteria that assailed him—concupiscence, anger, envy, vengefulness, and the rest—he became liable to sin and, through sin, to damnation. The elimination of evil, then, entails the elimination of the consequences of evil, physical death and moral wickedness. And so the *Frashkart* involves the total destruction of Ahriman and his creation, the raising of the dead, the purification of the souls that had been damned in hell, and the establishment of the kingdom of perfect harmony which will be brought about by the adherence of the whole human race to the Good Religion.

The *Frashkart*, however, was implicit in creation from the beginning, for it will be remembered that the physical death of Gayōmart made it possible for the human race to increase and multiply. From his seed the first human couple was born, and from then mankind began to multiply in ever-increasing profusion. Man lost his immortality as an individual, but he won a new immortality in the perdurance and continuous expansion of the race.[28] So too with the soul: Ahriman's greatest triumph had been to deceive the soul and thereby bring about its damnation in hell; yet even this could only be a short-lived triumph, for not only did death put an end to the evil deeds of the evil-doer, it opened his eyes in hell to the ugly fact that he had allowed himself to be made a fool of, and this in turn paved the way to his repentance. Nothing Ahriman does can prove to his own advantage in the long run; for he is worse than a knave, he is a fool.

Ahriman had sought to destroy Ohrmazd in five ways. First, his nature being cold and dry, he attempted to annihilate the hot and moist which together constitute the physical essence of Ohrmazd; at the same time and by the same means he had hoped to destroy all living things. Ohrmazd, however, countered this by uniting hot with dry and moist with cold, thereby forming the four elements from which he was to construct the whole material universe. Similarly, the creation of the demons and their onslaught on mankind served only to teach men to help each other and spurred them on to find ways and means of defeating their common enemy. Again, Ahriman hoped to defeat Ohrmazd's creation by one single concerted attack, but, failing to do so, he dissipated his forces, or rather was forced to do so because the chief and captain of all the demonic host, Āz-concupiscence, rebelled against this unitary plan so contrary to her nature, and reintroduced that 'disorderly motion', which is her very essence, into the Devil's camp. This disorder, again, which was intended to throw Ohrmazd's armies into disarray, inevitably turned on Ahriman's creation itself and devoured it;[29] and Ahriman, now abandoned and alone, is only saved from this final degradation of being devoured by what he had created by the intervention of his eternal enemy, Ohrmazd.

The Three Phases of Ohrmazd's Plan

Zātspram, as we have seen, divides the history of the cosmos into three stages—creation, the progress of religion, and the final Rehabilitation. The whole process he compares to the building of a house, and the whole history of the cosmos can thus be regarded as a gradual unfolding of the Rehabilitation. Ahriman's attack itself is in its way a *felix culpa*, for only by bringing death into the world does he make it not only possible but necessary for the human race to increase and multiply—only so can God's house be built by man. For:

'The creating of creation, the progress of Religion, and the final Rehabilitation are like unto the building of a house. For a house can only be completed by means of three things, that is, the foundation, the walls, and the roof. . . . As when a man desires to build a house, he chooses three men of whom one is most skilled in laying the foundation, one in raising the walls, and one in making the roof; and each is assigned to his proper task. Till the foundation was laid and the walls raised, it was not possible [to make the roof]. He who bade the house [be built] knows clearly how many things are needed to complete it, and because he has no doubt concerning the skill of the maker of the roof, long does he confidently wait. When the walls are completed, it is as easy for him whose business is the roof, to roof [the house] in as [it is] for the other two in the work that is assigned them.

'And again the Rehabilitation is like unto a dark night: when the night draws to its close, the sun rises over the three corners of the earth, returns to its proper place, completes its cycle, comes to shine anew, and smites the darkness and gloom.

310

'It is like unto the moon which waxes for fifteen [nights] and for fifteen wanes. When it has completely disappeared, it is born anew and is manifest in the sheen [it has] from the sun, the lord of lights: the restoration of the world of the Resurrection is figured forth thereby.

'It is like unto the year in which, in spring, the trees blossom, in summer they bear fruit, in autumn they bear the last fruits, and in winter they become dry and as if dead. When the order of the years is fulfilled, the sun returns to its first place, day and night are equal in measure, and the atmosphere [returns to] its original(?) equilibrium.

'And the Resurrection of the dead is like unto dry trees and shrubs that put forth new foliage and shoot forth tender saplings. Since stability must be restored, the end of all natural things is in the same manner as their beginning, even as man, whose coming to be springs from the semen, or as the plants whose becoming is from seed; their perfection and end are in the selfsame seed.'[30]

Zātspram's similes have a certain truth, for the evolutionary progress towards the final Rehabilitation, the building of the house of God, is a slow business and seems to meet with violent reversals. These reversals, however, always result in a further forward thrust towards the final goal which is the destruction of the Lie, because each time the Lie further weakens itself and makes its own demise the more inevitable. The similes of the sun, the moon, and the year are all in accord with the Zoroastrian idea of finite Time as *Ashōqar*, *Zarōqar*, and *Frashōqar*,[31] 'he who plants the seed, he who brings old age, and he who makes excellent.' According to this scheme of things, no doubt Zurvanite in inspiration, the world, so far from being impelled on by an inner evolutionary drive, rather seems to run out and die just at the moment when it is about to be again restored in a new life, a new glory, and a new luxuriance.

We have detailed accounts of the Rehabilitation in the *Bundahishn*, in Mānushchihr's *Dātastān i Dēnīk*, in Zātspram, and in one of the Pahlavi *Rivāyats* ('traditions'). They do not agree in all respects, and we shall have to draw on them all. Zātspram's version, as we would expect, shows Zurvanite tendencies. In his account it is Zurvān himself who arms Ahriman with the weapon of Āz, concupiscence and greed, who is ultimately to destroy his whole creation, and it is Āz, rather than Ahriman, who dominates the whole apocalyptic scene. In Mānush-chihr's account, on the other hand, no single demon is granted especial pride of place; rather the whole Satanic host breaks asunder, reft by its own inner contradictions, and the demons fall upon each other to their mutual ruin.

The Beginning of the End

The three last millennia of the cosmic year are presided over by the three posthumous sons of Zoroaster: Ōshētar, Ōshētarmāh, and Saoshyans, all of whom have been born from his seed, miraculously preserved in a lake.[32] Each has his part to play in the eschatological drama, but it is in the era of Saoshyans that Ahriman is finally destroyed, that the dead rise again, and that all creation is renewed and made immortal.

The millennia of Ōshētar and Ōshētarmāh are the prelude to the Rehabilitation, and at the beginning of each of them the Religion of Zoroaster is once again renewed. In these two millennia the noxious beasts created by Ahriman, that is, the wolf and cat tribes on the one hand, and reptiles and poisonous insects on the other, are destroyed.

In the millennium of Saoshyans the living win through to immortality and the bodies of the dead are raised. Man, as originally constituted, was autarchic: he had no need to eat. Thus when man's first parents, Mashyē and Mashyānē, first drank goat's milk, thereby breaking their fast, they felt obscurely that they had done wrong. 'After thirty days in the wilderness,' we read, 'they came upon a white-haired goat and they sucked the milk of its udders. And when they had drunk the milk, Mashyē said to Mashyānē: "I had greater joy when I had not drunk the milk than I have now when I have drunk it: my body is sick." '[33]

The reason that they felt ill at ease was that by eating and drinking they laid themselves open to Āz-concupiscence: their bodies were no longer self-sufficient but depended on nourishment from outside, and this in turn ultimately led to their own wastage and death when they themselves are devoured by Āz, for Āz is not only the demon of gluttony and lust, she is also the demon of death who is never sated;[34] she is the demon 'who swallows all things. When, through want, nothing comes her way, she pines away. She is that Lie who, though all the goods of this world were given to her, would be neither sated nor satisfied.'[35] According to Zātspram she divided her powers into three, 'that pertaining to the natural functions', 'that pertaining to the natural functions directed outward', and 'that outside the natural functions'. 'That pertaining to the natural functions consists in eating on which life depends: that pertaining to the natural functions directed outward is the desire to copulate, which is called lust (*varan*), and through which, by a glance outward, the inwards are excited and the natural functions of the body thrown into a turmoil; that outside the natural functions is the craving for whatever good thing one sees or hears.'[36]

Zātspram's conception of Āz would appear to be much influenced by Manichaeanism, for Āz is for him not so much the abuse of legitimate physical functions, that is, eating and drinking and sexual intercourse, as those functions themselves. That man's dependence on food in some way makes him a slave to Āz, however, seems also to be the view of the *Bundahishn,* and his progressive abandonment of all food and drink is in both books an essential preliminary to bodily immortality. Mānushchihr and the *Frashkart Rivāyat* make no mention of this 'spiritualization' of man's body which, in any case, seems to be at variance with the well attested belief that the soul eats 'spiritual' food in heaven. The contradiction, however, may be no more than apparent, for the whole point of the Rehabilitation is that matter and spirit are finally made one: 'nature will be clad in spirit,'[37] as Zātspram puts it, and, as his brother, Mānushchihr, also makes abundantly clear, the traditional descriptions of heaven and the renewed existence of the Rehabilitation in which food and sexual intercourse figure prominently, are not to be taken literally and can only be regarded as a feeble attempt to express infinite realities in finite terms; we just do not know what the Resurrection life and the 'spiritual' body that enjoys it are really like. The conquest of Āz, however, is and must be the decisive step in the defeat of evil in general, for only by depriving her of her normal diet of dead men will she be forced to find an alternative diet—live demons. So we read that:

'just as Mashyē and Mashyānē, after they had grown out of the earth, consumed water first, then plants, then milk, and then meat, so do men when they [are about to] die, abstain first from the eating of meat and milk and then from bread; but right up to the moment of death they drink water. So too in the millennium of Ōshētarmāh the power of Āz will be so diminished that men will be satisfied by eating one meal every three days and nights. After that they will abstain from eating meat, and eat [only] plants and the milk of domestic animals. After that they will abstain from the drinking of milk also; then they will abstain from the eating of plants too and will drink only water. Ten years before the coming of Saoshyans they will reach a stage in which they eat nothing, yet will not die.'[38]

Zātspram enters into greater detail concerning the spiritualization of the body that the gradual abandonment of food and drink entails. With the abandonment of flesh-meat one-quarter of the power of Āz is destroyed, and 'nature will be clad in spirit and intelligences will be more clearly grasped'. Further, 'in the bodies of the children that are born to them Āz will be less strong and their bodies will smell less foul, and their nature will be more closely bound to the gods. Instructed by the gods, they will turn away from the drinking of milk; half the power of Āz will dwindle. And those who are born to them will be

313

sweet-smelling, having little darkness in them, spiritual in nature, without offspring, for they will not eat.'[39]

The Destruction of Āz and Ahriman (Zurvanite Version)
Āz, now terribly enfeebled, deriving no power from the creatures of Ohrmazd, turns upon Ahriman, who had made her captain of his commanders, saying: 'Satisfy me, satiate me, for I derive nor food nor strength from the creatures of Ohrmazd.'[40] Then, with Ahriman's unwilling consent, Āz, insatiate to the last:

'swallows up Wrath (*ēshm*, the *Aēshma* of the *Gāthās*) of the bloody spear, and second Winter, created by the demons, third Bane that moves in secret, and fourth she swallows Old Age whose breath is foul, so that none remain [save only] the Destructive Spirit and Āz, the demon-created. And Āz, the demon-created, [says] to the Destructive Spirit: "I will swallow thee, thou warped in mind, for the gods have taken away [all] creation save thee." '[41]

The wheel has now turned full circle. Ahriman, who had led a united host of demons against Ohrmazd's creation and against its captain, man, Ahriman who had once befouled the whole earth and brought death to all living things except only man, Ahriman, who had boasted: 'Perfect is my victory. . . . I have seized the kingdom, and on the side of Ohrmazd none remains to do battle except only man; and man, isolated and alone, what can he do?'—this same Ahriman now finds himself isolated and alone; and not only isolated, but hemmed in between the embattled hosts of Ohrmazd on the one side, strong in their new-won immortality, and, on the other, Āz, the obscene monster he had himself called into existence, strong once again with the strength of the whole demonic host she has devoured, avid now for a royal banquet at which the King of Darkness will himself be her last delicious fare. Rather than submit to this ultimate indignity, the Evil One turns in hopeless appeal to his ancient enemy, relying on his mercy. 'I created this creation,' he fatuously boasts, 'and Āz, the demon-created, who has swallowed up my creation, now craves to swallow me. I make thee Judge between us.'[42]

This is the end. Evil, which had co-existed with Good for all eternity, and which the Good God had finally brought out into the open, now stands at bay, defeated by its own incoherence, discord, envy, and greed, forced to appeal to God to save it from death at the hands of its own most powerful ally; but Ohrmazd, the Good God, whose nature is always to show mercy, knows that here there can be no mercy, for his enemy is utterly and irretrievably depraved, evil in essence and beyond all redemption; therefore he must be once and for all destroyed. So:

'Ohrmazd arises with Sraosha the Blessed, and Sraosha the Blessed smites Āz, and Ohrmazd the Destructive Spirit. With all the foul darkness and misery he had brought into [the world] when he first rushed in, he is thrown out of the sky by the same hole through which he had [first] rushed in; and at that hole is he laid low and made unconscious so that [never] again will he arise from that stupor. There have been some who have said that he will be forever powerless and, as it were, slain, and that henceforth neither the Destructive Spirit nor his creation will exist.'[43]

The Meaning of Ahriman's Destruction

It is a Zoroastrian dogma that in the end Ahriman and his entire creation will be made powerless for all eternity, but, as can be seen from the passage just quoted, there was uncertainty as to whether this powerlessness meant his annihilation or not. Two views are alternatively expressed, first that he is expelled from the universe of light and reduced to a never ending unconsciousness, and secondly that he is 'as it were' slain, and that neither he nor his creation will ever exist again. The more philosophical texts, however, assure us that Ohrmazd and Ahriman are substances, and it is of the nature of substance that it cannot change. What, then, is meant by the 'annihilation' of Ahriman? Mānushchihr compares it to the physical death of material creatures, which is the dissolution of the elements that had gone to make up the living organism. Ahriman is, of course, not a material being: he is a spirit, but apparently a composite spirit. His destruction, then, means that his faculties are dissipated 'just as with mortal men on earth when the vital spirit is separated from the body, there is dispersion: the [various] organs are separated and the faculties destroyed so that a [total] stupor ensues, all activity is stopped, and all movement comes to an end'.[44] In more homely language, Ahriman 'is dragged outside the sky and his head is cut off'.[45] What is, of course, universally conceded is that Ahriman as an active force utterly ceases to be; the principle of death itself is slain and dies.

The Disintegration of Evil (Orthodox Version)

Whether or not Ahriman's final humiliation at the hands of Āz, which figures not only in Zātspram but also in the *Bundahishn* and the *Frashkart Rivāyat*, is specifically Zurvanite, Mānushchihr prefers to ignore it and attributes the collapse of the forces of evil to the total disintegration of the temporary alliance they had been able to form when there was still hope of destroying man. With man at last withdrawn from their grasp they have no choice but to fall upon each other.

'The demons of calumny whose nature it is to incite creatures against each other by falsehood and lies, since they no longer succeed in inciting the saved against each other, incite the damned against the damned, and when they can no longer incite the damned against each other, they incite demon against demon. And Wrath of the bloody spear, no longer able to stir up strife among the saved, stirs up strife and warfare among the damned; and when it can no longer stir up strife among the damned, it stirs up strife among the demons and lies and makes them fall on one another. So too the demon Āz, no longer able to swallow the good, is impelled by her own nature to go and swallow up the demons. And so too the Loosener of Bones who deals out death by causing separation, seeing that the saved no longer die and that even the damned among God's creation are no longer subject to death, falls upon the lies and brings them death, which is no more than the separation of their organs and faculties [which can only survive in union].'[46]

Thus the very nature of the demons, which is to commit aggression, to torment, to stir up strife, and to destroy, turns in upon itself; they 'fight against themselves, strike, rend, tear, and disrupt themselves',[47] until not a particle or a particle of a particle of them remains within the kingdom of the light.[48] So, for Mānushchihr, 'the Lies are vanquished by their own weapons, their own impulse, their own striving, as well as by the glory (khwarr) of the Creator and the gods.'[49] 'A house that is divided against itself cannot stand,' and the House of the Lie is no exception to the rule. The inner contradictions which only a common fight against a hated enemy could temporarily dissemble, reveal themselves in all their crudity once the enemy is beyond the Lie's reach. Then the demons turn the one upon the other and rend each other to pieces.

Ahriman, the principle of death, is now himself dead; and it only remains for Ohrmazd to raise the bodies of the dead, to reunite them with their souls, and to inaugurate his kingdom of unending joy.

The Resurrection of the Body

Of all the doctrines of Christianity that the modern scientific mind finds hard to swallow, the resurrection of the body is the hardest. This dogma, which Christianity inherited from Zoroastrianism, the Zoroastrians themselves found hard. The Prophet himself is represented as questioning his God concerning this doctrine which seems to fly in the face of reason.

'Zoroaster asked Ohrmazd: "Shall bodily creatures that have passed away on earth receive their bodies back at the final Rehabilitation, or will they be like unto shades?"

'Ohrmazd [said]: "They will receive their bodies back and will rise again."

'And Zoroaster asked: "He who has passed away is torn apart by dog and bird and carried off by wolf and vulture: how will [their parts] come together again?"

'Ohrmazd said: "If thou who art Zoroaster hadst to make a wooden casket, would it be easier to make it if thou hadst no wood and yet hadst to cut and fit it, or if thou hadst a casket and its parts were sundered one from the other and thou hadst to fit it together again?"

'Zoroaster said: "If I had a branch of wood, it would be easier than if I had no wood; and if I had a casket [and its parts were sundered the one from the other,] it would be easier [to fit it together again than if I had no wood and yet had to fashion and fit it]."

'Ohrmazd said: "When those creations were not, I had power to fashion them; and now that they have been and are scattered abroad, it is easier to fit them together again. For I have five storekeepers who receive the bodily substance of those who have passed away. One is the earth which keeps the flesh and bone and sinews of men: one is the water which keeps the blood: one is the plants which preserve the hair of the head and the hair of the body: one is the light of the heavenly sphere which receives the fire: and yet another is the wind which [gives back] the spirit of my own creatures at the time of the Rehabilitation." '[50]

The Role of Saoshyans and the Final Bull-Sacrifice

Ohrmazd, however, does not himself inaugurate the Resurrection of the body, but, with characteristic courtesy, entrusts it to Saoshyans, the last of Zoroaster's posthumous sons, who represents the human race redeemed; and he will first raise the bones of Gayōmart, the first ancestor of the human race, who first fell, though sinless, a victim to the malice of the Aggressor, then the bones of Mashyē and Mashyānē, man's first parents who first learnt to sin. Then 'for fifty-seven years will Saoshyans raise the dead, and all men will be resurrected, both those who were saved and those who were damned. And each man will arise in the place where his vital spirit left him or where first he fell to the ground.'[51]

Saoshyans, it appears, has only the power to raise the scattered elements, not the power to reconstitute them as individual men; this Ohrmazd himself must do, restoring to each his individual 'form' (adhvēnak)[52] and character. Body is thus once again joined to soul, but the reconstituted human being has yet to receive the seal of immortality. This is conferred on him by a solemn repetition of the Haoma sacrifice through which he received the earnest of immortality, though not its

317

substance, on earth. This is the 'sacrifice of the raising of the dead . . .
and in that sacrifice the bull Hadhayans will be slain, and from the fat
of the bull the white Haoma will be prepared, [the drink of] immortality, and it will be distributed to all men'.[53] 'Life will be given back
to their bodies and they will possess an immortal soul,' freed from evil
and transience, 'forever living, forever increasing (hamē-sūt).'[54]

Purgation by Molten Metal

But before the final sacrifice can take place, all sin must once and for all
be purged away from the human soul. For three days the saved are
returned to paradise and the damned to hell in preparation for the
final ordeal.

'Then will the Fire-god and the god Airyaman melt the metals that are in
the mountains and hills, and they will flow over the earth like rivers. And all
men will be made to pass through the molten metal to be purged thereby.
And it will seem to him who was saved as if he were walking through warm
milk, but to the man who was damned it will seem that he is walking through
molten metal in very deed.'[55]

After this final purgation in which all stain of sin has been forever
wiped out, both those who had been in heaven and those who had been
in hell 'become of one voice and are loud in their praise of Ohrmazd
and the Bounteous Immortals',[56] for they too are immortal and about
to enter into a state of never ending joy.

The 'Final Body' and Renewal of All Things

The Frashkart, the 'Making Excellent', or final Rehabilitation is also
the Tan i pasēn, the Final Body. This phrase needs elucidation. It
can scarcely mean anything but the final and perfect form that the
'first body',[57] the total cosmos or macrocosm, the 'body of Zurvān
or finite time',[58] takes on at the end of time when time itself merges
into the Infinite. The 'evolutionary progress' of the material world
which culminates in the Rehabilitation, is then seen in its first stage as
a progressive differentiation from unitary matter through the four
natural properties and the four elements to the appearance of individuated organic life and the emergence of a rational being, man. The
second stage is the multiplication of individual men and of organic life
in general, and the third is the unification of mankind in total concord
and in adoring acceptance of the will of God. The 'first body' was one
in the sense that it was totally undifferentiated and unconscious, but the
'Final Body' is one in the sense that it is a totally integrated complex
of individual rational unities in which each element, by fulfilling itself,

also plays its part in fulfilling the whole. This is the *khwarr* fulfilled, each man, each group, each nation, and finally all the human race have become what in God's plan they always were, their own perfection and final cause. This interpretation of the meaning of the Rehabilitation is stressed in the *Dēnkart*, and this book alone among the Pahlavi books sees this achieved solidarity and reconstituted harmony of the whole human race under God, this perfect unity in perfected diversity, as the essence of the resurrection life. The *Bundahishn* has nothing worthwhile to say on the subject. Zātspram, however, does stress that the essence of the resurrection life is harmony and concord; for Ohrmazd and the Bounteous Immortals are represented as saying:

'We are seven, but one in thought, word, and deed; and because we are one in thought, word, and deed, we are unageing and deathless, knowing neither corruption nor decay; and when you who are men become one in thought, word, and deed, then will you become unageing, free from sickness, knowing neither corruption nor decay, even as we, the Bounteous Immortals are.'[59]

The Marriage of Matter and Spirit

In the main, however, the descriptions of the resurrection life are disappointing, and, despite the repeated warnings that the joys of immortal existence infinitely transcend the joys of this life, we cannot help feeling that those late Zoroastrian apocalypses had no real feeling for a life of spirit which would transcend sense. True, the earth is lifted up to the station of the stars, and paradise, the House of Song, descends from on high to meet it there;[60] and the gulf between spirit and matter, narrow though it had always been, is now filled in. Matter is 'clad in spirit' and spirit in matter; God indwells man and the other Bounteous Immortals indwell the animals, fires, metals, earth, water, and plants, over which they respectively preside:[61] the whole material creation is suffused and illuminated by spirit.

Or again, Ohrmazd, the Bounteous Immortals, and all the gods assemble in one place together with resurrected humanity; sun, moon, and stars take on human form and walk with men, and Ohrmazd will have consummated the work of creation. Ohrmazd's work is finished and he can now rest in peace for ever, and man's sole work will be 'to gaze upon Ohrmazd and offer him prayer as Lord and to do whatever else should seem to him most pleasurable. Each man will love his fellow[62] even as himself'.[63] The words, however, are once again inadequate to the reality, for 'the joys of the Final Body, apart from what has been described above, are such as cannot be known by the finite intellect and reason of man, nor can they be spoken of'.[64]

The sources, however, agree that to each man will be restored his wife or wives and that he will have his pleasure of them[65] though no children will be born to them. Yet how can the intercourse between man and woman be compared to what takes place in the resurrection life? for it is clear that the resurrection body is totally different from this earthly body, weighed down as it is by darkness.[66] For 'their bones will shine like crystal among gems; the flesh on their bones will be like the bark (?) on trees; the tendons on their bones will be like golden chains on carved crystal. The blood will course in their veins like perfumed wine in a golden chalice, and the humours in their bodies will be more fragrant than musk and ambergris and camphor'.[67]

Mānushchihr eschews the rather crude materialism of tradition and emphasizes only that the restored creation will be not only perfectly at peace, but also suffused with light and a mutual love centred in God.

'After the Rehabilitation there will be no demons because there will be no deceit, no Lies because no lying, no Ahriman because no aggressiveness, no hell because no state of damnation, no strife because no wrath, no vengeful-ness because no hurt, no pain because no sickness, no lamentation because no fear, no need because no craving (āz), no shame because no ugliness, no deceit because no desire to deceive, no irreligion because no false doctrine, no evil because its source will have been destroyed in accordance with the tradition that the source of all evil thoughts, words, and deeds, and all evil states, stems from the Destructive Spirit. Once he is destroyed, all evil will be destroyed; and with the destruction of evil all good things are brought to their fulfilment; and at a time when good has reached its plenitude, there can be no possibility of devising pain and misery by any means whatever against any creature.'[68]

Good is symbolized by light, evil by darkness: so the destruction of evil and the sole sovereignty of the good can only mean that the material world is transformed into pure light.

'The sun, moon, and stars will [indeed] exist, but there will be no need for daylight or a succession of glimmering dawns, for the whole world will be light and devoid of any darkness, and each [individual] creature will be light. Being light, they will be full of joy. And all creatures will have but one will and one desire. Individual men will feel no envy at the joy of the totality of created things (vispān dāmān), but will rejoice together with it. The goodness[69] and joy allotted to each will wax and grow in the glory of the omnipotence of Him who is all-good, [all]-aware, all in all through his overflowing bounty and perfect skill in means.'[70]

Of all the accounts of the resurrection life, Mānushchihr's is the most essentially Zoroastrian. The conquest of evil means the conquest of death, and death is diminution and separation. The elimination of evil and the sole sovereignty of good means life and ever more life, increase, harmony, and the union of all separate wills with the will of God, each person remaining himself, each soul glad in the glory that is peculiarly his and making his own individual contribution to the perfect whole—a contribution that none but he can make and without which the whole would be less than perfect. Spirit and matter are indeed fused, but the fusion implies no confusion of identity.

'Spirit is one thing and matter another: matter is one thing and spirit another; but thanks to God's omnipotence all souls and external souls desire and choose the Creator's glory (*khwarr*) and his command; [and this they do] effortlessly and full of joy. As the seas and rivers, and other waters, mountains, and plants, which differ in form and shape[71] disport themselves in an effulgence [of their own], so do the souls and external souls, though created spirits, take their pleasure and delight in union with [their bodies] which experience through sense; engaged in worship for ever and ever they abide in a plenitude of bliss.'[72]

This is infinite existence in which finite time merges into Infinite Time, and God himself at last becomes 'all in all'. Limited from the beginning by a principle of darkness which carried within it the seed of death, God now enters into his own plenitude and his own infinity; and his creation, freed from evil and death and united with his will, comes to participate in his own absolute goodness and absolute bliss, each man partaking of it according to his capacity—and because God's nature is superabundant bounty, the resurrection must be seen as an ever-expanding joy to which there can be no end. In fulfilling his own nature, God bestows on his whole creation a richness of life and joy, both spiritual and material, that must go on increasing ever more though time has long since stopped.

ABBREVIATIONS USED IN THE NOTES

A²H.	Inscription of Artaxerxes II at Hamadan.
AVN.	*Artāy Virāf Nāmak.*
BSOAS.	*Bulletin of the School of Oriental and African Studies.*
Clemen, Fontes.	*Fontes historiae religionis persicae.*
DB.	Inscription of Darius I at Bīsitūn.
Dd.	*Dātastān i dēnīk.*
DkM.	*Dēnkart,* ed. Madan.
DN.	Inscription of Darius I at Naqsh-i Rustam.
DP.	Inscription of Darius I at Persepolis.
DS.	Inscription of Darius I at Susa.
GB.	*Greater Bundahishn.*
MKh.	*Mēnōk i Khrat.*
Murūj.	[Mas'ūdī], *Murūj al-dhahab.*
Ny.	*Nyāyishn.*
Phl.	Pahlavi.
PR.	Pahlavi *Rivāyats.*
PT.	*Pahlavi Texts.*
RV.	*Rig-Veda.*
ShGV.	*Shikand-Gumānīk Vichār.*
TM.	[R. C. Zaehner] *The Teachings of the Magi.*
Vd.	*Vidēvdāt.*
XP.	Inscription of Xerxes at Persepolis.
Y.	*Yasna.*
Yt.	*Yasht.*
ZKhA.	*Zand i Khwartak Apastāk.*
Zs.	*Selections of Zātspram.*
ZZD.	[R. C. Zaehner] *Zurvan, A Zoroastrian Dilemma.*

NOTES

INTRODUCTION

1. AVN. 1.7: cf. DkM. 412.3–5 (translation in Zaehner, ZZD, pp. 7–8: Tabarī, *Annals* (de Goeje), I, 676: Mas'ūdī, *Murūj* (Barbier de Meynard),

II, 124–5: *Epistle of Tansar* (Minovi), p. 11.

2. DkM. 455.11: 459.10 (translation in ZZD, p. 430).

PART I: DAWN

CHAPTER I: THE PROPHET

1. This agrees with Theodore bar Kônai who gives Zoroaster's date (sc. his birth) as 628 BC. See Zaehner, ZZD, p. 442.
2. See W. B. Henning, *Zoroaster, Politician or Witch-Doctor?*, pp. 42ff.
3. Y. 46.1.
4. Ibid., 19.18.
5. Ibid., 31.15.
6. Ibid., 29.1,2: 30.6: 44.20: 48.7,12: 49.4.
7. Ibid., 29.1.
8. *mānthrem āzūtōish : mānthra*—means 'sacred word'. Āzūiti is plainly akin to Vedic *āhuti*—'oblation', but in the later Avesta it comes to mean 'fat' and is so translated into Pahlavi (*charpīh*), or, as Bartholomae rightly says 'solid food in contrast to liquid'. Nyberg's translation (*Religionen des alten Iran*, p. 197) is merely perverse.
9. Y. 29.6–7.
10. *Vohū manañhā*, 'in accordance with good mind, or the Good Mind.' See p. 46.
11. See pp. 45–50.
12. See n. 10.
13. *Ishā-khshathrīm*: to '*aēsh-*, 'to be powerful', on the analogy of *vasō-khshathra*.
14. Y. 29.9.
15. Ibid., 46.1–2.
16. Ibid., 34.8.
17. Ibid., 31.1–2.
18. Ibid., 33.14.
19. Ibid., 49.3.
20. Ibid., 44.15.
21. Ibid., 43.8.
22. Ibid., 33.2.

23. W. B. Henning, *Zoroaster, Politician or Witch-Doctor?*, p. 45.
24. Y. 32.8. Humbach's translation of this passage is totally different.
25. In India he becomes the lord of the dead.
26. Y. 32.14.
27. Ibid., 48.10.
28. See pp. 126–44.
29. Y. 30.9 : 31.4.
30. Ibid., 44.20.
31. Ibid., 47.4.
32. Ibid., 46.6.
33. See p. 54.
34. Y. 43.8.
35. Ibid., 33.2.
36. Ibid., 31.3.
37. Ibid., 31.10.
38. Ibid., 31.11.
39. Ibid., 49.3.
40. Ibid., 31.12.
41. Ibid., 44.12.
42. Ibid., 31.2.
43. Ibid., 30.2.
44. Ibid., 30.3–6.
45. Ibid., 45.2.
46. Ibid., 32.1–2.
47. Ibid., 32.3–5.
48. Ibid., 33.6.
49. Ibid., 50.6.
50. Ibid., 44.2.
51. Ibid., 46.2.
52. Ibid., 44.11.
53. Ibid., 43.5.
54. Ibid., 33.6–7.
55. Ibid., 28.5.
56. Ibid., 31.3.
57. Ibid., 45.8.

58. Y. 31.8.
59. Ibid., 47.2–3.
60. Ibid., 44.3 : 47.2.
61. Ibid., 45.4 : 31.8.
62. Ibid., 45.4.
63. Ibid., 60.5 : cf. 33.4.
64. Ibid., 31.15.
65. Ibid., 33.8 : 34.1 : 45.5, etc.
66. Ibid., 47.3.
67. Ibid., 48.6.
68. Ibid., 34.11.
69. Ibid., 43.4.
70. Ibid., 28.4 : 46.12 : 49.3.
71. Ibid., 34.12.
72. Ibid., 46.9.
73. Ibid., 47.1.
74. Ibid., 43.9.
75. Ibid., 32.2–3 : 47.5.
76. Ibid., 43.7.
77. Ibid., 45.6.
78. See p. 46.
79. See p. 34.
80. Y. 43.7.
81. e.g. Y. 45.9.
82. Ugo Bianchi, *Zamān i Ohrmazd*, Turin, 1958, p. 82.
83. See p. 55.
84. Millar Burrows, *The Dead Sea Scrolls*, New York, 1956, p. 374.
85. Y. 32.1–2.
86. Ibid., 44.12.
87. Ibid., 31.7.
88. Ibid.
89. Ibid., 31.8.
90. Ibid., 31.11.
91. Ibid., 44.7.

92. Y. 43.1.
93. Ibid., 44.3–7.
94. Ibid., 31.20.
95. Ibid., 30.11 : 45.9.
96. Ibid., 43.12.
97. Ibid., 46.10.
98. Ibid., 46.12 : 49.3,5.
99. Ibid., 32.15.
100. Ibid., 44.9.
101. Ibid., 46.11.
102. See pp. 302–4.
103. PR. 48.66. Cf. BSOAS, xvii, pp. 246–7.
104. Y. 46.17.
105. Ibid., 44.2.
106. Ibid., 30.4.
107. Ibid.
108. Ibid., 32.15.
109. Ibid., 32.13.
110. Ibid., 51.15.
111. Ibid., 51.14.
112. Ibid., 33.5.
113. Ibid., 30.11 : 43.12.
114. Ibid., 30.11.
115. Ibid., 31.20.
116. Ibid., 45.7.
117. Daniel 12.2.
118. Y. 34.6.
119. Ibid., 34.15.
120. Ibid., 30.9.
121. Ibid., 34.13 : 46.3 : 48.12.
122. Ibid., 45.1.
123. Ibid., 51.6.
124. Ibid., 51.9.
125. Ibid., 31.19.
126. Ibid., 43.4 : 34.4.
127. Ibid., 46.7.

CHAPTER II: THE SEVEN CHAPTERS

1. Y. 38.2.
2. Ibid., 35.1.
3. See pp. 39–40.
4. Y. 41.1.
5. Ibid., 40.2 : 41.6.
6. Ibid., 37.4.
7. Ibid., 36.6. Cf. I. Gershevitch, *The Avestan Hymn to Mithra*, p. 293.
8. Ibid., 38.1.
9. Ibid., 38.3.
10. Except in Y. 66 and 68 which are dedicated to the waters.
11. See pp. 39–40.
12. See I. Gershevitch, *op. cit.*, p. 4.
13. Yt. 10.145.
14. Y. 1.11 : 2.11 : 3.13 : 4.16 : 6.10 : 7.13 : 22.13.

15. RV. 2.28.6 : 4.1.2. : 5.65.2 : 8.23.30 : 8.25.1,7,8, etc.
16. Ibid., 5.63.1.
17. Ibid., 1.23.5.
18. Ibid., 2.32.8 : 7.34.22.
19. Taittirīya-Samhitā, 5.5.4.1. : 6.4.2.3.
20. RV. 5.69.2. Cf. 5.63.5.
21. Y. 38.5.
22. A. A. Macdonell, *Vedic Mythology*, Strassburg, 1897, p. 24.
23. Y. 41.2 : cf. 35.5.
24. E.g. RV. 6.48.14 : 7.28.4 : 10.99.10 : 10.147.5.
25. Y. 41.3.
26. Ibid., 1.11 : 3.13 : 7.13.
27. RV. 1.24.8 : 7.87.1.
28. Ibid., 1.50.6.

29. I. Gershevitch, *op. cit.*, p. 49.
30. J. Duchesne-Guillemin, *Ormazd et Ahriman*, p. 15.
31. Y. 46.5.
32. Ibid., 42.2.
33. I. Gershevitch, *op. cit.*, p. 56.
34. I supply *mat* before *mithrāndruj* on the analogy of Dd. ch. 90 where we have *'tāk mithrāndruj i chandēnāk 'hast mat* 'until he who lies against Mithra who is the "mover" came'. Theoretically *mat ān druj* could be read instead of *mithrāndruj*, but I know of no passage in the Dd. and very few indeed outside where the phonetic signs *'N* represent *ān*, 'that'. If used the signs almost invariably represent *ō*, not *ān*.
35. Dd. ch. 63.
36. Yt. 17.16.
37. Y. 46.11.

38. Y. 51.2.
39. W. B. Henning, *Zoroaster*, p. 43.
40. Ibid.
41. Y. 35.5.
42. Ibid., 41.2.
43. Ibid., 35.2.
44. Ibid., 35.3.
45. Ibid., 35.4.
46. Ibid., 35.9.
47. Ibid., 36.3.
48. I. Gershevitch, *op. cit.*, p. 320.
49. Y. 39.3.
50. Ibid., 39.2.
51. Ibid., 42.1–3.
52. Ibid., 40.2.
53. Cf. ibid., 35.9.
54. Ibid., 41.8.
55. Ibid., 35.1.
56. Ibid., 39.2 : 40.1.
57. Ibid., 42.5.

CHAPTER III: THE CULTUS

1. Y. 55.2–3.
2. Ibid., 16.3, etc.
3. Yt. 5.17.
4. Ibid., 15.3.
5. Ibid., 13.12.
6. Y. 9.13 (*vīdaēvō ahura-tkaēshō*).
7. Ibid., 30.9 : 31.4.
8. Refs. *apud* Bartholomae, *Altiranisches Wörterbuch*, 293–4.
9. Cf. Y. 7.15 : 1.13.
10. The word *usig* proves that Zoroaster is attacking an ancient cult dating back to Indo-Iranian times. In the RV. it occurs in the form *uśig* and is frequently used of Agni, the fire-god, in his capacity of divine priest (RV. 1.60.4 : 3.3.7, etc.). Grassman, in his concordance translates 'heischend, eifrig strebend . . . von Sängern und Opferern'.
11. Y. 44.20. Cf. ibid., 51.14.
12. Ibid., 29.1.
13. Ibid., 29.4.
14. Ibid., 46.4.
15. Ibid., 32.8.
16. Ibid., 32.10.
17. Ibid., 32.12.
18. Ibid., 32.14. I omit *avō* at the end of the line as it seems to be a copyist's error derived from the same word standing immediately above. See further n. 22.

19. Y. 48.10.
20. J. J. Modi, *The Religious Ceremonies and Customs of the Parsees*, pp. 296, 306–7.
21. *Soma* and *Haoma* are etymologically the same word, Iranian *h* corresponding to Indian *s*. Cf. Iranian *ahura*, Indian *asura*.
22. There is no reason to take *saochayat* in a figurative sense. If, as is generally supposed, the reference is to the 'inflaming' of the senses in ritual drunkenness, it is difficult to see why Zoroaster speaks of the Haoma being so inflamed rather than the worshipper.
23. Y. 3.2.
24. J. J. Modi, *op. cit.*, p. 292.
25. Phl. *Yasna* 10.13.
26. Ibid., 11.7, etc.
27. GB., p. 226 : translation in Zaehner, TM., pp. 148–9.
28. Herodotus, 1.132.
29. Strabo, XV, 3.15.
30. DkM. 466.12ff. Translation in Zaehner ZZD., p. 52. Cf. Phl. *Yasna* 29.1 where the ox is said to be created 'to be eaten and owned': here again only the 'immoderate' slaughter of it is condemned.
31. Vd. 10.9–10 : 19.43.
32. See especially RV. 10.119.
33. A. A. Macdonell, *Vedic Mythology*, p. 106.

34. See H. Grassmann, *Wörterbuch zum Rig-Veda*, col. 1648–9.
35. See p. 103.
36. Y. 9.13.
37. Ibid., 10.8.
38. Chapter 47.
39. J. J. Modi, *op. cit.*, pp. 306–7.
40. Phl. *Yasna* 9.1.
41. Ibid.
42. Ibid., 32.12: according to the *daēva*-worshippers 'joy and life derive from the slaughter of cattle'.
43. See p. 87.
44. Dd. chapter 47.
45. Y. 11.4.
46. Yt. 10.89–90.
47. For a detailed description of the *Yasna* see J. J. Modi, *op. cit.*, pp. 246–310.
48. See pp. 94–6.
49. Y. 9.1.
50. Ibid., 9.4–5.
51. Yt. 9.10.
52. Zs. 4.13–26: DkM. 611–2.
53. Y. 9.26.
54. Ibid., Phl. gloss.
55. Ibid., 10.14.
56. Ibid., 11.4.
57. Ibid., 9.19–21.
58. Yt. 10.88–89.
59. Y. 57.19. He is also represented as worshipping Ashi (Yt. 17.37) and Drvāspa (Yt. 9.17).
60. But see p. 115.
61. See V. Langlois, *Collection des historiens anciens de l'Arménie*, II, pp. 186–7.
62. Ibid., p. 201.
63. Al-Dinawari, *Al-Akhbār al-Tiwāl*, ed. V. Jerjas, p. 58.
64. Herodotus, VII, 43.
65. Xenophon, *Cyropaedia*, VIII, 3.11, etc.
66. Y. 35.4.
67. Yt. 13.88, *ukhdhahyācha sraoshem*, 'hearkening to what is said'.
68. Y. 33.14.
69. Ibid., 28.5.
70. Ibid., 56.1, etc.
71. Yt. 11.14.
72. Y. 3.20: 4.23: 57.33. Vd. 18.14. *Sīrōchak* 1.17.
73. Yt. 11.14.
74. Ibid.: Y. 57.23.
75. Ibid., 6–8.
76. Ibid., 12.
77. Ibid., 23.
78. Ibid., 22.
79. GB. 169.5: PR. 56.3.
80. Ibid., 169.7.
81. Yt. 57.10.
82. Y. 57.16–7.
83. Yt. 11.20.
84. See pp. 302–3.
85. GB. 163.4.
86. PR. 56.3.

CHAPTER IV: MITHRA

1. J. J. Modi, *op. cit.*, pp. 247ff.
2. H. W. Bailey, *Zoroastrian Problems of the Ninth Century Books*, pp. 1–51.
3. See p. 161.
4. Herodotus, I, 131.
5. Yt. 10.42. I follow Darmesteter's translation which neither emends nor forces the grammar as Gershevitch does.
6. Ibid., 10.108.
7. Ibid., 5.94–5.
8. Ibid., 10.70–2.
9. Ibid., 14.47.
10. Y. 30.4.
11. Yt. 10.110.
12. Ibid., 10.29.
13. Ibid., 26. I follow Bartholomae's translation here.
14. Y. 47.4.
15. See p. 40.
16. Yt. 6.5.
17. So E. Benveniste and L. Renou, *Vrtra et Vrθragna*, Paris, 1934, *passim*.
18. So I. Gershevitch, *op. cit.*, pp. 158–62.
19. *History of Armenia*, I, 31. Further references in F. Cumont, *Les Mystères de Mithra*, Brussels, 1913 ed., p. 128.
20. A. A. Macdonell, *Vedic Mythology*, p. 59.
21. Yt. 10.86.
22. See pp. 88–9.
23. I. Gershevitch, *op. cit.*, p. 33.
24. Yt. 17.16.
25. So H. S. Nyberg and his school. Against this view see Gershevitch, *op. cit.*, 210–2.
26. *De Antro Nympharum*, 6.
27. See Gershevitch, *op. cit.*, pp. 40–1.
28. Yt. 17.16.
29. See p. 45.

30. Yt. 13.87–8.
31. See A. T. Olmstead, *History of the Persian Empire*, Chicago, 1948, pp. 59, 245, 399.
32. By Gershevitch.
33. Nyberg's theory.
34. Y. 36.6.
35. Porphyry, *Vita Pythagorae*, 41.
36. Yt. 10. 95–6.
37. Ibid., 10.95–7 : 11.11–13.
38. Ibid., 10.88 : Y. 57.19.
39. Ibid., 10.125 : Y. 57.27.
40. Ibid., 10.50 : Y. 57.21.
41. Ibid., 10.41, 100.
42. Ibid., 17.16.
43. MKh. 2.76. Dd. 13.3. Cf. AVN. 5.2.
44. ZKhA. 57, 70, 79.
45. See BSOAS., xvii, p. 247.
46. Y. 32.8.
47. Ibid., 30.3.
48. DkM. 193–4.
49. Ibid., 194.2.
50. PR. 51.
51. Cf. PR. 65.14 where the Triad attaches itself to the Heptad of the Bounteous Immortals.
52. Yt. 10.54.
53. Ibid., 17.16 where the Religion of the worshippers of Mazdāh is called Ashi's sister. I have said 'adopted' because

this appears to be a clear case of the fusion of two distinct cults.
54. Yt. 10.68.
55. Ibid., 69.
56. Ibid., 42.
57. Ibid., 84.
58. *Barsom* (Avestan *baresman*) was originally a strew of twigs on which sacrificial meat was laid. Later the twigs were gathered into a bundle which the officiating priest held in his hands. Today the twigs have been replaced by metal rods.
59. Yt. 10.88.
60. Ibid., 10.89.
61. See pp. 85–6.
62. Yt. 10.106.
63. Ibid., 10.119. This is obviously an animal sacrifice. Gershevitch takes it to mean 'along with small cattle', etc. For this we would expect the addition of the word *hadha* or *hathra*. The sacrifice 'with' cattle, etc., is exactly parallel to the sacrifice 'with' libations we find throughout the *Yasna*.
64. Ibid., 10.124.
65. Yt. 10.123–7.
66. Yt. 10.137–9. Mainly after Gershevitch.
67. Dd. 47 : GB. 177.7.
68. Yt. 10.140–1.
69. Ibid., 10.145.

CHAPTER V: MITHRA—YIMA—MITHRAS

1. See p. 159.
2. Yt. 14.55–6 as I interpret it.
3. GB. 47.12 : cf. Zaehner, ZZD, p. 15.
4. DkM. 182.6ff. : Zaehner, ZZD., pp. 14, 30–1.
5. *Omomi* is obviously a dittography for *Hōm*. E. Beneveniste's rejection of this obvious equation (*The Persian Religion*, p. 74) need not be taken seriously.
6. Plutarch, *De Iside*, 369 D : Clemen, Fontes, p. 48.
7. ZKhA. 242.1–2.
8. GB. 142ff.
9. Ibid., 147ff.
10. *Shatapatha-brāhmana*, 4.1.4.8.
11. Y. 32.8.
12. From the Avestan *Yima khshaëta*, 'royal Yima'.
13. See GB. 93.
14. F. Cumont, *Textes et Monuments figurés rélatifs aux mystères de Mithra*, Brussels,

1896–9, vol. ii, plate VIII (between pp. 364–5).
15. Ibid., vol. i, pp. 38ff.
16. See p. 262.
17. For a detailed argument of this thesis see BSOAS., xvii, pp. 237–43.
18. GB. 103–4.
19. Ibid., 104.8.
20. RV. 10.13.4.
21. Ibid., 10.14.1.
22. Ibid., 10.14.2.
23. Ibid., 1.38.5.
24. Ibid., 10.165.4.
25. Ibid., 10.135.1.
26. Ibid., 10.135.7.
27. Y. 48.10.
28. RV. 1.35.6.
29. Ibid., 10.14.7.
30. Ibid., 10.97.16.
31. Ibid., 10.123.6.
32. Ibid., 10.14.12.

33. RV. 1.66.8.
34. *Mahābhārata*, II, 313–4.
35. Dd. 38.20: PR. 31.a.10.
36. DkM. 340.11.
37. Vd. 2.
38. Yt. 9.10: 17.30.
39. Lit. 'let them eat', etc.
40. Yt. 19.32–3.
41. Ibid., 10.50.
42. DkM. 595.21–2.
43. Vd. 2.8.
44. The homeland of the Avesta.
45. Vd. 2.20.
46. Ibid., 2.41.
47. Yt. 10.142.
48. Y. 57.21.
49. Vd. 2.30, 38.
50. GB. 218–9.
51. Dd. 36.81 : DkM. 668–9.
52. On the nature of the *vara* I follow Lommel.
53. Al-Baghdādī, *Al-Farq bayn al-Firaq*, ed. Kawtharī, Cairo, 1948, p. 213: translation in A. S. Halkin, *Moslem Schisms and Sects*, Tel Aviv, 1935, p. 219.
54. Vd. 2.20.
55. GB. 100.14.
56. Yt. 13.130 where he appears first in the list of kings.
57. Ibid., 19.33.
58. Ibid., 19.35.

59. Yt. 10.138-9.
60. See A. Christensen, *Le premier homme et le premier roi dans l'histoire légendaire des Iraniens*, vol. ii, p. 37.
61. F. Spiegel, *Die traditionalle Literatur der Parsen*, Vienna, 1860, p. 328.
62. Al-Bīrūnī seems to have mistranslated *apākhtar* as 'South'.
63. Al-Bīrūnī, *Chronologie orientalischer Völker*, ed. C. E. Sachau, Leipzig, 1878, p. 217.
64. Formerly it was at the summer solstice. Ibid., p. 216.
65. ZKhA. 25.1.
66. Strabo, XI.14.9: Clemen, Fontes, p. 32.
67. Athenaeus, *Deipnosophists*, X.45 : Clemen, Fontes, p. 26.
68. Al-Bīrūnī, *op. cit.*, p. 223.
69. Y. 9.1.
70. See p. 151.
71. Yt. 19.35.
72. Ibid., 19.46.
73. The latest attempt is that of Gershevitz, *op. cit.*, p. 151.
74. See p. 37.
75. Reading *ku* for *kē*.
76. Reading *āz-ich* for *haft* (or *ut-at*). This passage, which has been consistently mistranslated, will be dealt with in an article in due course.
77. DkM. 810.13–811.2.

CHAPTER VI: FRAVASHI—VAYU—KHWARENAH

1. Yt. 5.18.
2. Ibid., 13.2–16.
3. Ibid., 13.12–13.
4. By G. Widengren in his *Hochgottglaube im alten Irān*, and S. Wikander in his *Vayu*.
5. Yt. 15.43–4.
6. Ibid., 57.
7. See Zaehner, ZZD., pp. 121ff.
8. Yt. 15.5.
9. Ibid., 44.
10. *Aogemadaēchā*, 77–81.
11. Vd. 19.29.
12. DkM. 278.14.
13. H. W. Bailey, *Zoroastrian Problems in the Ninth Century Books*, Oxford, 1943, pp. 1–77.
14. Yt. 19.56.
15. GB. 101.

16. DkM. 341.11.
17. *Epistle of Tansar*, ed. Minovi, p. 13. Cf. A. Christensen, *L'Iran sous les Sassanides*, 2nd ed., p. 320.
18. DkM. 342.21.
19. Ibid., 343.19–334.3.
20. Ibid., 341.13–22.
21. ZKhA. 160.4–5.
22. DkM. 513.9.
23. Dd. 36.35 : 38.14.
24. DkM. 342.3ff. Cf. Ibid., 350.13ff.
25. Yt. 10.127.
26. DkM. 347.6–7.
27. Ibid., 425.11.
28. GB. 164.13ff.
29. Zs. 5.1 : DkM. 434.13–18.
30. DkM. 347.15–22.
31. Ibid., 350.14–15.

CHAPTER VII: ACHAEMENIDS AND MAGI

1. See especially Vd. 1 and Yt. 10.14.
2. S. H. Taqizadeh, *Old Iranian Calendars*, London, 1938, p. 13.
3. DB. 1.11–12, etc.
4. DSf. 9–10.
5. Ibid., 15–22.
6. DB. 4.61,63.
7. DSj. 4.
8 DNa. 1–8.
9. DPd. 15ff.
10. DSs. 1–2.
11. DB. 4.58,77.
12. DNb. 7–8.
13. Ibid., 14.
14. DPd. 1–2.
15. DNa. 52.
16. Ibid., 58–60.
17. Y. 72.11.
18. DB. 1.63–4.
19. DNa. 31–6.
20. DSe. 31–40.
21. *Daivadāna* is usually taken to mean a 'place or temple of the *daivas*', but *-dāna* normally means a 'receptacle', and this seems a very odd way of referring to a temple. I would take the word to mean 'rite' or 'law' and would compare Vedic *yātudhāna*, 'following the law of the Yātus'.
22. XPh. 35–56.
23. See p. 83.
24. See p. 82.
25. DB. 5.18–20.
26. Herodotus, VII.35.
27. Ibid., 113.
28. Ibid., 191.
29. Ibid., 180.
30. GB. 42.14: translation in Zaehner, TM., p. 47.

31. A²Hb.
32. J. H. Moulton, *Early Zoroastrianism*.
33. G. Messina, *Die Ursprung der Magier und die zarathustrische Religion*.
34. Herodotus, I.140.
35. Ibid.
36. I.101.
37. See p. 124.
38. St Basil, *Ad Epiphanium*, 4.
39. Herodotus, I.132: Strabo, XV.3.13.
40. GB. 237.13 where all *magupats* (written *M'WPT'N* (*mōpatān*)) are said to be of the family of Mānushchihr. Cf. St Basil.
41. Pseudo-Lucian *apud* Clemen, Fontes, p. 74.
42. Pliny the Younger, *Historia Naturalis*, XXV.2.13: Clemen, Fontes, p. 42.
43. PT., p. 134: *gēhān pērāyak, kishvar abhrang, ōstām maghvand*.
44. *De Abstinentia*, IV. 16: Clemen, Fontes, p. 80.
45. See Messina, *op. cit.*, p. 42.
46. *Alcibiades* I. 121.
47. Herodotus confuses Mithra with Anāhitā.
48. Herodotus, I. 131–140 (Rawlinson's translation).
49. Strabo, XV. 3.13: Clemen, Fontes, p. 34.
50. Y. 11.1,4.
51. Diogenes Laertius, *Proem*, 8: Clemen, Fontes, p. 75.
52. AVN. 1.12–18.
53. See p. 87.
54. Strabo, XV.3.15: Clemen, Fontes, p. 35.
55. DkM. 412. See p. 175.

PART II: TWILIGHT

CHAPTER VIII: IN SEARCH OF AN ORTHODOXY

1. DkM. 412–5. Translation as in ZZD. with slight alterations.
2. Y. 45.2.
3. Al-Ghazālī, *Mishkāt al-Anwār* in *Jawāhir al-Ghawālī*, ed. Sabrī, Cairo, 1936, p. 143: translation by W. H. T. Gairdner, Lahore, 1952 (reprint), pp. 166–7.
4. PT., pp. 42–4.

5. Al-Baghdādī, *Al-farq bayn al-Firaq*, ed. Kawthari, pp. 177, 200, 153, 171, 172: pp. 131, 183, 68, 115, 116 in Halkin's translation.
6. Murtazā Rāzī: see ZZD., p. 451.
7. Shahristānī, *Kitāb al-Milal wa'l-Nihal*, ed. Cureton, p. 182: Haarbrücker's German translation, p. 276.

8. Baghdādī, *op. cit.*, p. 214: translation, p. 220.
9. Damascius, *Dubitationes et Solutiones*, 125 bis: Clemen, Fontes, p. 95.
10. As suggested by me in ZZD., p. 20.
11. Diogenes Laertius, *Proem*, 8: Clemen, Fontes, p. 75.
12. See p. 92.
13. H-C. Puech, *Le Manichéisme*, Paris, 1949, p. 45.
14. DkM. 466.20: 658.14: 680.14, etc.
15. See now M. Sprengling, *Third Century Iran, Sapor and Kartir*, Chicago, 1953.
16. For references, see Puech, *op. cit.*, p. 137.
17. See pp. 196-8.

18. Sprengling, *op. cit.*, pp. 47, 52.
19. See BSOAS., xvii, pp. 234-7.
20. See pp. 196-8.
21. ShGV. 10.70-1.
22. See T. Nöldeke, '*Syrische Polemik gegen die persische Religion*' in *Festgruss an Rudolf von Roth*, Stuttgart, 1893, p. 34.
23. See pp. 207-8.
24. For a full discussion of the case of Mihr-Narsē, see ZZD., pp. 39-47.
25. Mas'ūdī, *Murūj*, ii, p. 196.
26. Agathias, ii, 28.
27. DkM. 428.19-429.4. For more details on the reign of Khusraw I, see ZZD., pp. 47-50.

CHAPTER IX: THE VARIETIES OF ZURVANISM

1. *Epistles of Mānushchihr*, 2.1.12: see also ZZD., p. 96, n. 4.
2. See p. 176.
3. J. Bidez and F. Cumont, *Les Mages hellénisés*, vol. i, p. 33.
4. Mas'ūdī, *Murūj*, II, pp. 167-8. Cf. Hujwīrī, *Kashf al-Mahjūb*, tr. R. A. Nicholson, London, 1936, p. 404.
5. Al-Ghazālī, *Al-Munqidh min al-Dalāl*, ed. Jābir (undated), Cairo, p. 18: tr. W. Montgomery Watt, *The Faith and Practice of Al-Ghazālī*, p. 30.
6. DkM. 250.3-4. ShGV. 6.
7. Ibid., 250.3.
8. See DkM. 406.2 and H. W. Bailey, *Zoroastrian Problems*, p. 85.
9. R. A. Nicholson, *Studies in Islamic Mysticism*, Cambridge, 1921, p. 133.
10. ShGV. 6.1-8.
11. M. Sprengling, *op. cit.*, pp. 65, 67.
12. *Maitrī* Upanishad, 6.14.
13. Ibid., 6.16.
14. See p. 182.
15. DkM. 345.19.
16. Bailey, *op. cit.*, p. 171.
17. *mātagh* and *dēsak*.
18. DkM. 98.19-22: 398.20-1.
19. Ibid., 202.18.
20. J. M. Schmid's German translation, Vienna, 1900, p. 87.

21. *a-hambūt* DkM. 398.20.
22. *a-bahr* Ibid., 399.4.
23. Ibid., 207.18.
24. Ibid.
25. Ibid., 133.2-6. Translation in ZZD., p. 383.
26. DkM. 202-3: 207-8.
27. Ibid., 203.
28. Ibid., 121.3-9.
29. Ibid., 208.21-2.
30. GB. 181.6.
31. Ibid., 188.11.
32. *De Generatione*, 330ª 30.
33. DkM. 207-8.
34. Ibid., 120.16-20.
35. Ibid., 120.22-121.1.
36. Ibid., 124.17-18.
37. Ibid., 98-100.
38. Ibid., 278.16-18.
39. MKh. 8.12.4: ZZD., pp. 368, 400.
40. Ibid., 8.13-14.
41. Ibid., 23.
42. Ibid., 51.
43. See p. 193.
44. See ZZD., pp. 419-29.
45. DkM. 829.1-3.
46. MKh. 8.6-7: ZZD., p. 368.
47. MKh. 8.9: ZZD., p. 369.
48. Zs. 1.29-30: ZZD., pp. 342-3.

CHAPTER X: CLASSICAL ZURVANISM

1. Shahristānī, *Kitāb al-Milal wa'n-Nihal*, Cureton, p. 184: Haarbrücker, p. 279: ZZD., p. 434.

2. R. A. Nicholson, *Selected Poems from the Dīvāni Shamsi Tabrīz*, Cambridge, 1952, p. 15.

3. DkM. 128.20–129.1 : ZZD., p. 382.

4. Zs. 1.9: ZZD., p. 341.

5. ShGV. 16.80: ZZD., p. 395.

6. DkM. 121.14.

7. Ibid., 199.4–5.

8. MKh. 10.4: ShGV. 3.19.

9. Eznik of Kolb, *Against the Sects*, II, 8: ZZD., p. 438.

10. Ibid.

11. ZZD., p. 435.

12. AVN. 131–2 (*Pahlavi Texts*, p. 95): ZZD., p. 397: *Abhyātkār i Zāmāspik*, 2.2: ZZD., p. 382.

13. GB. 7: ZZD., p. 314.

14. DkM. 294.1–2: ZZD., p. 392.

15. ZZD., p. 63ff.

16. Ibid., p. 410.

17. Ibid., p. 79 n.D.

18. Ibid., p. 412.

19. Ibid., p. 448.

20. DkM. 79.21.

21. ZZD., p. 79 n.E.

22. See p. 203.

23. DkM. 98–9.

24. Ibid., 99.5–10.

25. PT., p. 42.3: DkM. 581.9.

26. Ibid., 534.5.

27. See p. 181.

28. See ZZD., p. 441.

29. See BSOAS., xvii, 1955, p. 233.

30. See p. 200.

31. Quotations from ShGV. 16.53–111: ZZD., pp. 392–6.

32. See p. 204.

33. DkM. 133.2: ZZD., p. 383.

34. Ibid., 282.12–16: ZZD., pp. 389–90.

35. Cf. DkM. 228.5: 'Action, at its fulfilment returns to its original state of rest'. ZZD., p. 389.

36. DkM. 282.21–283.17: ZZD., pp. 389–391.

37. Cf. Zs. 1.30 (ZZD., p. 343), where Zurvān says to Ahriman: 'If thou hast not accomplished that which thou didst threaten . . . to demolish [Infinite] Time.'

38. DkM. 222.3–4: ZZD., p. 386.

39. DkM. 222.7: ZZD., ibid.

40. See p. 249.

41. See p. 236.

42. GB. 9.8–9: ZZD., p. 315.

43. DkM. 223.1: ZZD., p. 387.

44. DkM. 345.16–8.

45. Zs. 1.29–30: ZZD., pp. 342–3.

46. Zs. 34.35: ZZD., p. 351.

47. DkM. 204.19: ZZD., p. 377.

48. Ibid., 204.19.

49. GB. 11.10–12: ZZD., p. 316.

50. Ibid., 11.2–4; ZZD., ibid.

51. DkM. 143.12.

52. Ibid., 349: ZZD., p. 373.

53. See ZZD., p. 174.

54. DkM. 361.10–11.

55. DkM. 347.12–13: ZZD., p. 370.

56. Zs. 34.36–7: ZZD., pp. 351–2.

57. DkM. 378–80.

58. Zs. 34.35: ZZD., p. 346.

59. DkM. 120.15–20.

60. The *Haurvatāt* ('Wholeness') and *Ameretāt* ('Immortality') of the *Gāthās*.

61. DkM. 316.9–17.

62. Vd. 19.29.

63. Zs. 34.44.

64. Alexander of Lycopolis, ed. Brinkmann, Leipzig, 1895, p. 5.

65. Zs. 34.41.

66. Ibid., 34.39.

67. Ibid., 34.42.

68. Ibid., 34.38.

69. PR. 48.90–6: ZZD., pp. 354–5.

70. MKh. 8.10.

71. GB. 4.6–7: ZZD., p. 313.

72. See p. 230.

73. DkM. 379.15.

74. Ibid., 17–18.

75. Ibid., 342.3ff.

76. See ZZD., pp. 174–5.

77. Zs. 34.54: ZZD., p. 354.

78. Vd. 18.19.

79. Y. 16.8.

80. Yt. 18.1.

81. See ZZD., p. 166.

82. See p. 215.

83. ZZD., p. 436.

84. Ibid., p. 441.

85. GB. 39.11ff.: ZZD., pp. 355–60.

86. Zs. 34.31: There is a lacuna at the crucial point. The question is, To whom did she join herself? In ZZD. I argued that it must have been the Righteous Man. This indeed must have been the end of the episode, but it is rather her union with Ahriman that Zātspram is speaking of now. He defiles her first in order that she may defile the Righteous Man later.

87. GB. 107.15ff.

88. See p. 194.

CHAPTER XI: ZURVĀN

1. *Persian Rivāyats*, vol. ii, p. 53, l. 10: ZZD., p. 408.
2. MKh. 8.7: ZZD., p. 368.
3. ZZD., p. 412 (*Ulamā-yi Islām*, §23).
4. Ibid., pp. 220–5.
5. Ibid., pp. 228–31.
6. DkM. 278–9.
7. MKh. 8.12–14: ZZD., p. 369.
8. DkM. 278.21–279.2.
9. ZZD., pp. 159–61.
10. DkM. 23.12: ZZD., p. 381.
11. GB. 10.9–11.1: ZZD., pp. 315–6.
12. See p. 149.
13. PT., p. 76: ZZD., pp. 398–9.
14. Firdausī, *Shāhnāma*, ed. Vullers, vol. i, pp. 208–11: ZZD., pp. 444–6.
15. DkM. 294.1–2: ZZD., p. 392.
16. GB. 167.3–4: ZZD., p. 338.
17. DkM. 568.3–12: ZZD., p. 407.
18. PT., p. 74: ZZD., p. 257.
19. MKh. 38: ZZD., p. 401.
20. MKh. 24: ZZD., p. 404.
21. MKh. 22: ZZD., p. 402.
22. AVN. 150–7 (PT., p. 94): ZZD., pp. 404–5.
23. ZZD., p. 405.
24. PT., p. 147: cf. DkM. 547.

CHAPTER XII: OHRMAZD AND AHRIMAN

1. GB. 2.12–3.6: ZZD., pp. 312–3.
2. Zs. 1.1–2: ZZD., p. 341.
3. GB. 3.6–4.1: ZZD., p. 313.
4. See p. 218.
5. GB. 31.3–4: ZZD., p. 333.
6. See ZZD., pp. 207ff., and p. 295.
7. GB. 11.2–4: ZZD., p. 316.
8. GB. 16.2–3: ZZD., p. 318. Cf. GB. 4.6–7: ZZD., p. 313.
9. See ZZD., pp. 371–4, and p. 201.
10. See p. 225.
11. Dd. 90.
12. Ibid., 63.
13. GB. 16.1–12: ZZD., p. 318.
14. See ZZD., pp. 96–8. My present conclusions are different from those advanced there.
15. Zs. 1.3: ZZD., p. 341.
16. GB. 4.12–14: ZZD., p. 313. Zātspram's account differs.
17. GB. 7.2–6: ZZD., p. 314.
18. GB. 10.1–8: ZZD., p. 315.
19. GB. 32.4: 166.11: ZZD., pp. 333, 338.
20. Zs. 1.9: ZZD., p. 341.
21. GB. 9.2–11: ZZD., p. 315.
22. GB. 5.1–3: ZZD., p. 313.
23. DkM. 375.19–20.
24. Ibid., 191.16–17.
25. GB. 11.8–10: ZZD., p. 316.
26. GB. 11–12: ZZD., p. 316.
27. See p. 225.
28. DkM. 378–80 and see p. 276.
29. GB. 12: ZZD., p. 316.
30. This and the preceding quotations are from GB. 5–8: ZZD., pp. 313–4.
31. GB. 14.3–8: ZZD., p. 317.
32. Zs. 1.28: ZZD., p. 342.
33. GB. 15.5–7: ZZD., p. 317.
34. See p. 46.
35. Y. 19.2.
36. See pp. 201–2.
37. DkM. 349–50: ZZD., pp. 373–4.
38. DkM. 278–9.
39. GB. 18.3–9: ZZD., p. 318.
40. GB. 18.12–19.2: ZZD., pp. 318–9.
41. PR. 46: ZZD., pp. 361–7.
42. See BSOAS., xvii, p. 244.
43. RV. 10.90.
44. ShGV. 1.20–4.
45. GB. 189.8–13.
46. DkM. 278.
47. Zs. 30.5–11.
48. Chapter 63.
49. The Pahlavi translation of the Bounteous Immortal *Asha Vahishta*.
50. The old mistranslation of this word as 'priest' has, incomprehensibly, been revived by M. Molé (*La naissance du monde*, Paris, 1959), p. 320. This is both wrong and perverse. The word occurs either as *asarōk* (Pahlavi transliteration of Avestan **asarō*) or as *asar*, both meaning 'endless' or 'headless'. 'Priest' is *āsrōn* (= Avestan *āthravan*): it does not have the final *k*.
51. *Gētēh* almost certainly translates Avestan *gaya*, 'life'. Mānushchihr deliberately translates as 'world' meaning

'microcosm'. The usual translation of *gaya* is *jān*.
52. GB. 12.11 : ZZD., p. 316.
53. Dd. 34.2.
54. GB. 38–9.
55. Ibid., 41.10–42.6.
56. Zs. 2.2.
57. GB. 42.6–14.

58. GB. 42.14–43.8.
59. Zs. 2.9.
60. Ibid., 2.10 : GB. 21.4–5.
61. *Astōvihāt*, the chief of the demons of death.
62. GB. 43.10–45.9.
63. MKh. 8.8.
64. Zs. 2.18.

CHAPTER XIII: MAN

1. MKh. 28.2.
2. Reading *arvand*.
3. Reading *khrōsishn*.
4. Zs. 3.2–3.
5. Reading *ruzdaihā* for *ranjaihā*.
6. ShGV. 4.63–79.
7. GB. 93–4 : Zs. 3.50–1.
8. GB. 101.2–5.
9. Ibid., 102.9–15.
10. See p. 223.
11. GB. 104.9–11.
12. Ibid., 105.11–12.
13. Ibid., 101.9–12 (= *Indian Bundahishn*, 33.16–20), which has the better readings.
14. See p. 151.
15. DkM. 148.16–17.
16. Ibid., 378.22–379.2.
17. GB. 34.4–13.
18. See pp. 262–3.
19. DkM. 122.5–8.
20. See pp. 146–7.
21. DkM. 122.17–19.
22. Ibid., 123.5–7.
23. The text is corrupt here.
24. DkM. 123.10–13.
25. Ibid., 229.10–11.
26. Ibid., 123.
27. Reading *ut-shān* for *andar-shān*.
28. Reading **chirāgh* with Bailey, *Zoroastrian Problems*, p. 100.
29. Reading **kirrēnītak*.
30. Omitting *razm-ich*.
31. Reading **hēn*.
32. DkM. 241–2.
33. Ibid., 321.3–4.
34. MKh. 46.2.
35. Cf. also DkM. 300.2, reading *khwatāy i tanōmand* for *khwatāyōmand tan*.
36. Omitting *apar* after *martōm*.
37. Reading **anakhw*, meaning (i) a 'not-lord' and (ii) 'without intellect'.
38. Reading *pat martōm khwatāyīh* for *martōm pat khwatāyīh*.

39. Omitting *KYM*.
40. DkM. 186.18–187.10.
41. Ibid., 126.1.
42. Reading *'dēh*.
43. DkM. 300.10–12.
44. Ibid., 178.5–6.
45. Substituting *khrat* for the *ut srūt* of the text.
46. DkM. 231.13–21.
47. Omitting the words *apārīk yazdān*.
48. Reading **ashgahānih*.
49. Reading *āhōkīhēt*.
50. DkM. 286.8–22.
51. See p. 253.
52. DkM. 341.11.
53. Ibid., 260.12.
54. Ibid., 331.21–332.2.
55. Ibid., 383.22–384.4.
56. Ibid., 344.5–6.
57. *Khrat* must be read for *zat*.
58. Text corrupt. Read *frāch āhanjēt ut apāch āhanjēt*.
59. Omitting the first *adhyār*.
60. Omitting *harvisp*.
61. Reading **kashēt*.
62. DkM. 306.2–12. Cf. Ibid., 258.6–14.
63. Cf. DkM. 379.5ff.
64. Ibid., 266.1ff.
65. Ibid., 267.
66. Ibid., 337.4–5.
67. Ibid., 548.11–13.
68. Ibid., 269.23–270.1.
69. MKh. 2.65.
70. PT., p. 144.
71. DkM. 581.17ff.
72. Ibid., 505.21–2.
73. Ibid., 515.10–11.
74. Ibid., 547.21ff.
75. Ibid., 577.11–12.
76. Ibid., 574.19–20.
77. Ibid., 519.19–22 : 540.17–22.
78. Ibid., 97.9–11.
79. Ibid., 479.13–15.
80. Reading *nē* for *rādh*.

81. DkM. 526.18–527.2.
82. Ibid., 243.18–244.1.
83. Ibid., 190.17–191.5.
84. Ibid., 268.3–8.
85. Ibid., 322.9.
86. Ibid., 9–18.
87. Ibid., 86.14–22.
88. Ibid., 307.11–13.
89. Ibid., 64.18–22.

90. Reading *vēhīh for gās.
91. DkM. 68.17–22.
92. Ibid., 361.21–362.2.
93. Reading khēm.
94. DkM. 380.19–382.3.
95. Ibid., 281.4–6.
96. Ibid., 260.17–19.
97. Ibid., 258.17–22.
98. Ibid., 101.10–11.

CHAPTER XIV: THE RELIGION AND THE KING

1. See ZZD., p. 144, n.D.
2. Mas'ūdī, Murūj, II, p. 162.
3. ShGV. 1.11–30.
4. DkM. 46.17–18.
5. Ibid., 239.11–12.
6. Ibid., 326.4–5.
7. Ibid., 165.7ff.
8. Ibid., 98.7.
9. Ibid., 155.6.
10. See p. 287.
11. DkM. 222.14.
12. Ibid., 429.11–15.
13. GB. 7.1–6.
14. MKh. 27.15.
15. DkM. 147.7.
16. DkM. 295.7–297.5. See ZZD., pp. 262–3.
17. DkM. 130: TM., p. 96.
18. DkM. 307.7–8.
19. Ibid., 167.
20. Ibid., 58–9.
21. Ibid., 370–1.
22. See p. 249.
23. MKh. 57.2–16.
24. DkM. 361.19–20.
25. Ibid. 361.21–362.3
26. Ibid., 302.2–3.
27. Ibid., 84.13–17.
28. Ibid., 302.3.
29. Ibid., 387.20.
30. Ibid., 484.7–9.
31. Ibid., 302.3–7.
32. Ibid., 250–1.
33. Ibid., 274.16–20.
34. Ibid., 350.13–14.
35. Ibid., 104.

36. DkM. 144.9–18.
37. Reading akhw for hām.
38. DkM. 154.6–13.
39. Ibid., 373.17–18.
40. Ibid., 314.9–10. See also ZZD., pp. 207–8.
41. Dd. 47.
42. DkM. 459.15.
43. Ibid., 237.7–8.
44. Ibid., 460.16: cf. 312.20.
45. Ibid., 237.8–10.
46. Ibid., 329.14–330.6.
47. Ibid., 355.6–11.
48. Reading nē for rās.
49. DkM. 251.12–14.
50. Ibid., 358.7–9.
51. Ibid., 251.12–22.
52. ShGV. 10.20ff.
53. See p. 271.
54. DkM. 47.6.
55. Ibid., 335.20–336.2.
56. Ibid., 337.7–8.
57. Dd. 2.13.
58. DkM. 401.3–5.
59. Ibid., 92.16–17.
60. Ibid., 140–1. (141.6–15).
61. ShGV. 1.19.
62. DkM. 460.8–10.
63. Ibid., 401.12.
64. Ibid., 287.17–22.
65. Ibid., 322.20–323.1.
66. Ibid., 292.20–293.1.
67. Ibid., 293.1–6.
68. Ibid., 218.19–21.
69. Ibid., 216.9–17.

CHAPTER XV: THE END

1. Reading jān-*'kanīhiā.
2. MKh. 2.73–122.
3. Dd. 23.2.
4. Ibid., 23.3.

5. Dd. 23.4.
6. Ibid., 24.4.
7. Ibid., 30.16: 31.9.
8. GB. 204.14–15: AVN. 6.11.

9. MKh. 7.14: AVN. 6.12.
10. Dd. 30.18.
11. Ibid., 30.18–19.
12. Ibid., 25.3–4
13. Ibid., 25.6.
14. Ibid., 30.6–7.
15. AVN. 101.10–12.
16. Dd. 30.3.
17. Ibid., 30.8.
18. Ibid., 30.11.
19. Ibid., 30.17.
20. Ibid., 26.2.
21. Ibid., 26.3–8.
22. AVN. 18.3–13.
23. Dd. 32.3–6.
24. Ibid., 31.4–5.
25. Ibid., 36.95.
26. Ibid., 31.10.
27. Ibid., 36.35: cf. Zs. 3.2.
28. Ibid., 36.68–9.
29. DkM. 175–7.
30. Zs. 34.21–9.
31. See p. 217.
32. GB. 220.
33. Ibid., 103.1–6 (*Indian Bundahishn*, p. 35.1–7).
34. DkM. 836.11.
35. GB. 185.13–186.1.
36. Zs. 34.36.
37. Ibid., 34.39.
38. GB. 221.1–11.
39. Zs. 34.40–1.
40. Ibid., 34.42.

41. PR. 48.91–2: ZZD., pp. 354–5.
42. Ibid., 48.93.
43. Ibid., 48.94–6.
44. Dd. 36.99.
45. *Abhyātkār i Zāmāspik*, 17.16.
46. Dd. 36.88–91.
47. Ibid., 36.94.
48. Ibid., 36.99.
49. Ibid.
50. Zs. 34.1–7.
51. GB. 223.4–7.
52. PR. 48.55.
53. GB. 226.3–5: TM., p. 149.
54. Dd. 36.100.
55. GB. 225.6–11: TM., p. 148.
56. GB. 225.16.
57. DkM. 350.1. ZZD., p. 374.
58. GB. 32.5. ZZD., p. 333.
59. Zs. 35.1–2.
60. PR. 48.98.
61. Zs. 35.39.
62. Reading *dōst*.
63. PR. 48.102.
64. Ibid.
65. GB. 226.9–10: Zs. 35.52: PR. 48.106.
66. Zs. 35.51.
67. Ibid.
68. Dd. 36.101–2.
69. Reading *vēhīh* for *gās*.
70. Dd. 36.104–6.
71. Reading *dēsān* for *dahishn*.
72. Dd. 38.107–9.

BIBLIOGRAPHY

Modern as opposed to pioneer work on Zoroastrianism can be dated from 1895 when GELDNER published his authoritative text of the Avesta or, more logically perhaps, from 1904 when the grand old man of Zoroastrian studies and prince of philologians, Christian BARTHOLOMAE, published his wonderful *Altiranisches Wörterbuch* which provided Iranian scholars with an irreplaceable reference book in which every single passage of the Avesta was, where translatable, translated into German by the greatest Iranian philologian of his day. Work on Zoroastrianism before 1904 was, of necessity, of a pioneer nature since there was no Avestan dictionary in existence. Scholars had to work largely in the dark, relying on intuition rather more than is normally necessary. There would, then, seem little point in including in this bibliographical note works written before 1904 except those which still retain some of their value.

This seemed the best course for another reason too. As recently as 1958 Professor DUCHESNE-GUILLEMIN published an exhaustive bibliographical study on the history of Zoroastrian scholarship in the West entitled *The Western Response to Zoroaster*: to this work I am greatly indebted. Readers interested primarily in the history of Zoroastrian studies in the West are therefore referred to this excellent monograph, and only the barest outline of the history of these studies will be given in this note. This applies as much to the original sources as to works about Zoroastrianism, particularly in the case of the Achaemenian inscriptions which have been repeatedly edited. In the bibliography that follows the sources are listed first, more general works follow. Articles in learned periodicals have not been included except when they are of sufficient length and importance to rank as a book.

I. THE SOURCES

A. *THE AVESTA*

The standard edition is that of:

K. F. GELDNER, 3 vols., Stuttgart, 1895.

Translations of the whole Avesta exist in English, French, and German. None of them can be considered as anything like definitive. The most reliable is the German version. The versions are:

J. DARMESTETER and L. H. MILLS, *The Zend-Avesta*, in *Sacred Books of the East*, vols. iv, xxiii, and xxxi, Oxford, 1883–7. MILLS' version of the *Yasna* (which includes the *Gāthās*) is wholly out of date. The volumes by DARMESTETER are still useful.

J. DARMESTETER, *Le Zend-Avesta*, 3 vols., Paris, 1892–3. This includes fragments from the Avesta not included in the English version, and contains introductory essays and footnotes which are still extremely useful. The general introduction is marred by an impossible theory about the *Gāthās*. These, DARMESTETER considered, were forgeries written between the first century BC and the third AD under the influence of Neo-Platonism. This theory (which even DARMESTETER later withdrew) is the greatest tribute ever paid to the originality of Zoroaster's thought.

F. WOLFF, *Avesta, übersetzt auf der Grundlage von Chr. Bartholomae's altiranischen Wörterbuch*, Strassburg, 1910. This is based entirely on BARTHOLOMAE's dictionary.

An admirable selection of passages in translation was made by K. F. GELDNER. This selection presents the best picture available of Zoroastrianism as it appears in the Avesta itself. The selection is entitled:

K. F. GELDNER, *Die zoroastrische Religion (Das Avesta)*, Tübingen, 1926.

Less comprehensive, though more up to date, are the selections in:

K. BARR, *Avesta*, Copenhagen, 1954 (in Danish).

(1) The Gāthās

The *Gāthās*, being the work of Zoroaster himself, have been repeatedly translated. In English we have a word-for-word translation by:

Maria Wilkins SMITH, *Studies in the Syntax of the Gâthâs of Zarathushtra*, Linguistic Society of America, 1929.

J. DUCHESNE-GUILLEMIN, *The Hymns of Zoroaster*, translated from the French by Mrs. M. Henning, London, 1952. The only relatively up-to-date version of the *Gāthās* in English.

Dastur F. A. BODE and Piloo NANAVUTTY, *Songs of Zarathushtra*, London, 1952. This is a tendentious interpretation rather than a translation. In conformity with a trend that has been accentuated since India gained her independence, the translators, though Parsees, distort the Prophet's words to fit in with those trends in modern Hinduism which come nearest to theosophy.

In addition there is an English version of BARTHOLOMAE's translation in:

J. H. MOULTON, *Early Zoroastrianism* (see p. 345).

In French there is DUCHESNE-GUILLEMIN's version in:

J. DUCHESNE-GUILLEMIN, *Zoroastre* (see p. 345).

It is, however, the Germans who have concentrated most heavily on these difficult texts; and in German we have:

Chr. BARTHOLOMAE, *Die Gathas des Awesta*, Strassburg, 1905. Still indispensable to any serious student.

J. WACKERNAGEL translated all the *Gāthās* according to the mind of his great teacher F. C. ANDREAS. These all appeared in the *Nachrichten der Göttinger Gesellschaft der Wissenschaften* in 1909 (3rd *Gāthā*), 1911 (4th *Gāthā*), and 1913 (1st, 2nd, and 5th *Gāthā*).

Another pupil of ANDREAS, H. LOMMEL, published his version of all the *Gāthās* except the first in the same journal in 1934-5.

The most recent version in German is:

H. HUMBACH, *Die Gathas des Zarathustra*, 2 vols., Heidelberg, 1959.

The four German versions conform to the highest philological standards, and the reader who knows German might well compare them with one another to see how enormous the discrepancies between them can be.

The following German translations of individual *Gāthās* may also be consulted:

J. MARKWART, *Das erste Kapitel der Gāthā Uštavati*, Rome, 1930.

W. LENTZ, *Yasna 28, Kommentierte Übersetzung und Kompositionsanalyse*, Wiesbaden, 1954.

(2) The Yashts

The only complete version of the *Yashts*, apart from those appearing in translations of the whole Avesta, is in German. It is:

H. LOMMEL, *Die Yäšts des Awesta*, Göttingen/Leipzig, 1927.

The only individual *Yasht* translated separately into English is the *Mithra Yasht*. This is by:

I. GERSHEVITCH, *The Avestan Hymn to Mithra*, Cambridge, 1959. This is a magnificent piece of scholarship, but the translation, though intentionally literal, contains unnecessary bizarreries. The introduction gives the author's considered view on the development of Zoroastrianism. Though rather confused, it is on the whole balanced, but the author's reactions against theories (frequently preposterous) advanced by some modern scholars, tend to be extreme. A book that must be read by any serious student of the subject.

In German, again, more translations of individual *Yashts* are available. We have:

K. F. GELDNER, *Drei Yasht aus dem Zendavesta*, Stuttgart, 1884. This contains *Yashts* 19, 14, and 17, and is still of value.

J. HERTEL, *Die awestische Herrschafts-und Siegesfeuer*, Leipzig, 1931. Contains translations of *Yashts* 18 and 19.

Yashts 14, 16, and 17, Leipzig, 1931.

Die Sonne und Mithra im Awesta, Leipzig, 1931, contains translation of *Yasht* 10.
HERTEL had a mania for identifying almost everything with fire. This idiosyncracy was detrimental to the soundness of his philological judgements.

Also in German there is:

S. WIKANDER, *Vayu*, Uppsala, 1941. This includes a translation of *Yasht* 15. A most useful work.

(3) *Fragments of the Avesta*

(i) *The Aogemadaēchā* has been edited and translated by:

W. GEIGER, Erlangen, 1878.

J. DUCHESNE-GUILLEMIN in *Journal Asiatique*, 1936, pp. 241ff.

S. WIKANDER, *Vayu* (see above).

(ii) *The Nīrangistān* has been edited by:

A. WAAG, Leipzig, 1941.

B. *THE ACHAEMENIAN INSCRIPTIONS*

Earlier editions are now superseded by:

R. G. KENT, *Old Persian*, 2nd ed., Newhaven, 1953.

C. *THE SASSANIAN INSCRIPTIONS*

E. HERZFELD, *Paikuli, Monument and Inscription of the early History of the Sassanian Empire*, 2 vols., Berlin, 1924.

M. SPRENGLING, *Third Century Iran, Sapor and Kartīr*, Chicago, 1953.
Both these books leave much to be desired.

D. *GREEK AND LATIN SOURCES*

These have been collected by:

C. CLEMEN, *Fontes historiae religionis persicae*, Bonn, 1920.

Die griechischen und lateinischen Nachrichten über die persische Religion, Giessen, 1920.

E. *THE PAHLAVI BOOKS*

These have all been edited by Parsee scholars in the original script, and the whole collection of Pahlavi books in Copenhagen (which is almost complete) has been beautifully reproduced in facsimile. It would be superfluous to list the Pahlavi books here, and the reader is therefore referred to my earlier work, *Zurvan, a Zoroastrian Dilemma* (see p. 347), pp. 453–5, for a list of the more important Pahlavi and Parsee-Persian sources.

A more or less complete English translation of the Pahlavi books was made by the great Pahlavi scholar E. W. WEST in the *Sacred Books of the East*, vols. v, xviii, xxiv, xxxvii, and xlvii. Pahlavi, however, remains without a dictionary and many of WEST's translations are completely out of date. This is particularly true of the *Dēnkart* and the works of Mānushchihr.

341

Some reliance can be placed on his translations of the cosmological and eschatological portions of the *Bundahishn* and Zātspram and of the *Mēnōk i Khrat*.
There are fairly reliable translations of various books into different European languages in the following:

B. T. ANKLESARIA, *Zand-î Vohûman Yasn*, Bombay, 1919. This is a heterodox apocalyptic text. English.

E. K. ANTIÂ, *Kârnâmak-i Artakhshîr Pâpakân*, Bombay, 1900. The legendary history of Ardashîr I. English.

F. JUSTI, *Der Bundahesh* . . ., Leipzig, 1868. German.

Ervad M. F. KANGA, *Cītak Handarz i Pōryōtkēšān*, Bombay, 1960. A typical Zoroastrian manual of moral maxims. English.

P. J. de MENASCE, O. P., *Skand-Gumānīk Vicār, la solution décisive des doutes*, Fribourg, 1945. French. Contains valuable introductory notes to the various chapters.

G. MESSINA, S. J., *Abyātkār i Zāmāspik, libro apocalittico persiano*, Rome, 1939. Another apocalyptic text. Italian.

J. C. TAVADIA, *Shāyast nē shāyast: A Pahlavi Text on Religious Customs*, Hamburg, 1930. English.

Quite unreliable are:

S. I. BULSARA, *The Laws of the ancient Persians*, Bombay, 1937. This is a legal rather than a religious text.

P. B. and D. P. SANJANA, *Dīnkard*, 19 vols., Bombay, 1874–1928.

F. *PARSEE-PERSIAN 'TRADITIONS'*

B. N. DHABHAR, *Persian Rivâyats*, Bombay, 1932. An English translation of a large selection of so-called 'traditions' written in New Persian.

G. *THE PRINCIPAL NON-ZOROASTRIAN SOURCES IN TRANSLATION*

Armenian historians: V. LANGLOIS, *Collection des historiens anciens et modernes de l'Arménie*, 2 vols., Paris, 1867–9.

AL-BAGHDĀDĪ: *Moslem Schisms and Sects*, Part I, trs. Kate Chambers SEELYE, New York, 1920. Part II, trs. Abraham H. HALKIN, Tel Aviv, 1933.

AL-BELʿAMĪ: *Chronique de . . . Tabarî, traduite sur la version persane de Belʿamī* par H. ZOTENBERG, 4 vols., Paris, 1867–74.

AL-BĪRŪNĪ: *The Chronology of ancient Nations*, trs. C. E. SACHAU, London, 1879.

FIRDAUSĪ: *Le livre des rois*, trs. J. MOHL., Paris, 1876–8.

AL-MASʿŪDĪ: *Les prairies d'or*, ed. and trs. C. BARBIER de MAYNARD and PAVET de COURTEILLE, 9 vols., Paris, 1861–77.

Le livre de l'avertissement et de la revision, trs. B. CARRA de VAUX, Paris, 1897.

AL-SHAHRISTĀNĪ: *Religionspartheien und Philosophen-Schulen*, trs. Th. HAARBRÜCKER, 2 vols., Halle, 1850–1.

Syrian sources: some relevant passages are collected in BIDEZ-CUMONT, *Les mages hellénisés* (see p. 346).

AL-TABARĪ: *Geschichte der Perser und Araber zur Zeit der Sasaniden*, trs. TH. NÖLDEKE, Leyden, 1879.

II. GENERAL

A. *THE PIONEERING PERIOD*

The birth of Zoroastrian studies in Europe occurred in 1771 when the great French orientalist and traveller, ANQUETIL-DUPERRON, published the Avesta, a copy of which he had brought back with him from his Indian travels. Prior to this momentous event the only serious work published on the Zoroastrian religion which utilized all the sources available at the time was Thomas HYDE's *De vetere religione Persarum*, Oxford, 1700. The publication of the Avesta, the sacred book of the Zoroastrians themselves, however, was to revolutionize the West's appreciation of Zoroaster, so greatly did the contents of the Avesta differ from the accounts of his religion handed down by the classical and Christian writers. The difference was, indeed, so marked that some of the foremost orientalists of the time for long doubted its authenticity.

The first real advance in Avestan studies was made by Martin HAUG who realized that of all the Avesta only the *Gāthās* could be attributed to the Iranian Prophet himself. It was he who, to the immense relief of the Parsees who had come to be a little ashamed of their reputation as dualists, first formulated the thesis that Zoroaster himself was a monotheist in theology though a dualist in philosophy. This vague formulation of the Prophet's theologico-philosophical position for long satisfied all parties.

The big names among Zoroastrian scholars in the latter half of the nineteenth century were Fr. SPIEGEL, James DARMESTETER, C. P. TIELE, F. JUSTI, and W. GEIGER. SPIEGEL, despite the fact that he originated the theory that Hebrew prophecy had influenced Zoroaster—a theory that can no longer be maintained—was an Iranist of the first rank, and his *Eranische Alterthumskunde* (3 vols., Leipzig, 1871–8) can still be consulted with profit. DARMESTETER's monumental translation of the Avesta (see p. 339) is still useful, but his other works have now only an academic interest. TIELE's *De Godsdienst van Zarathustra* (Harlem, 1864), written in Dutch, follows HAUG in his separation of the *Gāthās* from the rest of the Avesta. This book, moreover, set the pattern for almost all books subsequently written on Zoroastrianism, containing, as it does, sections on Iranian religion as it was supposed to have been before the coming of Zoroaster; the teaching of the *Gāthās*, their monotheism and/or dualism; the Bounteous Immortals; the restored pagan deities; demons; creation; the after-life; and the last things. TIELE also includes a section on the liturgy, and most general writers on Zoroastrianism have followed him in this. JUSTI is justly famous as the author of the *Iranisches Namenbuch* (Marburg, 1895) which is still indispensable to the serious student. He also wrote a synthesis of Zoroastrianism in *Preussische Jahrbücher* in 1897.

In his *Age of the Avesta and Zoroaster* W. GEIGER showed more conclusively than had been done before that Zoroaster must have operated in the eastern end of the Iranian lands. He followed his predecessors, however, in rejecting the traditional date of the Prophet and in pushing him back into remote antiquity. His gigantic and indispensable *Grundriss der iranischen Philologie* to which the finest Iranian scholars of the time all contributed, was completed in the year 1904, the very year in which BARTHOLOMAE's dictionary appeared. GEIGER also wrote a monumental two-volume work which appeared in 1885–8, the English translation of which is entitled *Civilization of the Eastern Iranians in ancient Times*, which treats of every aspect of ancient Iranian life.

Meanwhile, ecclesiastical interest in rediscovered Zoroastrianism was not lacking. Already the Belgian Catholic priest C. de HARLEZ, had made his own translation of the Avesta, now no longer consulted, and had written a number of philological and other works, now no longer read. He was followed by the Catholic Bishop of Salford, L. C. CASARTELLI, whose *Philosophy of the Mazdayasniam Religion under the Sassanids* (Bombay, 1889) was unique in its time, and indeed still is, since it had never occurred to any of his contemporaries that the Zoroastrians of Sassanian times might have had a philosophy at all. Owing to the rudimentary state of Pahlavi studies in his time, the book is completely out of date but remains a challenge to Zoroastrian scholars of the future to write the authoritative work CASARTELLI might have written had he been alive today. Beside CASARTELLI's brave attempt the works of the Swedish Lutheran Bishop L. O. N. SÖDERBLOM, *Les fravashis* (Paris, 1899) and *La vie future d'après le mazdéisme* (Paris, 1901) are insignificant.

Such, then, in broad outline, were the achievements of the pioneers who worked without an established text of the Avesta and without a dictionary. With the publication of both, Avestan studies entered into their modern phase.

In Old Persian epigraphical studies the decisive years were earlier, for it was in 1835 that Sir Henry RAWLINSON made the first squeezes of Darius' great inscription at Bisitūn, and in 1847 that he published for the first time text and commentary. Editions rapidly succeeded each other and there are now few philological problems left to solve. In Pahlavi, however, WEST was the first and, apparently, the last scholar to devote his life to the study of it. This neglect of Pahlavi and the bland assurance with which Avestan scholars make use of the Pahlavi sources without bothering to compile their own word-index, has led to a totally lop-sided view of Zoroastrianism as a whole.

B. *THE MODERN PERIOD*

(1) *The Avesta and the Achaemenian Era*

With the publication of BARTHOLOMAE's dictionary which made it possible for scholars to dispense with the disagreeable task of doing their own spade-work, books on Zoroastrianism multiplied. These can best be divided into general works and those on specialized aspects of the subject.

The general works may be divided into the 'orthodox' school which follows in the main GELDNER and BARTHOLOMAE and the unorthodox with radically different views. The orthodox school was not seriously challenged in the first quarter of the twentieth century except by G. HÜSING, who saw the moon and certain animals almost everywhere, and J. HERTEL whose peculiar fetish was fire. The major works of these scholars who have found no followers are:

J. HERTEL, *Indo-Iranische Quellen und Forschungen*, I-IX, Leipzig, 1924-7.

G. HÜSING, *Die iranische Uberlieferung und das arische System*, Leipzig, 1909.

Der Mazdahismus, Vienna, 1935.

The views of the 'orthodox' may be summed up in the following way: Zoroaster was a prophet who claimed to hold colloquy with God: as Prophet he was also a reformer. The religion of the society into which he was born was similar to that of the *Rig-Veda* in India, and this society's essentially polytheistic religion reappears in barely disguised form in the later Avesta. To this form of religion belong the Haoma cult, animal sacrifice, etc. The essential features of Zoroaster's reform were (*a*) the belief in one God, Ahura Mazdāh, (*b*) the irreconcilable antagonism of good and evil, called Truth and the Lie or, in more personalized form, the Holy Spirit and the Evil Spirit, (*c*) the association of entities whose names are all abstract conceptions with the one God (Truth, the Good Mind, etc.), and (*d*) the affirmation of the freedom of man's will and his obligation to choose between Truth and the Lie. In addition, Zoroastrianism rapidly fell under the domination of the Magi in the west. Owing to the conflicting evidence about the Magi the 'orthodox' disagree about them more than about anything else.

The books listed below all follow the orthodox line to a greater or lesser extent.

C. BARTHOLOMAE, *Zarathustra's Leben und Lehre*, Heidelberg, 1924. Essential reading as it gives the great philologian's mature view.

A. CHRISTENSEN, *Die Iranier*, Munich, 1933. A good short introduction.

M.N. DHALLA, *Zoroastrian Civilization*, New York, 1922.

History of Zoroastrianism, New York, 1938. Probably the best work by a Parsee on his own religion. Stresses the Parsee view that their Prophet's religion was an 'ethical monotheism'. There is a section on the Sassanian period, as usual inadequate, and an interesting finale on the theological squabbles among the still religiously minded Parsees of the thirties. The book is an expansion of an earlier work, *Zoroastrian Theology from the earliest Times to the present Day*, New York, 1914.

A. V. W. JACKSON, *Zoroastrian Studies*, New York, 1928. A cautious and unexciting book. Part II on free will is well worth reading.

H. LOMMEL, *Die Religion Zarathustra's nach dem Awesta dargestellt*, Tübingen, 1930. Probably the best book on the Avesta to date. Cautious and scholarly but rather heavy going.

R. P. MASANI, *The Religion of the Good Life*, London, 1938. A short and popular exposition seen from the point of view of a modern Parsee.

J. H. MOULTON, *Early Zoroastrianism*, London, 1913. Probably the best book on the subject in English. As a corrective to his extreme views on the Magi, MESSINA's *Ursprung der Magier* (see p. 346) should be read.

The Treasure of the Magi, Oxford, 1917. Goes over the same ground from a missionary's point of view.

R. PETTAZZONI, *La religione di Zarathustra*, Rome, 1920. The standard work in Italian. Pettazzoni here adheres to SPIEGEL's untenable theory that Judaism influenced Zoroaster.

O. G. von WESENDONK, *Das Weltbild der Iranier*, Munich, 1933. An excellent semi-popular work all too little known. Should be read before LOMMEL.

Two books have appeared in the last thirty years which have evoked considerable controversy, so widely do they diverge from the orthodox view of Zoroastrianism. These are:

E. E. HERZFELD, *Zoroaster and his World*, Princeton, 1947. This book which has been described as 'little more than a learned novel', has been greeted (if that is the right word) on the whole with ridicule, sometimes with contempt, sometimes with righteous indignation. It has done great harm, in that nineteenth-century theories that have long since been abandoned are again revived by an archaeologist of very considerable repute and thus find their way into the work of the unsuspecting non-specialist. To these antiquated theories HERZFELD adds fantasies of his own more outrageous far than those he revives. The final answer to this kind of nonsense has been given by HENNING in his *Zoroaster* (see Appendix).

H. S. NYBERG, *Die Religionen des alten Iran* (German translation from the Swedish), Leipzig, 1938. This also falls into the historical novel class. Zoroaster has become a witch-doctor and NYBERG himself the prophet. Unlike HERZFELD, NYBERG originally found disciples among his own Swedish pupils who, however, now seem to be turning their backs on the embarrassing heritage. Among these the best known is:

G. WIDENGREN whose *Hochgottglaube im alten Iran*, Uppsala, 1938, sees 'high gods' everywhere. WIDENGREN does not follow NYBERG in his more extravagant excesses.

The perfect refutation of both HERZFELD and NYBERG is contained in:

W. B. HENNING, *Zoroaster, Politician or Witch-doctor?*, Oxford, 1951. HENNING exposes the essentially unscholarly methods employed by both HERZFELD and NYBERG, and it is with the greatest pleasure that I reprint the relevant passage as an appendix to this book. It was a timely and necessary blow in defence of sanity and of intellectual honesty with oneself. In addition it establishes beyond reasonable doubt the soundness of the traditional date of Zoroaster as well as the fact that he operated in eastern Iran.

The following are specialized monographs concerned mainly with the *Gāthās*:

J. DUCHESNE-GUILLEMIN, *Zoroastre*, Paris, 1948. Contains chapters on Indo-Iranian religion and a translation of the *Gāthās*. In his interpretation of the 'Bounteous Immortals' he follows DUMÉZIL (below).

A. MEILLET, *Trois conférences sur les Gāthās de l'Avesta*, Paris, 1925. Insists overmuch on the social character of Zoroaster's reform.

O. G. von WESENDONK, *Das Wesen der Lehre Zarathuštrōs*, Leipzig, 1927. Criticizes MEILLET's extreme views and vindicates the originality of Zoroaster.

On the legendary life of Zoroaster found in the Pahlavi books there is:

A. V. W. JACKSON, *Zoroaster, the Prophet of ancient Iran*, New York, 1899.

345

One or two monographs have been devoted specifically to the *Amesha Spentas* or 'Bounteous Immortals'. These include:

G. Dumézil, *Naissance d'archanges*, Abbeville, 1945. Dumézil's thesis is that all Indo-European mythology reflects a threefold division of society into the ruling class (*fonction souveraine*), the warrior class, and the mass of the peasantry. This theory he applies to the 'Bounteous Immortals'. His principal disciple in Iranian studies is Duchesne-Guillemin. Dumézil has been under heavy and constant fire from specialists in all fields of Indo-European studies, but he remains unmoved.

B. Geiger, *Die Aməša Spəntas*, Vienna, 1916. Sums up the theories about the Bounteous Immortals advanced up to his time.

The following monographs have appeared on various aspects of the later Avesta:

E. Benveniste, *The Persian Religion according to the chief Greek Texts*, Paris, 1929. Sceptical to a fault.

E. Benveniste and L. Renou, *Vrtra and Vrθragna*, Paris, 1934. A largely philological study on the god Verethraghna.

A. Christensen, *Les types du premier homme et du premier roi dans l'histoire légendaire des Iraniens*, 2 vols., Leyden/Uppsala, 1917–34. An excellent monograph. Contains an exhaustive treatment of the Yima legends.

 Études sur le zoroastrisme de la Perse antique, Copenhagen, 1928. Mainly concerned with the chronology of the *Yashts*.

 Les Kayanides, Copenhagen, 1932. On the legendary kings of the Avesta.

 Essai sur la démonologie iranienne, Copenhagen, 1941.

 Le premier chapitre du Vendidad et l'histoire primitive des tribus iraniennes, Copenhagen, 1943.

 Les gestes des rois dans les traditions de l'Iran antique, Paris, 1936.

G. Dumézil, *Le troisième souverain . . .*, Paris, 1949. Essay on the god Airyaman.

L. H. Gray, *The Foundations of the Iranian Religions*, Bombay, 1930. An exhaustive catalogue of the Avestan deities, demons, etc. A very useful reference-book.

S. H. Taqizadeh, *Old Iranian Calendars*, London, 1938. A carefully argued analysis of the data which justifies the traditional date of Zoroaster. This view is now generally accepted.

P. Thieme, *Mitra and Aryaman*, New Haven, 1957. An angry refutation of Dumézil's *Le troisième souverain*.

S. Wikander, *Der arische Männerbund*, Lund, 1938. Highly speculative.

 Vayu, Uppsala, 1941. On the god Vayu.

 Feuerpriester in Kleinasien und Iran, Lund, 1946. Speculative.

On the Magi there are two excellent monographs:

J. Bidez and F. Cumont, *Les mages hellénisés*, 2 vols., Paris, 1938. An exhaustive and excellent treatment of the Magi in the west.

G. Messina, S.J., *Die Ursprung der Magier und die Zarathuštrische Religion*, Rome, 1930. Corrects the excesses of Moulton.

(2) *The Sassanian Period*

Most of the general works mentioned above have a section (almost always inadequate) on the Sassanian period. The only full study of the period itself is:

A. Christensen, *L'Iran sous les Sassanides*, 2nd ed., Copenhagen, 1944. Supersedes the earlier *L'empire des Sassanides*. Indispensable to students of Sassanian Persia.

On Sassanian religion the following monographs have appeared:

H. W. Bailey, *Zoroastrian Problems in the Ninth Century Books*, Oxford, 1943. Indispensable to the specialist. The chapters on the *khwarenah* and the dating of the Avesta are particularly important.

U. BIANCHI, *Zamān i Ōhrmazd, Lo Zoroastrismo nelle sui origini e nella sua essenza*, Turin, 1958. A balanced criticism of ZAEHNER and the 'Swedish school'.

S. S. HARTMAN, *Gayōmart, étude sur le syncrétisme dans l'ancien Iran*, Uppsala, 1953. Very specialized and wholly unconvincing.

H. JUNKER, *Uber iranische Quellen der hellenistischen Aion-Vorstellung*, Leipzig, 1923. Quite out of date.

L. MARIÈS, *Le de Deo d'Eznik de Kolb*, Paris, 1924–5. A study on the sources of the Zurvanite myth.

J. P. de MENASCE, O.P., *Une encyclopédie mazdéenne, le Dēnkart*, Paris, 1958. A summary of the contents of the third book of the *Dēnkart*.

H. S. NYBERG, 'Questions de cosmogonie et de cosmologie mazdéennes' in *Journal Asiatique*, 1929, 1931. An admirable exposition of a difficult subject, but largely superseded by ZAEHNER, *Zurvan, A Zoroastrian Dilemma*.

J. D. C. PAVRY, *The Zoroastrian Doctrine of the future Life*, New York, 1929.

I. SCHEFTELOWITZ, *Die Zeit als Schicksalsgottheit in der indischen und iranischen Religion*, Stuttgart, 1929. Useful.

R. C. ZAEHNER, *Zurvan, A Zoroastrian Dilemma*, Oxford, 1955. An exhaustive treatment of the whole Zurvanite question. Reproduces in translation almost all the available evidence.

The Teachings of the Magi, A Compendium of Zoroastrian Beliefs, London, 1956.

On the Mazdakite heresy we have:

A. CHRISTENSEN, *Le règne de Kawadh I et le communisme mazdakite*, Copenhagen, 1925.

O. KLIMA, *Mazdak, Geschichte einer sozialen Bewegung im Sassanidischen Persien*, Prague, 1957.

There are a number of books on the supposed relationship of Zoroastrianism to Judaism, Platonism, and Gnosticism, all of them highly speculative. Among these are:

E. BÖKLEN, *Die Verwandtschaft der jüdisch-christlichen mit der persischen Eschatologie*, Göttingen, 1902.

J. DUCHESNE-GUILLEMIN, *Ormazd et Ahriman*, Paris, 1953. A short general work much influenced by DUMÉZIL. Chapters on supposed Zoroastrian influence on Gnosticism and Judaism.

W. KOSTER, *Le mythe de Platon, de Zarathustra et des chaldéens*, Leyden, 1951.

L. H. MILLS, *Zoroaster, Philo and Israel*, Leipzig, 1903.

Zarathuštra, Philo, the Achaemenids and Israel, Leipzig, 1906.

R. REITZENSTEIN, *Das iranische Erlösungsmysterium*, Bonn, 1921. The Iranian *Erlösungsmysterium* is largely REITZENSTEIN's invention.

R. REITZENSTEIN and H. H. SCHAEDER, *Studien zum antiken Synkretismus aus Iran und Griechenland*, Leipzig, 1926.

H. H. SCHAEDER, *Iranische Beiträge I*, Halle, 1930. A miscellany.

I. SCHEFTELOWITZ, *Die altpersische Religion und das Judentum*, Giessen, 1920.

E. STAVE, *Uber den Einfluss des Parsismus auf das Judentum*, Harlem, 1898.

O. G. von WESENDONK, *Urmensch und Seele in der iranischen Uberlieferung*, Hanover, 1924. A much needed criticism of REITZENSTEIN who saw Iranian influence everywhere.

On fatalism in the Epic there is:

H. K. V. RINGGREN, *Fatalism in the Persian Epics*, Uppsala, 1952.

On Mithraism we have:

C. AUTRUN, *Mithra, Zoroastre et le préhistoire aryenne du christianisme*, Paris, 1935.

F. CUMONT, *Textes et monuments figurés relatifs aux mystères de Mithra*, 2 vols., Brussels, 1894–6. A magnificent work of scholarship and absolutely indispensable to any student of

347

Mithraism. Its only defect is that on the Iranian side CUMONT had to rely on inadequate translations.

   Les mystères de Mithra, 3rd ed., Brussels, 1913. This is drawn entirely from the text of the larger work.

   The Mysteries of Mithra, London, 1903. English translation of the first edition of the foregoing.

 M. J. VERMASEREN, *De Mithrasdienst in Rome*, Nijmegen, 1951. Adds nothing to CUMONT.

   Corpus inscriptionum et monumentorum religionis mithriacae, The Hague, 1956. There are too many inaccuracies.

 On the modern Parsees we have:

 D. K. KARAKA, *History of the Parsis*, 2 vols., London, 1884.

 J. J. MODI, *The religious Ceremonies and Customs of the Parsees*, 2nd ed., Bombay, 1937. Indispensable for students of Zoroastrian ritual.

APPENDIX

Professor W. B. Henning's critique of the work of E. E. Herzfeld and H. S. Nyberg, from his *Zoroaster, Politician or Witch-doctor?*, Oxford, 1951.

'Any discussion of Professor Nyberg's theories is bound to have constant regard to the latest and—regrettably—last work published by Professor Herzfeld in 1947, a few months before his death, which we lament as the greatest blow to Iranian Studies in recent years. Herzfeld's work, *Zoroaster and his World*, has been aptly described by a friend of mine as "an 800-page review of Nyberg's book"; indeed, Herzfeld has discussed and criticized, and at great length, almost every word that Nyberg had written. As I am often in agreement with Herzfeld's views, as far as his criticism of Nyberg's theories goes, my task has been eased considerably; for most of what I proposed to say on this subject has now already been said by Herzfeld, probably much better than I could do it. However, Herzfeld's work is by no means confined to mere criticism. His main object was to state and restate his own theories on Zoroaster, to which he had devoted a great deal of his writing in the last twenty years: he restates opinions he had held for a long time, he elaborates them, he fortifies them by fresh argument, and at the same time he criticizes Nyberg, as indeed Nyberg, on his part, had criticized him in his own book. A controversy between these two scholars was natural and inevitable; for their disagreement on everything that concerns Zoroaster is complete.

'Herzfeld's Zoroaster was a man who lived his life in the full light of history, in the time of Cyrus and Darius. By birth and by marriage, he was himself a member of the two royal houses that dominated the history of Ancient Iran, of the Median dynasty and of its successor, the Persian house of the Achaemenides. Astyages, the last of the Median kings, whom Cyrus deposed, was Zoroaster's grandfather. After Cyrus had gained his great victory, he married Zoroaster's mother. Cyrus' daughter, Atossa, was therefore half-sister to Zoroaster. Atossa married Cambyses, Cyrus' son and successor, and after the early death of Cambyses she married his successor, the Great King Darius. Through Atossa, therefore, Zoroaster was brother-in-law to both Cambyses and Darius.

'Herzfeld's Zoroaster was primarily a politician. He soon got into difficulties with the government authorities—not because (as we might perhaps expect) he had claims to the throne himself; for as a grandson of Astyages he might have planned the removal of Cyrus or Cambyses, he might have plotted for the restoration of the Median royal house, of which he himself was the chief; but such considerations do not seem to have entered his head. His sole interest, as politician, was to improve the situation of agricultural labour in Media, or, to use Herzfeld's own words, he wanted "to

349

replace serfdom by the voluntary, sworn-to obedience of the vassal".[1] In pursuit of this aim he got into conflict with the ruling classes, the great land-owners, noblemen, and priests. He was indicted as a revolutionary in Raγā, his home-town, and brought before a court presided over by none other than Gaumāta the Magian, who later usurped the kingship and was murdered by Darius. Gaumāta condemned him to banishment, and Cambyses, at that time Viceroy of Media—for all this happened still during the lifetime of Cyrus—confirmed the judgement.[2] Zoroaster was extremely indignant at the treatment he had suffered, most of all with Cambyses who, as his step-brother, should, by ancient right, have upheld him.

'Now comes that memorable journey into exile to which Herzfeld has devoted so much labour, the journey along the post-road from Raγā to Tūs with the now famous halt at Qūmis where a certain Persian gentleman refused to let him stay in his castle as a refugee. In each of his recent books Herzfeld has added fresh details to this story: now everything has become clear, except the one point whether the coach in which Zoroaster travelled was his own or one hired from a friend.[3]

'For the whole fascinating tale, Gaumāta's court, Cambyses' failure to revise the judgement, Raγā, Qūmis, Tūs—for all this Herzfeld has discovered clear evidence in Zoroaster's own poems, the Gāthās, which in this matter are his sole source. All previous students, and there have been many, have failed to find any reference to any such event in the Gāthās, or for that matter anywhere else.

'At Tūs Zoroaster found favour with the there residing satrap of Parthia, Vištāspa, the father of Darius who was destined to become the King of Kings of Persia after the death of Cambyses. At Vištāspa's court important positions were held by two brothers, Jāmāspa and Frašauštra, members of a leading Persian family. Zoroaster thought it wise to strengthen his position by allying himself to this family, and so added a daughter of Frašauštra's to his harem. His newly acquired relatives did all they could to reverse the judgement of banishment which Cambyses had so naughtily confirmed: both Jāmāspa and Frašauštra travelled from Tūs to the far-distant court of the Great King Cyrus himself to intercede on his behalf.[4] Cyrus, who after all was Zoroaster's stepfather, could well be expected to stretch out a helping hand to the fugitive. But all was in vain: Zoroaster had to remain at Tūs, cut off from the centres of the Persian Empire, cut off from the chance of indulging in political intrigues, his favourite occupation. All he could do, and did do, was to compose a few more verses cursing Cambyses and his bosom friend Gaumāta.

'After Cyrus died and Cambyses succeeded to the throne, Zoroaster's prospects of re-establishing himself in the rank to which he was born seemed to disappear altogether. However, fate smiled on him again: soon he could

---

[1] Herzfeld, Zoroaster and his World, i. 349; cf. ibid. 199.
[2] Cf. ibid. 202.   [3] Cf. ibid. 186.
[4] Cf. Herzfeld, op. cit. i. 203.

rejoice at the news of the sudden death of Cambyses, and soon he could arrange, behind the scenes, for the murder of his bitterest enemy, Gaumāta the Magian.

'The story of Cambyses, his misdeeds and his misfortunes, how he had his younger brother Bardiya secretly killed, how during his absence from Persia Gaumāta the Magian usurped the throne pretending to be Bardiya, how Cambyses died when he hurriedly returned from Egypt, how the impersonation of Bardiya by Gaumāta was discovered, and how seven noble Persians, Darius among them, murdered Gaumāta and proclaimed Darius as King of Kings—the story is too well known to bear repetition. Here we are concerned solely with the role that Zoroaster is said to have played in the matter.

'The man to whom Cambyses had entrusted the task of killing his brother was, according to Herodotus, Prexaspes, a noble Persian. This Prexaspes, we learn from Herzfeld, was the brother of Jāmāspa and Frašauštra, an uncle, therefore, of one of Zoroaster's wives. Herodotus makes it clear that Prexaspes kept his secret carefully enough; his life would have been forfeit had it become known that he had slain the heir-apparent to the throne. However that be, thanks to Herzfeld we know now that Prexaspes could not, after all, keep the secret from his brothers. He might as well have told everybody; for his brother Frašauštra, of course, told his daughter, and his daughter told her husband, Zoroaster, and Zoroaster gleefully told the world. And when the news of the death of Cambyses had reached Tūs, he saw at last how he could revenge himself on Gaumāta. He composed a few more stirring verses to incite his listeners to the murder of the usurper;[1] one at least among them, Darius the son of Vištāspa, hung on his lips and hastened away to do the deed to which Zoroaster had inspired him.

'It is a matter for regret that when Darius, after his success, set up an inscription to commemorate these events and enumerated the names of his helpers in it, he did not so much as mention the name of Zoroaster to whose advice he was so greatly indebted. Those who disputed Herzfeld's theories inevitably pointed out that the omission of Zoroaster's name was significant. However, this point has been cleared up now: it was at Zoroaster's own suggestion that his part in the affair was not mentioned: *he wished to work in the dark*. Here we have the picture of two men who conspire to hide the truth, but who, in their speeches and writings, almost monotonously, enjoin the speaking of Truth as the chief duty of Man, who never cease condemning all lies and liars, all deceit and hypocrisy. And one of these two cunning and hypocritical intriguers was the man whom the Persians, mistakenly it seems, regarded as their prophet for many centuries.

'So much for Herzfeld's Zoroaster. Nyberg's Zoroaster is a very different kind of person. He lived somewhere in the region of Oxus and Jaxartes, beyond the countries that had come into contact with the civilized states of Babylonia and Mesopotamia, in a nation that had no history. He was a

---

[1] Cf. ibid. i. 202.

prehistoric man. While Herzfeld gives us precise dates for almost every event of Zoroaster's life, Nyberg declares that the question of Zoroaster's date is altogether unessential and without interest.[1]

'In his tribe Zoroaster held the hereditary office of witch-doctor or medicine-man. He faithfully fulfilled the duties that were attached to this position among the savage tribes of Inner-Asia before they were subdued and civilized by the Persian Empire. Their religion can be best described as a form of shamanism; its chief points are two, both of equal importance: the ordeal and the Maga. The tribal mythology, theology, and all rites derive from ordeal and Maga; they are their functions. The ordeal, the divine judgement here carried out by pouring molten metal on the litigants, is self-explanatory; it was administered by a college of Fellows of the Ordeal, presided over by Zoroaster as medicine-man and shaman-in-chief.

'It is less easy to explain the purport of the Maga. Secondarily, the Maga is an enclosure within which the sacred rites are performed; primarily it is a term for "magic singing", and as a collective, "a group of people engaging in magic songs". Within the Maga the members of the tribe who were admitted to the sacred community met from time to time to perform certain acts that aimed at reaching a state of ecstasy. The chief means employed to this end were singing and probably dancing, hence the curious name. Quicker results were reached by the application of steam and hemp (the question whether Zoroaster used hemp for such purposes will be discussed later).

'As soon as the participants in these ceremonies had fallen into a trance, they began to shout incomprehensible words and syllables; but presently they fell into a complete coma. In this state they imagined themselves to reach a mystical union with God, or rather with Vohu Manah. Their souls, released by trance from the body, rose up to the higher regions to join with other souls who had been freed either in the same way or by death; there is no real difference between these two groups: as we might say "sleep is the brother of death" the shamanists would have said "trance is the brother of death". Vohu Manah is the collective of the Free-souls, or the cosmic, divine Free-soul.

'To reach a trance or coma was regarded as the greatest boon; to be excluded from the fellowship of the Maga a terrible misfortune. It is clear that in a given tribe the leading shaman must have exercised great influence; for beside presiding over the ceremonies connected with the ordeal he was the chief of the Maga and as such determined who was to be admitted to the supreme happiness the Maga alone could bestow.

'We also begin to understand now why the Gāthās, the poems by Zoroaster which his community so faithfully transmitted through the centuries, have presented so great difficulties to the scholars who have hitherto tried to fathom their meaning. If the Gāthās are crazy mutterings shouted by a senseless man in a hemp-induced stupor, it is pointless to seek much meaning

---

[1] Cf. Nyberg, *Die Religionen des alten Iran*, p. 45.

in them. It was also rather pointless that those who—mistakenly—believed themselves to be following in the footsteps of Zoroaster should have taken so much trouble to preserve what turns out to be gibberish. As to the scholars who in modern times studied the Gāthās without finding the true key to them, the less we say about their inept attempts the better.

'We now come to an intricate problem: the religious development which Zoroaster underwent. To understand Nyberg's position, it is necessary to make a few general remarks. One of the chief problems that confront the student of the Zoroastrian religion is the relation to each other of several types of religious belief that appear to have coalesced in Zoroastrianism (I am using this term only of the later form of religion). As a rule it is assumed that there were two, or at the most three, religions involved; we can pass by those extremists who operate with larger numbers, in some cases far larger numbers.

'The most important form of religion involved is that represented by Zoroaster himself; he may have originated it; or he may have inherited it; or he may have inherited it in part and added to it on his own. The chief points in Zoroaster's religion are these: belief in one God whose name is Ahura Mazdāh; belief in an anti-divine force led by Angra Mainyu, the "Evil Spirit"; the belief that the acts of mankind exercised great influence on the outcome of the incessant struggle between God and the Evil Spirit, resulting in the attribution to Man of a unique position as the arbiter between Good and Evil; and finally, the association with God of a number of so-called Aməša Spəntas, on whose function scholars always have disagreed and probably always will disagree; some regard them as aspects of God (that is also my view); according to Nyberg they are social collectives representing the Tribe in its various aspects.

'The second chief ingredient in Zoroastrianism is the comparatively primitive polytheism which the Iranians had inherited from the remote past, from the time when their forbears were still in contact with the tribes, later known as Indo-Aryans, that immigrated into India. This primitive religion existed before and after Zoroaster; it still flourished centuries after the destruction of the Persian Empire by Alexander. There were many gods and goddesses: Mithra, Anāhita, Vərəthraɣna, Tištrya, and so on; there were animal sacrifices on a lavish scale; an intoxicating drink, Haoma, the Indian Soma, played an important role in the sacrificial ceremonies. No doubt this religion assumed different forms in the different provinces at different times; the points of divergence have been stressed, in my view exaggerated, by several students; they need not concern us here.

'The third form of religion involved is one about which we know very little, the religion of the Magi. It seems to have exhausted itself in a narrow-minded ritual; purification rites, particularly in connexion with dead bodies, characterize it. Some regard Magism as a remnant of the autochthonous religion which the Iranians found existing in Media and elsewhere when they entered the country as conquerors, and which they gradually absorbed.

'Now it is evident that there is a great gulf between the primitive poly-theism and the religion represented by Zoroaster. Indeed—on this point there is unanimity—Zoroaster attacks the polytheists in his poems, and does it in terms that leave us in no doubt about his views. Nevertheless, in the Zoroastrianism we find the polytheism inextricably mixed with Zoroaster's own religion. And the merging of the two forms, which apparently also swallowed up the third, must have taken place at a fairly early date, by 400 BC at the very latest. How did it come about that these two incompatibles combined in a harmonious association which was solid enough to endure until the present day? To find a satisfactory answer to this question is one of the chief tasks before the students of Zoroastrianism. The answer usually given is that the merger was due to the integration of the Iranian provinces that was brought about by the Persian Empire; that it was deliberately encouraged or promoted by the Persian government.

'These few observations will be sufficient, I hope, to indicate the nature of the problem by which we are confronted, so that I can now proceed to explain the solution at which Professor Nyberg has arrived. According to Nyberg, the religion which, together with the medicinemanship, Zoroaster had inherited from his forefathers, resembled the later Zervanism in certain points, especially in its theology in the narrow sense: Ahura Mazdāh here occupies the position which Zervan, the god of Time, held in Zervanism. Ahura Mazdāh is a *Deus otiosus*: he has set the world in motion, but now keeps aloof from it; its management is left to two contrasting and contending powers, the Good Spirit and the Evil Spirit. In Zervanism Zervan creates Ahura Mazdāh and the Evil Spirit and then takes no further part in the affairs of the world. In his aloofness Zoroaster's Ahura Mazdāh, as seen by Nyberg, reminds one of the shadowy gods of Gnostic systems, who are known as "The Nameless God" or "The Stranger".

'This is the central point in the religion into which Zoroaster was born. He would no doubt have transmitted it unchanged to succeeding generations, had not exterior events compelled him to search his heart and reformulate his creed. The event that produced a revolution in his mind was missionary activity by primitive polytheists, by that group which put the God Mithra into the foreground. The propagandists of Mithraism, with their animal sacrifices and nocturnal haoma orgies, exercised an unholy fascination upon the simple, unsophisticated members of Zoroaster's community. The number of those who attended the Maga to spend their days in a peaceful coma grew less and less; the situation worsened from day to day. Zoroaster held stoutly to his ancient religion at the beginning, but soon his mind was affected by doubts. This is the "great crisis" in his life.

'In his perplexity he turned to his God: Ahura Mazdāh heard his prayer: he received a revelation. In a vision he saw that his earlier theology had been wrong: Ahura Mazdāh, in truth, was not the God who keeps aloof from the world, the God that had created both the Good and the Evil Spirits. No, Ahura Mazdāh was an active God, who guided the good, who was ever ready to stretch out a helping hand to those who fought for Truth. He had not created the Evil Spirit: the Evil Spirit was independent, hostile to him and all his creatures, equal or almost equal in power. In short, while he had been a Zervanist before, Zoroaster now became a strict Dualist, the author of that dualism that has characterized Zoroastrianism through the ages.

'Armed with his new theology Zoroaster turned to the attack. However, while he had been able to do very little against the lusty Mithraists before, his sudden change of front did not improve matters. One can easily imagine that the few faithful friends that were ready to stand by him now despaired and turned away. At any rate he had to leave his tribe, reviled by his enemies, abandoned by his friends. The great crisis in Zoroaster's life—if I may use words I used once before—can be summed up in four words: alcohol prevailed over hemp.

'He found refuge in another tribe whose chief, one Vištāspa, welcomed him with open arms. Geographically, his move was from the Oxus to the Jaxartes—we had seen that in Herzfeld's view the journey was from Raγā to Tūs. Vištāspa's tribe had originally observed religious customs similar to those current in Zoroaster's home country. Yet some time before Zoroaster's arrival this tribe, too, had become converted to Mithraism. Nevertheless, Vištāspa's tribe proves more receptive than his own to Zoroaster's persuasive words, and Vištāspa himself soon experiences the happiness of ecstasy on the newly established Maga. However, there is a considerable change in Zoroaster's attitude. He no longer fulminates against the wicked Mithraists. His earlier lack of success has made him more cautious in his dealings with them. He is ready to compromise. We might say: he has become a realist. He begins to make advances to the Mithraists, he uses bits of their terminology, he makes little concessions here and there. It was only by proceeding in this worldly-wise fashion that he succeeded in establishing himself in Vištāspa's tribe at all. And, fortunately for him, his new friends were still lukewarm in their Mithraism, were equally ready to make compromises. They accepted Zoroaster as their spiritual leader, they accepted Ahura Mazdāh, the dualism, the Aməša Spəntas, the Maga and all that went with it. And Zoroaster accepted Mithra and Anāhita and other constituents of Mithraism in its local form. He even admitted the haoma against which he had inveighed shortly before; but to relieve his conscience, he insisted on a radical change in the ingredients: in future haoma was to consist chiefly of water, milk, and plant-juice.

'Thus Zoroaster, none other, became the founder of the composite Zoroastrianism, which other students attribute to later development. How far Zoroaster went in absorbing Mithraist elements is not very clear from Nyberg's book. At any rate, *he* began that process of uniting and combining which was continued after him by his disciples.

'In concluding this brief description of Nyberg's theories I hope I have given a fairly accurate idea of the chief points in which he differs from earlier interpreters of Zoroaster. My description is necessarily selective, and the selection is in some respects coloured by personal views; others may regard other matters as of greater importance.[1] The points I have stressed are those on which I shall make a few remarks in these lectures.

'Any student who contemplates the figures of Zoroaster drawn by Herzfeld on the one hand, by Nyberg on the other, will be filled with perplexity. How is it possible, one is bound to ask, that two scholars of renown who work with precisely the same material, use exactly the same sources, arrive at results that are diametrically opposed to each other? Here is Herzfeld's Zoroaster: a backstairs politician, an exiled nobleman who goes to the races when not engaged in malicious gossip. There is Nyberg's Zoroaster: a prehistoric man, a drunken witch-doctor muttering gibberish on his ludicrous Maga. There is comfort in the thought that if the one is right the other must be absurdly wrong; there is no middle way. There is more comfort in the possibility that both may be wrong.

'It must be borne in mind that the theories advanced by Herzfeld and Nyberg are in opposition not only to each other, but also to the common opinion on Zoroaster, the opinion gradually developed by scholars during the last one hundred and fifty years. At least I think it is permissible to talk of a common opinion; for even though there was always a great deal of divergence of views, nevertheless, there had emerged commonly accepted notions on many essential points. One hesitates to abandon this common opinion in favour of theories that are as strongly contested as Nyberg's and Herzfeld's are. At the beginning of this lecture I pointed out that Nyberg had strongly criticized Herzfeld's ideas, and Herzfeld even more strongly Nyberg's views. It is noteworthy and significant that their mutual criticism carries conviction nearly throughout, while the exposition of the views they favour leaves the student filled with doubt and misgiving.

'Although at first glance the theories presented by Nyberg and Herzfeld appear to be in contrast with each other, when one looks deeper one finds that nevertheless there are certain features in which they share. It is perhaps not accidental that the points that are common to them are also those that provoke the liveliest objection; the remainder of this lecture will be devoted to their enumeration.

'Firstly, as I mentioned just now, they are at one in the dim view they take of the labours of their predecessors in Zoroastrian studies. Their attitude oscillates between the patronizing and the downright contemptuous. For example, Nyberg sums up the common opinion on Zoroaster in these words:[2] *the picture of a progressive country parson with an interest in agrarian reforms*—nicely formulated but scarcely an accurate description.

'Secondly, both authors are certain in their minds that they have understood Zoroaster correctly, and tell us so frequently. It is pleasant to find this conviction in the midst of a maze of uncertainty. They would probably

---

[1] I pass by in silence such interesting matters as the 'Begiessung' of the pastures with cow urine (Nyberg, op. cit., pp. 198 sqq.), an activity which the followers of Zoroaster, to believe Nyberg, apparently considered necessary and desirable.

[2] Nyberg, op. cit., p. 202.

regard it as more accurate to describe their opinions as plain facts than as hypotheses.

'*Thirdly, both scholars have built their theories largely on the re-interpretation of words and to some extent on the emendation of passages in the Avesta.*[1] The second feature, emendation, is not so prominent in Nyberg's work, but very much so in Herzfeld's writings. Indeed, Herzfeld, when dealing with obscure passages, was fond of declaring: this line *must* mean so-and-so; therefore, it does mean so-and-so; if grammar does not agree with it, well, so much the worse for grammar.

'*Of far greater importance is the re-interpretation of words. Inevitably, there is a large number of words in the Avesta whose meanings are unknown, and a further large number whose meanings are imperfectly known; and such unknown or imperfectly known words are particularly numerous in the Gāthās. Then there are the words whose meaning is not in doubt; but even they, as all words, have a certain range of meaning, and from that range one can select an eccentric meaning. Now if one attributes an entirely arbitrary set of meanings to the unknown words, in such a way that this set of meanings is consistent within itself and conforms to a preconceived notion of the contents of the Gāthās, and if one proceeds to select suitable extreme meanings for the known words, one can translate the Gāthās (or for that matter any ancient text that carries a sufficient number of unknown words) in any way one likes; one can turn them into a philosophical treatise or a political note-book, a lawgiver's code or a soothsayer's utterance. Take a word that properly means "house" or "dwelling": one can say "in the Gāthās this word always designates the residence of the royal family", or one can say "in the Gāthās this word regularly denotes the felt-hut in which the shaman enters into a coma", and so on, and by translating accordingly one can give the sense of these ancient verses a twist in any direction one may have in mind.*[1]

'This "method" was first introduced into this subject by Hertel. He noticed what everybody else had noticed before him, namely, that the ancient Iranians had the highest regard for Fire and Light. Proceeding from this correct observation he soon conceived the notion that they had had regard for Fire and Light only, and set out to translate the Avesta in conformity with his ideas. He proved to his satisfaction that almost every word in the Avesta meant "light" or "bright" or "fiery" or the like. It is difficult to preserve one's gravity when one reads his translations, which happily have not been taken seriously by most students. That his method should have been revived, in modified forms, by Herzfeld and Nyberg is a matter for regret. It is due to its application that on the one hand harmless words, such as *xᵛafna*, "sleep", are given a restricted and specialized meaning, such as "trance", suitable to a shamanist environment, and that on the other hand the Gāthās turn out to be crowded with the technical terms of racing, as is fitting for the poems of an idle gentleman.

'The *fourth* point common to the two scholars is their tendency to project the cultural phenomena of a later age into the more distant past. Thus Herzfeld seeks to elucidate events in the circle around his Zoroaster by

[1] Author's italics—R.C.Z.

constant reference to the happenings at the court of the Abbaside Caliphs, at the court of a Ma'mūn or a Mutawakkil; yet there is a world of difference between the cultural levels of these two epochs: so much has happened in between, the Persian Empire, Macedonians and Greeks, Parthians, Sassanians, and Islam, that immediate comparison is misleading rather than helpful. Similarly, Nyberg calls on the Dancing Dervishes of fairly recent times to lend support to his dancing and shrieking Zoroaster; indeed, his Zoroaster is modelled, in many respects, on the Muslim Dervishes. He anticipates our objection and surmises that the customs of those Dervishes may have had their origin in the shamanist Zoroastrianism; thus the Dervish customs are to help explain Zoroaster as a shaman, and the shamanist Zoroaster serves to explain the Dervish customs.

'There is another matter which could be mentioned here. It seems to me that Nyberg's opinion on Zoroaster has been influenced in yet another way by his extensive knowledge of Islam, influenced in particular by the figure of Mohammed; Mohammed, that is to say, as seen by Western scholars. There is an implicit resemblance:

(a) Mohammed, who had hallucinations and visions owing to some nervous disorder; some unkind spirits even used to say he was an epileptic—Zoroaster, who had visions through the physical and mental collapse attending shamanist practices; perhaps he was even a drug-addict.

(b) Mohammed, the fervent preacher of the end of the world, who was rejected by his people and compelled to leave Mecca in danger of his life—Zoroaster, precisely the same, if we put "home-tribe" instead of Mecca.

(c) Mohammed, after the Hijrah, in al-Medinah, turning from a prophet into a politician—Zoroaster, after his flight, in Vištāspa's tribe, turning from a prophet into a religious politician.

However, there is genuine resemblance in one point only: both prophets leave their own country in distress and become honoured in their place of refuge; which merely illustrates what has been said on the point in the Gospels.

'The *fifth* point is the claim that the Zoroastrians, who believed themselves the true disciples of Zoroaster, were wrong in this belief, that in fact they did not understand Zoroaster at all. It is plain that both Nyberg and Herzfeld are bound to make this claim; for the view they take of Zoroaster is basically different from the view held by the Zoroastrians through the ages. As to Herzfeld's Zoroaster, it is sufficient to point out that the Zoroastrians regarded their prophet as a prophet, not as a politician. And as regards Nyberg's Zoroaster, it is well known how deeply the Zoroastrians, at all times, abhorred such obscure practices as Nyberg attributes to their founder. Indeed, Nyberg himself admits that even in the later parts of the Avesta such practices are roundly condemned, and that the Maga, on which his

Zoroaster performed, is treated with scant respect. One can add that this lack of appreciation went so far that in Sassanian times the word "Mag(a)" could be used for nothing more dignified than a lavatory.[1] It is, of course, admitted that the faithful of any religion are apt to see their founder through rose-coloured spectacles, and to fail to understand him properly, in true historical perspective; but there are degrees of misunderstanding. Moreover, in no point are religions more conservative than in the forms of service and ritual observances; and of all religions known Zoroastrianism is perhaps the most conservative.

'And so I come to the *sixth* and last point: the inadequacy of the figures drawn by Herzfeld and Nyberg to the place of Zoroaster in history. Whatever Zoroaster was, at any rate he was the founder of one of the great religions of the world. A great nation revered him as its prophet. Long after the Iranians had forgotten Cyrus and Darius and all their crowd, they continued to accord nearly divine honours to Zoroaster. Herzfeld's Zoroaster is manifestly insufficient: one does not see why this slightly shady politician, who had nothing in particular to his credit, should have been remembered at all. Nyberg at least admits Zoroaster to the dignity of prophet; but his ecstatic witch-doctor is not greatly distinguished from the multitude of other ecstatic witch-doctors that, one in each generation, interceded with the spirits for their fellow-tribesmen, in each tribe all over northern Asia. His one distinction, it seems, is that he admitted not merely polytheists, but polytheism into his Church. That would have been treason—a compromise where no compromise can be allowed. It would have earned him contempt and derision instead of reverence and devotion.

'It is said that Mohammed, driven to despair by the unbelievers, faltered one day and emitted a revelation which accorded sanctity to three goddesses whom the idolaters worshipped. Mohammed repented at once of his momentary weakness and proclaimed his error on the next day. Thus he regained the respect of his friends and enemies. Had he persisted in this mistake, Islam would have died before it was born. That is exactly what would have happened to Zoroaster's religion, had Zoroaster been weak enough to adopt Mithra or any such divinity. His memory would not have survived the next generation.'

[1] e.g. *Yōišt-i Fryān*, iii. 69.

INDEX

Achaemenian Empire, 21, 73, 78, 94; and Iranian religion in West, 154–69

Acquisitiveness, 276

Action *in potentia*, Infinite Time as, 219–20

Ādhur-Hormizd, 188

Ādityas, 49

Aēshma (aggressive impulse), 34, 90, 101; ox handed over to, 40, 84; enemy of Sraosha, 96, 111; routed by Mithra, 107, 118

Aeveternity, 251, 257

Afterlife, 56–8. *See also* Immortality; Resurrection

Agathias, 27 and *passim*

Ahl-i Haqq ('People of Truth'), 130

Ahriman (Angra Mainyu), 34, 42, 72; his challenge to Ahura Mazdāh, 81, 82; *daēva*-worship of, 122–3; slaying of bull by, 125, 127–8; opposed to Ohrmizd, 127–8; in Mithraic mysteries, 129–30; Yima perhaps prototype of, 139–40; offering to, 163; dualist concept of, 180; identified with darkness, 181, 182, 201, 203, 205, 209, 224, 248, 254; increased importance of, 191; identified with cold and dry, 203, 205, 216, 217, 309; myth of birth from Infinite Time, 207–9, 248–9, 252; pact with Orhmizd, 209–10, 286–7; armed with concupiscence (Āz), 209, 213, 223–9, 251, 253–5, 311; evil by choice, 213–14, 232; the substance of death, 216, 315–16; derives from Orhmizd's accession to consciousness, 211; brings death into world, 226, 270, 271; woman's defection to, 232–233, 245, 261; originator of planets, 238; first assault on Ohrmizd, 251, 256; creates Lying Speech, 255; defeated by Ohrmazd, 256–7, 260–1, 308–11; assault on material world, 261–3, 265, 309–10; and fall of man, 263–4; trapped in material world, 265–6, 309–11; his lack of wisdom and reason, 292–3; his destruction, 314–316. *See also* Destructive Spirit

Ahuna Vairya prayer, 95, 255, 256–7, 261, 295

Ahura (the 'Lord') 16; term *Mazdāh* applied to, 64, 67, 71; worship of, 65; taken over by Zoroaster, 65, 67, 70–1; resemblance to Indian Varuna, 67–8; forms dual compound with Mithra, 67, 69–70, 72, 100, 110; separation of Mithra from, 105–6; reunited with Mithra, 117–18; revised cult of, 119–20

Ahura Mazdāh (Wise Lord) 16; the one supreme God and creator, 34, 43–4, 45, 52–4, 56, 60, 65, 66, 69, 114, 156; 'Bounteous Immortals' attributes of, 34, 35, 45–50, 60, 63–4, 113; must make choice between good and evil, 41, 43; identified with Holy Spirit, 45–6, 50, 60, 72; inseparably united with Truth and Good Mind, 49, 67; father of Holy Spirit, 50–1, 53, 60, 72; and of Destructive Spirit, 50–1, 52; Seven Chapters and, 63–77; sun and light visible forms of, 64, 68, 75; 'wives' of, 65, 67, 77, 161; counterpart of Vedic Varuna, 66, 67–8; and creation of first man, 71–2; worshipped as creator, 75, 83, 156; his position in *Yasna*, 80–1; *Yasht* of, 97; Mithra's plaint to, 113–14; his veneration of Mithra, 117–18, 145 and of other deities, 145–6; Darius and 155–60. *See also* Ohrmizd.

Ahura-mithra, 100

Ahura-tkaēsha, 100, 154

Ahurānis ('female Ahuras'), 65, 67–8, 77, 161

Ahuras, 39–40, 80; upheld in confession of faith, 82–3, 100, 104; and Haoma cult, 89

Akōman (Evil Mind, q.v.), 229, 257

Al-Baghdādī, 180, 181

Al-Bīrūnī, 138

Alexander the Great, 21, 22, 23, 175; destroys Aresta, 25

Al-Ghazālī, 179–80, 196

Al-Jīlī, 197

Amesha spentas. *See* 'Bounteous Immortals'

Anāhitā, Ardvī Sūrā, 81, 98, 100, 114, 145–6, 148, 166, 167

Anāhīdh, 188

Analogy, 190

Angra Mainyu, 34, 42–3, 45, 47, 80; first introduces death, 47, 72; chooses worst things, 60. *See also* Ahriman; Destructive Spirit

Animal sacrifice, 34–5, 38–9, 51, 160, 165, 166–7, 169; Haoma cult and, 84–94

'Animatism', 80, 81

Antiochus I, 175

Apām Napāt ('Child of the Waters'), 83

Apocalypse of St John, 57

Ardashīr I, 22, 176, 184–5
Areimanios (Ahriman q.v.), 124, 125, 126; in Mithraic mysteries, 129–30
Aristotle: influence of, 185, 195; concept of matter, 200–1, 204
Armenians, 187–8
Arrogance, 276
Arsacids, 22
Artaxerxes I, 21, 155
Artaxerxes II, 98, 161, 166, 167
Artaxerxes III, 161
Artāy Virāf, 306, 307
Āryas, 20
Asceticism, 276, 278, 279, 300
Asha, See Truth
Asha/rta, 285
Ashavans ('followers of the Truth'), 34, 35
Ashi (goddess of Plenty), 98, 111, 112, 114
Ashōqar ('he who makes virile'), 217–18, 311
Astyages, 21
Asuras, Indo-Iranian deities, 37, 39, 66
Aśvins, 88
Athene (hellenized Anāhitā), 160, 161
Āthwya, 89, 93
Atmosphere, Vayu as, 150, 201, 237
Āturpāt, 187, 188, 189, 199, 206, 208, 239, 243, 245, 278, 301
Avesta, 25–6, 28, 29, 33, 34, 35, 39, 59, 62, 65, 66, 88, 125, 154; polytheism in, 50; three main portions of, 79; Mithra in, 99, 103; Yima in, 134; Vayu in, 150; Magi and, 162, 163; Sassanian reconstitution of, 178; Greek and Indian matter in, 185, 189, 196, 199, 202, 207; Āz in, 229–30; veneration of time divisions in, 242; and soul's fate at death, 302–8
Avidyā (ignorance), 229
Āz (Concupiscence): the weapon of Ahriman, 209, 213, 223–9, 253–4, 311; threefold nature of, 225, 254, 312; Manichaean, 226–9, 231, 235, 254, 312; the demon of death, 226, 229, 312; and Buddhism, 229–30, 254; gender and sex of, 230–1; as intellectual pride, 255; enemy of body and soul, 275–6; conquest of, 312–15
Azhi Dahāka, 139, 142

Babylonian Planetary System, 49
Bahrām Chūbīn, 94
Bahrām V, 187, 188
Bailey, Professor Sir Harold, 150–1
Bartholomae, Christian, 15
'Becoming', 202, 203
Bīsitūn, 75, 156

Body: created after soul, 268; and vital spirit, 269, 271; relationship to soul, 273–275, 276–9, 298; and concupiscence, 275–276; health of, connected with virtue, 276–8; reunited with soul, 317
Boghaz Köy, 65, 175
'Bounteous Immortals' (*amesha spentas*): attributes of Wise Lord, 34, 35, 45–50, 71, 113; 'instrumental' role of, 47; 'origin' of, 48, 71; in Seven Chapters, 63–4; equivalents in *Veda*, 50, 71; little part in liturgy, 80, 96; *Yasht* of, 97; early equivalents of, 124; not mentioned by name by Darius, 157; identified with elements, 237; creation of, 257–8; functions taken over by Mean, 286
Brāhmans, Magi equivalent to, 21, 163, 164
Bridge of the Requiter, 56, 59, 96, 111, 226, 302–4
Buddhism: Āz and, 228–30; and matter, 254
Bull, cosmic, 127–8, 262–3; plant and animal life from, 266–7
Bull-sacrifice, 38, 84–8; by Mithras, 99, 125–6, 128, 133; immortality from, 126, 128, 130, 140; Yima and, 126–7, 134, 139, 142–3; by Ahriman, 127–8; at end of time, 128–9, 317–18; *daēvic* practice, 129–31; of man's first parents, 130–1
Bundahishn, 207, 224, 270, 311, 313, 319; bull-sacrifice in, 130; contents of, 194; on woman's defection, 232, 234, 247; on original state of existence, 248, 251, 255–9; on material creation, 257–9, 269

Cattle, 258, 259; identified with Good Mind, 46, 47, 74, 86
Cautes and Cautopates, 141–3
Chishtā, 117
Chorasmia, 19, 21, 33
Christianity: Trinity compared to Bounteous Immortals, 47; and heavenly reward, 57; and idea of creation, 106; rising dogmatism of, 178; martyrs of, 188; tolerated by Khusraw I, 189; and asceticism, 278, 279, 300
Cold and dry, Ahriman identified with, 203, 205
Concupiscence: as excess and deficiency, 287–9; the source of evil, 292, 293; as misuse of reason and desire, 293–4. *See also* Āz
Consciousness, 269, 271; emergence of, 220–1
Contemplation, 282–3

Contentment, 244
Contract, sanctity of, 99, 100, 101, 105, 108–109
Creation, 130–1, 146, 199; Zurvanite myth of, 201–2, 207–9, 211–12; *Dēnkart* description of, 203–5; Mazdean version of, 249–255; other versions of, 215–17; material, 257–63, 265–8; six grades of, 258–9; Wisdom the source of, 290–2
Creeping things (*khrafstars*), 125
Cumont, Franz, 129
Cyrus the Great, 19, 21, 73–4; the Lord's anointed, 20

Daēnā Māzdayasni ('Good Religion of the Worshippers of Mazdāh', q.v.), 64
Daēvas (cf. *devas*): worshipped by followers of the Lie, 37, 38, 39; acknowledge Wise Lord as Supreme God, 53; punishment of, 55; Zoroaster attacks worship of, 71, 73, 87, 94, 99–100, 101; renounced in confession of faith, 82–3, 91, 100; and Haoma cult, 87–8, 89, 91; cult of violence, 101–2, 119; and Mithra, 104–5, 109, 112, 114, 123–5; worshippers of, 121–3, 131, 154; and bull-sacrifice, 129–31; proscribed by Xerxes, 154, 155, 159–60, 167, 168
Daēvō-dāta, 100, 230
Dahrīs, sect of, 196–7, 240
Daniel, 58
Dar-i Mihr, 98
Darius the Great, 20, 21, 26, 154–60
Darius III, 21, 170, 175
Darkness: evil as, 183–4; Ahriman as, 203, 205, 248; Lie and, 255
Dātastān i Dēnīk, 90, 194, 260
Dead, disposal of, 161–2, 165, 166
Dead Sea Scrolls, 51–2
Death: introduction of, 47, 71–2; brought by Ahriman, 101, 226, 270, 271; Vayu's path of, 149–50; Āz the demon of, 226, 229, 315–16; Zurvān the god of, 238–9; Time synonymous with, 239; soul's fate at, 302–5
Deceitfulness, 276
Deficiency and excess, opposed to health and reason, 286, 287–9
Deïoces, 21
Dēnkart, 25, 28–9, 178, 195, 197, 198, 246, 290; account of restoration of Good Religion, 175–7, 184, 186; main theological source, 193; interpretation of creation, 201, 202, 203–5; and Zurvanite myth, 208, 213, 215; on Time-Space, 219, 223–224; on consciousness, 220–1; on Āz, 225–6; on Fravashi, 270; on royalty, 297; on Rehabilitation, 319
Despair, 276
Destiny, 151, 205–7, 237. *See also* Fate
Destructive Spirit, 41, 42–3, 45, 80; first introduces death, 47; opposed to Holy Spirit, 48, 50–1, 71–2, 123, 146; origin of, 50–1, 52; in Endless Darkness, 99; Mithra's assault on, 108, 118; 'sorcerers'' worship of, 122–3, 129; becomes evil by choice, 179. *See also* Ahriman
Devas, 66; and Soma cult, 88, 89. *See also Daēvas*
Discipline, 94
Disorder (*ōshtāp*), 226, 228, 231, 254, 287
Doubt: evil produced by, 212, 221, 227, 254–5
Druj, See Lie
Drvants ('followers of the Lie'), 34, 35
Duchesne-Guillemin, Professor, 49
Dumézil, Georges, 49–50, 69

Earth, 258, 259; Right-mindedness identified with, 46, 47, 62, 65, 232
Elements: equated with stages of evolution, 202–4; and prototypes, 217–18; correspond to man's constituents, 237
Elishē Vardapet, 187–8
'Endless Form' (macrocosm q.v.), 224–5; source of all creation, 249–50; Ohrmazd's creation of, 253, 257, 258, 260; Ahriman's piercing of, 262–3
Endless Light, 220–1, 248; and 'Endless Form', 224, 249; heavenly sphere from, 258–9
Energy, 64, 285
Epistle of Tansar, 244–5
Eternity, Zurvanite concept of, 199
Eudemus of Rhodes, 182, 205, 207, 215, 242
Everlasting life, 57–9
Evil: 'Lie' the principle of, 34, 84, 157; punishment of, 56–60; origin of, 179, 181–182; darkness identified with, 183–4; produced by doubt, 212, 221, 227, 254–5; final destruction of, 302, 309–16, 320–1
Evil Mind, 41, 42–3, 80, 281, 282
Evolution: creative, 201–3, 294; fourfold scheme of, 202–3; dualist interpretation of, 203–4; Zurvanite view of, 204–20
Excess and deficiency, opposed to reason and health, 286, 287–9
'Existence, second', 58–60, 87
Eznik of Kolb, 188

Fame, 64
Fat, oblation of, 34, 86, 87
Fatalism: Zurvanite, 187, 188, 194, 205–7; of Firdausi, 240–2
Fate: Zurvān as, 237–8; orthodox attitude to, 243–4; man's response to, 244–6; Time identified with, 246
Female: equated with darkness and evil, 231, 242; defection to Ahriman, 232–3, 245, 261
Fertility: cosmic sacrifice for, 127–8; Fravashis and, 269
Final Body, 153, 219, 222, 239, 249, 318–19
Finite, relationship with Infinite, 218–20, 249
Finite Space, 150, 251; Zurvān as, 237
Finite Time, 150, 218–20, 222, 311; Zurvān as, 236–7, 238; duration of, 250; creation of, 251–3
Firdausi, 190, 206–7; fatalism of, 240–2
Fire: as symbol of Truth, 46, 47, 54, 61, 74, 83, 258; as centre of cult, 49; ordeal by, 56, 59; identical with Holy Spirit, 75, 77; the male and hot element, 215–16, 231
Fortitude, 285
Fortune (Khwarenah), 64, 98
Frashkart ('Making Excellent' q.v.), 152, 229, 236, 239, 296, 302, 308–9. See also Rehabilitation.
Frashkart Rivāyat, 313
Frashōqar ('he who makes excellent'), 217–218, 236, 237, 239, 311
Fravashis (pre-existent external souls), 76, 78, 81, 225; Yasht of, 98; cosmos dependent on, 146–8, 150, 260; co-operate with vital spirit, 237; as warriors against Lie, 261, 269–70, 273–4; concerned with fertility, 269
Free will, 41–2, 60; a creation of God, 54–5; Zurvān opposed to, 187, 188, 192, 205–7; denied by Zandīks, 200; the soul's, 271–2; man's, 272–3
Fury, See Aēshma

Gāthās, 25, 26, 27, 28–9, 35, 37, 39, 52, 67, 80, 163, 281; moral dualism between Asha and Druj in, 34, 50; do not identify Holy Spirit with Ahura Mazdāh, 43, 45, 181; monotheism of, 50; and judgement after death, 56–7, 59; doctrines summarized, 60–1; and the Seven Chapters, 62, 63–4, 91, 94–5; impact of, 171
Gāthā of the Seven Chapters, 26, 62–78, 161, 166, 167, 181

Gayō Maretan (first man), 71, 136. See Gayōmart.
Gayōmart (first man and 'dying life'), 72, 128, 180, 232, 259; man's first parents from seed of, 131, 267, 275; solar lineage of, 136; sect of, 217; Ahriman's assault on, 262–3, 309, 317; consort for, 233
Geldner, K. F., 15
Gershevitch, Dr, 69
Gētēh (matter), 200–2, 216
Glory, 151–2
Gnosticism, 183, 254, 274–5
Good and evil: problem of, 39–43, 50–4, 74, 178–9, 180–4; Vayu split between, 148–9, 150; free choice by twin Spirits, 213, 214; duality of, secondary to sex, 215, 246; male and female, 230; Zurvān author of, 237, 238–9
Good desire (īsha), 64
Good Mind (Vohu Manah), 40, 43, 238; a purely Iranian concept, 35; aspect of God, 45, 46–50, 60, 63, 67, 281; connected with cattle, 46, 47, 86; Zoroaster especially close to, 48–9, 53–4; united with Truth, 49; union with, at death, 56, 77; Yima and, 137; and operation of natural law, 257; indwelling of, 281–2; identified with Wisdom, 285, 286, 292, 295; corresponds to the mean, 290
'Good Religion of the Followers of Mazdāh': official designation of Zoroastrianism, 64; Seven Chapters conscious expression of, 77; inseparable from Haoma, 93; Mithra initiated into, 114, 116–17; Sassanian restoration of, 175–7; co-terminous with social order, 285; as the mean, 289; of creative evolution, 295–6, and royalty, 297–9
Good Reward, 64
'Good thoughts, good words, good deeds', 24, 74, 116–17
Gratitude, 276
Greater Bundahishn, 251
Greek works, study and influence of, 160, 161, 175–7, 185, 189–90, 195, 196

Hadhayans (Bull), 90, 93, 128, 318
Hamēstagān ('place of the mixed'), 305
Haoma: rite of, 38, 39, 78, 111, 125, 160; sacrificial bull and, 84–8, 99; elixir of immortality, 85, 88–90, 317–18; central act of Zoroastrianism, 15, 86, 147; as sacrifice, victim, priest and God, 90–4, 105, 116; Mithra's priest, 115–16

Happiness, 156, 276–8, 299–300
Harā, Mithra's heavenly home, 112–13, 117
Heaven, 56–7, 58, 112–13, 186, 211, 305, 306–7
Heavenly sphere, 237–8, 250, 251, 258–9 *See also* macrocosm, 'Wheel' of heaven.
Hell, 56–7, 58, 186, 304–5, 307–8
Hellenistic influence, 160, 161, 175–7, 189–190, 195
Henning, Professor, W. B., 16, 17, 29
Herodotus, 27, 98, 154, 160, 161–2, 163, 164, 165–7
Herzfeld, E. E., 16
Hippolytus, 215, 231
Holiness, 44–5, 54, 77
Holy (or Bounteous) Spirit, 42–3; Ahura Mazdāh identified with, 45–6, 50, 69, 72, 97, 146, 179; opposed to Destructive Spirit, 48, 50–1, 71–2, 123, 146; Ahura Mazdāh father of, 50–1, 72; perhaps Mithra in disguise, 69, 72, 111, 118–19, 137; earlier prototype of, 71–3; fire identical with, 75, 79; creation through, 106; Ohrmazd identified with, 198
Honesty, 276
Hope, 276
Horomazes (Ohrmazd), 124, 125
Hot and moist, Ohrmazd identified with, 203, 204, 205
House of Eternity, 241–2, 247
House of Song, 132, 290, 291, 306
Humility, 45

Ignorance (*avidyā*), 229
'Image', one of man's five constituents, 269
Immortality, 57, 94; a Bounteous Immortal, 45–50, 63; identified with plants, 46, 47; Haoma the elixir of, 85, 88–90; bull-sacrifice for, 126, 128, 130, 140; the mean and, 286, 287
Incarnate Word, 96, 119
Incestuous marriages, 162, 165
Indian works, study of, 189–90
Indra (Aryan war-god), 37, 39, 66; associated with Soma cult, 88, 89; and characteristics of Mithra and Verethraghna, 102–4, 105, 109, 110, 112; Vayu paired with, 149
Indrā-vāyū, 149
Infinite, relationship to finite, 219–220, 249
Infinite Space, 182
Infinite Time, 28, 129; Zurvanism introduces, 181–2; as source of all things, 182,

186–7, 222, 240, 246–7; Zurvān as, 194, 198, 207, 236–7; Zandīks and, 197; as father but independent of Ohrmazd and Ahriman, 207–9, 214, 222, 251; and pact between them, 209–10; as action *in potentia*, 219; House of Eternity equated with, 241–2, 247; in dualist texts part of divine personality, 249; finite Time from, 251–3
Intellect and will: in Sassanian Zoroastrianism, 218; spiritual side of creation, 225, 255, 268–9; Āz's attempt to divide, 229, 238; subject to reason, 273, 275
Isaiah, 20
Islam, 28, 171, 179, 206
Israel, 20

Jalāl al-dīn Rūmī, 212
Jāmāspa (Zoroaster's son-in-law), 62
Jam-shīd, *See* Yima
Jēh, the Whore, 232–4
Judaism, influence on, 20–1, 51–2, 57–8
Judgement at death, 56, 59, 226, 302–5
Jung, C. G., 231

Karapans (leaders of old religion), 37
Kartēr (high priest), 26, 184, 186–7, 188, 192, 195, 196–7, 208
Kavāt (Sassanian King), 176, 177
Kavis (leaders of old religion), 37
Khurda Avesta, 26
Khusraw I, 176, 178, 180, 185, 188–90, 195, 199, 300–1
Khusraw II, 94
Khwarenah (royal fortune), 148, 222; concept of, 98, 150–5; Yima's, 141, 151; assailed by Āz, 230. *See Khwarr*.
Khwarr: final cause of each man, 222, 253, 267, 268, 275, 319; and concupiscence, 229, 294, 300. *See Khwarenah*.
Khwashkhwarrīk, 215
Kingdom: a Bounteous Immortal, 45, 46–50, 63, 68; identified with metals, 46, 258; Varuna associated with, 68, 71; Darius' concept of, 157–8
Kingship (royalty): sanctity of, 272; indispensable to religion, 284, 289, 296–7; function of, 297; material complement of Good Religion, 297–9; virtues of, 299–300; bond between God and man, 300–1
Knowledge, 219, 221

Lie (*Druj*): 'followers of' (*drvants*), 34, 35-7, 39, 53, 84; represents principle of evil, 34, 42, 84, 157; no compromise with Truth, 36, 40, 48-9, 52, 60, 157; not mentioned in Seven Chapters, 73; man's vital part in annihilating, 147, 156-7, 280-1; rebellion equated with, 156, 157; creation of, 255; Fravashis' battle with, 270, 271, 273-4; inflicts unhappiness, 277; defeated by solidarity of mankind, 280-1

Light: associated with Truth, 64-5, 255; visible form of Ahura Mazdāh, 68, 75; Mithra as, 110-11; goodness and, 183-4; Ohrmazd as, 203, 205, 248; male principle and, 231; part of divine personality, 249

Liturgy, central act of, 79, 85, 86, 91-2, 147, 190. *See Yashts, Yasna.*

'Long tradition', 83

Macrocosm ('Endless Form'), 224-5, 237, 239. *See also* Heavenly Sphere, "Wheel' of heaven.

Magavan, 163-5

Magi, 15, 19, 21; animal sacrifice by, 160; Zoroastrianism disseminated by, 161-7, 186; new elements introduced by, 165-167; dualist doctrine of, 179-80; worship of light, 179, 182; and problem of evil, 190; Khusraw gives full authority to, 189-190; theory of creation attributed to, 205; in Firdausi's epic, 240-2, 247

'Making Excellent', 152-3, 231, 236, 237, 239, 268, 283, 296, 302, 308-9. *See also Frashkart*, Rehabilitation.

Male: equated with fire and light, 231

Man: creation of, 71-2; meeting-place of spirit and matter, 77; vital to annihilation of Lie, 147, 156-7; 'humanity' defined, 225-6, 269; needs and desires of, 226, 227, 229, 313; supreme creation, 232, 272; woman's defilement of, 234-5; as microcosm of universe, 237, 259-61, 285, 301; his response to fate, 244-6; sky the prototype of, 258; fall of, 263-4; re-creation of, 266-8; original sin of, 267-8; constitution of, 268-70; essential goodness of, 270-1, 276; free will of, 272-3; six cardinal virtues and vices in, 276; and self-love, 280, 299; love of fellow-men, 280-1, 299

Māni, 177, 183-4

Manichaeanism, 23, 177, 178, 192, 194; dualism of light and darkness, 96, 183-4;

196; Āz in, 226-9, 231, 235, 254, 274, 312; on matter, 254; and asceticism, 278, 279, 300

Manual of Discipline, 51-2

Mānushchihr (high priest), 194, 235, 260, 305, 306, 311, 313, 315-16, 320

Mardān-Farrukh, 194, 197, 218-19, 221, 249, 259, 284-5

Mashyē and Mashyānē (first human couple), 126, 130-1, 137, 139, 167, 267, 312, 313, 317

Maskhiyya sect, 180-1

Material and spiritual: linking of, 46, 47, 59, 62, 75, 278-9, 297-8, 313, 319-21; Seven Chapters and, 76-7; Aristotelian view, 200-1, 202; in man, 268-9, 277-9; the mean in, 286

Material creation, 257-61; Ahriman's assault against, 261-3, 265; Ahriman imprisoned in, 265-6; revival of, 266-8

Materialism, Zurvanite, 186, 188, 192, 196-7, 198-203, 246

Matter: Aristotelian concept of, 200-1, 202, 204; and creative evolution, 201-3; concupiscence and, 227, 231, 254-5; union with spirit at Rehabilitation, 313, 319-21

Mattiwaza (Aryan ruler), 65

Māyā (mysterious power), 68

Mazdā-vara, 75-6

Mazdāh: term applied to Ahura, 64, 66, 67, 71; Mithra the rival to?, 69; the 'creator', 70, 83. *See* Ahura Mazdāh.

Mazdakite heresy, 177, 180, 188-9

Māzdayasni, 64, 154

Mean: identified with Truth, 285; doctrine of, 286; as cosmic principle, 286; essence of reason, 287-90

Medes, 19-21

Mēnōk (primal matter), 200-2, 204, 216

Mēnōk i Khrat ('The Spirit of Wisdom'), 193-194, 206, 207, 209, 240, 243, 290-1

Messina, G., 161, 162, 163

Metals, Kingdom identified with, 46, 258

Microcosm, man as, 237, 259-61

Mihr-Narsē, 187-8

Mihragān, feast of, 138-9, 141

Misfortune, 244, 245

Mithra, 16; ritual slaughter and, 38; relations with Sraosha and Rashnu, 56, 111-112; next in importance to Ahura Mazdāh, 66, 99, 105; forms dual compound with Ahura, 67, 69-70, 72, 100; Zoroaster's supposed antipathy to, 69; bringer of life, 72, 113; *Yasht* of, 98, 100-102, 104-20, 122, 136; contrast with

Mithra—*cont.*
Roman Mithras, 99, 123; embodies sanctity of contract, 99, 100, 101, 105, 108–9; as a god of war, 100–2, 109–10, 112; and Indra's characteristics, 102–4, 109, 112, 133; separation from Ahura, 105–7; as contract and king, 108–9; as light, 110–111; heavenly house of, 112–13, 134; his plaint to Wise Lord, 113–14, 121; descent to earth of, 114–15; and Haoma cult, 115–16; initiated into 'Good Religion', 116–17; reunited with Ahura, 117–18, 119, 145; and Holy Spirit, 118–19; and *daēva*-worshippers, 123–5; and Yima, 136–9, 140–4; mentioned by Artaxerxes, 161, 166, 167; as aspect of Zurvān, 237
Mithra-ahura, 67, 68, 105
Mithrándruj, 72
Mithras: differs from Mithra, 16, 99, 123; supposed creator of world, 106; emphasis on purity, 117; mysteries of, 123; and bull-sacrifice, 125–6, 128, 130–1, 133
Mithrō-druj, 100, 109
Mitra: Vedic divinity, 66–7; inseparable from Varuna, 67–8; estrangement from cattle, 126; his place usurped by Yama, 133
Moderation, 279
Modesty, 276
Moses of Chorene, 103
Moulton, J. H., 161
Muslims, 23, 171

Nāñhaithya, 66, 88
Narsēh, 232
Nāsatyas, 66, 88
Natural order (*chihr*), 218, 268; Āz enemy of, 226, 253, 255; and Good Mind, 257
Nature, Spirit of the Power of, 224–5
Nereids, 161
Nietzsche, 19
Night sky, Mithra and, 110–11
Nomads, threat to pastoral life, 34
Nōrūz, feast of, 138–9, 141
Nyberg, H. S., 16

Oblation, 64
Ohrmazd: earlier Ahura Mazdāh (q.v.), 72, 81, 175, 177; identified with Holy Spirit, 72, 198; his creation of six gods, 124, 127, 257; and death of cosmic bull, 127–8, 263; as goodness and light, 180, 181, 182, 201, 203, 205, 209, 224, 248, 256; supreme creator, 131, 152, 180, 191, 201, 221–2, 257–8, 267; identified with hot and moist, 203, 205, 216, 217, 309; myth of birth from Infinite Time, 207–9, 212–13, 222, 228, 248–9; his pact with Ahriman, 209–10, 286–7; neither omniscient nor omnipotent, 213, 214, 234, 249; as Wisdom, 218, 220–1, 256; accession to consciousness of, 221, 256; his weapon the 'Endless Form', 224–5, 226, 249–50, 253, 257, 260; creates woman as man's consort, 232, 234; bisexual, 250; Ahriman's first battle with, 251, 256–7; his limitation of Time, 252–3, 308; creates True Speech, 255; his material creation, 258; entraps Ahriman in material world, 265–6, 309–11; King the symbol of, 297–8, 300; and final judgement of soul, 303, 306; and Resurrection, 316–17
Ordeal, trial by, 56, 59
Order, Zurvān as, 237
Original sin, as error of judgement, 267
Ōshētar, 312
Ōshētarmāh, 312
Ox: as sacrificial victim, 34–5, 38–9, 48, 84; identified with Good Mind, 46, 47, 86

Pahlavi Books, 24, 27, 28, 29, 34, 65, 72, 99, 168, 169, 184, 188, 190; differing eschatologies of, 37, 59; dualism of, 81, 89, 125–31, 150, 269–70; animal sacrifice in, 87, 125–9; doctrines defined in, 178–80; Greek and Indian ideas in, 185, 195; main contents of, 193–4; solitary mention of Zurvanite myth in, 208; concept of earthly life as battle in, 292–3
Pantheism, 80
Parsees, 23–4
Parthians, 22, 175, 178, 183
Pastoral life, nomadic threat to, 34
Paternity in God, 45, 60
Patmān (treaty), 286–7
Paul, St, 57
Persepolis, 33, 127, 197
Persians, 19–22
Planets: Babylonian system, 49; as oppressors of man, 238, 242, 243; analogy with man's body, 260
Plants, 258, 259; Immortality identified with 46, 47, 85, 88–90; holiness of, 77; re-creation of, 266–7
Pleasure, 299–300

Plenty, goddess of, 98
Plutarch, 27, 123–5, 126, 127, 163
Porphyry, 106, 110, 164
Pouruchishtā (Zoroaster's daughter), 62
Pourushaspa (Zoroaster's father), 89
Poverty, 279, 298
'Preservers-Creators', 69–70, 72, 105, 106, 112, 113
Primal matter, 201–3, 204, 253
Primary properties, equated with evolutionary stages, 202, 203
Productivity, identified with virtue, 297
Prosperity, 64, 297–8; and spiritual progress, 277, 278–9
Purity, 117
Purushasūkta, 259
Pythagoras, 195

Qumrān sect, 51–2

Raghā (Ray), 33
Ras (primal matter; the 'wheel' q.v.), 201, 204, 205, 216, 258
Rashnu (the just judge), 56, 96, 99, 100, 101, 107, 111–13, 117, 303, 304
Raven, on Mithraic monuments, 131, 141
Reason (khrat), 226; soul subject to, 272–3; the essence of man, 275, 281; one of six virtues, 276; linked with happiness, 277; identified with husbandman caste, 285; Mean the essence of, 287–9; identified with Good Religion, 295; misuse of, 293–294. See also Wisdom.
Rehabilitation, 153, 229, 236, 253, 295, 296, 302, 308–9, 310–14. See also Frashkart, 'Making Excellent'.
Religion, identified with Wisdom, 249
Resurrection, 57–60, 87, 239, 253, 316–21
Rewards and punishments, 57–8, 59–60, 186, 187, 200
Rig-Veda, 27, 48, 103, 147, 259; two classes of deity in, 37, 39, 66; Rta in, 48, 50, 71; divinities of, 65–8, 70, 88, 103–4, 149; Soma cult in, 88–9; Yama in, 132–4
Right-mindedness (ārmaiti): a Bounteous Immortal, 45, 46, 53, 63, 71; identified with earth, 46, 47, 62, 65, 83, 232; as the mean, 286
Ritual slaughter, 34–5, 38–9; Haoma cult and, 84–94. See also Sacrifice.
Royalty, see Kingship
Rudra, 88, 109

Sacrifice: of ox, 34–5, 38–9, 48, 84, 125–31; Haoma cult and, 84–94; by Xerxes, 160; by Magi, 160, 165–7, 169; final, for immortality, 317–18
Samsāra, 228
Saoshyans (Saviour): and resurrection ('second existence'), 58–9, 87, 90, 128, 296, 312, 313, 317–18; and bull-sacrifice, 87, 90, 128; posthumous son of Zoroaster, 299, 317
Śarva (Rudra), 88, 109
Sassanian Empire, 51, 94, 98, 158; revival and reform of Zoroastrianism, 170, 171–2, 175–92, 245–6; nationalistic approach, 177–8, 191; dualism and Zurvanism in, 181–3, 191–2; Zoroastrian connexion with social hierarchy of, 284–5
Śatapatha-brāhmana, 126
Saurva, 39, 88
'Second existence', 58–60, 87. See also Resurrection.
Selections of Zātspram, 193
Self-love, 280, 299
Self-will, Āz derived from, 254–5
Seven Chapters, Gāthā of, 62–78, 110, 121, 161, 166, 167, 181
Sex differentiation, 215
Shahristānī, 180, 211
Shāpūr I, 26, 176, 177, 183, 184–5, 186, 195, 200
Shāpūr II, 176, 187
Sheol, 58
Shkand-Gumānīk Vichār, 194, 195
Shuppiluliumash (Hittite king), 65
Sirius, 98
Śiva, 39
Sky; prototype of man, 258–9, 260; attacked by Ahriman, 261–2
Social order, Zurvān identified with, 237, 284–5
Soma plant, 85; cult of, 88–9, 126
Sophists, 196
Soul, 96, 146; crossing of Bridge of Requiter, 56, 59, 302–5; survival as moral entity, 57; created before body, 268; the guiding faculty, 268, 269, 271; its free will, 270–2; and reason, 272–3, 275; relationship to body, 273–5, 276–8, 298; concupiscence the enemy of, 275–6; its fate at death, 302–8; reunited with body, 317
Souls, external. See Fravashis.
Sovereignty (kshatra), 68
Space, 218–19; veneration of, 92; as Endless Light, 249

Spenta Mainyu, see Holy Spirit.
Spirits, 'twin', 96, 201; origin of, 42–3, 137, 182, 207–9, 242; God and, 50–1; in Dead Sea Scrolls, 51–4; good and evil by choice, 179, 214; Infinite only source of, 182, 198, 209
Sraosha: genius of hearing, 44; and judgement at death, 55, 56, 94–5, 99, 100, 107, 302–4; *Yasht* of, 91–2; as mediator, 95–6, 137; Mithra and, 98, 111–13, 117, 119; destroyer of Āz, 227, 315
Strabo, 27, 167, 168–9
Suffering, 277
Sūfism, 28
Sun, 68; visible form of Ahura Mazdāh, 68, 75; Mithra god of, 110–11; Yama and, 133; Yima and, 135–6; man's 'image' in station of, 269
Surūsh, 44. *See* Sraosha.

Talents, equivalent to *khwarr*, 268, 276
Tansar (priest), 178, 184
Tauru (*daēva*), 88
Temperance, 276, 285
Theodore bar Konai, 217, 232
Thetis (hellenized Anāhitā), 160, 161
Thirst, 229
Thrita, 89, 93
Time: veneration of, 92; creation of path of death, 149; concept as source of all things, 197–8; synonymous with death, 239; identified with Fate, 246. *See also* Finite Time, Infinite Time, Zurvān.
Time-Space: infinity of, 182; Zurvān as, 198–9, 216, 224, 254; source of creation, 201–2, 204–5, 242, 246–7; Mardān-Farrukh on, 218–19; Ohrmazd's weapon, 224, 225. *See also* Zurvān.
Tishtrya (Sirius), 114
Tree, analogy of, 284–5
Trita Āptya, 89
Tṛṣṇā (thirst), 229
Truth (*Asha*): 'followers of' (*ashavans*), 34, 35–6, 53, 114–15; no compromise with Lie, 36, 40, 48–9, 52, 60, 157; free choice of, 41–2; a Bounteous Immortal, 45–50, 63; creation of, by God, 45, 53, 60, 107, 255; identified with fire, 46, 47, 54, 61, 74–5, 83, 258; united with Good Mind, 49, 53; associated with Light, 64–5, 68, 75; dominates Seven Chapters, 64, 67, 73; individual *Yasht* of, 97; identified with the Mean, 285

Tughazghaz tribe, 194
Twin Spirits, *see* Spirits, 'twin'.

'Ulamā-yi Islām ('The Doctors of Islam'), 193, 207, 215, 231
Unhappiness, inflicted by Lie, 277
Upanishads, 202, 215

Varuna (Vedic deity), 37; inseparable from Mitra, 66, 67–8, 70, 133; associated with Kingdom, 68, 71, and with Yama, 133
Varunānī (consort of Varuna), 67
Vayu: daēvic origin of, 80, 81, 114; split into good and evil, 89, 98, 104, 106, 148–9; transformed into Void, 98–9, 253; and path of death, 149; and Zurvān, 149–50; as atmosphere, 201, 203, 237
Vedic deities, 39; supposed parallels with Bounteous Immortals, 50, 71, and with Mithra, 102–4, 133
Verethraghna, 80, 83, 89, 98, 99, 114, 302; agent of Mithra's vengeance, 101–2, 116; has character of Indra, 103–4, 105, 110
Vices: six cardinal, 276; virtue the mean between contrary, 289–90
Vidēvdāt, 26, 27, 79, 81; drawn up by Magi?, 162; legalistic dualism of, 171
Vīdaēva, 154
Virtue: connexion with bodily health, 276–278; the mean as principle of, 286; identified with productivity, 297
Virtues: six cardinal, 276; balance between competing, 289–90; of kings, 299–300
Vishtāspa, King, 19, 21, 33, 36, 37, 73, 78, 120, 170
Visp-rat, 25
Vital Spirit, 269–71
Vivahvant (father of Yima), 127, 131, 136, 140; initiator of Haoma cult, 89, 92–3
Vohu Manah, see Good Mind.
Void (Vay or Vayu), 201, 203, 248, 249, 253; third entity of creation, 209

Water, 258, 259; Wholeness identified with, 46, 47; veneration of, 76, 77, 83, 92, 160, 166, 167, 169, 231; the female and moist element, 215–16, 231
Waters: goddess of, 98; identified with *ahurānī*, 65, 67–8
'Wheel' of heaven, 201, 216, 225, 250. *See also* Heavenly Sphere, macrocosm

Wholeness, 57; a Bounteous Immortal, 45–50, 63, 71; identified with water, 46, 47; individual *Yasht* of, 97

'Whore', the, *see* Jēh.

Wind, Vayu god of, 148–50, 201, 203

Wisdom: Ohrmazd as, 220–1; identified with Power of the Word, 225; part of divine personality, 249; source of, 282; identified with Good Mind, 285, 286, 292, 295, and with orderliness, 287; as creative principle, 290–2

Wise Lord, *see* Ahura Mazdāh.

'Wolf species', 125, 128, 130

Woman: defection to Ahriman, 232–3, 245; defiled, 261

Word, Spirit of the Power of, 224–5

Wrong-mindedness (*varan*) 270, 282, 292–3

Xerxes, 21, 26, 121, 122; proscribes cult of *daēvas*, 154, 155, 159–60, 167, 168

Yajur-veda, 67, 126

Yam, *see* Yima

Yama, Vedic first man, 132–4

Yashts, 26, 27, 57, 67, 69, 79; polytheism of, 80–1, 170; of Haoma, 91, 92; of Mithra, 97–8, 100–2, 103–20, 122, 136; Yima in, 136; of other deities, 145–9; fall into disuse, 170

Yasna, *passim*; liturgy of, 38–9, 62, 63, 79–80, 82, 84, 91–4, 147; 'animatism' in, 80, 81; fourfold synthesis in, 82–3; Haoma cult in, 86, 88–94

Yezdigird I, 187

Yezdigird II, 94, 187–8

Yima (first man): Zoroaster's attack on, 37–38, 136; censured for 'giving of ox to eat', 84, 85, 89–90, 112, 126–7, 131, 134, 139, 167; his golden reign, 92–3, 134–5, 136; 'like the sun', 127; legends of, 127, 134; as Yama in *Rig-Veda*, 132–4; subterranean paradise of, 135; and the sun, 135–6, 138; his 'lie', 136–7; Mithra's twin, 137–9, 140–4; his *khwarenah*, 141, 151; as the ideal king, 288–9

Zairi, 88–9

Zāl, 240–2, 247

Zand (commentary), 175, 177, 196, 200

Zandīks, 186, 195, 196–7, 200, 205, 208, 210, 240, 246

Zarathushtri, 82, 154

Zarōqar ('he who makes old'), 217–18, 239

Zātspram (high priest), 194, 209, 223, 225, 230, 235, 248, 257, 260, 270, 310–11, 312–13

Zeal, 64

Zodiac, Signs of, 206, 238, 242, 250

Zoroaster, 21, 24 and *passim*: date and sphere of operations, 19, 33–6; opposition to, 35–6; his attacks on 'followers of the Lie', 36–40, 48, 101, 157; no spirit of compromise, 36, 40; condemns ritual practices, 38–9, 84–8, 160; claims to be prophet, 39, 41, 43–5, 53, 73, 77, 122, 170; prophet of free will, 41–2, 60, 187, 206, 302; myth of twin spirits, 42–3, 50–1, 198, 208; relationship with God, 43–5, 65; his idea of God's paternity, 45, 60; concept of Bounteous Immortals, 45–50, 96; linking of material and spiritual worlds, 46, 47, 59, 62; personal invention of Good Mind, 48–9, 53–4, 285; on holiness of God, 54; on heaven and hell, 56–7, 211; on 'second existence', 58–60, 127, 316–17; his doctrine summarized, 60–1, 156–7; silence on subject of Mithra, 69, 105; his reform of old religion, 70–2, 78, 119–20; his 'goodness', 117; his House of Song, 132, 291, 306; and Yima, 134; *Khwarenah* of, 152; and Magi, 161, 163–5, 168; alleged preceptor of Pythagoras, 195; said to recognize four principles or elements, 217

Zrvan Akarana (Infinite Time q.v.), 51, 201, 207. *See* Zurvān.

Zurvān ('old age'), 217–18

Zurvān: and the lion-headed deity in Mithraism, 129; Vayu and, 149–50; father of Ohrmazd and Ahriman, 188, 207–9, 215, 225, 239, 246; as Infinite Time (q.v.), 194, 198, 207, 216–17, 224, 226, 236–7; and pact between Ohrmazd and Ahriman, 209–10, 224; and Āz, 209, 213, 223; the One and the Many, 211–12, 217, 221; his doubt, 212–13, 221, 227, 237, 254; originally bisexual, 215; the weapons he gives his sons, 224, 225–6, 251, 254, 311; as author of life and death, 226, 238–9; as finite Time (q.v.), 236, 237; sevenfold aspects of, 236–7; as God of Fate, 237–8; as God of Death, 238–9; as God of Resurrection, 239. *See also* Time, Time-Space.

Zurvanism, 28: and Two Spirits, 51; and problem of evil, 181, 190, 192, 212–14; myth of, 182–3, 188, 207–9, 211, 215–17, 223, 247, 255; predominance in third century, 183–5; materialist type of, 186, 188, 192, 196–7, 198–203, 246; fatalism, 187, 188, 192, 205–7, 239–46; revival by Mihr-Narsē, 187–8; 'classical', 188, 198–200, 207, 211–35, 246; varieties of, 193–210; view of evolution, 204–5; 'fall' in, 212; differences between orthodoxy and, 213–15, 236; variants of, 215–17; and Manichaean Āz, 223, 226–231; essential orthodoxy of, 230